INTERNATIONAL ASSISTANCE TO THE PALESTINIANS AFTER OSLO

Why has the West disbursed vertiginous sums of the money to the Palestinians after Oslo? What have been donors' motivations and above all the political consequences of the funds spent?

Based on original academic research and first-hand evidence, this book examines the interface between diplomacy and international assistance during the Oslo years and the *intifada*. By exploring the politics of international aid to the Palestinians between the creation of the Palestinian Authority and the death of President Arafat (1994–2004), Anne Le More reveals the reasons why foreign aid was not as beneficial, uncovering a context where funds from the international community were poured into the occupied Palestinian territory as a substitute for its lack of real diplomatic engagement. This book highlights the perverse effects such huge amounts of money have had on the Palestinian population, on Israeli policies in the occupied Palestinian territory and on the conflict itself, not least the prospect of its resolution along a two-state paradigm.

Conventional wisdom argues that if the Palestinian economy did not improve after Oslo, it was primarily due to the corruption of the Authority headed by President Arafat. In fact, the story of Palestinian corruption is much more complex, involving Israeli and Palestinian businessmen, politicians and high-ranking security personnel. For its part, the deterioration of the living conditions in the West Bank and Gaza Strip, and the multifaceted process of Palestinian territorial, demographic, socio-economic and political fragmentation after Oslo was largely caused by a number of mutually reinforcing Israeli policies and continuing occupation and colonization of the Palestinian territories in a generalized context of persisting violence on all sides.

International Assistance to the Palestinians after Oslo gives a unique narrative chronology that makes this complex story easy to understand and makes this book a classic for both scholars and practitioners, with lessons to be learned far beyond the Israeli–Palestinian conflict.

Anne Le More holds a PhD in International Relations from Oxford University. Her research interests include the Middle East, and more broadly, the Arab and Muslim world. She has published a number of articles and is the co-editor of *Aid, Diplomacy and Facts on the Ground: The Case of Palestine* (Chatham House, London, 2005).

ROUTLEDGE STUDIES ON THE ARAB–ISRAELI CONFLICT

Series Editor: Mick Dumper

University of Exeter

The Arab–Israeli conflict continues to be the centre of academic and popular attention. This series brings together the best of the cutting-edge work now being undertaken by predominantly new and young scholars. Although largely falling within the field of political science the series also includes interdisciplinary and multidisciplinary contributions.

1 INTERNATIONAL ASSISTANCE TO THE PALESTINIANS AFTER OSLO

Political guilt, wasted money

Anne Le More

INTERNATIONAL ASSISTANCE TO THE PALESTINIANS AFTER OSLO

Political guilt, wasted money

Anne Le More

Routledge
Taylor & Francis Group

LONDON AND NEW YORK

First published 2008
by Routledge
2 Park Square, Milton Park, Abingdon, Oxon OX14 4RN

Simultaneously published in the USA and Canada
by Routledge
270 Madison Ave, New York, NY 10016

Routledge is an imprint of the Taylor & Francis Group, an informa business

© 2008 Anne Le More

Typeset in Times by Wearset Ltd, Boldon, Tyne and Wear
Printed and bound in Great Britain by TJI Digital, Padstow, Cornwall

British Library Cataloguing in Publication Data
A catalogue record for this book is available from the British Library

Library of Congress Cataloging in Publication Data
A catalog record for this book has been requested

ISBN10: 0-415-45385-2 (hbk)
ISBN10: 0-203-92833-4 (ebk)

ISBN13: 978-0-415-45385-1 (hbk)
ISBN13: 978-0-203-92833-2 (ebk)

A MES PARENTS ET MES SŒURS,
À LA MÉMOIRE DE NOTRE GRAND-MÈRE
PATERNELLE

The conviction that everything that happens on earth must be comprehensible to man can lead to interpreting history by commonplaces. Comprehension does not mean denying the outrageous, deducing the unprecedented from precedents, or explaining phenomena by such analogies and generalities that the impact of reality and the shock of experience are no longer felt. It means, rather, examining and bearing consciously the burden which our century has placed on us – neither denying its existence nor submitting meekly to its weight. Comprehension, in short, means the unpremeditated, attentive facing up to, and resisting of, reality – whatever it may be.

(Hannah Arendt, The Origins of Totalitarianism, 1951)

CONTENTS

CONTENTS

CONTENTS

ILLUSTRATIONS

Figures

Maps

Tables

PREFACE

The story being told in this book is little known, although a great many of its constitutive parts will be familiar to most readers. So much is written on the Israeli–Palestinian conflict, and in particular on the Oslo 'peace process' after 1993, that this is hardly surprising. What may be of significance, therefore, are not only the intricate detailed facts that are presented here for the first time, but what they demonstrate: the way international politics and economic assistance are so deeply interwoven.

What may also be of interest is the underlying theme of continuity. Precisely because the Israeli–Palestinian conflict is so high-profile and under constant media spotlights, one has perpetually to struggle to remain on the top of what is going on. There always seems to be a new development, a new declaration, a new commitment, a new event. We are constantly told of a series of novel episodes, some worthy, some entirely insignificant, but all accentuating the impression that most of these events are already *passé* as we are acquainting ourselves with their occurring.

Fundamentally, however, very little changes. There are many ups and downs, high hopes dashed by periods of despair, quiet disrupted by violence, but the underlying trends remain remarkably constant. This also should not come as a surprise considering that the balance of power between the two parties has remained stable, although the gap between the two has widened and the expectations of the two populations have been propelled to ever more extreme thresholds. This continuity is often overlooked. In the excessive attention devoted to the minutiae of the conflict, the big picture gets lost.

And the big picture – mirroring the balance of power – has remained steady, and steadily deteriorating. It is one of continuing Israeli occupation, dispossession, colonization and segregation; of increasing territorial, demographic, socio-economic and political fragmentation of the Palestinians; of a persisting humanitarian crisis and more mismanagement, authoritarianism, lawlessness and chaos in the West Bank and Gaza; of more hatred, radicalization and indiscriminate violence against civilians on both sides; of detachment and incomprehension; and of a two-state solution growing ever more remote. It is above all a picture of a vast amount of money being poured in by the international community as a substitute for its lack of real diplomatic engagement.

A political strategy would necessitate tackling head on the root causes and asymmetrical structure of the conflict. This would entail confronting its history, and the legitimate national rights and grievances of both peoples. This would imply having to deal, at last, with the hard issues which the Oslo 'peace process' sought to evade – the Palestinian refugees, the frontiers between Israel and a future Palestinian state, the status of Jerusalem, Israeli settlements, and security arrangements. As nothing serious is being done in order to influence Israeli policies so that a just and viable compromise can be reached, international donors are providing funds *en masse* to the Palestinians. This is partly humanitarian impulse, partly to assuage our guilty conscience. It is also being done in the hope that this may 'induce' the Palestinians to accept whatever deal the international community may be able to extract from the Israelis.

This was the rationale behind the creation in the early 1950s of the United Nations Relief and Work Agency to take care of more than half of the native population living in Palestine at the time, who were displaced and dispossessed as the result of the first Israeli–Arab conflict and the creation of the State of Israel. After Oslo, and to this day, the same logic was extended to the remaining Palestinian population of the West Bank and Gaza Strip. This book begins with the Oslo process, when the Palestinian Authority (PA) was created and then Palestine Liberation Organization (PLO) Chairman Yasser Arafat moved from Tunis to the occupied territory. It ends with his death at the close of 2004. This story, however, is still unfolding.

In the spring of 2006, a few months after Hamas received a democratic mandate from the population of the West Bank and Gaza, Western donors decided to stop direct funding to the Palestinian government. The conventional view – as epitomized in the media by the plethora of articles on PA officials not being paid for months – is that since then the Palestinians have been stranded with very little money. The staff on the PA payroll indeed stopped being paid. However, while officially no money went to the budget of the Authority, more funds were actually disbursed in 2006 than ever before. The money simply came in through different channels: out of the unprecedented US$1.2 billion disbursed that year, some US$700 million transited directly through the office of President Abbas and the rest through international agencies, whether the United Nations or non-governmental organizations. While ever vaster amounts of international funding continue to be disbursed to the Palestinians, their living conditions and lives under occupation continue to deteriorate. The prospect of seeing the emergence of a viable independent state is also becoming ever less plausible, and so is the prospect of economic development and reaching a just agreement which will at long last bring peace for them and for the Israelis. This book explains exactly how this happened, and in so doing also provides the reader with some of the answers to why it happened.

ACKNOWLEDGEMENTS

In its first incarnation, this book was conceived as a PhD dissertation which I defended at Oxford University in the autumn of 2006. Numerous individuals and institutions have contributed to make this four-year project feasible, including the ESRC, Nuffield College, the Department of Politics and International Relations of Oxford and the British Council in Paris, whose combined financial assistance has enabled me to carry out the initial stage of this research in truly privileged conditions. For this, I am most grateful to all concerned and especially indebted to the following persons:

The senior members of the Centre for International Studies and the Middle East Centre at Oxford, above all my supervisor, Neil, who was both firm and unfailingly supportive, even when my extended leaves took me to the heart of Africa where it required some stretch of the imagination to see how this could assist me in advancing my research on Israeli–Palestinian politics. Yuen, Sudhir, Andrew, Adam, Avi and Marga, all of whom I have known since I started my postgraduate studies in the UK a decade ago and who have always remained encouraging and extremely generous with their time. I could never express sufficient gratitude to Karma for her constant back-up, the stimulating exchanges on Middle Eastern politics we held over the years, and much much more. At Oxford, I would also like to thank Leah, Ashish, Marcus, Sharon, Adam, Kathryn, Armelle and David.

Miles for reading the first complete draft of this manuscript and being so consistently enthusiastic, although my research could not possibly have made any contribution to the history of nineteenth-century Britain. My friend Charlotte, who flew from Jerusalem to New York expecting to explore the city, only to spend most of her time stuck in a small one-bedroom flat in the Lower East Side diligently scrutinizing one page after another. Peter, a shrewd analyst of the Palestinian–Israeli conflict and also a dear friend, who kindly agreed to let my chapters disrupt the last summer he and his family spent in Phnom Penh in 2006. Their critical comments, on both substance and style, have been invaluable. Elisabeth and Bruce, to whom I am forever grateful for encouraging me to start this project in the first place, and a little less so from the point of view of its expeditious completion, for parachuting me into the frantic world of New York international-policy-making-academia as I was just finishing my penultimate chapter in Paris in the autumn of 2005. Souhail, for reacquainting me *in extremis* with some of the most remarkable classics of political theory, his own precious theories and our enduring complicity. Asif, Sébastien, Shaun, Dror and Robert for their feedback on parts of the draft. Mark, one of my examiners, for his input on the entire piece and for insisting it should go to print. Yahia for his assistance in making it actually go to print.

My colleagues and friends in Gaza City, Jerusalem, Ramallah and Tel Aviv for their support our many stimulating discussions and all the fun we had together despite the grim and ever more depressing reality of the situation on the ground. In particular: Karen, Elodie, Fabio, Maryvonne, Christian, Pierre and Lisa, Alban, Marcus, Donatella, Benoit, Michael, Alex, Moti, Anwar, Yasser, Ghassan, Chiara, Jeff, Cat, Kim, another Marcus, Andrew, Stephano, Aimé, Dalal, Zamir, Francine, Pascal, David, Marc, Didi, Maya, Yasmine, Zizette, Tim, Mamoon, Alexandra, Lizzie, David (number two), Chris, Iman, Karim, Jean-Luc, Conal, Arjan, Geoff, Lucas, Genevieve, Andy and Nir. A special thought for my former UNSCO colleagues in Gaza.

Michael, who has been both a most amazing boss and a continuous source of energy and inspiration. *Aid, Politics and Facts on the Ground: The Case of Palestine*, the book we co-edited in 2004–2005, together with Robert and the support of Rosy at Chatham House, was one of the most rewarding and intellectually challenging experiences of the last few years. A very particular thanks to Nigel, whose astuteness and knowledge of donor politics in the West Bank and Gaza has no equal, for the great conversations we had over the years. The more than 100 people whom I interviewed in Israel, Palestine, Europe and the US and who generously shared their thoughts, time and knowledge. For obvious reasons, most preferred to do so on condition of confidentiality, and this is why the source of some of the quotes used in this book is not revealed: I am most obliged to them for their trust and openness.

Susanne, Walid, Damien, Tobias, Fanny, Sebastian, Alistair, Rebecca, Tash, Newton, Lina, Jonathan, Helen, Andy, Richard (times two), John and Adam who offered shelter, a listening ear and *divertissement* during my research and linguistic trips to Brussels, Damascus, London, Washington DC and New York. Moi, Nesh, Nici, Bronte, David and Ross for the out-of-the-ordinary Kinshasa parenthesis.

JC, who from the outset has followed my thesis peregrinations the closest, although a substantial part of the time from very far afield. Bertille and Greg, who have followed the process less closely, but also from much too far away. Ninon, François, Elodie, Thomas, Véronique, Marie, Nicole and Chloé for bearing with me during what I thought would be *la dernière ligne droite* in Paris in 2005. My colleagues at the UN Secretariat and friends in New York for making sure *la dernière ligne droite* was actually just that. In particular, Salman, Nathalie, Nick, Sylva, Joel, Myriam, Julie, Asima, David, Shelley, Hervé, Manu, Anne, Amin, Momar, Naututu, Minh-Thu and Amy. Amihaï for being present, most caring and so patient throughout the entire Paris–New York–Paris–New York final stretch. While thankful for all the support I received from those hitherto mentioned, and many more, I assume full responsibility for the final content.

Finally, I wish to extend my deepest gratitude to Henri, Véra, Pauline and Marthe, as well as the more extended 'L.M.' 'R.', 'P.', 'B.d.L.' and 'W.' families – for everything and much more.

Ich weiß nicht, was soll es bedeuten,
Daß ich so traurig bin;
Ein Märchen aus alten Zeiten,
Das kommt mir nicht aus dem Sinn.
    Heinrich Heine, *Die Lorelei*, 1824

CHRONOLOGY

1991

October   Madrid Peace Conference

1993

13 September   Declaration of Principles on Interim Self-Government, Oslo
1 October   Donor Conference to Support Middle East Peace, Washington
                 DC
5 November   First Ad Hoc Liaison Committee, Paris
16 December   First Consultative Group meeting, Paris

1994

29 April   Paris Protocol on Israeli–Palestinian Economic Relations
4 May   Gaza–Jericho Agreement (Cairo Agreement)
10 May   Arrival of first Palestinian police force in Gaza
1 July   Establishment of the PA; arrival of Chairman Arafat in Gaza
29 August   Transfer of power from the Israeli Civil Administration to the
                 PA; expansion of Palestinian self-rule over education,
                 taxation, social welfare, tourism and health completed by
                 December

1995

6 January   First meeting of the Local Aid Coordination Committee,
                 Jericho; formation of Sector Working Groups
5 June   First meeting of the Joint Liaison Committee
28 September   Interim Agreement on the West Bank and Gaza Strip (Oslo II)
4 November   Assassination of Israeli Prime Minister Rabin

1996

20 January	First Palestinian presidential and legislative elections in the West Bank and Gaza Strip; PLO Chairman Arafat becomes PA President
7 March	Inauguration of the first Palestinian Legislative Council
29 May	Likud wins Israeli elections; Netanyahu Prime Minister

1997

17 January	Protocol concerning Israeli redeployment in Hebron

1998

23 October	Wye River Memorandum
30 November	Donor Conference to Support Peace and Development in the Middle East Peace, Washington DC

1999

4–5 February	Last Consultative Group, Frankfurt
4 May	Expiry of Oslo agreement; end of five-year transitional period
17 May	Labour wins Israeli elections; Barak Prime Minister

2000

24 May	Israeli withdrawal from South Lebanon
July	Failure of Camp David Summit
28 September	Outbreak of the second *intifada* or 'Al Aqsa *intifada*'

2001

January	Failure of Taba Summit
6 February	Likud wins Israeli elections; Sharon Prime Minister
September	First informal meeting of the Quartet (the United States, the European Union, Russia and the United Nations), New York

2002

March/April	Israeli Defence Forces Operation Defensive Shield into the occupied Palestinian territory
23 June	'100 Days Reform Plan' of the Palestinian government
24 June	President Bush speech on 'vision' for peace in the Middle East
10 July	Quartet launches Task Force on Palestinian Reform

Summer	Sharon's request to UN Secretary-General for assessment of the humanitarian situation in the WBGS – Bertini Mission
20 December	Principals-level Quartet, New York: finalized 'Roadmap' draft

2003

14 February	President Arafat's decision to appoint Prime Minister
29 April	Abbas (Abu Mazen) as first Palestinian Prime Minister
May/June	Roadmap process begins and ends; Acaba Summit
7 September	Abbas resigns; Qoreï (Abu Ala) Prime Minister

2004

April	Sharon's Disengagement Plan is announced
14 April	Exchange of Bush/Sharon letters
11 November	Death of President Arafat

2005

9 January	· Palestinian presidential elections; Abbas becomes President
Summer	Israel disengages from Gaza

2006

January	Palestinian legislative elections; Hamas won 44 per cent of the popular vote and 74 seats in the Palestinian Legislative Council

ACRONYMS AND ABBREVIATIONS

AHLC	Ad Hoc Liaison Committee
CEC	Central Elections Commission
CG	Consultative Group
CIDA	Canadian International Development Agency
COGAT	Office of the Coordinator of Government Activities in the Territories (Israeli)
DAC	Development Assistance Committee (OECD)
DFID	Department for International Development (UK)
DFLP	Democratic Front for the Liberation of Palestine
DPA	Department of Political Affairs (UN)
EAP	Emergency Assistance Programme
EC	European Commission
ECHO	European Commission Humanitarian Aid Department
EIB	European Investment Bank
EU	European Union
FAO	Food and Agriculture Organization
GA	General Assembly (UN)
GCO	General Control Office (PA)
GIE	Gaza Industrial Estate
GOI	Government of Israel
GSS	General Security Services (Israeli)
HAMAS	Harakat Al-Mukawama al-Islamiya (Islamic Resistance Movement)
HEPG	Humanitarian Emergency Policy Group
ICJ	International Court of Justice
ICRC	International Committee of the Red Cross
IDF	Israeli Defence Forces
IFC	International Finance Corporation
IFI	International Financial Institution
IHL	International Humanitarian Law
ILO	International Labour Organization
IMF	International Monetary Fund

IR	International Relations
JLC	Joint Liaison Committee
LACC	Local Aid Coordination Committee
MEP	Member of the European Parliament
MEPP	Middle East Peace Process
MFA	Ministry of Foreign Affairs (Israeli)
MoF	Ministry of Finance (PA)
MOPIC	Ministry of Planning and International Cooperation (PA)
NDI	National Democratic Institute
NGO	Non-governmental organization
NIS	New Israeli Shekel
OCHA	Office for the Coordination of Humanitarian Affairs (UN)
ODA	Official Development Assistance
OECD	Organization for Economic Cooperation and Development
OLAF	European Anti Fraud Office
oPt	Occupied Palestinian territory
PA/PNA	Palestine National Authority
PBC	Peacebuilding Commission (UN)
PBSO	Peacebuilding Support Office (UN)
PCSC	Palestinian Commercial Services Company
PDP	Palestinian Development Plan
PECDAR	Palestinian Economic Council for Development and Reconstruction
PFLP	Popular Front for the Liberation of Palestine
PIEDCO	Palestinian Industrial Estates Development Corporation
PIF	Palestinian Investment Fund
PLA	Palestinian Liberation Army
PLC	Palestinian Legislative Council
PLO	Palestine Liberation Organization
PNC	Palestine National Council
REDWG	Regional Economic Development Working Group
RSG	Reform Support Group
RWG	Refugee Working Group
SC	Security Council (UN)
SG	Secretary-General (UN)
SRSG	Special Representative of the Secretary-General (UN)
SSR	Security System Reform
STA	Single Treasury Account
SWG	Sector Working Group
TA	Technical Assistance
TAP	Tripartite Action Plan
TFGWB	Trust Fund for Gaza and the West Bank (World Bank)
TFPI	Task Force on Project Implementation
TFPR	Task Force on Palestinian Reform

TIPH	Temporary International Presence in Hebron
UN	United Nations
UNDP	United Nations Development Programme
UNICEF	United Nations Children's Fund
UNCTAD	United Nations Conference on Trade and Development
UNESCO	United Nations Educational, Scientific and Cultural Organization
UNRWA	United Nations Relief and Works Agency for Palestine Refugees in the Near East
UNSCO	Office of the United Nations Special Coordinator
UNTSO	United Nations Truce Supervision Organization
US	United States
USAID	United States Agency for International Development
WBGS	West Bank and Gaza Strip
WFP	World Food Programme
WHO	World Health Organization

End 2003, indicative exchange rate US$1 = NIS4.5

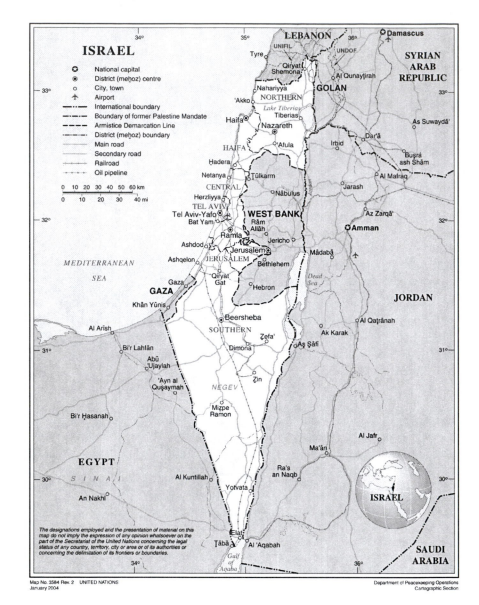

Map 1 General map, Israel and the region (UN).

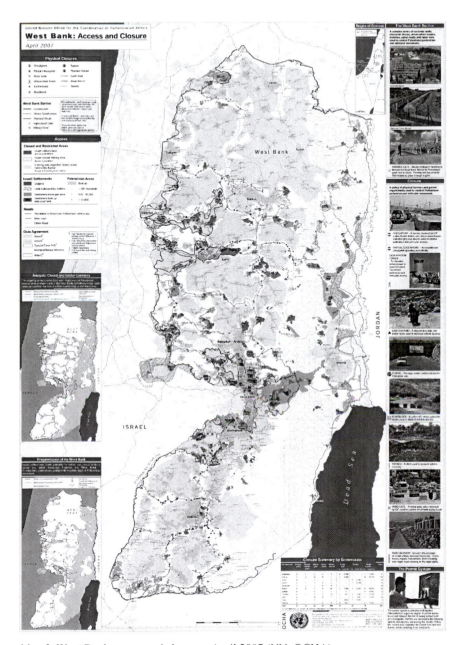

Map 2 West Bank access and closures, April 2007 (UN–OCHA).

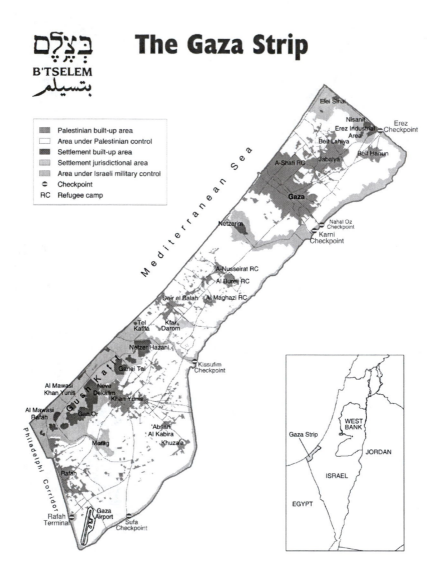

The Gaza Strip

B'TSELEM בְּצֶלֶם بتسيلم

Legend:
- Palestinian built-up area
- Area under Palestinian control
- Settlement built-up area
- Settlement jurisdictional area
- Area under Israeli military control
- ○ Checkpoint
- RC Refugee camp

Mediterranean Sea

Elei Sinai
Nisanit
Erez Industrial Area
Erez Checkpoint
Beit Lahiya
Beit Hanun
A-Shati RC
Jabalya
Gaza
Netzarim
Nahal Oz Checkpoint
Karni Checkpoint
A-Nusseirat RC
Al Bureij RC
Deir el Balah
Al Maghazi RC
Tel Katifa
Kfar Darom
Netzer Hazani
Ganei Tal
Kissufim Checkpoint
Al Mawasi Khan Yunis
Neve Dekalim
Khan Yunis
Al Mawasi Rafah
Gan Or
Gush Katif
'Absan Al Kabira
Morag
Khuza'a
Rafah
Gaza Airport
Rafah Terminal
Sufa Checkpoint
Philadelphi Corridor

WEST BANK
Gaza Strip
JORDAN
ISRAEL
EGYPT

Source: Adapted from map of OCHA (UN Office for Coordination of Humanitarian Affairs)

Map 3 Gaza closures, July 2004 (UN–OCHA).

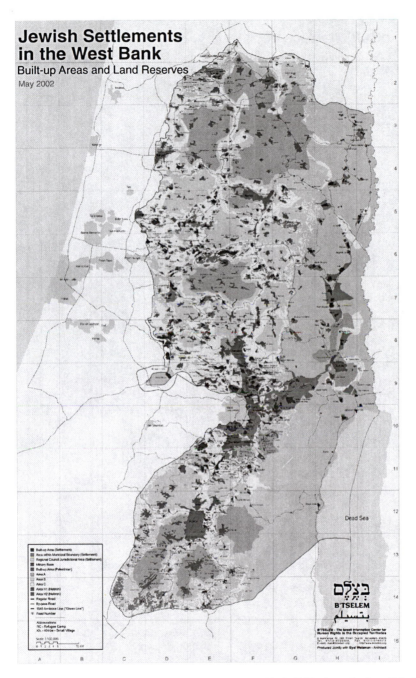

Map 4 Jewish settlements in the West Bank, May 2002 (B'Tselem, the Israeli Information Center for Human Rights in the Occupied Territories).

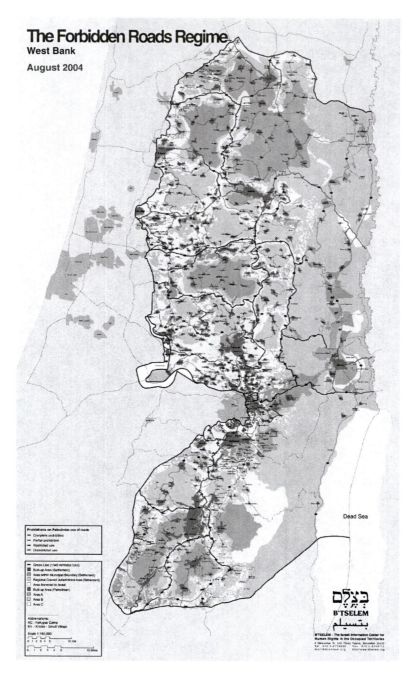

Map 5 The Forbidden Roads Regime, West Bank, August 2004 (B'Tselem, the Israeli Information Center for Human Rights in the Occupied Territories).

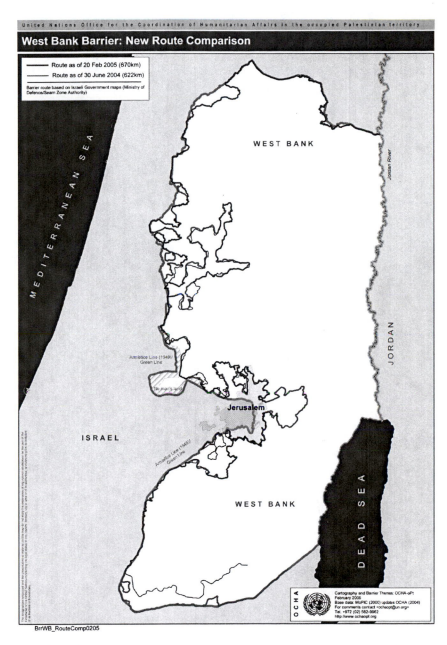

West Bank Barrier: New Route Comparison

Route as of 20 Feb 2005 (670km)

Route as of 30 June 2004 (622km)

Barrier route based on Israeli Government maps (Ministry of Defence/Seam Zone Authority)

WEST BANK

MEDITERRANEAN SEA

Jordan River

Armistice Line (1949)/ Green Line

No man's land

Jerusalem

JORDAN

ISRAEL

Armistice Line (1949)/ Green Line

WEST BANK

DEAD SEA

Cartography and Barrier Themes: OCHA-oPt
February 2005
Base data: MoPIC (2000) updates OCHA (2004)
For comments contact <ochaopt@un.org>
Tel: +972 (02) 582-9962
http://www.ochaopt.org

OCHA

BrrWB_RouteComp0205

Map 6 West Bank Barrier: new route comparison (2004 versus 2005 route), February 2005 (UN–OCHA).

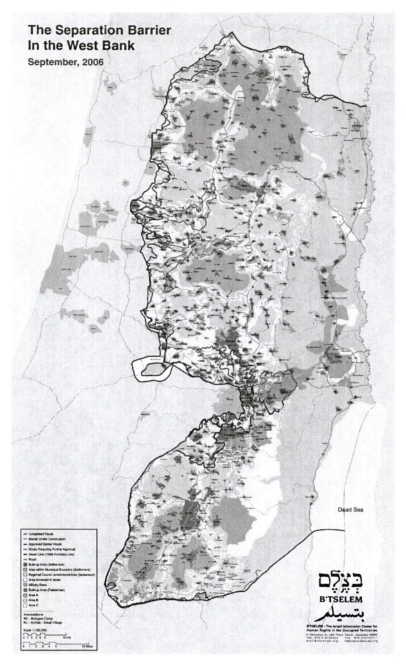

The Separation Barrier
In the West Bank
September, 2006

Dead Sea

B'TSELEM

Map 7 The Separation Barrier in the West Bank, September 2006 (B'Tselem, the Israeli Information Center for Human Rights in the Occupied Territories).

The Separation Barrier - Jerusalem Area September, 2005

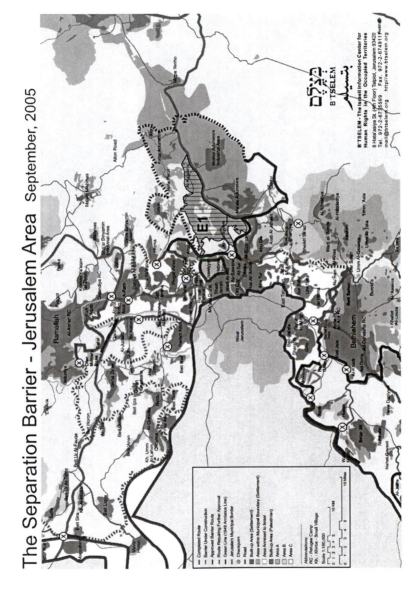

Map 8 The Separation Barrier, Jerusalem area, September 2005 (B'Tselem, the Israeli Information Center for Human Rights in the Occupied Territories).

INTRODUCTION

On the eve of the Palestinian legislative elections in January 2006 which brought into power a Hamas-led government, the provision of humanitarian relief and direct budgetary support to the Palestinian National Authority (PA) had come to constitute the bulk of the international funds provided to the Palestinian population of the West Bank and Gaza Strip (WBGS). More than US$1 billion a year was being spent on the occupied Palestinian territory (oPt). Most was in the form of emergency assistance and constituted one of the highest and longest sustained levels of multilateral foreign aid per capita in the world.[1]

Despite such high levels of international support, the living conditions of the Palestinian population were dismal. Indeed, they had been steadily deteriorating since the beginning of the Oslo peace process in 1994, and most dramatically since the onset of the second *intifada* in September 2000. The PA itself, which had been established 12 years earlier and until then had been dominated by Fatah, historically the dominant political force within the Palestinian Liberation Organization (PLO), was literally bankrupt. To the extent that it continued to function at all, it was only because it was maintained on life support by unsustainable levels of direct budgetary funds from international donors.

In its gloominess, the broader geopolitical context mirrored – and largely contributed to – the PA's dire financial situation. It was marked by renewed conflict and indiscriminate violence against civilians on both the Palestinian and Israeli sides, the absence of direct political negotiations between the two parties, and continuing Israeli military occupation, colonization and expansion into the Palestinian territories accompanied by routine oppression, segregation and continuing dispossession of the Palestinian population.

Dependency, fragility and paucity of resources seriously curtailed the PA's ability to deliver basic social services, to govern and to maintain law and order in the already circumscribed Palestinian areas under its jurisdiction as the result of the Oslo Accords. In the last year of Yasser Arafat's presidency, before he passed away in November 2004, loss of security control, factional disputes and indications of internecine struggle within Fatah characterized an increasingly chaotic, divided, and violent domestic scene in which radical movements were expanding their popular support.[2]

1

As for the majority of the Palestinians, the Palestinian refugees living outside the WBGS in neighbouring Arab countries and amongst the Palestinian diaspora, they were largely ignored by the prevailing Western narrative after Oslo, international focus and assistance programme having been targeted at the PA and the population living inside the oPt rather than at the Palestinians taken as a people.[3] This added to mounting popular distrust of the representativeness and legitimacy of the PA leadership in a context where, twelve years after its move from Tunis, it had failed to establish itself as an accountable and democratic entity, to ensure the basic safety needs and protection of the population under its jurisdiction, as well as to deliver on peace, prosperity, the recovery of Palestinian national rights, and the creation of an independent state. A sovereign Palestinian state had not even been established, but it seemed the PA and the political regime put in place in the WBGS after 1993 already displayed many of the attributes of a 'failed state'.[4]

This situation was markedly different from what the international community had envisaged ten years earlier when it embarked on an ambitious Official Development Assistance (ODA) programme in support of the implementation of the Oslo peace process. At the first donor conference on 1 October 1993, two weeks after the signing of the Declaration of Principles, 42 donor countries and agencies met in Washington DC and pledged over $2 billion in aid to be disbursed over the stipulated five-year interim period.[5] Participants at the conference agreed 'to support the historic political breakthrough in the Middle East through a broad-based multilateral effort to mobilize resources to promote reconstruction and development in the West Bank and Gaza'. Specifically, the funds were intended to meet urgent relief efforts, and other short-term needs, including the rehabilitation of existing infrastructure, to promote social and economic development as well as to 'build the capacity of the Palestinian population to organize and manage their own political, economic, and social affairs in the context of the implementation of the September 13 Palestinian–Israeli Declaration of Principles'.[6]

Three basic objectives animated international donors in 1993: sustaining the Israeli–Palestinian peace process; fostering economic and social development in the WBGS; and building Palestinian institutions within the framework of the self-government and autonomy which had been granted to the PA under Oslo. Although not explicitly stated at the time as pertaining to final status negotiations between the parties, building Palestinian institutions was viewed by most third-party actors as a first step towards the establishment of a Palestinian state.[7] By the early 2000s, a clear international consensus had emerged around the idea of a two-state solution as the best option for peace in the Middle East. This was embodied in the title of the peace plan unveiled by the Quartet in April 2003: a 'Performance-based roadmap to a permanent two-state solution to the Israeli–Palestinian conflict'.[8]

Background

In 1993, there was considerable optimism that the process of reaching a final peace deal would proceed uninterrupted during the five-year transitional period. After two years of the failed multilateral and bilateral talks initiated at the regional Middle East Peace Conference in Madrid in October 1991, the Israeli–Palestinian agreement which came out of the Oslo Secret Channel was seen as a remarkable opportunity for peace in the region. For the first time in the history of the Arab–Israeli conflict, Israel recognized the PLO as the representative of the Palestinian people and agreed to begin direct negotiations with it. For its part, the PLO not only reiterated its commitment to recognize Israel's right to live in peace and security and renounce the use of terrorism and other acts of violence, but, for the first time, also accepted the Israeli demand for an interim agreement without clear commitments on the nature of the future permanent settlement.[9] In providing the Palestinian population with 'tangible' improvements in basic infrastructure, living conditions and employment opportunities, the assumption was that foreign aid would enhance public support for the negotiations, and create a positive environment for achieving a comprehensive peace settlement.

Both were perceived as inextricably linked. An optimist, linear, functionalist conception of forward movement towards peace and development dominated the thinking on the economic aspects of peace in the Middle East. According to this approach, economic development and increased regional cooperation would strengthen and consolidate peace through 'spill-over effects'.[10] It was also well understood, although less openly said, that an economic 'stake in peace' was the necessary prerequisite for obtaining Palestinian agreement on the political concessions that they would be asked to make in order to fulfil the requirements of what was essentially an Israeli-dominated peace process. As explained by a World Bank official working on the WBGS portfolio at the time:

> The sense was that if there was going to be a peace process leading to statehood – this was not said at the time but that's what everyone assumed, then you would need a strong economy and a 'stake in peace'. If people are benefiting economically, then they are happy with the peace process.... It would also help the Palestinians to make the 'painful decisions' that they would need to make, especially giving up the right of return. The idea was to have a strong economic rationale to buy Palestinians into agreeing to lesser political goals. There was also the idea of a gradual binding of the two economies so as to bring integration of the two peoples.

Yet, 12 years later, by the time Hamas was elected into government, little integration had been achieved and little peace remained to be upheld, despite the fact that more than US$8 billion had collectively been disbursed to the

Palestinian population of the oPt. The years 2002–2003 in particular saw a dramatic upsurge in violence and confrontation characterized by frequent Palestinian suicide attacks against Israelis, and large-scale military operations by Israeli armed forces involving incursions into Palestinian areas, re-occupation of major cities, refugee camps, towns and villages, the imposition of prolonged curfews, ever tighter movement restrictions, as well as the systematic targeting, damage and destruction of the Palestinian institutions and infrastructure paid for by the donor community in the 1990s.

There had been no formal negotiations between the parties since the Taba Summit in January 2001 and the internationally contrived Roadmap never got off the ground, although both parties had officially committed themselves to it.[11] The only political 'movement' on the diplomatic front had been Israel's unilateral disengagement from Gaza and parts of the northern West Bank in the summer of 2005. By default, and in the absence of direct bilateral negotiations between the parties, disengagement – and the supposed opportunity for peace this represented – became the diplomatic and donor 'game in town'. Between mid-2004 and the end of 2005 (and before it was replaced by a new focus on Hamas), disengagement captured international attention and third-party diplomatic and financial endeavours, even if few Middle East experts and observers on the ground actually believed this would mark a major breakthrough in the resolution of the conflict, a prediction which has since been vindicated by the violence, lawlessness and impoverishing socio-economic conditions which have engulfed the Gaza Strip. Finally, although at the declaratory level there had been a growing acceptance of the two-state solution, the feasibility of its materialization had dramatically decreased since the onset of Oslo.[12] Paradoxically, while the 1990s saw an *evolution* of the idea of a Palestinian state which also gained increasing international support and legitimacy, there was an *involution* of its materiality.

Indeed, the ignored or purposely downplayed reality on the ground has been that Palestinian territorial, demographic, socio-economic and political fragmentation increased throughout Oslo and subsequently intensified with the onset of the *intifada*. As this book argues, though the Palestinian leadership bears responsibility for the way the situation evolved after Oslo, notably in terms of the non-transparent, authoritarian and repressive nature of the administration it headed, this multifaceted process of fragmentation has in large part been caused by a number of mutually reinforcing Israeli policies, namely: closure, security/military control, and continuing occupation and colonization of the Palestinian territories through such measures as land confiscation, settlement expansion, the construction of a segregated by-pass road network and, from 2002, the building of the Separation Barrier in the West Bank. This process of dispossession, progressive transfer of the Palestinian population and 'bantustanization', whereby the West Bank, East Jerusalem and Gaza Strip have become a collection of internally fragmented areas and population enclaves physically separated from one another, stands in sharp contradiction to the *sine qua non* of territorial contiguity as the basis for an economically and politically viable Palestinian state.[13]

The representation of the Israeli–Palestinian conflict in the West, and in particular in the US, is often so distorted and simplified that to the extent that the extreme bleakness of the Palestinian living conditions is understood at all, the general assumption is that this multifaceted process of fragmentation and dispossession started after the failure of the Camp David Summit in July 2000, largely as the result of the onset of Palestinian violence. Such was the scale of the revolt which erupted in the autumn of 2000, so high had been the hopes and expectations invested in the American-sponsored peace summit and so pervasive became the one-sided Israeli narrative about Prime Minister Barak's 'generous offer',[14] that it quickly developed into conventional wisdom that, from then on, everything went downhill and the 'progress' – diplomatic, developmental, security and otherwise – achieved in the late 1990s was reversed.

The latter part of the 1990s was undoubtedly calmer, more hopeful and more prosperous than the mid-1990s, and when compared of course to the crisis of the 2000s. However, this was only relative. Far from being a product of the *intifada*, this comprehensive process of Palestinian fragmentation can be traced back to the onset of Oslo itself – and arguably to developments that go back to 1967, when Israel began its colonization and military occupation of East Jerusalem, the West Bank and Gaza, and before that to 1948, when more than half of the native population living in Palestine at the time was displaced and dispossessed.[15]

Not only have these measures enhanced Israeli control and profoundly transformed the physical and demographic landscape of the oPt, but the 'cantonization', closure and severe restrictions on the internal and external movement of Palestinian goods and people have also been the proximate cause of the recurrent economic crises that have engulfed the WBGS since the mid-1990s. These measures, and notably the fact that the Palestinian economy has been progressively shut out of the Israeli labour market without simultaneously gaining access to other external markets, had already precluded the possibility of Palestinian growth and development before the outbreak of the *intifada*, and resulted in a fully fledged – and entirely man-made – humanitarian crisis after 2002. This has been compounded by an extreme level of Palestinian fiscal dependency on both Israel and international donors. The much advertised issue of PA corruption and internal mismanagement practices only made things worse, but contrary to another well-received wisdom, this has only been – as this book demonstrates – a marginal factor in determining the overall poor economic performance of the occupied territories.

As for the Palestinian domestic scene, internal disintegration has perhaps not been initially as appreciable as were territorial crumbling and socio-economic decline. It is certainly the case that the fragmentation of the Palestinian body politic at large was accentuated after Oslo, partly through the marginalization of the PLO, and the progressive exclusion of the Palestinians residing outside the

WBGS from a political and civic process to which they too are entitled under international law.[16] Nonetheless, if arguably the very creation of the PA – and the dominant Western narrative thereafter – has functionally prejudiced the Palestinians not living within the oPt, the international focus on consolidating a Palestinian regime through unqualified support for President Arafat and his administration initially provided an illusion of political stability.

The prevailing orthodoxy throughout the Oslo years was that only Arafat was capable of delivering security for the Israelis (which meant above all containing the radical, mainly Islamist, opposition to the peace process) and concluding a peace deal. Within the Oslo 'security first' paradigm, progress in the political process, Israeli redeployments from the oPt, and ceding control to the PA were all conditional upon Palestinian security performance as judged by Israel. This emphasis on delivering security in turn militated against democratization and the establishment of the rule of law in the WBGS, as well as against the development of self-sustaining, representative, and accountable Palestinian institutions. As famously stated by Prime Minister Rabin in September 1993:

> I prefer the Palestinians to cope with the problem of enforcing order in the Gaza Strip. The Palestinians will be better at it than we were because they will allow no appeals to the Supreme Court and will prevent the Israeli Association of Civil Rights from criticizing the conditions there by denying it access to the area. They will rule by their own methods, freeing, and this is most important, the Israeli army soldiers from having to do what they will do.[17]

As will be shown in this book, the nature of the Palestinian regime which developed after 1994 has not only largely been the result of the security orientation of Oslo and of Arafat's personal style of management, but is also linked to the PA 'client' relationship to Israel which retained control over the majority of the Palestinian territory as well as most Palestinian resources and rents, and thus has had the ability to inflict significant penalties on the Palestinians for non-compliance in the diplomatic and security spheres.[18] Within this context, the growth of authoritarianism and neo-patrimonial practices among the Palestinian bureaucratic elite was inadvertently encouraged by an international community anxious to sustain the 'peace process' and not to undermine an already vulnerable, fragile and contested PA, both domestically and vis-à-vis Israel.[19] For the same reasons, donors also turned a blind eye to reports of corruption, mismanagement and human rights abuses until relatively late in the decade. Matters of governance and reform only came to the forefront of the international agenda in mid-2002 in the context of a bankrupt and de-legitimized PA in need of budgetary support, and amidst calls by some governments, notably the US and Israel, for regime change and the removal of President Arafat. By then, though, the PA, and its leading faction Fatah, had lost not only the ability to deliver security for the Israelis, but also credibility and legitimacy among its own people, as evidenced by the electoral victory of Hamas as a national alternative to a moribund, fragmented and discredited regime. Indeed, ten years of failed peace process had gravely radicalized Palestinian politics.

Thus, when assessed against the goals of peace, socio-economic development and the establishment of an independent state, the outcome of more than a decade of sustained international efforts in Palestine can hardly make one rejoice. Unquestionably, 12 years of active involvement and high levels of financial support have not been without any result: the basic needs of the population have been covered; some degree of infrastructural development took place; and institutions of Palestinian self-government were established and functioned for some years (albeit with a debatable level of efficiency and continuing reliance on external financing already in the period before Hamas was elected, and after that those institutions ceased to function altogether. Internationally certified national and legislative elections were held in 1996, 2005 and 2006. Most critically, the international community declared itself in favour of Palestinian statehood as the desirable outcome for a permanent and just resolution of the Palestinian–Israeli conflict. Nevertheless, these achievements seem modest when measured against the acute state of violence and political stalemate that has characterized the Palestinian–Israeli relationship since 2000, as well as the overall security, geo-political, socio-economic and human picture that has prevailed in the oPt throughout this period.

Funding the demise of the Palestinian state

This book seeks to comprehend the following paradox: how vast and unprecedented amounts of foreign assistance provided in support of Oslo were supposed to accompany a diplomatic process that was to lead to the resolution of the Israeli–Palestinian conflict according to a two-state paradigm, but instead saw a deepening of the Israeli colonization in the West Bank and a pervasive process of Palestinian demographic, territorial, socio-economic and political fragmentation that is fundamentally at odds with the aim of establishing a viable, independent Palestinian state.

As mentioned, at its conceptual core, the international community's approach was premised upon an unsophisticated but common assumption about linear progress between peace, security and development. This conception has come under increasing scrutiny by aid analysts and practitioners, especially as it pertains to complex emergencies and particularly violent and intractable conflicts. Nonetheless, to this day, aid remains the hallmark of every post-conflict reconstruction and state-building enterprise. International assistance is often conceived as a device to generate behavioural change in recipient countries, and this is particularly the case in conflict and post-conflict environments. If used adroitly and as part of a comprehensive strategy, foreign aid may help cement a peace deal. However, if the reasons why money may contribute to the success of a political process in some contexts rather than others are manifold and complex, aid as a substitute for politics has more often than not proven to be a recipe for disaster. This book reveals how this occurred in the Israeli–Palestinian case.

Foreign aid to the WBGS has been geared towards three basic objectives (peace process, socio-economic assistance and institution-building), but the thrust of the international community has come from one overriding strategic goal: sustaining the Oslo peace process. On the surface, this may seem to be uncontroversial. Indeed, it has been the *raison d'être* for the massive international financial engagement in the first place. But it has also been premised on the international assumption that both sides converge around the basic idea of a two-state solution, even if the 'details' of the final peace deal would remain to be worked out during final status negotiations. Had this indeed been the case, Israeli policies in the oPt are difficult to explicate. As will be shown in Chapters 2 and 3, Palestinian fragmentation and dispossession after Oslo have been too comprehensive and systematic to be seen as merely accidental or only linked to Palestinian security performance. Instead, it has been the result of a determined colonization strategy pursued by all Israeli governments regardless of party affiliation to disengage from heavily populated Palestinian areas while expanding Israel's territorial and demographic grip on key areas of the oPt, and remain in effective control.

While there has been a recognition across the Israeli political spectrum that self-government or even some sort of a Palestinian state is necessary so as to avoid having to maintain the occupation ad infinitum or having to absorb the Palestinian population of the occupied territories into Israel, thereby jeopardizing its 'ethnic Zionist' character, this has not meant that a fully sovereign Palestinian state provides a long-term solution to Israel's 'Palestinian problem' – or indeed, Israel's 'Arab problem' and deep-seated sense of insecurity in the Middle East. As forcibly argued by Mushtaq Khan, a state might actually hinder Israel's perceived room for manoeuvre to 'manage' the problem within the ethno-demographic reality of contemporary Israel–Palestine. This is so because

> Even after the creation of a Palestinian state, a significant Palestinian minority would remain in Israel with Israeli citizenship. The Israeli Palestinian minority was already around 20 per cent of the Israeli population at the time of the Oslo Agreements, and its faster growth was expected to steadily increase this percentage in the decades ahead. There was also the issue of the refugees. Many of them were unlikely to give up their historic struggle to gain the right of return, irrespective of any agreements signed by their leaders. This can explain why the Israeli political class may have felt that Israel as a Zionist state would always have to live with the 'Palestinian problem', and the exercise of power over the Palestinians was going to be a permanent part of Israel's survival strategy as it had always been in the past.[20]

The basic assumption upon which the international intervention has rested has thus arguably been problematic from the outset. This was not necessarily appreciable in 1993–1994. What this book explores, however, is why, as the 'facts on the ground' became more and more compelling in the oPt and notably the contradiction between its avowed state-building objective and Palestinian multifaceted fragmentation became so conspicuous, the international community clung to its initial objective of 'sustaining the peace process' through an unprecedented amount of funds to the WBGS and, in so doing, has been complicit in a set of disastrous outcomes which resonate to this day.

It is beyond the scope of this book to offer a comprehensive and sophisticated assessment of the reasons Oslo did not bring peace and security to both peoples, in addition to socio-economic benefits to the Palestinian population. Reasons are manifold, views are polarized, and there is little consensus on this matter, either in academia, on the Palestinian and Israeli sides, or amongst the diplomats and international bureaucrats who have participated in the endeavour. Some believe that Oslo – as a negotiation process between two unequal parties – was structurally flawed and doomed from the outset, principally because it postponed the most contentious but important issues (Jerusalem, refugees, borders, etc.) until final status negotiations and did not stipulate a clear political endgame, thereby favouring the considerably stronger party, Israel, by perpetuating the status quo. Indeed, not everyone has seen in the agreement the 'historical breakthrough' that was triumphantly asserted by the international community at the time. Others have argued that 'everything went downhill' after Israeli Prime Minister Rabin was assassinated in 1995. As noted by a World Bank official:

> I hold a fairly simplistic view, but believe that the beginning of the end started with Rabin's assassination. Both sides then lost the dynamism and commitment to move forward. Israelis failed to implement what had been agreed in terms of territorial withdrawal, an end to settlement expansion, and a more equitable share of natural resources. For instance, the settlers were getting access to water at a much lower cost and Palestinians were getting one tenth of what the settlers were getting. What stake do you have as a Palestinian? What makes you think that the resolution of the conflict is working in your favour? Not much, especially since closure and other economic policies were also undermining the Palestinian economy, and there was no solid progress towards a state. It was by and large in Israeli hands to make things happen on the ground and give them a stake, but they did not. Hence there was less and less commitment on the Palestinian side to peace, although opinion polls always showed that the majority continued to support a peaceful resolution of the conflict. Leaving aside the question of whether Arafat was committed or not, it was a hard sell for any

Palestinian as they did not see any improvement in their lives. If Rabin had not been shot, things might have been the same, but clearly with his death things went downhill.

Many have perceived the advent of Prime Minister Netanyahu in 1996 as marking a turning point. In the words of a US diplomat: 'Since the elections of Netanyahu, we could feel that things were not going on the right track; until then, there was a sense that we were moving forward.'

Still others have argued that the momentum for peace was sustained up until the Hebron Protocol of 1997. This was the view shared by another American official:

> The problem is not that we were naïve in 1993 but that after 1997 we did not have anything to show to the Palestinians. Both sides bear responsibilities and the US too for not having put enough pressure on either side. Why did the settlements double during the Oslo period? We believed that it wasn't worth putting any pressure on Israel as long as the Palestinians got what they wanted (i.e. redeployments), but in fact the trust was eroded. On the other hand, incitement remained very important on the Palestinian side and we did not pay enough attention to it.

No matter what the perception and analysis of the lack of diplomatic progress in the mid-1990s, and despite the continuing deterioration of the situation on the ground, the most commonly agreed view (expressed below by a World Bank staff member) is that Barak's tenure of power in 1999–2000 re-ignited an opportunity to move the peace process forward politically:

> The Declaration of Principles envisaged a five-year transitional period. It was clear that we were never going to meet the peace process time-line, but at Taba, we could have reached an agreement. We were not that far away, it was feasible. Donors had managed to keep the Palestinian state from collapsing. We were compensating for closure, which in the mid-90s was already quite harsh, we re-channelled our money from reconstruction to short-term labour-intensive projects to keep things from collapsing entirely. But we managed and we actually came close to a peace accord. You cannot say that people were so far away from the mark. But then the *intifada* broke out.

Others talk less of an opportunity than of a 'strong hope', after the political drawbacks characterizing the Netanyahu years, that the process would be jump-started again. But the Camp David and Taba summits ended in failure, while the *intifada* began. As noted by a European official:

In the late 1990s, there was a strong hope that things were going to get there. There was some frustration at delays, at the erosion of the trust between the parties. But, on the international side, many people did not want to disturb the process by criticizing it, because of the hope that things would improve. But they did not. Camp David was a big mistake, the Palestinians did not want to go, they were not ready to go, but were coerced into going and then blamed for the failure of the summit.... The whole period was characterized by ups and downs. We were naïve. We did not see that too many people were opposed to a two-state solution and there was not a strong enough intervention on the part of the international community.

Whatever one's take on the state of the bilateral negotiations in the 1990s, there is little dispute that the 'peace process' did not unfold according to plan, even before the outbreak of the *intifada* and, a fortiori, after the crisis broke out. Violence on both sides has been continuous; not one Oslo target has ever been met; trust between the two parties and populations has receded; Israeli colonization deepened and the territorial and socio-economic conditions of the Palestinian population have unremittingly deteriorated. There is little controversy about these facts; they have been witnessed, documented and known by all parties concerned. Moreover, although there is no agreement on which event, or series of events, has marked a turning point – arguably, none of them have – and all observers would concur that Palestinian suicide attacks have also greatly contributed to Oslo's downfall, it must be noted that most have traced the 'beginning of the end' prior to Camp David to events primarily connected to Israel. That the diplomatic process has been largely dominated by Israel and, on the international side, by the US unwaveringly supportive of its ally, is not in serious dispute either.

Over time, as deterioration in the situation was becoming more evident, the international community found itself in a terrible quandary. Perhaps because of the optimism and hopes generated in 1993–1994, no one on the international side has been able to contemplate 'letting go' of the process. The stakes of reaching a peace deal in the Middle East seemed too important, and immense personal and capital investment by all stakeholders had been made. There has also been a degree of institutional inertia, as well as an element of personal vanity, on the part of the international civil servants involved: it was difficult to renounce the expectation, aspiration, privilege even, of being part of such a high-profile, historical and, hopefully, successful undertaking. 'They' could not afford to doubt or stop trying and, most importantly, 'they' had to hope that things would get better, even if the situation on the ground suggested the absolute opposite. Even criticizing the 'process' has been problematic; according to an EC bureaucrat: 'You ran the risk of disturbing it.' And, in the words of an American official: 'The peace process was like a bicycle. Even if you pedalled slowly you had to move. Otherwise you fell over.'

But on the international side, the diplomatic process could not easily be moved by anyone except the United States, and American policy has in turn been highly constrained by domestic politics.[21] During the Oslo years, and culminating at Camp David, the multilateral Madrid track was marginalized. The US, under the Clinton administration with Dennis Ross as the chief Middle East peace negotiator, Aaron David Miller as Deputy Special Middle East Coordinator, and Martin Indyk as either US Ambassador to Israel or Assistant Secretary of State for Near East Affairs, increasingly monopolized the bilateral political track to the exclusion of other actors – including the career Middle East specialists of the Near East Affairs section of the State Department. Their approach towards the conflict, which was also a reflection of their own personal commitment to Israel and, for some, of their ties to prominent pro-Israeli organizations in the US such as the American–Israel Public Affairs Committee (AIPAC) and the Washington Institute for Near East Policy (WINEP), rested first and foremost on the need to deepen America's strategic partnership with Israel. 'Given its small size and vulnerability', only a secure Israel would make concessions for peace and take the risks entailed in withdrawing from the oPt. This necessitated that 'no wedge would be driven between the United States and Israel' and America's strong financial and political support, as well as a strong commitment to her security concerns.[22] This held when Labour was in power as well as when Likud was in office, although Clinton and his staff did not hide their antipathy towards Prime Minister Netanyahu.[23] As pointed out by Kathleen Christison:

> All these men believe that a peace settlement can be achieved by cajoling Israel into taking small, incremental steps rather than by squeezing or codling it. They appear to believe that because they have often been harshly critical of Israel, they are unbiased on Palestinian–Israeli issues. They all have had a deep interest on Arab–Israeli issues since their teenage years, and most have at least some familiarity with Arabs...But to call them neutral, or able to view the issue objectively from both Palestinian and Israeli perspectives, is to misunderstand the mindset from which they are operating....These men are openly regarded in Israel as identifying with Israel's Labor party. According to Palestinian negotiator Hanan Ashrawi, who met regularly with them during preparations for the 1991 Madrid conference and during bilateral peace talks in Washington in 1992 and 1993, the Palestinians saw the American team as representing a map not of America's domestic political scene but of Israel's, with allegiances to Labor, Likud, or Peace Now.[24]

The thrust of American policy towards Israel and the Israeli–Palestinian conflict did not fundamentally change under the administration of George W. Bush. The style was different, as was the initial degree of direct engagement from the White House. The more 'hands off' approach of Bush – in particular during his first term in office – departed somewhat from his predecessor's active personal involvement. To a certain extent, under Secretary of State Colin Powell, the centre of gravity for policy-making moved from the political appointees of the Clinton era back to the career diplomats of the State Department Near Eastern Affairs. The post 9/11 context of the global war on terror, as well as the attempt to reduce anti-American sentiment in the Arab world while the US launched military interventions in Afghanistan and Iraq, may also explain America's initially lower profile. Furthermore, with the onset of the *intifada*, there was in any event no bilateral dialogue to sponsor and be actively engaged in. The relationship between the new US President and Prime Minister Sharon was at times poor, as evidenced by a number of public rows, notably in the autumn of 2001 and again in the midst of Operation Defensive Shield when Israel was asked to show restraint in the oPt and Bush made public his 'vision of a Palestinian state'.[25]

However, despite America's initial detachment, the US continued to be protective of its leading diplomatic role, and resolute in its support for Israel. The vision of such leading neo-conservatives as Vice-President Cheney, Paul Wolfowitz, John Bolton, Richard Perle and Elliot Abrams was decidedly premised on the notion of 'Israel first'.[26] During the years preceding Arafat's death, the US refused to deal with the Palestinian President. Furthermore, in 2004, in what was widely seen as a historic change in US official Middle East policy, President Bush rescinded Palestinian right of return and officially accepted Israel's intention to retain the major settlement blocs as part of any future peace deal.[27] The establishment of the Hamas-led government in 2006 only made the US approach to the conflict even more lopsided, it being almost entirely defined through the narrow prism of terrorism and its 'global war on terror'.

Strong US support for Israel and American overall diplomatic predominance, in addition to Oslo's procedural bias towards process rather than substance, has greatly limited the room to manoeuvre of other third-party actors – whether the EU or UN – all the more since they too are subject to internal dissensions and pressures, as will be detailed in Chapter 4.[28] More generally, there is also an unusual level of anxiety in governing circles in the West when it comes to criticizing Israeli policies. This is linked in large part to the deliberate instrumentalization by some of anti-Semitism and the Holocaust, and to the virulence of the attacks unleashed by extremist elements among pro-Israel supporters against individuals and institutions that disapprove of Israeli actions publicly. It has resulted in a considerable degree of self-censorship and resignation among diplomats, as well as in donors being exceedingly apprehensive when it comes to tackling any issue of direct concern to their work related to the impact on the Palestinians of Israeli policies on the ground, whether they be movement restrictions, obstacles to project implementation, Israeli destruction of donor projects, and, more generally, the socio-economic and humanitarian conditions in the oPt.[29]

It is one of the main contentions of this book that, as the international community at large has only been able to marginally influence Israeli policy or

American mediation efforts, aid to the Palestinians has come to be used as a 'fig leaf' for its inability to substantially move the process forward politically and a cover of the rollercoaster dynamics of a peace process largely dominated by Israel and the US. The aid agenda is what has given other third-party actors the leeway to continue to 'pedal'.

As pointed out, one might assume that as the situation did not unfold as envisaged, as donors realized the extent to which continuing Israeli colonial practices and policies on the ground jeopardized the development and state-building agenda to which they had committed – in addition to the peace process itself – they would have adjusted their intervention to factor in the composite, evolving but steadily deteriorating local realities and, above all, the role played by Israel, not least because she continued to exert control over Palestinian borders, natural resources, currency and fiscal policy, and remained the occupying power under international humanitarian law (IHL). This is all the more so as it had been explicitly recognized in 1994 that the success of their assistance programmes required 'stability in the Occupied Territories, steady progress in bilateral and multilateral negotiations, and a maturation of internal political processes'.[30]

However, the donors' apparent unity of purpose to support the 'peace process' remained staunch, unchallenged and resistant to any changes on the ground, and even to the 'peace process' itself. In the midst of the *intifada*, when it required some stretch of the imagination to detect signs of the 'peace process', donors continued to justify their continuing to finance the Palestinians according to the above original purpose. Supporting 'the peace process' had become the dominant, immovable paradigm, to the point of tautology. Every action or absence of action was justified by and dissolved into the 'peace process'. In effect, donors espoused the same 'crisis management' mode that characterized international diplomatic involvement in Middle East peacemaking by focusing on day-to-day problem solving and the latest peace move or plan ('the game in town'). As a result, and contrary to the widespread assumption that relief assistance has largely been a product of the *intifada*, donors actually shifted most of their funds to emergency assistance as early as 1994–1995, to alleviate the social impact of the severe economic and budgetary crises which engulfed the WBGS, and to provide a minimum level of support to the nascent PA.

Admittedly, the levels of emergency aid peaked after 2000, and the relative balance between relief and development varied over the years according to the intensity of the recurrent crises which beleaguered the oPt after 1994. Nonetheless, despite donors' best efforts to maintain a veneer of medium-term development, and to continue (rhetorically, at least) framing their assistance programmes within a broader state-building objective, aid to the oPt was from the outset overwhelmingly reactive and short-term in nature. Donors kept international assistance coming at all costs, largely to mitigate and offset the damaging socio-economic and humanitarian effects of Israeli colonial enterprise and policies on the ground. This enabled them to keep the 'peace process' alive politically, and most importantly their role within it. Nevertheless, if 'low politics' and the aid agenda was what enabled other (non-US) third-party actors the opportunity to be part of a process from which they would otherwise have been largely excluded, 'high politics' and American–Israeli predominance also sharply reduced donors' latitude. The donor agenda was not only a palliative to remedy the socio-economic crisis and donors' own political powerlessness. It was also totally subservient to the immediate, and seemingly ever changing, political and security exigencies as largely determined by Israel and the US.

In the process, the specificity of the Israeli–Palestinian context, notably the international legal framework stemming from continuing Israeli military occupation, colonization and expansion, and the absence of Palestinian sovereignty, was erased by the dominant and ahistorical post-Oslo approach to the conflict. Donors focused on socio-economic 'stop gap' solutions, and on keeping the PA on (the 'peace process') track by means of a complex assortment of carrots and sticks. Frustration grew at Israeli actions, vis-à-vis the Palestinian territory and economy, formulaic statements to that effect were routinely pronounced, and increasing concerns were voiced by both donors and diplomats in private, but the international community failed to initiate any sustained action to influence Israeli policy, whether through diplomatic or economic means. They continued to behave as if the Palestinian development and state-building effort could proceed despite what was actually happening on the ground.

Scope and terminology

This book explores the politics of international aid to the Palestinians within the context of the Oslo peace process and *intifada*, with a focus on the years between the creation of the PA and the death of Arafat. It sets out the broad context within which international aid has been delivered; describes the multifaceted process of Palestinian territorial, socio-economic and political fragmentation which occurred at a time of substantial international engagement; analyses trends and changes in the aid instruments used and the reasons behind these changes, the links between political decision-making and the provision of aid, the role and influence of the main international actors as well as the two parties themselves; finally, it looks at the effects of international assistance on the Palestinian population and territory, on Israeli policies in the oPt, and on the conflict itself, particularly on the prospect of its resolution along a two-state paradigm.

From the outset, six caveats or qualifications should be made regarding the scope of this book.

First, the international community in the Oslo and *intifada* period focused overwhelmingly on the territory of the WBGS and on providing assistance to the Palestinians living there, to the detriment of Palestinian refugees in neighbouring Arab countries and the diaspora at large. This focus has been restrictive and enormously detrimental in many respects, in particular since it inadvertently reduced the Palestinian people and nation to the one third living in the oPt, thereby contributing to changing the terms of the debate and international discourse on and perception of the Palestinian right to self-determination, and on the questions of refugees and the right of return. This also led to the marginalization of the majority of the Palestinians and fragmentation of the Palestinian body politic as mentioned above. These issues will be touched upon in the following pages, notably when examining the aborted Palestinian democratization process in the context of donors' narrow support to the PA regime. Nevertheless, following international donors over the course of the last decade, this book focuses on examining international assistance to the WBGS.

Second, it does not purport to be an account of *why* political negotiations, and the Oslo process, failed to deliver peace and security for both peoples. The political failure is sufficiently sweeping, and violence devastating, to distribute responsibility for misjudgement and misguided policies across a multitude of players and organizations. However, it does examine the context within which aid to the Palestinians has been provided, given that foreign assistance is seldom dispensed in a political, socio-economic and legal vacuum. Hence, part of this book necessarily analyses Israeli policies in the oPt, and their security, political, legal and socio-economic effects on the Palestinian population. This is necessary in order to ascertain how they complied (or not) with, and impacted on, the overall diplomatic and ODA processes, and how the international community responded (or not), within the context of its own avowed political, developmental and humanitarian objectives.

Third, since aid was not channelled to Israel by the donor community as a whole, except bilaterally from the United States, this book does not look directly into the effects of international assistance on the State of Israel.[31] This may prima facie give the reader an impression of imbalance, yet this is unavoidable given the nature of international assistance and the focus of this book. This sense of imbalance may be reinforced by the profoundly asymmetrical nature of the conflict in so far as the Palestinians continue to live under military occupation or in exile, and have not yet achieved a comparable level of political, diplomatic, military and economic independence, or indeed statehood.

Fourth, this book will principally examine the policies of, and interaction between, four main actors: the United States, the European Union, the United Nations and the World Bank. This is because these four have dominated most aspects of the political and aid processes at both the local and the capital levels, as will be shown in Chapter 1. Norway has also been central, given its involvement in the secret negotiations leading up to Oslo, but its role remained less influential and will not therefore be examined in great detail. Other donors, such as the Arab states, which, through the Islamic Development Bank and their contribution to the PA budget, became one of the main financial backers to the WBGS during the *intifada*, will equally not fall within the purview of this investigation. Given the broader Israeli–Arab context, and as most Arab donors do not have local representation in either Israel or the WBGS, they have never been part of the 'club' of key Western donors who shaped the multilateral aid process and agenda.

Fifth, the change in international funding for Palestinian civil society organizations will similarly not be examined in detail, except as it relates to the issue of PA financing, and how funds originally enjoyed by these organizations were, after Oslo, directed instead to support the fledgling administration as part of the overall regime consolidation donor agenda. In the same vein, the plethora of people-to-people projects, conferences or second-track initiatives which flourished under Oslo and sustained the 'peace industry' is not analysed. Finally, as the focus is on official foreign aid exclusively, informal channels of assistance to the Palestinian population, such as the one through Islamic welfare organizations which are believed to be very important, is equally not explored.[32]

Last, a reference to language. Influenced by constructivist approaches to International Relations, I share the view that preferences and interests are socially, politically and discursively constructed through the mediation of such human attributes and 'cognitive restraints on rationality' as language, ideas, beliefs, perceptions, operational codes, knowledge and complex learning. There can be no objective world independent of the social categories through which it is analytically identified by human beings. 'Social configurations are not "objective" like mountains or forests, but neither are they "subjective" like dreams or flights of speculative fancy. They are... inter-subjective constructions.'[33] In this view, language, discourse and perceptions matter.

In the case of the Palestinian–Israeli conflict, there is often more than one term to describe the same 'reality'. Even a single organization, such as the UN, will employ a variety of different labels depending on which part of the organization is using it. This essentially reflects the different, and conflicting, Palestinian and Israeli historical and national narratives, and the attempt by other parties not to take a position either way, thus often creating a third, alternative expression. For instance, what the international community and international law refers to as 'settlements', Israelis call 'Jewish neighbourhoods' and Palestinians 'settlements' or 'colonies'. Similarly, the UN Secretary-General (SG) and the donor community in the field talk about the 'Separation Barrier', while Israelis refer to it as the 'security fence' and Palestinians, the UN General Assembly (GA) and the International Court of Justice (ICJ) use the term 'Wall'. The official UN terminology for the Palestinian areas is 'occupied Palestinian territory' (covering the West Bank, Gaza and East Jerusalem), but many donors and international organizations prefer to use the more nondescript 'West Bank and Gaza Strip' while Israel uses the biblical 'Judea and Samaria' to denote the West Bank. The word 'Palestine' is also used in anticipation of the creation of a Palestinian state within the 1967 borders, or with reference to the right of the Palestinian people to self-determination, including their right to an independent State of Palestine.

In this book, I will vary the terminology used. For example, I will use the international humanitarian law and official UN terminology when describing the 'oPt', but I will also sometimes refer to it as the 'WBGS' for the sake of diversity, and because both correctly denote the territory, albeit in different respects. Similarly, I will use the terms 'Separation Barrier' and 'Wall' inter-changeably because the physical reality constitutes both. For its part, the term 'Fence' will be employed in specific reference to the Israeli designation only, as anyone who has actually seen the structure *de visu* will find it far-fetched to describe it as such. While the high level of political sensitivity surrounding the Israeli–Palestinian conflict makes it necessary to abide by the highest standards of accuracy and impartiality, it is equally important not to uncritically utilize and interiorize terminology – whether international, Israeli or Palestinian. The reasons for caution are real, manifold and well known. Terms should thus be considered and selected in full knowledge of their meaning and implications of their usage.

Chapter outline

Chapter 1 introduces the analytical background to this thesis, summarizing the key issues raised by the academic and aid communities over the last 15 years with regard to the linkages between aid, politics, conflict and peacebuilding. It also gives an overview of the specific legal and institutional frameworks within which international assistance to the Palestinians has been provided.

Chapters 2 and 3 document the phenomenon of Palestinian territorial, demo-graphic, socio-economic and political fragmentation which occurred after Oslo. They focus on Israeli policies of colonization and their socio-economic and political effects, as well as on the way the Palestinian leadership around Arafat adjusted through an examination of the nature of the Palestinian regime emerg-ing after 1994.

Chapter 4 looks at the relationship between the diplomatic and donor processes. It outlines the political stances, aid policies, respective role of and interaction between four main international actors (US, EU, UN and the World Bank), with a special emphasis on American–European relationship.

Chapter 5 details the evolution of the donor agenda and assistance pro-gramme to the Palestinian population between 1994 and 2004. It spells out some of the aid's impact at the humanitarian, socio-economic, political and normative levels, as well as on the prospect for resolving the conflict.

Chapter 6 also looks at some of the effects of ten years of international assis-tance but focuses specifically on the process of Palestinian institution-building.

1

AID BECAUSE OF POLITICS

The analytical, legal and institutional frameworks

Foreign aid is invariably a highly political enterprise. Its motives, objectives and effects are political, albeit to a greater or lesser extent and although the promotion of 'economic development and welfare' is the received definition of what constitutes its principal goal.[1] The political nature of assistance has been conceptualized in different ways. Some view aid as a gift, others as an instrument of imperialist domination, still others as a form of purchase. Its rationale has also been analysed through the prism of various paradigms: aid can be seen as motivated by moral imperatives and altruistic feelings (humane internationalism); it can be grounded in mutual economic advantage and enlightened self-interest (liberalism); or it can be driven by foreign policy objectives – whether geopolitical, commercial or cultural – and, in particular, security interests (realism). In reality, the motives for, and objectives of, foreign aid are often mixed and vary quite extensively over time according to each donor and to each particular setting, as well as to whether the assistance provided is developmental or humanitarian.[2]

As mentioned, foreign assistance to the WBGS was a direct response to the signing of the Oslo agreement and had the explicit political aim of sustaining the Israeli–Palestinian peace process. This combined different motives and meant different things to different international actors, as will be detailed in Chapter 4. Whatever the motivations, aid often implies an asymmetric power relationship between donor and recipient, as terms such as leverage, pressure, coercion and conditionality, often confusingly associated with foreign assistance, denote. In particular, over the last 15 years, the use of economic or political conditionality by donors has become a dominant feature of the commitment, disbursement and allocation of development funds. This has been seen, for instance, with the growth of 'democracy assistance' and so-called 'second-generation' conditionality whereby aid is linked to policy reform and a host of aspirations associated with Western liberal democracy which embraces such attributes as 'good' governance, the rule of law, transparency and respect for human rights.[3] Increasingly also, conditionality has been introduced in the context of emergency assistance, as in the Palestinian case, where budgetary support to the PA came to be conditioned on administrative reform from 2002 onwards.

This chapter first provides a brief overview of the key issues raised by the academic and aid communities over the last 15 years with regard to the linkages between aid, politics, conflict and peacebuilding. It then outlines the peculiarity of the environment under which international assistance was delivered, focusing on the legal status of the West Bank, Gaza Strip and East Jerusalem as well as on the evolution – over the course of the decade following Oslo – of international discourse and perceptions vis-à-vis this legal framework. Appreciating the complexity of this environment is essential to understanding the constraints faced by donors, and the room to manoeuvre available to them in their dealings with both the aid recipient, the Palestinians and the aid community's host country, Israel. Finally, this chapter details the institutional framework underpinning international aid politics to the WBGS and introduces the main political and donor protagonists of this case study.

Analytical background: aid, politics, conflict and peacebuilding

While the relationship between aid and politics is always complex, it is particularly intricate in conflict settings. Since the end of the Cold War, the changing nature of conflict, the new characterization of security as a development – or even a 'human' – concern and the weaknesses of international assistance to respond to the complex crises of the 1990s appear to have led to an increasing politicization of assistance whereby aid is now tied to donors' overall conflict-resolution strategy and political agenda of peace and security. This development took place within the context of calls in the aftermath of the crisis in Rwanda for increased 'coherence' between political and humanitarian interventions to manage complex emergencies.[4]

Aid harming politics

The *Joint Evaluation of Emergency Assistance to Rwanda* was extremely influential in this respect. It concluded that the critical failings in the international response to the genocide lay in the lack of a political strategy to deal with the crisis, relief operations thus disastrously serving as a smokescreen for inaction and, in effect, substituting for political intervention.[5] One of the report's main recommendations was greater policy coherence between the political and humanitarian dimensions of the international response to complex crises. This report, and experience in other conflict areas, encouraged new research on the interface between aid and politics. From a focus on exploring the political motivations of donors and governments, analysts turned their attention to the political impact of aid.

The debate which emerged in the aftermath of the Rwandan genocide over the way foreign aid influences the domestic processes and political economy of recipient countries and, more generally, the dynamics of conflict was first particularly vibrant within the humanitarian community. It emerged as evidence grew that aid had in some contexts inadvertently prolonged war, raising the 'spectre of the well-fed dead'. As famously stated in the opening lines of Mary Anderson's *Do No Harm*:

> When international assistance is given in the context of a violent conflict, it becomes a part of that context and thus also of the conflict. Although aid agencies often seek to be neutral or nonpartisan towards the winners and losers of a war, the impact of their aid is not neutral regarding whether conflict worsens or abates. When given in conflict settings, aid can reinforce, exacerbate, and prolong the conflict; it can also help to reduce tensions and to strengthen people's capacities to disengage from fighting and find peaceful options for solving problems. Often, an aid program does some of both: in some ways it worsens the conflict and in others it supports disengagement. But in all cases, aid given during conflict cannot remain separate from that conflict.[6]

Aid can easily be manipulated and become part of the political economy that sustains conflict and affects the economic capacity of belligerents: it can be stolen and diverted by armed factions for military purposes or contribute to the war effort by creating rent-seeking opportunities for local groups or by freeing up local resources.[7] Its distributional effects and impact on internal balances of power between different groups can ease social tensions or widen them, reinforce the peace process or undermine it.[8] Aid may also contribute to the continuation of conflict by enabling the parties, whether governments or opposition movements, to 'evade or defer their responsibility to address the urgent needs of civilian populations and to seek political solutions to the conflict'.[9] Furthermore, relief operations can also help maintain an illusion of international protection and instil a false sense of security among civilians, with potentially fatal consequences. As is succinctly put by Peter Uvin in an OECD study on the influence of aid in situations of violent conflict:

> All aid, at all times, creates incentives and disincentives, for peace or for war, regardless of whether these effects are deliberate, recognized or not, before, during or after war. The issue is then not whether or not to create (dis)incentives but, rather, how to manage them so as to promote conditions and dynamics propitious to non-violent conflict resolution.[10]

However, the idea that humanitarian actors should take conflict impact into account when devising programmes and interventions remains a controversial proposition. The classical conception of humanitarianism, as embodied in the Geneva Conventions and Protocols in reference to war situations, stresses the ethical imperative and legal right to protect and assist civilian victims on the basis of need alone, independently of political and military considerations and regardless of consequences.[11] The 'integrationist' approach to humanitarian and political action advocated in the mid-1990s has been seen by many as posing a threat to the independence of humanitarian action by subordinating it to governments' political objectives. Traditional humanitarianism continues to emphasize the primacy of the principles of universality, humanity, neutrality and impartiality, especially as the humanitarian dilemma remains compelling: if providing aid can relieve immediate suffering but at the risk of prolonging conflict, withholding aid may perhaps dampen violence but invariably at a high cost to the most vulnerable civilians. Nonetheless, despite these reservations, calls for a more politically informed response and 'damage limitation' policy to conflict situations, so as to mitigate aid's potentially harmful consequences, also gained credence within the relief community.

From the proposition that aid in wartime might have negative effects, the idea that the converse might also be true emerged. The debate on 'harm' and conflict impact thus converged with another major theme of reflection within the aid community in the 1990s, namely the relief-to-development debate and the appeal for more developmental approaches to relief in post-conflict contexts, linking humanitarian assistance with long-term strategies such as poverty alleviation, employment generation, environmental protection and institutional development. The objective would be to minimize the negative effects of emergency assistance, for example intensifying aid dependency and weakening local capacity. This rested on the recognition that transition processes could no longer be regarded as sequential or a continuum from relief to development, since a neat distinction from conflict to peace seldom occurred in practice. Rather, humanitarian and development aid often have to be provided simultaneously.[12]

New research also emphasized the need to refine the definition of peacebuilding and conceptualize it inductively: this implies refraining from assuming that every war-torn society will benefit equally from the standard menu of international assistance, and focusing instead on the in-depth analysis of the causes of a particular conflict and the interrelationship between the security, political, social and economic spheres, as well as seeking to devise appropriate short- and long-term strategies accordingly. Within this double context, aid came to be seen as a potential mechanism for conflict reduction and resolution: the proposition that assistance could be 'smart' and designed with the explicit political objective of addressing the root causes of conflict, shaping its processes and transforming it, gained support. From being an end in itself, humanitarian assistance became a means to foster developmental and peacebuilding goals as part of the overall 'coherence' strategy.[13] In the process, however, the distinctions between conflict prevention and conflict resolution, and between development and humanitarian aid, became increasingly blurred.

Aid in support of politics

As the role of aid in conflict areas expanded in the 1990s to be incorporated into a wider peace and security agenda, and greater emphasis was placed on the linkage between relief and development, a growing appreciation of the political impact of developmental aid also emerged. Concern that intervention by development agencies might also aggravate inequities and exacerbate conflict became widespread.[14] Agencies involved in development activities in a peacebuilding context faced the same 'politicization' dilemma as their humanitarian counterparts, although perhaps less acutely given the different terms of engagement of humanitarian and development actors with donors and Member States. This was nonetheless clearly the case for the Bretton Woods Institutions.[15]

With the World Bank and the IMF becoming prominent actors in multilateral reconstruction efforts, the issue of coordinating their development and financial strategies with the peace agenda of political and military actors came to the fore. Since its inception, the Bank had been directly concerned with conflict situations: it was established during the Second World War as the 'International Bank for Reconstruction and Development' and was active in post-conflict reconstruction during the Cold War. Nonetheless, it initially adopted a very cautious attitude vis-à-vis the 1990s debate on the role of external assistance in crisis prevention, peacebuilding and conflict management. This reticence stemmed mainly from the fact that the Bank does not like to see itself as a 'political' agency, although as an institution made up of Member States it is obviously affected by its member countries' political agendas, influence and voting majorities in the supervisory bodies. Still, its mandate is based on the doctrine of 'economic neutrality', with poverty reduction, economic stabilization and sustainable development being its central objectives.[16]

However, it rapidly became clear that in post-conflict settings, it was particularly difficult to insulate economic decision-making process from all political considerations.[17] For instance, the conflict-fuelling impacts of IFI standard neoliberal macroeconomic policies of fiscal and monetary restraint on war-torn societies became an area for major concern in the early 1990s. Calls for flexibility in the implementation of their macroeconomic programmes, as well as enhanced transparency, information sharing and coordination with other agencies involved in peacebuilding, such as the UN, became widespread.[18] The Bank sought to adapt in the latter half of the 1990s, created a 'Post-Conflict Unit' in 1997, and formulated a new reconstruction operational framework for supporting war-to-peace transitions. Although it ruled out military and security reform as beyond its mandate, it nonetheless increased its capacity to address issues such as land mine clearance or the demobilization and reintegration of ex-combatants and refugees. More generally, the Bank assumed a growing role in the provision of social safety nets for vulnerable population groups affected by conflicts and in the overall coordination of international aid to post-conflict countries, such as in leading with the UN Post-Conflict Joint Needs

23

Assessments. In 2001, the Post-Conflict Unit was renamed the Conflict Prevention and Reconstruction Unit, reflecting a willingness to go a step further and integrate sensitivity to conflict in the Bank's activities. In 2002, the organization also established the Low Income Countries Under Stress (LICUS) initiative to focus on assistance and aid effectiveness in the specific cases of 'fragile states'. However, although its thinking and operational resources have evolved considerably over the last decade, including through the development of a conflict analysis framework, the setting up of dedicated trust funds and the publication of policy papers based on best practice and lessons learned, as well as enhanced cooperation with United Nations agencies, it has so far not looked in a systematic way at the effects of its own assistance on conflict.[19]

This criticism is not restricted to the Bank. An increased awareness among donors of the significant and multifaceted impact of foreign assistance on war and peace did not translate into the willingness to take the political implications of their assistance fully into consideration. Some, like the IFIs, invoke the limited scope of their mandates. In other bureaucratic institutions, such as the UN or national governments, the division between development cooperation and diplomatic services (or between political, humanitarian and development departments and agencies) remains the norm. Some governments such as that of the UK have tried to bring coherence to their action and bridge the security–political–development gap by establishing a joined-up government approach and bringing together the Department for International Development (DFID), the Foreign Office and the Ministry of Defence in the areas of conflict prevention and post-conflict.

But these initiatives have yet to result in donors collectively and systematically taking into consideration the full range of effects their assistance has on conflict or peace processes, with the aim of informing their programming. As suggested by James Boyce, this is not only a question of '*how much* aid is delivered, but also of (1) *what types* of aid are given? (2) *to whom?* and (3) *with what conditions* attached?' For instance, in looking at the types of aid donors disbursed, Boyce identifies several tensions between the short- and long-term demands of peacebuilding that donors should take into consideration when devising their programmes: for example, the trade-off between emergency relief and capacity-building; allocation of resources between current expenditures and investment; support for political stability and so-called pacification of the elite versus democratization and equalitarian growth. In addition, Boyce suggests that donors need to think not only in terms of assisting the country as a whole, but also in terms of assisting specific individuals, groups and classes, as well as the distributional effects of aid on the balance of power between various parties to the conflict and on the prospect for democratization.[20]

As the above makes clear, the multifaceted involvement in the 1990s of multilateral organizations, governments and aid agencies in conflict and post-conflict situations exposed, but did not simplify, the intricate enmeshing of aid and politics. Within the policy and academic community, new research yielded useful insights for peacebuilding but left much unexplored. In particular, by the early 2000s, it was increasingly acknowledged that the tensions between conflict management and resolution, humanitarian principles and developmental objectives, remained unresolved.

Aid instead of politics

Within the humanitarian community, the 'coherence' agenda increasingly came under attack for being perceived as an easy way to cover up for political inaction. According to Joanna Macrae, while the integrationist approach which emerged in the aftermath of the Rwanda crisis was premised on the development of a clear political strategy integrating all the different policy aspects necessary to deal with complex emergency, this did not materialize:

> In fact what seems to have happened is...that, through the idea of coherence, humanitarian aid has been renamed and re-packed as politics. Thus by funding for example the Strategic Framework, donors can claim they are supporting the peace process while expending very little diplomatic energy on a real peace process.[21]

In this way, aid is used as the primary form of external engagement in conflict-affected countries, especially in peripheral areas where governments have less incentive to intervene politically:

> through a conceptual sleight of hand, aid has become not a substitute for politics, but the primary form of engagement in conflict in 'unstrategic' countries. It has evolved from a short-term palliative to a way of building liberal peace on the periphery. The rich get diplomats, the poor get aid workers.[22]

She argued that instead of 'coherence', 'complementarity' may be perhaps a more successful way of conceptualizing the relationship between aid and politics: it 'might at least expose the different roles of humanitarian and political action and emphasize that political problems need political solutions, not aid solutions masquerading as political solutions'.[23] She stressed the need to reinvest in diplomatic actions.

Some scholars in International Relations (IR) also began to emphasize the need to re-focus on the political dimension of international assistance as a way to remedy the confusion over objectives and methods that emerged as peacebuilding came to encompass nearly every sector of aid to war-torn societies. In *Peace-building as Politics*, Elizabeth Cousens, Chetan Kumar and Karin Wermester contended that to be well designed and accountable for its achievements, peacebuilding 'requires establishing a strategic framework of objectives for international assistance, privileging within this framework the objectives of conflict resolution over other goals, and in relationship to that objective, setting priorities among international efforts'.[24] They argued that peacebuilding should be closer to its original purpose – consolidating whatever degree of peace has been achieved. Priority should be given to the *political* dimension of conflict and its resolution, that is primarily the emergence of stable and viable political processes so as build or strengthen the mechanisms to resolve conflict without violence:

> all programming that involves societies in conflict should be conceived with political impact in mind. Across the range of actors, from foreign ministers through relief and development agencies, programs and policies should be alert to their effect on prospects for the emergence of sustainable conflict management structures, eventually in the political arena.[25]

Without stable political processes, international efforts to rebuild the infrastructure and foster economic and social development will come to little long-term effect.

Outside academia, there has also been an increasing recognition of the need to tackle peacebuilding at the highest political levels, as evidenced by the decision of the UN Member States at the World Summit in 2005 to endorse the Secretary-General's proposals to create a Peacebuilding Commission (PBC), Support Office (PBSO) and Fund at the UN Headquarters in New York. The main purpose of the Commission, as an intergovernmental advisory body, is to bring together all relevant international actors to marshal resources and propose strategies for post-conflict peacebuilding and recovery, so as to add coherence and integration to international efforts across multiple areas – military, political, humanitarian, economic and institution-building.[26] Moreover, the growing realization that fragile and failed states pose a major threat to peace and security is leading to a new emphasis on the necessity to build not only national and local institutions, but also the core functions of the state. This is seen as the best way not only to ensure the population's safety and well-being, deliver basic services and maintain law and order, but also to address underlying causes of persistent conflict and be the receptacle for legitimacy. From the concept of peacebuilding, there is an increasing shift to state-building, in effect reaffirming the essentially political nature of such processes.[27]

This brief literature review has highlighted a number of general issues of relevance to the analysis of donor aid politics in conflict and post-conflict settings. The next two sections will look at some of the specificities of the Israeli–Palestinian context, starting with the legal status of the WBGS.

International law, discourse and perceptions

The occupied Palestinian territory (oPt)

Israel has de facto been occupying the West Bank, Gaza Strip and East Jerusalem since the 1967 Arab–Israeli war, but has consistently rejected the *de jure* applicability of the Fourth Geneva Convention to the oPt.[28] There is, however, an international consensus that international humanitarian law (IHL) applies. The position of all other High Contracting Parties to the Fourth Geneva Convention, the UN (through its various bodies, in particular the General Assembly, Security Council, the Economic and Social Council and the Commission on Human Rights) and the International Committee of the Red Cross (ICRC) is that the Geneva Conventions are applicable *de jure* to the oPt, including East Jerusalem.[29] The PLO also holds this position.[30] In addition, the international community, as embodied by the UN General Assembly, has recognized the right to self-determination of the Palestinian people.[31] Although East Jerusalem is occupied territory under IHL, the status of East Jerusalem in Israeli law differs from that of the West Bank and Gaza Strip. In 1967, the Knesset (the Israeli parliament) passed a law extending Israeli jurisdiction over East Jerusalem and in 1980 annexed the area, stating that 'Jerusalem, complete and united, is the capital of Israel'.[32] Palestinians residing in East Jerusalem therefore have a special status, holding Jerusalem IDs which are distinct from West Bank and Gaza IDs, on the one hand, and the citizenship held by the Israelis of Palestinian origin (the 'Arab Israelis') on the other. Under international law, however, unilateral annexation does not deprive civilians from the protections offered by the Geneva Convention.[33]

The law of occupation is codified in the Hague Convention and Regulations of 1907 relative to the Laws and Customs of War on Land (which Israel considers as applicable), the Fourth Geneva Convention of 1949 Relative to the Protection of Civilian Persons in Time of War (which Israel ratified in 1951 but which it does not consider as applicable to the oPt) and Additional Protocol I of 1977 (which only applies to the extent that it is considered customary international law since Israel did not ratify it). These outline the duties and obligations of the occupying power vis-à-vis the occupied territory and its inhabitants. Of particular relevance to the WBGS are Articles 42 to 56 of the Hague Regulations which stipulate *inter alia* that the occupying power must protect the interests of the occupied population and preserve the legal status quo of the occupied territory, although it has some discretion, notably with regard to the protection of its own forces.

The Fourth Geneva Convention and Additional Protocols are concerned principally with the protection of civilian populations. Article 49 prohibits the occupying power from deporting or transferring 'parts of its own civilian population into the territory it occupies', a provision that is relevant to the Israeli policy of settlement expansion. Of significance to the aid and donor community providing assistance in the oPt are Articles 55 to 63, which state that 'to the fullest extent of the means available to it', the occupying power has the responsibility of ensuring the provision of relief, basic supplies and services (medicines, food, clothing, shelter). If the population is not adequately supplied, the occupying power shall agree and facilitate relief operations, although this does not relieve it of any of its legal responsibilities.[34] Under IHL, Israel is thus responsible for providing assistance to the Palestinian population and, if the population is inadequately supplied, for facilitating relief operations.

Discourse and perceptions

The corpus of international law relating to occupation provides clear guidelines on the duties and obligations of Israel as the occupying power. However, in the 1990s, several factors contributed to confusing the different international and Israeli interpretations and perceptions of the occupation of the Palestinian territory, and thus of the obligations of the State of Israel.

Confusion arose as the result of the Oslo Accords and of an increasing territorial, legal and social intermeshing of Israel and parts of the oPt. As will be detailed in the next chapter, this was the result of unilateral measures taken by Israel to change the territorial, demographic, legal and socio-economic status quo of the oPt, such as settlement expansion, the application of Israeli law over Israeli citizens residing in the oPt, the building of the Wall in the West Bank and East Jerusalem from 2002 on, and the harnessing of natural resources and infrastructure in the WBGS for the requirements of Israeli settlers and the Israeli economy. While these measures are illegal under IHL, they led to the creation of new 'realities on the ground' and contributed to confusing Israeli and international public perception of which part of historical mandate Palestine is Israel and which is oPt.

This is all the more so as there was some debate in the mid-1990s as to whether the Oslo agreement affected the applicability of the law of occupation to the oPt as a result of the establishment of the PA and the creation of autonomous areas with varying degrees of PA control (Areas A and B) following IDF redeployment as stipulated by various bilateral agreements.[35] In Area A (the main cities of the West Bank excluding East Jerusalem, covering 18.2 per cent of the West Bank and 20 per cent of its population), the PA assumed responsibility for internal security and public order, in addition to providing public services to the population.[36] Area B (22.8 per cent of the West Bank, 68 per cent of its population) included some 450 Palestinian towns and villages, but the PA there only had responsibility for public order and the delivery of services, with Israel retaining responsibility for security. Israel retained full control over the remaining areas, known as Area C (accounting for 60 per cent of the West Bank), which included sparsely populated regions, Israeli settlements and supporting infrastructure such as by-pass roads, as well as closed military areas.[37]

To the extent that the Israeli army withdrew totally from Area A, some change in the status of these areas resulted from Oslo. However, while some scholars have argued that IHL only applied in Area C,[38] others have contended that the law of occupation continued to apply to the whole of the oPt, as Israel retained overall responsibility for, and control over, the entire WBGS, including such issues as security, borders and settlements, and the Israeli military administration (COGAT) continued to exist. This has been the official position of the ICRC, which continued to regard the whole of East Jerusalem, the West Bank and Gaza Strip, including the autonomous areas, as occupied territory to which the Fourth Geneva Convention applies.[39] A similar debate arose within the context of Israeli disengagement from Gaza in the summer of 2005. At the UN World Summit in New York in September 2005, Israel sought hard to get international recognition that its withdrawal marked the 'end of its responsibility' for the fate of Gaza and its residents, even if it deliberately chose not to focus on whether disengagement triggered the 'end of occupation' or not. Indeed, the issues of the continuing applicability of IHL, of the legal status of the evacuated but 'besieged' territory and of the responsibilities of Israel towards its inhabitants remain complex.[40]

In any event, back in the 1990s and for political rather than legal reasons, the term 'occupation' almost entirely vanished from the international discourse and common parlance. A desire not to displease Israel while peace negotiations were under way, as well as a wish to see in Oslo the beginning of a process that would lead to an end to the occupation and the establishment of a Palestinian state, may explain why international organizations and aid agencies collectively came to substitute for occupied Palestinian territory appellations such as 'West Bank and Gaza Strip', 'Palestinian territories' or even 'Palestinian Authority'. The fact that, until the 2000s, foreign assistance was not overwhelmingly humanitarian in nature (although, as this book argues, it was 'emergency' throughout the period under review) may also account for why IHL may have seemed less relevant.

Thus for instance, after its initial six-volume study entitled *Developing the Occupied Territories: An Investment in Peace*, finalized before the Declaration of Principles (DOP) was signed, and its *Emergency Assistance Program for the Occupied Territories* published in April 1994, the Bank shifted to using the terminology 'WBGS' or 'WB&G'. This also became the term consistently used by other international institutions such as the United States Agency for International Development (USAID), the IMF and the European Commission (EC). Similarly, in its quarterly reports on economic and social conditions, the Office of the UN Special Coordinator (UNSCO) refers to the 'WBGS' or the 'Palestinian territories'. In some of its reports, 'occupied Palestinian Territory' (the official UN terminology used in General Assembly and Security Council reports and resolutions over the 1990s) is mentioned, but only once at the beginning, alternative expressions being then employed throughout the rest of the document.[41] Even UNSCO's full name was altered in 1999, from being initially the 'Office of the Special Coordinator in the Occupied Territories' to the 'Office of the Special Coordinator for the Middle East Peace Process'. This reflected a widening of its mandate to encompass 'good offices' functions and a conscious decision to position itself as a mediator between the two parties. As noted by one UN official:

> UNSCO did not follow conventional UN language (Palestine or oPt). It had a much more conservative approach, preferring to use WBGS. The idea was that UNSCO was not going to be a UN office but a 'neutral' body. This created some kind of tension with other UN agencies and internally. We accepted that as a matter of UN policy but that was not necessary.

Until the *intifada*, the international community thus chose not to emphasize the legal environment under which aid was being delivered, in part because it was genuinely confusing, but above all because it was contested by one of the two parties. As long as the peace process seemed on track, donors preferred to downplay the reality of the occupation rather than antagonize Israel. As observed by IHL expert Claude Bruderlein:

> The 'occupation' forced the international community to put priority where it did not want – on a final status settlement and on the fundamental issue of the relationship between national territory and national identity. These were taboo. They preferred instead to deny the reality of the occupation and carve a state in area A out of it. Everything was about the denial of the absence of a national space and of a relationship between nation and space; it was also a denial about refugees.... When one party is in total denial, how do you try to make progress? You enter into self-denial yourself. You concentrate on less controversial issues. The PLO was in denial too. Before Oslo, it talked about the discrimination of Arab Israelis and of the Palestinians of Jerusalem. Thereafter it argued that this was a 'political' issue and ceased to mention them.

The sanitized use of language by the bureaucratic and policy-making elite – and relayed by the media – played a major role in shaping Israeli and international perceptions of the situation in the oPt during the Oslo years. It erased the reality of the occupation as well as marginalized the status of occupied East Jerusalem. In so doing, it reinforced its legitimacy and the 'business as usual feelings on which Israeli policy depends'.[42] At the same time, however, the international community did not go as far as signalling the emergence of a sovereign Palestinian state – official documents invariably referred to the 'Palestinian Authority' as opposed to the literal Arabic translation 'Palestinian National Authority'. Similarly, some donors such as USAID talked about the 'Legislative Council' rather than the 'Palestinian Legislative Council' (PLC). This selective use of language reflected, but also arguably contributed to, the erosion of IHL as the relevant framework for international engagement in the WBGS. In effect, for most of the 1990s, aid agencies operated in a legal vacuum. The absence of common international norms in turn also resulted in the oPt becoming what the aid community on the ground commonly referred to by 2003–2004 as an 'international law-free zone'. By then, a number of Human Rights groups were alleging that Israel was committing war crimes with impunity.[43]

The scale of the violence and the emergence of a humanitarian crisis in the oPt after 2002 resulted in 'occupation' and IHL progressively re-emerging in international discourse and common parlance. The UN Office for the Coordination of Humanitarian Affairs (OCHA), which grew in field presence from 2003 onwards, also contributed to bringing IHL back on to the international agenda through advocacy, its monitoring of the humanitarian situation, and its consistent use of the 'oPt' terminology. The high media coverage of the occupation of Iraq may have also inadvertently increased awareness of the occupation of Palestinian territory. Finally, the ICJ advisory opinion of 9 July 2004, which declared the Separation Barrier in the West Bank illegal, also resulted in the reassertion of IHL as pertinent to the Israeli–Palestinian conflict. Interestingly, this did not leave the Israeli establishment untouched. In June 2004, the Israeli Supreme Court, which for many years had ruled that only the Hague Conventions applied, recognized that at least certain provisions of the Geneva Conventions should be observed.[44] A few months later, a team from the Israeli Ministry of Justice appointed by the Attorney General recommended that the government radically change its approach to the Geneva Conventions and 'thoroughly examine' the possibility of formally applying them to the West Bank and Gaza Strip.[45]

Nevertheless, although reference to the oPt, IHL and Israel's responsibility as the occupying power became more frequent and despite lively debates among the aid community as to whether it should continue to provide such high levels of relief assistance, most official institutions and governmental agencies continued to favour terms such as 'the West Bank and Gaza', and did not alter either the way they operated in the WBGS or the way they interacted with the government of Israel (GOI). In addition, the recognition that Israel as the occupying power had legal obligations vis-à-vis the Palestinian population did not result in any significant decrease in the quantity of international funds being allocated to the WBGS. On the contrary, the first four years of the *intifada* saw a near doubling of the annual sums provided by donors. The specific political rationale underpinning these decisions will be outlined in Chapters 4 and 5. The next section introduces the general political framework for assistance to the Palestinians.

The aid coordination architecture: a political framework for assistance

The formal aid structures established in 1993–1994 were linked to the multilateral track of the Middle East Peace Process (MEPP) which was formalized by the Madrid Conference in 1991, and which comprised a Steering Committee and Multilateral Working Groups in such sectors as arms control and regional stability, environment, refugees, regional economic development and water.[46] These coordination mechanisms, which emerged at both the capital and local levels, were elaborate and complex, reflecting the intricacy of the political context, the need to balance rival American and European positions, and the unusually large number of donors, UN agencies, other multilateral organizations and NGOs involved and competing for visibility, as well as a desire for rapid disbursement of funds to deliver on the 'peace dividend' of the agreement.[47]

Formal capital and local level aid coordination structures prior to the intifada

At the capital level, two main bodies were established to provide general direction to the aid effort: the Ad Hoc Liaison Committee (AHLC)[48] and the Consultative Group (CG). Overall, strategic supervision of donor assistance was assigned to the AHLC, a high-level group of key political donors established in November 1993.[49] Its principal mandate was to set the policy framework and development priorities for the WBGS relevant to all donors and aid institutions. It remained the principal policy-setting forum, the 'main vehicle for determining priorities and urging donors to channel their funds to specific activities judged necessary to support the continuation of Israeli–Palestinian negotiations and the implementation of agreements between the parties'.[50] Its original functions included supervising the strategic coordination, promotion and monitoring of assistance to the Palestinian people; promoting dialogue, cooperation and transparency among donors; monitoring developments in the Palestinian economy and PA fiscal situation; fostering private sector trade and investment, as well as encouraging the implementation of the economic aspects of the DOP.[51]

The AHLC also became the main forum for tackling political issues related to the development aspects of the peace process, be they points of contention between the parties related to the economic or financial provisions of their agreements, or obstacles to donor project implementation such as issues of permits, movement of goods and agencies' personnel, and importation of donor-funded equipment. Finally, more general impediments to Palestinian socio-economic development, most importantly Israeli closure policy and restrictions on movement (described in more detail in Chapter 2), also came to be addressed at the AHLC. While originally created by the Steering Group as one of the multilateral working groups on the Middle East Peace Process, in practice it rapidly came to operate autonomously.[52] This is all the more so since formal multilateral talks have been in abeyance since 1996, even if some working group activities continued to take place at the local level until later on in the decade.

To supplement the AHLC, the Consultative Groups (CG) were established to deal with the actual coordination of donor programmes, aid mobilization and broad-based discussion between the PA and its multilateral and bilateral donors. Consultative Groups are a Bank mechanism at the capital level not unique to the WBGS but used in many aid-recipient countries as an all-donor forum to pledge funds and discuss policy options and particular project activities. In the case of the WBGS, the CG called for, and chaired by, the Bank did not consider policy-related matters which remained the preserve of the AHLC. Rather, it focused on pledges and specific donor issues, and embraced more technical, information-sharing and coordination functions. The Palestinians played a relatively greater leading role in the AHLC, presenting development plans and financial needs. In effect, CG meetings, which met on average once a year, served principally as a follow-up mechanism for pledges made at the two major international conferences held in Washington in 1993 and 1998 to solicit a five-year funding programme in support of the peace process.[53] As a more inclusive donor forum comprising approximately 40 countries and institutions, the CG also served as a means to coordinate – and legitimate – the aid priorities as determined by the AHLC. However, no CG was re-convened after 1999, when the one in Frankfurt ended up in political fracas, as will be detailed in Chapter 4. Since then, the AHLC and other channels at the local level have taken on the role of mobilizing funds for the Palestinians.

At the AHLC in Brussels on 29–30 November 1994, the decision was made to establish two committees as local counterparts to the AHLC and CG: the Joint Liaison Committee (JLC)[54] and the Task Force on Project Implementation (TFPI). The JLC was established to address problems in donor–recipient and tri-partite relations. This included issues related to the implementation of the Tri-partite Action Plan (TAP) which was signed at the AHLC in Paris in April 1995 by Israel, the PLO and Norway (as Chair of the AHLC) and subsequently revised, updated and monitored through to 2000.[55] These issues included donors' and recipients' reports on project status; aid commitments and disbursements, as well as PA institution-building progress; PA reports on expenditures, revenues and budget evolution; Israeli reports on fulfilment of TAP undertakings; items related to private sector development; and project implementation issues.[56] It met on average four times a year, from June 1995 when it was first held until the beginning of the *intifada*, although its effectiveness was undermined as Israeli–Palestinian relations deteriorated after 1996. During the *intifada*, the forum was not convened as a trilateral mechanism, largely because Israeli withdrawal from the formal aid coordination structure at the local level, and the demise of the TAP undermined its *raison d'être*. A few 'informal', donor-only JLC meetings took place until June 2002, but after that it ceased to meet altogether.

In order to deal specifically with issues affecting donor project implementation, the JLC established the TFPI in 1997.[57] Its original mandate stipulated that it should recommend to the JLC actions 'to resolve implementation problems, identifying strategic issues for consideration on a sectoral basis and bringing to the attention of the parties fiscal issues related to implementation'.[58] It addressed both Israeli and Palestinian obstacles to project implementation, with the Israeli Ministry of Foreign Affairs (MFA) and the Palestinian Ministry of Planning and International Cooperation (MOPIC) acting as respective counterparts.

While the JLC acted as a local counterpart for the AHLC, a third mechanism – the Local Aid Coordination Committee (LACC) – was established in 1994 to mirror the CG, and has been open to all bilateral and multilateral donors active in the oPt. Representatives of the PA and UN agencies attend as observers. The meetings serve as a forum for regular coordination at the operational level and follow-up of issues raised at the AHLC and CG. They have, on average, been called on a monthly basis and are chaired by Norway with UNSCO and the Bank acting as Co-Chairs. About a dozen sector working groups (SWGs) were established in 1995 as a substructure under the LACC to cover the different fields of donor involvement such as in infrastructure, the productive sector, the social sector and institution-building. Each sector working group is led by a PA ministry, with a donor co-chairing in an advisory capacity and a UN agency acting as Secretariat. Since their establishment, several reviews of SWG purpose and procedures have taken place, most notably in 1999 when the latter were modified. Yet, on the whole, SWGs have been a source of disappointment in terms of planning and coordination: they have tended to function only as large, information-sharing gatherings, apart from in a few sectors such as health, education or job creation, which have generally been judged as more effective.[59]

The politics of the Oslo aid coordination structure

Before reviewing the evolution of the aid coordination structure after the *intifada*, three main features pertaining to the establishment of the Oslo formal aid coordination architecture are worth emphasizing. They expose the extent to which diplomacy and development have been inextricably linked, and highlight what would become familiar patterns characterizing the politics of international assistance to the Palestinians.

First, the mandate of the AHLC made it clear that the Declaration of Principles provided both the objective and political framework for the overall aid effort. Although the AHLC eventually became a permanent structure, the US first insisted that it be a short-term, ad hoc structure liaising with the parties and donors. According to a UN staff member, the US wanted to 'keep open the possibility for the US to disband it if it did not like it'. This partly explains the rapid evolution of the aid framework from being at first envisaged principally as bilateral (donor–Palestinian) to becoming more trilateral (donor–Palestinian–Israeli) after 1994: while Israel was initially brought into the coordination structures as a bilateral donor, it soon became clear that it had to be considered as a full actor in the 'triangular partnership' which developed at both the capital and local levels between the donor community, the PA and the GOI, as embodied in the terms of reference of such bodies as the JLC and TFPI. This was also reflected in the TAP. As Rick Hooper, UNSCO Chief of Staff in the mid-1990s, noted:

> Over time, it would become evident in practice…that Israel would have considerable influence on the allocation of funds since donors

would be reluctant to finance projects to which Israel strongly objected (or could be expected to object). After all, in the Declaration of Principles the PLO had formally recognized, at least pending final status negotiations, that Israel remained the controlling authority in the West Bank and Gaza Strip. Those powers and responsibilities enjoyed by Palestinian institutions were to be devolved to them by the Israeli military. The Palestinian Authority could do very little in areas under its nominal authority without receiving permission from Israel.[60]

The onset of the *intifada* led to a return to a more bilateral aid framework: tripartite mechanisms ceased to function as the GOI withdrew from the coordinating bodies at the local level. It is noteworthy, however, that this did not lead to a return to the initial donor–Palestinian setting: as will be detailed later, what developed from 2000 on was in fact two bilateral avenues, with donors dealing through separate channels with the PA (LACC *et al.*) and the GOI (TFPI).

Second, the aid coordination structure was the result of numerous political compromises. In particular, disagreements surfaced between the US and the EU over which country and institution would chair forums, and who would be invited to participate and in what capacity, underlining the differences in perception and political position as well as the competition existing between both donors, as will be detailed in Chapter 4.

A stalemate first emerged over who would chair the AHLC as the two main donors each declared an interest in doing so. The US saw its leadership as indispensable as it alone commanded sufficient political leverage over both parties and, in particular, Israel. The EU for its part was perceived as too pro-Palestinian. European decision-making through its complex 'troika' mechanism (EC, Presidency, Council) was also seen by many in the State Department as too unwieldy to allow a smooth functioning of an already complex set of aid mechanisms under European leadership. For its part, while recognizing the pre-eminence of US diplomatic clout, the EU felt that it should acquire a leadership position commensurate to its dominant financial role since Europe was financing half the total amount of the aid provided to the Palestinian population. European Member States also saw themselves as more even-handed in their respective positions on the Middle East Peace Process, while the American position seems to be invariably dictated by the requirements of its special relationship with Israel.

As the competing US and EU claims to chairmanship could not be reconciled, Norway (which had played a crucial role in the secret Oslo 'back channel' which led to the Declaration of Principles) was put forward by Saudi Arabia as Chair. This compromise was accepted. Dissension then erupted as to who should be the Secretariat, but the World Bank was eventually chosen, even if the Europeans had pushed hard for the European Investment Bank (EIB) to play this role. Although the initial US/EU conflict over leadership faded away in the immediate aftermath of the founding meeting of the AHLC, the rationale for this compromise was regularly brought into question by the EU in the late 1990s and, most acutely, in 2002–2003 and 2005 as discussions emerged within the donor community on how to streamline the aid coordination mechanisms in view of their evolution during the *intifada*. While several factors explained why the EU questioned the relevance of the 'Oslo' aid structure, it primarily reflected the persisting competition between the two leading international actors. Not only did the EU continue to be the largest donor to the Palestinians with relatively little political say on either the diplomatic or the aid process, but with time Norway had come to be perceived less as a compromised Chair than as a US proxy.

Back in 1993, a compromise also had to be reached on UN participation to the AHLC and it was only after Norway's intervention that the UN was eventually accepted as an associate member. Initially, the US and Israel were pushing for the UN to be excluded entirely.[61] The UN SG established UNSCO in June 1994 with the mandate to represent the UN family in both the political and aid dimensions of the implementation of the Palestinian–Israeli peace agreement.

In the early 1990s, so acute was the need to balance US and EU interests that even the matter of venues for the AHLC became a major issue: a division was subsequently established between so-called 'formal' meetings of the AHLC to be held in Europe and 'informal' meetings (attended only by full members) to take place in Washington DC. In reality, this distinction became so blurred that associated members came to be invited to 'informal' meetings as well. The division between full members and associate members also gradually lost in significance: the UN would over time attend meetings as a full member and so did the Bank, though officially the Bank participated in AHLCs as its Secretariat.[62] Competition between the US and EU also partly explains the initial division of labour between the AHLC, as the policy-setting body, and the CG, as a broader and more technical donor forum. As Rick Hooper explains:

> The AHLC is a smaller and more manageable forum than the Consultative Group. Because of the AHLC's limited membership, it is easier to balance European and US views in both political and substantive matters. In the Consultative Group all European donors are represented individually in addition to the presidency of the European Union and the European Commission. In the AHLC, Europe is represented by the European Presidency only (accompanied by a representative of the European Commission). This is one reason why the United States has preferred to address substantive issues through the AHLC and not the Consultative Group. Since the AHLC's establishment, it has proved possible to address contentious bilateral Palestinian–Israeli issues affecting the Palestinian economy. In the much larger forum of the Consultative Group, whose plenary meetings consist mainly of representatives reading prepared statements, political discussions of this type would not have been possible.[63]

By the same token, the US was initially keener than the EU to see the Bank exert some influence. It was thus agreed that the Bank would not only serve as Secretariat of the AHLC but until 1999 pledging would occur in the CG meetings, controlled by the Bank.

A third set of remarks related to the establishment of the aid architecture concerns the international actors leading the development process: the persons and institutions most involved in the AHLC have been the ones also with responsibility for the diplomatic aspects of the peace process. This is not surprising since the socio-economic aspects of the peace process were woven together with its politics. In addition to the Israeli and Palestinian parties, the key actors at the capital and local levels have been the US, the EU, Norway, UNSCO and the World Bank. The existence of an 'inner circle' (or what Rex Brynen has labelled 'the aid politburo') dominating most processes of coordination, policy discussion, agenda-setting and information-sharing has conveyed an impression of strategic focus and shared vision within the donor community.[64] In reality, and as will be seen in later chapters, the aid process remained very much driven by the American political agenda. Policy consensus around aid priorities thus meant above all conformity to the preferences of the most powerful member of the 'politburo'. In this respect, it is noteworthy that Security System Reform (SSR) was not included in any aid coordination mechanisms, as it remained an Israeli and American preserve.

Informal aid coordination structures during the intifada

In the context of a total breakdown of trilateral mechanisms at the local level, increasing emergency needs and a significant deterioration of the operational conditions in the oPt, several new developments occurred. The TFPI became the main channel of interaction between the international donor community and Israel. In the process, its mandate expanded considerably. Donors came to interact with the COGAT rather than with the Israeli Ministry of Foreign Affairs, to address both operational and policy concerns related to the provision of international assistance on the ground. Specifically, the TFPI focused on facilitating international humanitarian and emergency activities, particularly relating to the access and movement of personnel and goods within and between the West Bank, Gaza and Israel.

New coordination bodies also emerged after the *intifada*.[65] One important difference between the Oslo and *intifada* arrangements is that the new forums were donor-only coordination bodies, whereas the mechanisms set up during the 1990s were trilateral. This shift in part reflected the deterioration in Israeli–Palestinian bilateral negotiations and the weakening of the PA. In response to Operation Defensive Shield in March/April 2002, the LACC first established an ad hoc Donor Support Group working through special emergency operations rooms to assess the physical and institutional damage caused by the incursions and military operations into the West Bank, and to coordinate donor funds for repair. After the completion of the assessments in May 2002, the Donor Support Group ceased to function, although some of the operation rooms that had been established continued to exist and merged with previous SWGs, as for instance in the health sector.

Two more permanent structures were also created: the Task Force on Palestinian Reform (TFPR)[66] and the Humanitarian Emergency Policy Group (HEPG). The TFPR and seven reform support groups (RSG, in the fields of financial accountability, local government, elections, market economy, ministerial and civil service reform, judiciary, and legislative issues) were established in July 2002 to monitor and support the implementation of Palestinian civil reforms and provide guidance to the international donor community in its support to the Palestinian reform agenda, as will be detailed in Chapter 6. The TFPR met at both the local and capital levels and reported to the Quartet. Although the TFPR closely cooperated with the AHLC, it is a parallel structure to the AHLC–LACC–SWGs track. In order to develop a donor strategy for dealing with the deteriorating socio-economic and humanitarian emergency, the HEPG was established in December 2002.[67]

These new coordination structures facilitated greater EU visibility. The EU became Chair of the HEPG and was one of the main driving forces behind the TFPR through its Quartet membership. Interestingly, Norway was only appointed 'convenor' of the TFPR – rather than Chair. This was once again the result of a compromise between the members of the 'inner circle'. The EU, which not only continued to be the main donor to the WBGS but was alone among Western donors in supporting the PA through direct budgetary assistance, made it clear that it would no longer be content with a minor role in the coordination process. Yet greater European visibility did not drastically alter the dynamic of the 'inner circle' and the preponderance of the US in the aid agenda-setting, all the more so since the HEPG remained largely dysfunctional as a policy group and, by 2003–2004, the TFPR had lost momentum.

The second feature pertaining to the *intifada* aid coordination mechanisms was that, although the aid framework had been donor-led throughout, it came to be even more so. As its capacity eroded, the PA ceased to be formally involved in aid forums. This marginalization of the PA was particularly acute at the central level. Although donors gave more money directly to the Ministry of Finance (MoF) for the general budget, mainly to pay for the salaries of the PA bureaucracy, they simultaneously increasingly channelled funds through international organizations and NGOs, as well as directly through local government Palestinian authorities, by-passing line ministries in the planning and delivery of aid, and the provision of aid-funded services.[68]

Conclusion

International assistance to the WBGS took place in a complex legal and political environment. First, aid was delivered to a regime and population living under military occupation where the recipient of aid was weak, and neither sovereign nor the host country. In addition from 2000 onwards, assistance took place in the midst of conflict. The division of the oPt into Areas A, B and C also imposed critical limitations on donors, who had to design and implement the bulk of their projects in Areas A and B. This in turn fed into the fragmentation of the WBGS, as will be seen in Chapter 5. Second, the political rationale for foreign aid resulted not only in a choice of projects often based on political considerations, but also in a convoluted and highly politicized coordination and aid management structure. But donors did not only operate in a complex legal and political setting. Assistance was also delivered in a context of increasing fragmentation of Palestinian territory, economy and politics. The next two chapters examine this multifaceted process of fragmentation which, beyond the realms of international law and high politics, added another level of intricacy to the provision of aid to the Palestinian population of the oPt.

2

ISRAELI POLICIES

The territorial, demographic and socio-economic fragmentation of the occupied Palestinian territory

There is a general assumption, in Israeli society and internationally, that during the Oslo years and at least up until the onset of the *intifada*, Palestinians were in control of their lives in the new situation of interim autonomy or 'self-rule' resulting from the establishment of the PA and redeployment of the IDF from most Palestinian populated areas. This was not the case. Between 1993 and 2000, the population did gain a degree of freedom inside the Palestinian territorial and functional enclaves provided for by the Oslo agreements (Jericho, Areas A and B of the West Bank, Area H-1 of Hebron, autonomous zones of the Gaza Strip). Yet the Israeli military occupation of the oPt has remained firmly in place, together with the daily humiliation, routine arbitrariness, collective punishment and widespread human rights abuses that the presence of Israeli soldiers and settlers entails for the Palestinian population.

Though its colonial rule was to a large extent mediated by the PA in the autonomous areas, the GOI remained the final arbiter of Palestinian life, notably through the imposition of severe movement restrictions on Palestinian goods and people, and its control of entry and exit points to and from Palestinian areas as well as the road network linking them. In addition to continuing occupation over East Jerusalem, 60 per cent of the West Bank and, up until 2005, just over 25 per cent of the area in Gaza, Israel's territorial, physical and demographic control of the WBGS taken as a whole in fact intensified after Oslo. A number of Israeli policies combined to restrict Palestinian lives at an unprecedented level while simultaneously expanding Israeli control: a severe closure regime; land confiscation, unabated settlement and by-pass roads expansion; and from 2002 the construction of a Separation Barrier, partly inside the West Bank. In the process, Palestinian communities and livelihoods became increasingly separated and isolated from one another, and the landscape of the WBGS ever more fragmented.

Several reasons can be put forward to explain why Oslo did not mark a break in Israeli colonization and expansionist policy. First, the traditional Zionist ideology of 'Greater Israel', which can be traced back to the beginning of the twentieth century and according to which Judea and Samaria are an integral and inalienable part of the *Eretz Israel* ('Land of Israel') between the Mediterranean and the Jordan River, has remained one of the core principles of the Israeli right-wing Likud Party. Ever since Prime Minister Menachem Begin's election in 1977, territorial expansion, the dispossession of the population, and the official encouragement of the construction of settlements and related infrastructure in the WBGS has been the Israeli right-wing and religious nationalist parties' unfailing policy. This did not change after Oslo.[1]

Second, and perhaps less commonly acknowledged, territorial expansion has also always been encouraged by the Israeli Labour Party, although more for economic and security reasons than out of an ideological attachment to the land. In line with the Allon Plan of 1967, the policy initiated by Rabin at Oslo was to annex as much strategic land with as few Palestinians as possible (such as the Jordan Valley and the main settlement blocs along the Green Line which are located above the West Bank's main water aquifers).[2] With the Palestinian population under the jurisdiction and governance responsibilities of the PA (which also meant that the GOI no longer saw itself as responsible for the welfare of the population), Oslo enabled Israel to begin separating both peoples without having to end the occupation and withdraw from the WBGS – 'to keep the land but not the indigenous population'.[3] As mentioned in the Introduction, this can to be seen as a response to the perceived long-term demographic threat of a Palestinian majority, which would compromise the 'ethnic Zionist' identity of the State of Israel.

The bipartisan strategy pursued by all Israeli governments since Oslo has thus been to disengage from heavily populated Palestinian areas while expanding Israel's grip of key areas of Jerusalem and the West Bank, and to remain in effective control in all other aspects. Indeed, this national consensus was clearly articulated in the Beilin–Eitan Agreement of 1997: a Likud/Labour common plan which intended to serve as a roadmap for Israeli negotiators as they pursued final status negotiations.[4] This does not mean, of course, that Israeli policy-making has been static. On the contrary, it has been characterized by inventiveness and flexibility at the tactical level, in large part to respond to events on the ground, including attacks and suicide bombings by Palestinian militants, and as a result of the complex and fragmented nature of the Israeli political system. But underlying seemingly new policy initiatives is an unwavering strategic continuity. As hinted above, the Israeli political and military establishment espoused a similar strategic orientation for different specific reasons, but at a more general level this is also to be linked to Israel's deeply ingrained sense of insecurity in the Middle East, which in turn has little to do with Palestinian security performance per se.

This chapter outlines the multifaceted process of Palestinian territorial and demographic fragmentation and the socio-economic and humanitarian repercussions it has yielded. This overview is necessary not only because it exposes the shocking, yet too often not fully grasped, conditions under which the Palestinian population in the WBGS live, but also to appreciate the environment in which the international community has had to take policy decisions, operate and deliver assistance. As will be detailed in Chapter 5, these conditions on the ground determined to a large extent the type of assistance delivered and its sectoral allocation, in addition to sharply undermining the effectiveness and sustainability of the aid provided. They also created sharp humanitarian dilemmas and IHL concerns for donors. More importantly, this process of fragmentation and the creation of a territorial and demographic fait accompli has also had far-reaching consequences for Palestinian socio-economic, political and institutional developments in the period under review and, looking ahead, for the prospect of a two-state solution to the conflict.

Territorial separation, cantonment, dispossession and segregation

Closure

Israel's closure policy refers to the restrictions placed on the free movement of Palestinian people, vehicles and goods. It is enforced at all levels by a complex bureaucratic–military travel permit system, and a two-colour car licence-plate system,[5] and has three main aspects:

i internal closure of Palestinian towns and villages in the WBGS through a dense network of military checkpoints, roadblocks, ditches, earth mounds, the Separation Barrier, etc. This has been reinforced by the widespread use of curfews, especially from 2002 onwards, and no longer applies to Gaza since August 2005;

ii external closure of the border between Israel, on the one hand, and both the West Bank and the Gaza Strip, on the other, as well as between the West Bank and Gaza Strip; and

iii external closure of international crossings between the West Bank and Jordan, and between the Gaza Strip and Egypt, with passenger and commercial traffic through international crossings being severely limited.

On the eve of the Gulf War in 1991, an Israeli military order cancelled the 'general exit permit', which had allowed West Bank inhabitants since the early 1970s and Gaza inhabitants since the mid-1980s access to and free movement in Israel.[6] Travel restrictions for 'security cases' (mainly former prisoners and activists) began in 1988 following the onset of the first *intifada* and magnetic cards, renewable annually, were introduced in 1989 for residents of the Gaza Strip to enter Israel. However, until the beginning of the 1990s, free movement throughout Israel, the West Bank and Gaza was allowed for the majority of the Palestinians. Closure became institutionalized after March 1993, when 'general closure' was forced on the WBGS. Access to Jerusalem and Israel became strictly regulated and increasingly difficult, and travel between the West Bank and the Gaza Strip became nearly impossible. In effect, the Gaza Strip was completely cut off from the West Bank, creating a de facto Palestinian mini-state there. From 1994, an electronic fence sealed off the Strip. A single checkpoint, the Erez terminal, controlled passage to and from Israel, while the Rafah crossing, also controlled by Israel, regulated travel to Egypt. This situation did not significantly change after Israeli disengagement from Gaza in 2005. If anything, it became even harder for Palestinians to leave the Strip and for goods to move in and out of the territory from then on.

The establishment of the PA in 1994 led to further development of the permit system. As early as the mid-1990s, permits had become difficult to obtain. In 1995, for instance, it was estimated that only 60,000 permits were being delivered to Palestinian residents of the WBGS combined, i.e. to less than 3 per cent of the population.[7] Interestingly, although the majority of the population could not move freely in the 1990s and permits became the privilege of the few, the extent of closure does not seem to have been fully appreciated until later on in the decade. As perceptively observed by the Israeli journalist Amira Haas:

> Given the focus on its economic effects, closure throughout the Oslo years was said to be lifted whenever Palestinian workers and businessmen were given permits to cross into Israel…The great majority of the population, who could not leave because they had no work in Israel or business with Israelis, fell into the blind spot of the writers of reality's 'official version' – most journalists and the officials and diplomats who talk to the press. Lost from sight was the fact that even when the closure was 'lifted', the vast majority of the population still couldn't go anywhere.[8]

The Interim Agreement of 1995 and the division of the West Bank into Areas A, B and C in effect fed into, and reinforced, the internal variant of the closure system. The Agreement bestowed a 'quasi-legal' veneer, albeit supposedly temporary, on the increasing segmentation of the West Bank. As Israel relinquished control over the main Palestinian population centres, it simultaneously gained more control over the general geographical space of the WBGS, and over the movement of Palestinian goods and people.

Besides this permanent 'general closure', the GOI also at times imposed 'comprehensive closure', freezing all permits and suspending all traffic of goods and people within the WBGS, effectively placing Palestinian residents into town arrests. These restrictions were also imposed on UN officials and project materials, resulting in delays and added costs for development projects and in serious disruption of the work of aid agencies. Until the outbreak of the second *intifada*, this measure was enforced mainly on a temporary basis (albeit often for prolonged periods, notably following suicide attacks), particularly in the period 1996–1998. Between 30 March 1993 and mid-June 1997, the UN estimated that it occurred for a full 353 days.[9]

With the *intifada*, comprehensive closure became recurrent and accompanied by a tightened permit system and internal closure, in the form of extensive sieges of Palestinian towns and villages, isolation measures and prolonged periods of curfews. Permits for internal movement in the West Bank between major towns and villages were also introduced in 2002. This applied to all Palestinians, including the local staff of donor and aid agencies. Restrictions on access and the movement of international aid workers and diplomats both in and out of and inside the WBGS also became common. In November 2003, OCHA counted some 757 barriers (including manned checkpoints, ditches and earth mounds blocking vehicular access, concrete blocks, road gates, Wall gates for Palestinians) blocking Palestinian roads and towns in the West Bank.[10] Gaza was also subject to increased internal closures, with the IDF frequently isolating the northern, central and southern parts of the Strip from each other by closing access to the main roads, and prohibiting internal movement, especially where the main north–south road was crossed by roads going to Israeli settlements. Checkpoints for Palestinians on the principal arteries could arbitrarily be opened only for half an hour in the morning, and again in the afternoon for a short period of time, or closed altogether, sometimes for several days.

Movement of goods also became increasingly regulated between Israel and the WBGS and within the oPt. In the 1990s, permits for trucks at Karni passage in Gaza and for transport of goods across the Green Line and between the West Bank and Jordan became difficult to obtain and a limited 'back to back' system was put in place for transport of goods between the West Bank and Israel. Under the supervision of the IDF, Palestinians have to unload merchandise from a truck on one side of the checkpoint and reload it on another truck on the other side, resulting in increased transportation time and cost as well as the increasingly frequent occurrence that goods, especially agricultural products, are damaged or spoilt.[11]

During the *intifada*, the back-to-back system was gradually formalized to apply to all goods entering Israel from either the West Bank or the Gaza Strip. The construction of the Separation Wall from 2002 further limited the access of West Bank goods to Israel. Moreover, since April 2002, Palestinians have no longer been allowed to drive trucks between cities in the West Bank. These restrictions also apply to the transport of humanitarian and donor project goods, which has been allowed only in trucks with white licence-plates driven by international staff. In addition, entering/exiting the Gaza Strip has become ever more constrained and remained so after 2005. A permit or 'list' system for international aid staff (including UN staff who hold a UN laissez-passer) was introduced for Israeli permission to enter the Strip.

Curfews, by which the residents of a certain area are prohibited from leaving their houses during a given period of time (thus being denied access to work, school and medical care) decreased during the 1990s, with the exception of specific periods such as following suicide attacks and of those regularly imposed on the Palestinians living in the H-2 area of Hebron.[12] However, they were reimposed on a large scale during the IDF's Operation Defensive Shield in March/April 2002, and remained so on most Palestinian population centres throughout 2003. OCHA estimated that in 2002, on average, 37 Palestinian localities representing 547,000 persons were placed under daily curfew.[13] As of the mid-2000s, Israel was continuing to impose curfews on a regular, if less intense, basis.

If the extent and type of closure has varied over time, travel permits have also had gradations: most passes allow for travel only between 5 a.m. and 7 p.m. on weekdays, some grant overnight stay, a few others permit free movement for one to three months. In addition, the geographic scope of permits varies. For instance, some passes for Gaza residents in the 1990s used to be for the West Bank and Israel, others for the West Bank alone. Until January 2002, most Palestinians did not require permits to travel within the West Bank, except for East Jerusalem. Since then, permits have been obligatory. Furthermore, permits delivered to Palestinian individuals do not entitle them to drive their cars on by-pass roads. A different permit is necessary for Palestinian travel on roads in Area C when this is not totally prohibited. Such a permit is delivered principally to some Palestinian buses and shared taxis and, in exceptional cases, to Palestinian individuals. As of July 2004, according to the IDF, only 3,412 Palestinians out of the 2.4 million living in the West Bank held the 'special movement permit for internal checkpoints in Judea and Samaria', or about 0.14 per cent of the population.[14] The system of permits is not only complex, but the categories of persons who are eligible and the procedures for application are also opaque. Permit requests are routinely denied without explanation or on unspecified security grounds. According to the Head of COGAT, which is responsible for issuing permits in the WBGS, 'there are no definitive criteria for examining requests for a permit'.[15]

Permits are not simply a bureaucratic hassle with restricting consequences on the movement of the Palestinian population and, to a lesser extent, the international aid community. They also have far-reaching consequences on the social fabric of Palestinian society. As pointed out by the Israeli journalist Amira Haas:

> The political, economic, social and intellectual elites always found ways to get permits and get out, sparing them the constant pressures of being locked up and feeling suffocated. This class phenomenon found its fullest expression in the VIP system institutionalized under Oslo...The pass system turned a universal basic right into a coveted privilege – or portion of a privilege – allotted to a minority on a case-by-case basis...It was thus that an entire society was stratified and segmented on the basis of whether one had access, and in what proportion, to the 'privilege' of freedom of movement.[16]

Closure and associated permit requirements are portrayed by Israel as a 'temporary' security measure, a pre-emptive move against or reaction to terrorist attacks in Israel. However, it has been a consistent Israeli policy ever since the early 1990s, and is too far-reaching and all-encompassing to be seen as an ad hoc measure linked to Palestinian security performance. Although some of the checkpoints do have a security rationale, such as checking the entry of Palestinians into Israel, a meticulous analysis of the closures' maps clearly reveals that most inside the oPt do not, if the objective is to protect the civilian population in Israel from suicide bombings. An internal IDF report leaked to the press in November 2001 reached the following conclusion:

> Most of the permanent checkpoints are not organized to stop hostile elements and the checking of cars is done randomly....There are no clear rules to deal with humanitarian problems...no rules for reporting unusual incidents or for the treatment of those incidents by commending officers....There are deviant incidents that are not reported to the relevant authorities and are not adequately handled.[17]

In this respect, humanitarian and human rights organizations have classified closure, stringent permit requirements and curfews as harassment. These measures are identified as a clear case of collective punishment prohibited under IHL, enforced indiscriminately against the Palestinian civilian population and denying them basic human rights such as freedom of movement and the right to work and to have access to health services and education.[18] As pointed out by Amnesty International:

> Internal closures frequently operate in an arbitrary way. The fact that soldiers enjoy broad, individual discretion to permit or prevent Palestinians' movement undermines the Israeli authorities' contention that the internal closure is a rational system of control, based strictly on security needs.[19]

In fact, closure must be primarily understood in the context of other colonial policies in the WBGS aimed at maintaining and expanding control over the oPt. Especially in its 'internal' variant, closure may indeed be regarded as a security measure, but not, as is generally understood, as a legitimate way to ensure the security of the population in Israel. Rather, it is a means to protect Israeli settlers and settlements, and to secure the Israeli segregated road network within the oPt.

Settlement expansion and supporting infrastructure

All Israeli governments since 1967, whether Likud or Labour, have participated in the resolute and systematic development, strengthening and expansion of settlements in the WBGS, including East Jerusalem. This colonization has been achieved by a complex legal–bureaucratic mechanism for large-scale land seizure and expropriation, and rendered operational by financial benefits and incentives to encourage Israeli citizens to move into the oPt.[20] Although the Oslo Accords stipulated that 'neither side shall initiate or take any step that will change the status of the West Bank and the Gaza Strip pending the outcome of the permanent status negotiations', the Oslo period was no different in this respect.[21]

In fact, as is now well established, the 1990s saw the most spectacular growth of the settler population since 1967. The Jewish population in the WBGS alone grew from about 115,700 in 1993 to an estimated 203,000 by the end of 2000: an increase of approximately 75 per cent.[22] If the number of Jewish settlers living in occupied East Jerusalem is added, there were judged to be about 400,000 settlers living in the oPt by the end of 2002.[23] In late 2003, it was estimated that there were 125 settlements in the West Bank (and approximately 100 outposts, the precursor to a settlement) and 20 settlements in the Gaza Strip.[24] In May 2002, the Israeli Human Rights Organization B'Tselem calculated that settlements controlled 41.9 per cent of West Bank land, including the built-up areas, the municipal boundaries and the land seized by settlement regional councils.[25] In the Gaza Strip as of 2002, about 20 per cent of the land had been seized for the IDF and settlers, who represented 0.5 per cent of the overall population.[26] A report published by the Israeli newspaper *Ha'aretz* in September 2003 estimated that Israel had spent at least an extra NIS2.5 billion annually on non-military outlays to maintain and expand settlements in the WBGS, and spent at least NIS45 billion on the settlements since 1967. These figures do not include military spending, and do not include the money spent on East Jerusalem. Such civilian spending translates into annual surplus costs of more than NIS10,000 per settler.[27]

Settlements in the Gaza Strip, which were evacuated in the summer of 2005, were predominantly located to the south along the coast. In the West Bank, however, they have been scattered all over the territory, but successive Israeli governments have encouraged the development of four specific, strategically located, blocs: in and around the Jerusalem area, along the Green Line, around the Ariel area, and in the Jordan Valley. The great majority of settlements are situated on hilltops and adjacent to Palestinian towns. Furthermore, they have tended to be on militarily strategic locations (e.g. Ariel has a strategic view over the North), overlook major Palestinian towns (e.g. Psagot over Ramallah and El Bireh) or act as wedges between Palestinian towns (e.g. Gush Etzion bloc separating Bethlehem from Hebron, and Shomron bloc separating Ramallah from Nablus). In addition, the growth of settlements is mainly geared to the formation of blocs, i.e. they grow outwards and towards each other, breaking the territorial contiguity of Palestinian towns and villages.[28]

In East Jerusalem, the extension of Jerusalem municipal boundaries has led to land requisition and house demolition on a colossal scale. Jewish settlements not only form a belt which effectively encircles and isolates the Palestinian neighbourhoods of the city, cutting them from the West Bank, but they also literally bisect the West Bank, in addition to blocking the urban development of Bethlehem and severing that town from adjacent Palestinian communities. A continuous chain of settlements deep into the West Bank has thus been created, notably through the appropriation of land in the 'Greater Jerusalem' area (i.e. outside the area of jurisdiction of the Municipality of Jerusalem) which entails an extra 100 square mile area and 20 settlements, the expansion of the large Ma'ale Adumin West Bank settlement and its linking to Jerusalem through the E1, a planned built-up urban land bridge. For a Palestinian with a West Bank ID and with no permit to enter Jerusalem, it is impossible, for instance, to go from Ramallah to Bethlehem in a straight line via Jerusalem. A huge detour eastwards is necessary.[29]

Settlement expansion in East Jerusalem differs from the rest of the West Bank by its intensity and its legal framework. In 1967, the GOI annexed approximately 70,000 dunams of the West Bank to the Municipality of Jerusalem, pursuant to a decision of the Knesset to apply Israeli law to these areas officially rather than merely de facto as in the rest of the WBGS. Although under international law settlements in East Jerusalem are no different than in the rest of the oPt, they are considered by the GOI and most of the Israeli Jewish public as an integral part of the State of Israel since, as mentioned in the preceding chapter, East Jerusalem was formally annexed in 1980.[30]

In addition to their illegality under international law,[31] the profound impact they have on the prospect for the establishment of a viable Palestinian state – with its capital in East Jerusalem – and the broad injury to the Palestinian population caused by land expropriation and denial of access to land, settlements have specific detrimental effects on Palestinian communities, livelihoods and human rights. For instance, in rural areas they restrict the possibilities for Palestinian economic and agricultural development. In the Jordan Valley area, settlements prevent Palestinians from using an important part of the available water resources. Settlements in the central part of the West Bank along Route 60 (the main north–south artery) block the potential for urban and economic development for the major Palestinian cities situated along this axis: Jenin, Nablus, Ramallah, Jerusalem, Bethlehem and Hebron. Particularly noteworthy is also the fact that any Jewish person (whether Israeli or not, but excluding Arab Israelis) and any Jewish local authority in the oPt is subject to the authority of Israeli civilian law and not to the authority of the military law applying to the oPt. This leads to the de facto annexation of the settlements to the State of Israel and the creation of an extra-territorial zone in the WBGS. In effect, Israel has created a system of segregation based on discrimination by applying two separate legal systems in the same area, and basing the rights of individuals on their nationality or ethnic-religious identity.

Finally, settlements are a major source of friction and violence inside the WBGS, resulting in the death and injury of Palestinians and Israeli settlers, inciting violence on both sides, thereby further inflaming the conflict between the two parties and antipathy amongst Palestinians. In particular, human rights NGOs regularly detail occurrences of settlers attacking Palestinians and destroying their property. In some places, such as the Area H-2 in the city of Hebron, settler violence, along with the failure to enforce the law against those who have committed violence, has been regarded as one of the major reasons for the departure of hundreds of Palestinian families, or an estimated 43 per cent of the inhabitants of Hebron's old city, between October 2000 and July 2003.[32] Migration of the population of an occupied territory as a result of threatened and, in some cases, very real violence may be equated to a slow process of ethnic cleansing or population transfer which is prohibited under international law.[33] As Lieutenant Colonel Jan Kristensen, the head of the Temporary International Presence in Hebron (TIPH), pointed out in February 2004:

> The activity of the settlers and the army in the H-2 area of Hebron is creating an irreversible situation. In a sense, cleansing is being carried out. In other words, if the situation continues for another few years, the result will be that no Palestinians will remain there. It is a miracle they have managed to remain there until now.[34]

From 1995 onwards, the GOI also began the construction of an ambitious road network in Area C of the West Bank (and to a lesser extent in the Gaza Strip) connecting Israeli settlements to each other and to Israel proper and 'by-passing' Palestinian towns and villages. By-pass roads, many of which are large highways espousing the West Bank de-limitation of Areas A and B, are not integrated within the existing Palestinian network. They are built as a totally separate and segregated network for the quasi-exclusive use of the IDF and Israelis (as well as the internationals). Some roads are totally or partially prohibited to Palestinian use while others are restricted (see Map 5). In addition, by-pass roads are linked to the development of the road network in Israel, notably the trans-Israel highway and a number of west–east roads connecting the Mediterranean to the Jordan River that dissect the natural north–south topography of the West Bank in the process.[35]

Although exact figures are difficult to obtain, as most funds for the construction and maintenance of by-pass roads come from the Defence Ministry's budget (which does not necessarily specify the cost of building a new road on a separate budget line), it is estimated that between 1993 and 2002, Israel has spent over NIS1.25 billion on the construction of by-pass roads in the West Bank alone, including around NIS150 million in 2001, and NIS200 million in 2002.[36] The construction of many of the by-pass roads in the 1990s was financed by international donors on a bilateral basis, most notably the USAID. In addition to the process of land confiscation for the building of settlements and by-pass roads, the systematic demolition of Palestinian houses and land levelling has also been in part tied to the Israeli settlement policy of expanding territorial control in the oPt. House demolitions, which have occurred on a regular basis throughout the 1990s, intensified during the *intifada*.[37] Israeli measures become significant when taken as a whole. Professor Jeff Halper has put forward the concept of 'the matrix of control' to highlight the full implications of these interrelated measures, and which he describes as:

An interlocking series of mechanisms, only a few of which require physical occupation of territory, that allows Israel to control every aspect of Palestinian life in the Occupied Territories. The matrix works like the Japanese game of Go. Instead of defeating your opponent as in chess, in Go you win by immobilizing your opponent, by gaining control of key points of a matrix so that every time s/he moves, s/he encounters an obstacle of some kind....The matrix imposed by Israel in the West Bank, Gaza and East Jerusalem, similar in appearance to a Go board, has virtually paralysed the Palestinian population without defeating it or even conquering much territory.[38]

The Separation Barrier

The Separation Barrier or Wall which the GOI began to build in the West Bank in the summer of 2002 proceeds from the same logic and can be seen as the ultimate form of closure, fragmentation and segregation. The Barrier is a complex structure of concrete walls rising as high as eight metres, barriers, trenches, electronic fences, roads and barbed wire, espousing the Green Line in some areas and going deep into the West Bank in others (see Maps 6 and 7). It has an average width of 50–70 metres, increasing to as much as 100 metres in some areas, and includes sophisticated observation systems such as cameras and watchtowers.[39] Like closure, the Wall is justified as a temporary and defensive 'security measure', to prevent the infiltration of Palestinian suicide bombers into Israel.[40] However, the idea of erecting a barrier to separate the West Bank from Israel had been contemplated by the GOI since the mid-1990s.[41]

Phase 1, excluding the Jerusalem envelope, was completed in July 2003.[42] Much of Phase 1 construction in the north-western West Bank deviates from the Green Line and in some places goes as much as six kilometres inside the West Bank.[43] In the north-west alone, it places about 56,000 Palestinians in closed areas. These include communities in areas encircled by the Barrier's route, such as the town of Qalqiliya. These enclaves also comprise about 5,300 Palestinians living in 'closed military areas' between the Barrier and the Green Line who need permits to live in their homes, and to enter/leave what the GOI calls the 'seam zone'.[44] In June 2004, the construction of the Wall east of the Ariel, Kedumin and Immanuel settlements began. Described as 'fingernails' by Israeli officials (as those settlements are built on a narrow west–east axis deep into the heart of the West Bank), these will eventually lead to the annexation of at least 150 square kilometres of Palestinian land to Israel.[45]

In October 2003, after more than a year of construction at various locations, the Israeli Cabinet approved and publicly disclosed a first version of the full route of the eastern Barrier. This was planned to fence off the West Bank on its western side, including most of East Jerusalem, for a total estimated length of 622 kilometres. Moreover, 'approximately 85 percent of the revised planned route of the barrier intrudes into the West Bank, up to 22 kilometres in the case of the Arial "fingernail" '.[46] In November 2003, the UN SG reported to the GA that:

> Based on the route of the official map, including depth barriers and East Jerusalem, approximately 975 square kilometers, or 16.6 percent of the entire West Bank, will lie between the Barrier and the Green Line. This area is home to approximately 17,000 Palestinians in the West Bank and 220,000 in East Jerusalem. If the full route is completed, another 160,000 Palestinians will live in enclaves, areas where the Barrier almost completely encircles communities and tracts of land. The planned route incorporates nearly 320,000 settlers, including approximately 178,000 in occupied East Jerusalem.[47]

These estimates were calculated at a time when construction was still ongoing. Since then, a number of revised barrier routes have been published by the Israeli Ministry of Defence and made available on its website, such as in March and June 2004, and more recently in February 2005.[48] Nonetheless, the 2003 estimates are indicative of the scale of the wall construction and of its impact on affected Palestinian communities. On 9 July 2004, the ICJ stated that the Wall is contrary to international law and that Israel is under an obligation to cease construction and make reparation for all damage caused.[49] Access – or lack of it[50] – together with the final alignment of the Wall, including whether a Barrier will also be constructed on the eastern part of the West Bank in the Jordan Valley, will determine not only the magnitude of its social and economic impacts but also the level of population displacement. Already in July 2003, the international donor community documented cases of migration resulting from the construction of the Wall, in particular following house demolitions among the Palestinian population holding Israeli or Jerusalem IDs and, more generally, among the population who found themselves trapped in enclaves and closed military areas.[51] For instance, at the end of 2003, it was estimated that between 4,000 and 6,000 Palestinians out of a total population of about 41,000 had already left the city of Qalqilya.[52] Humanitarian access for NGOs and international organizations has also been at times obstructed.

The Barrier intensifies the territorial fragmentation of the West Bank. The complex intermingling of West Bank and Jerusalem ID-holders in the Jerusalem and Bethlehem areas means that the Jerusalem envelope will, when completed, separate members of the same family from one another. In 2005, it was estimated that such an envelope will incorporate large settlement blocs, encompasses over 4 per cent of the West Bank and excludes over 50,000 East Jerusalem Palestinians.[53] The Wall also severely constrains the delivery of basic social services and commercial exchange. Being built over some of the best water sources and agricultural land, it cuts Palestinians off from their land and seriously constrains local access to water. In the process, it tightens Israeli control over Palestinian natural resources, with detrimental long-term implications, notably for water use.[54]

Israel initially went out of its way to emphasize that the Barrier was a temporary security measure which was not intended to mark a political border, or to permanently annex Palestinian land. However, from the outset the extent, nature and enormous cost of its construction, its location partly inside the West Bank and the fact that hundreds of thousands of Palestinians would be placed on its western side raised serious doubt as to its temporary character, and also its exclusively security rationale.[55] As construction was initiated, some Israeli officials also spoke in public about the permanent nature of the Barrier. The head of the Seam Fence Authority in the Israeli Ministry of Defence, which is responsible for the implementation of the Barrier, stated that 'the politicians found a formula, but I believe that the fence will be the border'. The Director of the Israeli National Security Council noted that the 'Green Line is not sacred. There are places where more territory should be included, given long-term considerations.'[56] Since then, the GOI – in particular under Prime Minister Olmert – has officially talked about the fence as marking the 'desired permanent and defensible' borders of Israel with the aim of securing a solid Jewish majority.[57] Thus, initial Palestinian and international concerns that the Barrier might become a final border were warranted. All along, the PLO's legal position has been that the Barrier 'is an attempt to annex the territory contrary to international law. The de facto annexation of land interferes with the territorial sovereignty and consequently with the right of Palestinians to self-determination.'[58] In his report in 2003 to the UN Commission on Human Rights, John Dugard, the UN Special Rapporteur on Human Rights in the oPt, stated: 'The fact must be faced that what we are presently witnessing in the West Bank is a visible and clear act of territorial annexation under the guise of security.[59]

As of the mid-2000s, the territorial contiguity of the oPt was thus not only under threat; it simply no longer existed, precluding the likelihood of the establishment of a viable independent Palestinian state in the foreseeable future. Moreover, and in addition to the sheer hellishness endured daily by the Palestinians of the WBGS, Israeli policies on the ground have had a dramatic socio-economic, humanitarian and political impact on the population, further exacerbating the above described process of territorial disintegration.

De-development and macroeconomic decline under Oslo and the *intifada*

Contrary to the optimistic scenarios that were envisaged in the early years of the peace process and despite an unprecedented level of international assistance, Palestinian economic performance was worse in the 1990s and early 2000s than in the pre-Oslo period. It was characterized by a decline in household income, a sharp increase in unemployment and the general deepening of poverty. In 1994, the challenges were substantial. Factors such as the structural dependency related to the history of occupation, the decayed state of infrastructure and public services, the absence of fiscal viability, the institutional arrangement brought about by the 'Paris (Economic) Protocol', the PA's lack of experience in planning, administrative or budgetary matters, as well as the reluctance of private companies to invest in an uncertain political environment, all account in part for Palestinian weak economic performance in the decade following Oslo. As will be described in the next chapter, the PA's mismanagement of public funds, its lack of transparency and accountability, the concentration of wealth in the hands of a few (in particular through the system of monopolies), as well as its weak expenditure control resulting from an ever expanding wage bill, did little to improve an already fragile economic, financial and fiscal situation.

However, there is a consensus that the main proximate cause of this decline, which became a fully fledged economic recession from 2001 onwards, has been the Israeli imposition of the rigorous permits and closure system as described in the preceding section.[60] These policies deterred private sector investment and constrained previously established labour and commodity links between Israel and the WBGS, significantly reducing income flows in the process. In effect, closure sealed off Palestinian goods, workers and services not only from Israel but also from the rest of the industrial world. Palestinian economic output was thus erratic according to the varying levels of restrictions imposed on the WBGS. While sharp economic recession characterized the years 1995–1997 (where one first finds the occurrence of the term 'humanitarian crisis') and then from 2001 onwards, the situation improved between 1998 and 2000 as the closure regime was partially relaxed. However, despite some growth in the late 1990s, economic performance continued to be much lower than it was prior to 1993, and the period of partial economic recovery was never sufficiently robust to reverse the decline in living levels. In the course of the 1990s, the structure of the Palestinian economy also became increasingly disjointed, the West Bank and Gaza Strip being cut off from each other and from East Jerusalem, traditionally the commercial heart of the country. As internal commercial exchanges were disrupted, the Palestinian economy disintegrated into a small number of economic units, dismantling an already small domestic market.

A one-sided economic integration

Closure has had a particularly acute impact on the Palestinian economy because the WBGS had, since 1967, been partially integrated with Israel through an open, albeit asymmetrical, labour and goods market between the two entities. Trade between Israel and the oPt was effectively internal, although Israeli goods had free access to Palestinian markets while Palestinian producers had only very limited access to Israel, and Palestinians were only allowed to import through Israel.[61]

This incomplete economic integration was predicated on what academic Sara Roy has called the Israeli policy of 'de-development', designed 'to ensure that there will be no economic base, even one that is malformed, to support indigen-ous existence'.[62] She argues that internal Palestinian economic development and structural reform were held back in the period up to 1993 by three distinct yet interlinked policies: first, the Israeli policy of expropriation, confiscation of and restrictions on the use of key economic resources such as land and water; second, deinstitutionalization, with an unusually low level of investment, institu-tional development and infrastructural growth, particularly affecting the two main productive sectors of the Palestinian economy, agriculture and industry (indeed, the Israeli Civil Administration oversaw a recurrent budget that remained constant between 1967 and 1994, with virtually no capital investment component, and with a fiscal regime which oversaw a net drain on the Palestin-ian economy's domestic resources);[63] third, integration and externalization, which meant that economic growth in the WBGS came to rely principally on employment opportunities in the Israeli market, leading to a re-orientation of the labour force to semiskilled and unskilled employment in Israel (and also in Arab states) and away from local agriculture and industry, thereby distorting and weakening the indigenous economic structure.

In 1992, one third of the total Palestinian employed labour force worked in Israel (70 per cent of Gaza's), the majority of whom worked in the construction sector; 90 per cent of Palestinian imports came from or through Israel; and 80 per cent of exports went to or through Israel.[64] Through this one-sided economic integration, unemployment in the WBGS was low, never exceeding 4 per cent in the period 1970–1990, but the level of Palestinian dependence on Israeli demand for Palestinian labour, goods and services was extremely high, as was Palestin-ian trade deficit.[65] This was all the more so as both economies were highly unequal, with Israeli GDP averaging eighteen times higher than Palestinian GDP in the period 1990–1992.[66] 'De-development' and structural imbalances in the oPt economy thus precluded meaningful economic development in the period up to 1993, although there was some significant growth between 1968 and the mid-1980s, triggered by the rapid integration with Israel, and the regional oil boom. Nevertheless, the first *intifada* in 1987 and later the first Gulf War ushered in a period of economic decline with, from 1991, a decline in remittances from abroad and the first episodes of closure, adversely affecting employment and trading activity.[67]

The 'Protocol on Economic Relations between the Government of the State of Israel and the PLO representing the Palestinian people' ('Paris Protocol') signed on 29 April 1994 was the economic wing of the Oslo agreements, and defined transitional economic arrangements between Israel and the PLO/PA. The Protocol intended to formalize policies of economic cooperation and integration between the WBGS and Israel relating to the exchange of goods, fiscal and currency policy and labour services. However, its main effect was to deepen Palestinian dependency and vulnerability vis-à-vis the Israeli economy: it institutionalized the asymmetrical economic relations which had prevailed since the late 1960s and created an 'attenuated' one-sided customs union which continued to favour Israel in many respects. The volatility of the security situation, the deterioration in the bilateral political relationship as well as the poor implementation of the Protocol also explain why it never worked in practice. However, the agreement itself, a product of an uneven balance of power between the two parties and premised on the Oslo cornerstone of limited autonomy, also had fundamental flaws that worked against Palestinian economic interests, highlighting an instance of poor strategic choice by Arafat and his negotiating team.[68] As noted by an EC official:

> The most important point of the Protocol was that it created a joint custom union (free internal markets with common borders). The Palestinians had to agree essentially for political reasons. It was a deal, essentially to avoid having to tackle the question of territory, postponing the issue of borders until final status. The Israelis told the Palestinians: 'You shut up during the intermediary period and we let your workers work in Israel.' But it did not work because trade and employment were undermined by the closure policy and by the prohibition of Palestinians to work in Israel.

Similarly, the customs union was intended to give Palestinians preferential access to the Israeli market, but closure, in effect, offset the supposed benefits that could have been gained through the elimination of Israeli trade barriers on Palestinian agricultural products, and Palestinian imports were limited to relatively expensive Israeli goods. This continued dependency on Israeli goods and labour markets did not in turn allow the private sector to diversify. Because Israel continued to control all borders of the WBGS, Palestinian trade also had to be conducted through Israel, which retained an administrative fee, rather than directly with third-party countries, resulting in higher costs for Palestinian traders and a loss of part of trade tax and VAT revenue for the PA.[69] Moreover, the PA lacked an autonomous fiscal base and was dependent on Israel for the transfer of custom and income taxes it collected from Palestinians. The amount collected and transferred by Israel amounted to between 60 and 67 per cent of the Palestinian total revenue on a monthly basis (and part or the bulk of the remaining 33 to 40 per cent was provided by donors for most of the period under review).[70] As will be detailed in Chapter 6, this dependency enabled Israel to use the transfer of revenues issue as a powerful political weapon, for instance withholding revenues between 2000 and 2002 in reprisal for the beginning of the *intifada*.

Finally, Israel was also able to use its position of strength and control over borders to foster its own economic interests, putting Palestinian businesses at a serious competitive disadvantage. A study in 1999 compared Israeli and Palestinian firms in the same industries conducting business abroad. Transaction costs were found on average to be 30 per cent higher for Palestinian firms than for similar Israeli firms, and delays for imports and exports of Palestinian firms were about 45 per cent higher than for the Israeli firms.[71] As recalled by Ed Abington, former US Consul-General in Jerusalem:

> The EU told the Palestinians that they could export cut flowers and strawberries and have unlimited access to the European market provided they managed to get the goods to Europe. At Karni and Erez [entry points between Israel and Gaza], the IDF trashed the boxes containing the goods in search for bombs. Then Palestinians tried to export them via the Sinai. Presumably, goods leaving Gaza via Egypt do not pose a security threat to Israel. Yet, the boxes of flowers and strawberries would remain for days at the border until they were spoilt. Eventually, Palestinians were told that they could export to Europe provided they sold first to the Israeli firm Agrexco [which handles most Israeli agricultural exports]. Agrexco would of course determine the price...This is an example of how the spirit of the agreement was undermined.

More generally, during the interim phase, military law (and the economic restrictions therein) continued to apply to the oPt. Israel also retained control over key factors of production, such as land, water, labour and capital, while access to natural resources remained highly restricted for Palestinians. For instance, far from leading to a more equitable distribution of WBGS water resources, the Oslo agreements simply made official Israeli control over the Palestinian aquifers which had existed before the 1990s. Under the Oslo II agreement, 82 per cent of the West Bank's ground water was allocated to Israel, which was roughly what Israel consumed at the beginning of the decade.[72]

Loss of income, unemployment and economic recession

In the context of these structural weaknesses, the Palestinian economic situation deteriorated during the 1990s, especially between 1993 and 1998. Palestinian population growth, which was relatively high in the 1990s, exacerbated this trend. According to one estimate, the population grew from 850,000 to 1.4 million in the Gaza Strip and from 1.5 to 2.4 million in the West Bank between 1994 and 2004, a growth rate of about 60 per cent.[73] Economic decline peaked during the *intifada*. Israeli military incursions, tightened closure and reduction in the number of permits issued, curfews, destruction and damage to physical infrastructure on a large scale, and the construction of the Barrier disrupted economic activity, reduced the mobility of labour and commodities, and resulted in loss of employment in Israel and decline in trade flows. It severely affected Palestinian exports, as the access of Palestinian producers and traders to markets in Israel and other countries was seriously impeded. In its internal variant, closure also led to a decline in domestic production and access to local Palestinian markets which became fragmented, resulting in the spoilage of agricultural produce, inflated transaction costs and increased risk.

The loss of remittances from Palestinians working in Israel and the resulting lack of income also depressed domestic demand, in turn reducing Palestinian GDP.[74] Labour flows, and thus the extent of employment, became increasingly unpredictable, all the more so since Israel began substituting foreign workers for Palestinian labour. By the end of 1997, it was estimated that private sector investment in the WBGS had declined by 75 per cent since 1992.[75] Finally, movement restrictions also contributed to increasing the PA's budget deficit, by leading to the deterioration of the overall economic activity and decreased revenues for the PA. The close relationship between economic growth and closure is highlighted in Figure 2.1, published in March 2002[76]:

During the first three years of the peace process, UNSCO estimated that real GNP in the WBGS declined 22.7 per cent and that real per capita GNP, indicative of the level of living that might be attained, declined 38.8 per cent.[77] Between 1993 and 1998, unemployment rates trebled from an average of 5.6 per cent of the labour force in 1990–1993 to an average of 18.3 per cent in 1994–1998.[78] Diwan and Shaban have calculated that 'over the period 1993 and 1996, total costs of permit and border closure policies are estimated at about US$2.8 billion, about the size of one year's GDP, and nearly twice the sum of disbursed donor aid over the same period'.[79]

Relative to the years 1993–1997, the Palestinian economy improved from 1998 onwards as the political situation got better, the level of closure declined and more permits were issued. Thus GDP grew by an estimated 3.8 per cent in 1998 and 4 per cent in 1999, and overall WBGS unemployment fell to 12.4 per cent in 1999 and below 10 per cent by mid-2000.[80] Large-scale construction projects were realized, such as the Gaza international airport, the Gaza Industrial Estate (GIE) and

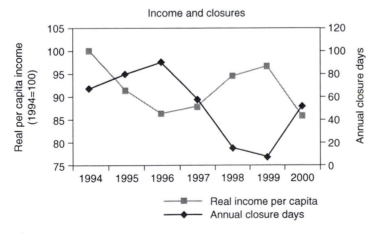

Figure 2.1 Income and closures (source: World Bank and UNSCO).

the construction of the Gaza Sea Port. However, despite some signs of recovery in the late 1990s, the economic performance remained well below what it was prior to Oslo. In June 2000, after two years of economic recovery and modest growth, the Bank nonetheless estimated that if growth rates were sustained, it would take a decade before real Palestinian GNP/capita reached its 1993 level.[81] In 1999, real per capita expenditure was estimated at its lowest level for any year since 1980.[82] Moreover, the two principal sources of new employment from 1998 onwards were the Israeli labour market (as closure relaxed) and the PA, neither of which was a long-term alternative to achieving sustainable economic growth.[83] This was all the more unsustainable as public sector employment growth in turn jeopardized the fiscal stability of the PA, which in 1999–2000 continued to be characterized by a large budget deficit and liquidity crisis.

The beginning of the *intifada* brought to a halt any relative economic progress that was achieved in the last quarter of the decade. Closure and the permit system tightened, and commercial transactions through Israel declined as the result of sealed border crossings. In the summer of 2000, it was estimated that 146,000 Palestinians (with and without permits and including East Jerusalemites) worked in Israel and Israeli settlements, representing about 22 per cent of employed Palestinians and 40 per cent of Palestinian wage income. By 2003, they averaged 57,000, and although only 9 per cent of employed Palestinians were working in Israel and the settlements, they represented 25 per cent of Palestinian wage income, as daily wages in Israel were approximately 82 per cent higher than in the West Bank and 138 per cent higher than in Gaza.[84]

In mid-2002, average per capita real income was 30 per cent below what it was when the Gaza–Jericho Agreement was signed in 1994. Including discouraged workers, unemployment reached 35 per cent of the total Palestinian population by the end of 2001 and 37 per cent a year later. In May 2003, the Bank estimated that

> overall GNI losses have reached some US$5.2 billion in 27 months – when one considers that GNI was estimated at US$5.4 billion in 1999, the opportunity cost of the crisis represents almost one entire year of Palestinian wealth creation. Cumulated raw physical damage has jumped in the last year to some US$930 million and lost investment to US$3.2 billion.[85]

By the end of 2002, total damage to infrastructure by military incursions was estimated upwards of US$1 billion.[86] According to the United Nations Conference on Trade and Development (UNCTAD) 2003 report, 'in real terms, in the last three years the Palestinian economy has forgone all the growth it had achieved in the preceding 15 years, with real GDP today below its 1986 level'.[87] As of the end of 2004, the Palestinian economy remained severely depressed, with about 27 per cent of the population being unemployed (35 per cent in Gaza), a number which reached 37 per cent among young people as opposed to 14 per cent in September 2000.[88]

These general figures mask economic variations in time and space. For instance, Operation Defensive Shield prevented nearly all economic activity in March–April 2002, while periodic incursions, and the Separation Barrier have had a severe economic impact. The situation in Gaza has also generally been much worse than in the West Bank as very few workers were able to enter Israel in the 2000s: while 29,865 workers crossed daily from Gaza into Israel in 1999, an average of 1,946 entered Israel daily in 2004.[89]

The *intifada* also resulted in the PA's ability to function and deliver social services to its people being drastically curtailed. By March 2002, the Bank estimated that the PA was 'effectively bankrupt', tax revenues having decreased to one fifth of previous levels. This was due both to the overall economic crisis, which led to a decrease in revenue collection, and to Israel ceasing to transfer clearance revenues that it collected on behalf of the PA between December 2000 and December 2002.[90] A total collapse of the economy and government was, however, averted, principally because donors provided an unprecedented level of budgetary support to maintain the PA on 'life support', particularly in 2002 when it amounted to 50 per cent (US$519 million) of all donor disbursements.[91]

Nonetheless, the PA's fiscal situation remained precarious and residual fiscal deficit reached US$550 million in 2003, financed primarily by borrowing from commercial banks and growing arrears to both the private sector and the public sector's pension fund. By the spring of 2004, the total stock of arrears to the private sector reached US$384 million (equivalent to 12 per cent of GDP) and the stock of the PA's debt to banks totalled another US$263 million.[92]

An increasingly fragmented economy

The hopes that integration between the two economies would produce economic normalization and income convergence with Israel failed to materialize, as did the expected improvement in Palestinian living standards following the peace process. Overall macroeconomic decline was so significant that, according to Sara Roy,

> at no time since the beginning of the Israeli occupation in 1967 had the Palestinian economy been as weak, and its people as vulnerable as during the seven Oslo years, a tragic irony given the enormous expectations that accompanied the early years of the process.[93]

During this time, WBGS markets became effectively severed from one another and internally fragmented, contributing to the creation of disconnected Palestinian economic clusters with no access to either the Israeli economy or to one another. This was particularly true with regard to the Gazan economy, with its high external dependency on imports and exports.[94] Up until the early 2000s, the West Bank continued to have more ties with the Israeli economy, although it was carved up horizontally into three main zones (northern, middle and southern), its urban centres became increasingly cut off and its villages became ever more isolated. From 2001/2002, the West Bank economy disintegrated into a number of fragmented economies, a process which intensified with the construction of the Wall. In 2004, the Bank observed that agricultural production for commercial purposes had shifted to subsistence production, as closures restricted farmers' access to lands, water resources and markets. This trend in the localization of economic activity manifested itself by an increase in the share of workers employed in their own villages, a proliferation of small-scale village businesses, and a shift towards purchase of goods locally, especially foodstuffs.[95]

What happened in Gaza during the 1990s may provide a good baseline from which to predict how the West Bank economy might respond economically to the establishment of the Barrier. Already in 2003 trends were apparent. In the northern governorates where movement restrictions were at their highest and the first phase of the Wall were being built, labour flows to Israel and Israeli settlements declined dramatically. For instance, between 1999 and 2003, there was a decline of 85 per cent in the number of workers from Jenin employed in Israel and Israeli settlements (ISI).[96] As of 2003, UNSCO estimated that

> despite limited employment in Israel and industrial zones for West Bank Palestinians, the Barrier and the division of the West Bank into microcosms will continue to harm trade networks, cause further asset-depletion of the private sector, and eventually result in 'de-skilling' of the labor force and impoverishment of households.[97]

By the mid-2000s, Palestinian economic prospects were thus bleak in terms both of actual economic indicators and of the likelihood of creating an economically viable Palestinian state. Fragmentation and a high level of dependency characterized the Palestinian economy. The GOI also announced that work permits for Palestinians would be revoked in 2008.[98] In its assessment of the economic impact of Israeli withdrawal from Gaza, the Bank estimated in October 2004 that 'disengagement would create worse hardship than is seen today', unless it resulted in a change in the highly restrictive border trade regime (i.e. a radical roll back of the closure system), which was not what it anticipated would happen, envisaging instead the sealing of Gaza's borders to labour and trade as well as perhaps a termination of water and electricity supplies.[99] And this is indeed what occurred after 2005, with disastrous socio-economic effects.

The emergence of a humanitarian crisis

The *intifada*, armed confrontations, tightened closure and economic recession combined to produce what aid agencies termed a serious humanitarian crisis in the oPt and which became particularly acute from 2002 on. Rising unemployment and falling incomes compromised household welfare and led to a drastic increase in the number of people in poverty.

Rising poverty levels

In 1997, 15.6 per cent of persons in the West Bank and 38.2 per cent in Gaza were estimated as living below the poverty line of US$2 a day, and poverty rates were much higher in some areas, such as in the south of the Gaza Strip where it reached 50.8 per cent.[100] By March 2002, an estimated 45–50 per cent were living below the poverty line, and this reached an average of 60 per cent by mid-2003.[101]

The impact of the humanitarian crisis has varied according to the rate of unemployment and the local impact of closure and curfews. Particularly affected have been communities which were already highly vulnerable prior to 2000, such as the refugee population and Palestinians living in remote villages of the West Bank and the southern part of Gaza. By November 2001, UNRWA estimated that the number of particularly vulnerable refugees had risen to over 1.1 million persons or about 74 per cent of the refugee population in the oPt.[102] In 2002–2003, around two-thirds of those classified as poor were in the Gaza Strip, where, in some areas, the number exceeded 75 per cent of the population. Communities in the West Bank which became isolated by the Wall have also become progressively more destitute. In 2004, the Bank noted that 64 per cent of Gazans lived below the poverty line, as compared to a national average of 47 per cent. Sixteen per cent of the total Palestinian population (or 600,000 people) and one quarter of all Gazans lived in deep or 'subsistence' poverty. One third depended on cash from friends and relatives, compared to almost none in 2001.[103]

Rising human insecurity: food, health, education and housing

A study undertaken by the Norwegian Research Institute FAFO in 2001 on how Palestinian households coped with the impact of the humanitarian crisis highlighted four main coping mechanisms: families sold assets, drastically reduced consumption (including food), increasingly relied on credit, and depended more and more on aid and emergency support.[104] The Bank described many family economies as being 'hollowed out'.[105] Falling incomes and lack of access to – and not unavailability of – food were the main causes for rising food insecurity and nutritional vulnerability. By the autumn of 2004, the UN estimated that 70 per cent of the Palestinian population was food insecure or in danger of becoming so, and that the average per capita food consumption had dropped by one third as compared to 1999.[106] An FAO study in 2003 noted that more than 90 per cent of the population reduced food consumption during the *intifada*.[107] Chronic malnutrition was estimated to affect one out of every ten children in the West Bank, although overall levels of malnutrition had stabilized as compared to

2002. The quality of children's diet declined in the 2000s, and as of December 2003 UNICEF found that 38 per cent of Palestinian children were anaemic.[108] By mid-2004, almost 1.5 million people, or 39 per cent of the population, were receiving regular food aid from WFP or UNRWA.[109] Dependency reached particularly alarming levels in some areas such as the town of Rafah in Gaza where 89 per cent of its 167,000 population regularly received food aid.[110] And indeed, according to WFP, food aid constituted the principal part of the household food basket in Gaza.[111]

As of the mid-2000s, it is difficult to gauge the precise impact of the humanitarian crisis on the long-term health and education of the Palestinian population, but trends of deterioration have already been apparent. According to the UN, in 2002 closures and curfews prevented half of the population from consulting their usual health services.[112] IDF action led to the destruction of clinics, hospitals and ambulances, as well as the death and injury of health personnel. It was also estimated that the first phase of the Wall alone had isolated or enclosed in enclaves 26 primary health care clinics, leading to a fragmentation of local health care networks and referral systems based around the cities of Qalqiliya, Tulkarem and Nablus.[113] At the same time, conflict-related violence resulted in growing demand for health care. In November 2004, the UN noted that the demand for blood transfusion services increased 178 per cent between 2000 and 2003, hospital emergency wards treated 52.6 per cent more injuries in 2003 than in 2000, and major surgical admissions increased by 31 per cent.[114] Access to water and its quality also decreased substantially as the result of military operations leading not only to shortages in domestic and agricultural consumption, but also to an increase in diseases, particularly among children under five who suffered more frequently from gastrointestinal infections. Access to education was equally seriously disrupted. For instance, OCHA estimated that in 2003 in the Tulkarem, Jenin and Qalqilia districts alone, about 2,898 children trying to reach 12 different schools were unable to do so in a consistent and reliable manner. UNICEF expressed serious concern in view of falling exam results and the rapid deterioration of the quality of education, as enrolment rates declined, children found it difficult to concentrate on their studies, students postponed higher education, and teachers could not benefit from adequate support and training.[115]

The number of homeless families also increased as the result of military operations and house demolitions. UNRWA calculated that during Operation Defensive Shield in March–April 2002, over 2,800 refugee housing units were damaged and 878 homes demolished or destroyed, leaving more than 22,000 people homeless or in need of shelter and/or rehabilitation. This figure came in addition to the more than 5,000 refugees whose homes had been damaged or destroyed by IDF bulldozing or shelling between September 2000 and January 2002.[116] House demolitions were even higher in Gaza. Between 2000 and October 2004, an estimated 24,547 Gazans were made homeless and the Israeli military demolished on average 120 residential buildings every month, leaving approximately 1,200 Gazans homeless each month. The Rafah refugee camp in southern Gaza was particularly affected: between October 2000 and January 2004: 9,970 Palestinians lost their homes there.[117] The construction of the Wall also resulted in an increasing number of homeless, internally displaced and isolated communities. Finally, land levelling increased during the *intifada*, in particular around settlements and in areas close to the Wall. For instance, over 50 per cent of Beit Hanoun's agricultural land in northern Gaza was destroyed between 2000 and 2004.[118]

Conclusion

Socio-economic and humanitarian indicators should not obscure the essentially political nature of the crisis in the oPt. As with the deteriorating economic situation in the 1990s, the humanitarian crisis which surfaced in 2002 largely resulted from the implementation by Israel of the above mentioned measures that have progressively been eroding Palestinian territorial and economic viability and the coping capacity of an ever greater proportion of the Palestinian civilian population. And these conditions continued to worsen after the mid-2000s. As an example, the UN estimated that poverty affected 65.8 per cent of the population in 2006, reaching 87.7 per cent in the now 'disengaged' Gaza Strip.[119]

The dilemma of providing high levels of funds over a sustained period of time to respond to what has essentially been an Israeli-induced crisis, and the related issue of the necessarily sub-optimal – when not harmful – impact of the aid package, is something which donors and aid agencies have had to grapple with at both the policy and the operational levels, as will be seen in Chapter 5. In addition, the deterioration of the socio-economic situation, coupled with continuing Israeli colonization and military occupation, the creation of 'facts on the ground' and the absence of any real headway in the diplomatic process have also had serious consequences on the evolution of Palestinian domestic politics after Oslo.

3

PALESTINIAN ADJUSTMENT

The rise and fall of Arafat's regime

The Oslo interim agreements of 1993–1995 established a set of new political structures in the West Bank and Gaza, transforming the political mechanisms and institutions upon which the Palestinian people had relied since the mid-1960s to lead their national liberation struggle. Through its agreement with Israel, the PLO, as the sole representative of the Palestinians and having drawn its political base and legitimacy from the support of the Palestinian population both inside and outside the oPt, established the Palestinian Authority (PA). Yasser Arafat, the leader of Fatah (the largest faction in the PLO) and his supporters moved from their headquarters in Tunis to Gaza City in July 1994 to become the ruling elite of this new administration. The PA was conceived as an inherently transient institution (the time of the interim period until final status negotiations), limited spatially (full control over Area A and partially over Area B) and circumscribed in the powers it could exercise in the non-contiguous areas which it was created to administer: the PA did not have control over its internal and external borders, airspace, sea access, defence and foreign policy, and key natural resources such as land and water. As described previously, it also lacked an autonomous fiscal and monetary base, and trade and the movement of goods and people to the outside world, between and within the autonomous areas were wholly dependent on Israel.

At the same time, though lacking the critical attributes of a sovereign entity – and indeed, legally remaining under military occupation – the PA assumed a 'state-like' quality, less in reality (the PA was from the outset, and remained throughout the period under review, more akin to what Edward Said described in 1993 as 'a kind of small-town government') than in the hopeful projection of the international community and many on both sides.[1] Though the Oslo agreements were primarily about the partial redeployment of Israeli troops and the establishment of Palestinian self-rule and limited autonomy in areas of high Palestinian population density, the PA was largely portrayed teleologically, as the embryonic structure upon which the future Palestinian state would be based. In addition to the executive branch of government headed by the President, a legislative assembly, the Palestinian Legislative Council (PLC), was elected. A Palestinian police and security apparatus was established. National elections took place in 1996. Other symbols of statehood included the Palestinian flag, which was raised over official buildings, passports, stamps and vehicle number-plates, which were issued, and an official Palestinian (state) internet domain.[2] Furthermore, the PA provided civil and legal administration to the great majority of the population of the oPt (although UNRWA continued to be in charge of much of the social services, expenditure and employment for the refugee population).

Most importantly – in terms of the creation and management of symbols, per-ceptions and prevailing narratives – was the fact that the PA became the de facto Palestinian diplomatic interlocutor – although the PLO, as the sole representat-ive of all Palestinians, continued to be the only entity which had the *de jure* authority to negotiate a permanent peace agreement with Israel. This ambivalent and incomplete transition from a national liberation movement into a 'para-state' or government lacking sovereignty, as well as the discrepancy between the actual very limited powers of the PA on the ground and the enhanced projected role conferred upon it, contributed to blurring the sense of what could be reason-ably expected from such a weak and circumscribed administration in the context of continuing Israeli occupation and control. As mentioned in the Introduction, one of the main tasks of the PA was to deliver security for the Israelis and police the population under its jurisdiction. Strong executive and security institutions were thus built into the PA as a response to consistent Israeli insistence on a 'security first' approach under Oslo.

But delivering security was bound to be arduous as Palestinian opposition to the Oslo process was virulent from the outset, mainly because it postponed key issues until final status negotiations. Oslo was opposed by the Islamic move-ments such as Hamas and Islamic Jihad, parties on the left such as the Popular Front for the Liberation of Palestine (PFLP) and the Democratic Front for the Liberation of Palestine (DFLP), and also by intellectuals, mainstream politicians and former peace negotiators such as Haydar Abd al-Shafi, Karma Nabulsi and Edward Said. The latter famously described the agreement as

> an instrument of Palestinian surrender, a Palestinian Versailles...the Palestinians [having] in effect discounted their unilateral and interna-tionally acknowledged claim to the West Bank and Gaza: they have now at most become 'disputed territories'. Thus with Palestinian assis-tance, Israel has been awarded at least an equal claim to them.[3]

At Oslo, the Palestinians agreed to forfeit 78 per cent of Mandate Palestine in exchange for the vague prospect of an unknown proportion of the remaining 22 per cent which had now become open for future negotiations. As pointed out, 'even this best-case scenario [22 per cent], and the process through which it was to be achieved, was highly controversial from the Palestinian perspective'.[4] Securing the peace process and security for Israel thus meant that it was neces-sary for the PA to have the means to crack down on internal dissent. Within the

context of Israeli control of the most important economic resources, their transfer back to the Palestinians in the forms of rents it controlled, and the substantial
constraints on Palestinian economic activities previously described, the PA also
had to allocate a considerable amount of money to maintain political stability, in
particular by creating jobs in the public sector and re-distributing rents and
favours itself.

This chapter reviews the nature of the Palestinian regime which developed in
the oPt after 1994, focusing on its authoritarian, corrupt and repressive character. The paradox is that this regime was established with the support of the international community and thereafter sustained with donor funds, while its very
nature hampered both the effectiveness of the aid provided and the development
of accountable, legitimate and sustainable institutions.

Authoritarianism and the personalization of power

The primacy of the executive

Although in theory the PA had to run government policies through the PLC,
which was supposed to legislate and provide overall oversight to the executive
authority, in practice it frequently by-passed it. Overall policy was devised and
implemented by the executive authority alone.[5] Moreover, the legislation
enacted by the PLC had to be signed by the President which in the case of Arafat
led to considerable delay and, more importantly, to many laws not being ratified.
Between 1996 and October 2002, only 31 laws were ratified by the President out
of the 95 submitted by the PLC.[6] One of the most important pieces of legislation
approved by the PLC in 1997, the Basic Law – the primary PA constitutional
document which determines the prerogatives and legal scope of each branch of
government – was not signed by Arafat until 2002, and under considerable
donor pressure as we shall see in Chapter 6. For most part, the President legis-
lated by orders and decrees. The PLC mandate was in any event limited geographically and functionally by the interim agreement which granted the Council
the power to legislate only on matters within the PA areas of responsibility, and
not on issues related to negotiations with Israel, foreign policy or final status
(still the preserve of the PLO). In the decade after its establishment, the PLC
thus remained a marginalized and powerless institution, in a context where the
overwhelming majority of its members were from Arafat's movement, Fatah.
Needless to say, this situation changed after the legislative elections of January
2006 which led to the electoral victory of Hamas and the concomitant formation
of a Hamas-led government, although the aid embargo imposed on the PA
(though not on the Palestinian presidency headed by Abu Mazen from Fatah) by
Western donors meant that the PLC continued to remain a powerless institution,
if perhaps a less marginalized one on the Palestinian domestic scene.

Arafat appointed the members of the Supreme Court and the Attorney
General, ruled by decree, and selectively picked and chose from the multiple

legal systems which remained in vigour.[7] The PA also frequently violated the civil and political rights of the population in the name of security, using the British Emergency Regulations of 1945 (which had also been used by the Israelis from 1967 onwards). In 1995, Arafat established by decree the state security courts enabling the security apparatus to rule without due process not only on security matters but also on criminal and civil cases as well as on issues related to taxation.[8] Constitutional ambiguity also enabled the extension of executive authority over both civil society organizations and the press, curtailing the freedom of the media and also NGOs.[9]

The executive branch itself also had a confusing structure because of the co-existence and partial overlap of authority between PLO and PA institutions. As these bodies were all headed by Arafat, the distinction between their functions became blurred and turf battles more acute, for example between the PLO Executive Committee and the PA Cabinet, or between the PLC and the Palestinian parliament-in-exile, the Palestine National Council (PNC) which is the only body that 'constitutionally' represents the rights of all Palestinians irrespective of where they live. In fact, the leadership of the PA and that of the PLO in the oPt (but not outside) became hardly distinguishable. Between 1996 and 2003 when the position of a Prime Minister was created, the PA did not hold any Cabinet meetings but only weekly 'leadership' meetings which included the President, Cabinet ministers, members of the PLO Executive Committee, the PLC speaker and his deputies, and the heads of the negotiating teams. In terms of internal affairs, this loose gathering – which was also much larger than a 'typical' Cabinet – examined such a broad range of issues as to make it almost impossible to plan strategically across ministries.[10] This leadership was also the group conducting negotiations with Israel and was accountable neither to the PLC nor to any other PA body. Attention was disproportionately devoted to the peace process, foreign relations and security, to the detriment of domestic socio-economic issues.[11]

Clientelism and the growth of the public sector

The President wielded considerable power, as exemplified by a variety of actions: the number of government agencies attached to his office by decree; his personal appointment of PA officials and the heads of those agencies; his micro-management of the work of his office and some of his ministers; and the fact that the minutiae of bureaucratic requests, such as civil servant and police officer vacation leave, mission per diems and petty expenditures all had to receive the President's personal attention and approval.[12] By the end of the 1990s, it was estimated that Arafat exercised about 30 official functions, the most important being the Chairman of the PLO Executive Committee, the President of the State of Palestine (as proclaimed in Algiers by the PNC in November 1988), the Head of Fatah Central Committee, and the President of the PA.[13] As noted by PLC member Dr Azmi Shuaibi in 2000:

So what have we done over the past five years? We have established ministries. It's hard to say precisely how many because some were originally established as agencies or departments, and then their directors, without any legal basis, simply started hanging signs over the entrance saying 'ministry of this or that'.... There are others – the head of the Petroleum Authority, for example – who simply assumed the title of minister themselves and started printing it on their calling cards and letterheads.... Another no less serious aspect has been the rise of centers attached directly to the President's office. They are no more than thirty ministries, but when I checked the government's accounts, I found that there were seventy-five public bodies that depend directly on the President, such as the Monetary Authority, the Hebron Reconstruction Committee, the Bureau of Public Institutions, the Jerusalem Committee, and the Civil Aviation Authority. But they also include offices of Presidential advisers with names like the Arafat National Center for Research and so on. These are fiefdoms, really, that employ hundreds of people and whose expenses are covered by the state.[14]

Public sector management was deeply affected by the personalized character of the system and by the fact that the system of appointment and promotion was more determined by personal, clan or party loyalty than by competence or merit. Clientelism was reinforced by the fact that the PA had to absorb a large proportion of former Civil Administration personnel (as per the Israeli demand in the Cairo Agreement) and returning PLO activists from Tunis.[15] Public sector hiring then became largely a 'means of rewarding loyalty and of securing a mass constituency', in addition to a genuine attempt to alleviate fast-expanding unemployment as detailed in Chapter 2.

Between the end of 1996 and the end of 2000, public sector employment grew by more than 50 per cent.[16] In 1996, it was estimated that there were 75,000 civil and security personnel on the PA payroll, a figure which had increased to 120,000 by 2000.[17] In May 2003, the Bank estimated that 125,000 people were on the PA's payroll, amounting to 26 per cent of those working in the oPt and 40 per cent of all domestic wages.[18] The PA had become by far the largest employer in the oPt. A year and a half later, it was calculated that the wages of 128,000 civil servants represented 68 per cent of the PA's current expenditures.[19] The expansion of public employment, coupled with the severe economic crisis of the early 2000s, forced the PA disproportionately to squeeze non-wage expenditure, incur debts to private suppliers, borrow from banks and defer social security payments (including pensions). Above all, it rendered the PA more vulnerable to Israeli control of revenue transfers and more heavily dependent on international donors for budget support. This has been most acutely revealed in 2006 when donors ceased to provide such support and Israel froze once again the release of transfers, leading to an unprecedented PA financial crisis, with dramatic repercussions for the civil servants under its payroll. At the same time, however, and despite doubt as to the efficiency of what many perceived as a bloated public administration, the above figures make clear that public sector employment also played a role in providing a safety net to a large proportion of the population increasingly beset by unemployment and deep poverty. This was one of the main reasons put forward by the donors for letting the PA's wage bill expand beyond sustainable levels, and for providing a considerable amount of unsustainable budget support during the *intifada*.

The corruption of the Palestinian authority

There is a widespread public perception, in the oPt, Israel and internationally, that the PA not only has been an authoritarian and largely inefficient organization, but that it has also been vastly corrupt. In a public opinion poll conducted by the Palestinian Centre for Policy and Survey Research in July 2000, 76 per cent of Palestinians believed that corruption existed in PA institutions; by May 2002, this figure had reached 83 per cent.[20] In fact, it is extremely difficult to gather dispassionate evidence on PA corruption because it gained disproportionate domestic and international salience as the decade unfolded, becoming one of the main themes recurrently invoked by both Palestinian opposition parties in the oPt (notably the left and the Islamists) and Israel and pro-Israeli groups in the US Congress and the European Parliament. However, according to a survey carried out by the Bank in 2001, the two most frequently found types of corruption throughout the world – informal payment to government officials for 'getting things done' or corruption in procurement – occurred less often in the WBGS than in many other developing countries.[21] The general view of international donors, diplomats and analysts who worked on the Israeli–Palestinian file in the 1990s and the first half of the 2000s is also that the scale of PA corruption was grossly exaggerated for political reasons. Nevertheless, it was certainly the case that the system experienced a lack of institutional transparency and accountability and that large sums of public money were unaccounted for. Evidence also suggests that Arafat and his close associates used public revenues not only to enrich themselves and their families personally, but also as a political resource to buy people off and strengthen the regime's position.

The misuse and waste of public funds

The issue of PA corruption first came to the forefront of the Palestinian domestic agenda in the summer 1997 – long before it attracted Israeli or donor attention – when a Special Committee, which had been set up by the PLC to look into the use of public funds, examined a report by the General Control Office (GCO) and concluded that around US$326 million or about one third of the PA yearly budget had been misused or wasted.[22] The report pointed to widespread bureaucratic corruption within virtually all PA institutions and concentrated at the top echelons of the government. It included favouritism, unequal opportunities, abuse of power, monopolies, the private pocketing of public resources and mis-management of public funds by wasting public finance by lavishly furnishing ministries and buying luxury cars for the personal use of an excessively large number of PA and PLO officials. As an example, around 20 per cent of the Health Ministry's budget between 1995 and 1997 was spent to cover medical expenses abroad, some of the transfers being made upon Arafat's order himself without notifying the Minister; similarly, a black box was uncovered in the MOPIC in which money from projects – presumably donor projects – was ille-gally channelled and then made available for the personal use of the Minister, Dr Nabil Sha'ath.[23] Following the publication of this report in which several minis-ters were accused, the PLC called on Arafat to dissolve the government. However, this had little impact, apart from the fact that it was the last time that either the GCO or the PLC was officially able to investigate Palestinian domestic finances.

Forms of corruption were not just endemic to the internal workings of the PA; corruption also extended to relations with Israeli officials and counterparts. For instance, bribery became institutionalized under the PA within the specific context of Israeli restrictions on movement. The widespread use of *bakshish* increasingly became the norm to access such basic services as obtaining a travel permit, telephone installation or car registration, and was essential for a special service such as obtaining a transfer to a hospital in Israel or abroad.[24] Trade was equally subjected to an elaborate system of influence and enticement involving Israeli and Palestinian security and custom officials, notably through granting travel permits in, out of, and between the WBGS, as well as to Israel, Jordan and Egypt. As Joseph Saba, the former director of the Bank's West Bank and Gaza Office, said: 'You set up gates and you set up gatekeepers on each side of the gate and history tells us that gatekeepers charge tolls.'[25] PA officials also enjoyed more freedom of movement than the population at large through their connections with the IDF and COGAT (some were even granted VIP pass status). Palestinian businessmen, especially those with links to Israeli com-panies, have also had greater access to permits than the rest of the population. As stated by one UN official, 'Palestinian businessmen and traders get the best treatment. Even when UN staff cannot get permits or when Erez [between Gaza and Israel] is closed to UN staff, Palestinian businessmen can pass.'

Part of the issue with transparency came from the fact that the PA did not ini-tially submit a yearly budget to the PLC, although from 1996 it was obliged to do so under combined domestic and international pressure. However, according to PLC member Dr Shuaibi, who was the Chairman of the Council's Budget Committee until the end of 1999, there were two main problems with the draft budgets submitted by the PA between 1997 and 1999: first, not all revenues reached the Treasury; second, the PA's public investments (i.e. the monopolies) were not included. In 1997, the IMF estimated that diverted income to accounts outside the Ministry of Finance's control represented about one quarter of total public revenue.[26] This is turn contributed to the Ministry of Finance's liquidity crisis, compelling it to borrow domestically and accumulate arrears. For instance in late 1998, it was estimated that Palestinian domestic debt amounted to US$93 million and arrears to US$79 million.[27]

This, together with the revenues of the monopolies which remained off-budget and were either deposited in private bank accounts or reinvested in commercial activities, constituted the discretionary funds placed at the disposal of the President. These discretionary funds were justified by the PA as a necessary strategic 'reserve', a means to secure its revenue base in case Israel ceased the transfer of clearance revenues (as it would in 2000–2002 and after 2006) or donors cut off aid. Indeed, the Paris Protocol created an almost total fiscal dependence of the PA on Israel, making off-budget revenues to manage the extremely volatile political context almost a necessity. But, as pointed out by Dr Shuaibi, that the PA might have needed a reserve did not substantiate Arafat's opposition to it being recorded on the budget.[28] It is also noteworthy that this reserve did not include the large presidential budget dedicated to the expenses of his office in the WBGS and PLO offices (diplomatic representation) abroad, which were also without effective oversight. Between 2001 and 2003, the IMF estimated that this amounted to nearly US$100 million yearly, or 8 per cent of the overall PA budget.[29]

PA monopolies

Monopolies are the heart of the issue of PA corruption because of the amounts involved, the secrecy surrounding where this money went, and the opacity with which most of the private monopoly companies that constituted the PA equity holdings were granted exclusive rights contracts.[30] There is also strong evidence that high-ranking PA officials frequently used their position to favour family business or the private commercial interests of specific groups within Palestinian society.[31] For instance, the 1997 PLC report suggested that Jamil al-Tarifi, then PA Minister for Local Government, struck a deal with Israeli government officials to close the border between Jordan and the West Bank for a couple of weeks, and his eldest son's company was the only one allowed to import cement into the oPt during that period. The widespread perception of the private sector as an 'uneven playing-field' – with some economic actors being favoured over others because of their connections – did little to make private investments any more attractive.[32]

More generally, public monopolies in profitable areas such as cement or fuel were also heavily criticized, not least because they led to the absurd situation where the PA sold fuel in the WBGS at a price higher than the Israeli on the other side of the Green Line, taking advantage of being the sole supplier to make higher profits. Most of the monopolistic deals involved the Palestinian Commercial Services Company (PCSC), a company run by Arafat's financial advisor Muhammad Rashid (Khaled Salam) which acquired and held about 79 semi-public enterprises.[33] Palestinians dealt with Israeli companies such as Nesher

Cement or Dor Energy for the supply of cement and fuel. According to Peter Lagerquist, deals often went through Israeli mediators, one of the most prominent being Yossi Ginossar, a former head of the Israeli GSS and a close associate of Rabin and Peres who was Rashid's main Israeli business partner. Muhammad Rashid's lawyer was Dov Weinglass, who was also Sharon's lawyer and would become his bureau chief and senior adviser in 2001. Also acting as go-between for Israeli and Palestinian businessmen were Danny Rothschild and Gadi Zohar, former heads of the Civil Administration, who together with intelligence officer Samuel Ettinger created the consultancy firm Yurta International Trade and Projects. This firm not only took part in the PA economy of rents but also established itself as one of the biggest security providers for the PA, Palestinian banks and businesses in the WBGS through the security firm it partially owed, NETACS, which was one of the few Israeli firms specially authorized by the GOI to provide security equipment and services in the oPt.[34]

Until the consolidation of Palestinian revenues and investments took place in the early 2000s, some of the monopoly excises and profits from PA commercial activities were deposited into a private Israeli bank account in Tel Aviv under the control of Arafat and Rashid. Money also made its way to Swiss bank accounts, reportedly transiting through the account of the brother of Abu Mazen, who at the time was Arafat's deputy and who later became the PA President in January 2005.[35] According to the IMF, between 1995 and 2000 almost US$900 million of excise tax revenues and profits from commercial activities were diverted from the Ministry of Finance.[36] These financial transactions were undertaken with the knowledge and compliance of Israel. Thus, if monopolies led to the private pocketing of public funds on a large scale, the issue is more complex than it may seem at first glance. The involvement of Israeli match-makers, Israeli companies and the connections with Israeli and Palestinian security establishments, suggest that the artificial scarcity and 'rent-seeking' opportunities created by such arrangements were exploited by both Israelis and Palestinians in business and politics.[37] Moreover, as pointed out by Rex Brynen, 'Israel provided about half of all of the diverted funds going to Arafat prior to the *intifada* through its payment of the petroleum excise tax into a private *Bank Leumi* account controlled by Arafat and Muhammad Rashid.'[38] These deals occurred at the highest echelons of both Palestinian and Israeli government circles. As noted by one US diplomat:

> Rashid worked with people close to the GOI and managed to cut a deal (probably in return for the economic favours he gave them) that Israel will turn over these revenues into private bank accounts. There was not necessarily an initial design on the part of the Israelis to corrupt and discredit the Palestinian leadership, this came later on in the decade after Camp David. Rather, some Israeli officials were close to Rashid and he delivered Arafat on various issues for them.

Furthermore, monopolies were also structured by the special constraints of the Paris Economic Protocol. As explained by Professor Mohamed M. Nasr:

> A closer examination of the Palestinian context suggests that in some sectors, the external constraints were such that realistic alternatives to the operation of Palestinian monopolies were not immediately present. The import of strategic commodities such as cement and petroleum was regulated by the terms of the Paris Economic Protocol in terms of quantities allowed and the clearance revenues in ways that effectively gave Israel a monopoly position in the supply of these goods to the Palestinian market. In such a context, the creation of counterpart Palestinian import monopolies by the PNA at least had a rationale as it allowed the PNA to capture some of the monopoly rents that would otherwise have gone to Israel.[39]

In fact, the Bank had reached a similar conclusion in 2001, noting that given the provisions of the Oslo Accords, a single buyer in the oPt corresponding to a single monopoly source in Israel 'may represent the best method of limiting the resulting monopoly rents'.[40] The Paris Protocol, coupled with the fact that in practice it was much less difficult and safer to import from Israel (because of Israeli control of borders as well as excessive movement and security restrictions which discriminated against non-Israeli suppliers and middlemen) therefore largely explains why monopolies may have been seen as beneficial to the Palestinians. For instance, the cement imported by private companies from Jordan or Egypt (the Paris Protocol allowed a small percentage to be imported from countries other than Israel) was often subjected to intrusive security inspections by Israeli customs, frequently resulting in the bags being damaged or torn apart.[41] Indeed, closure, and the necessity to be granted permits by the Israelis, was itself a significant constraint for many Palestinian businesses. As observed:

> Resolving such difficulties often became conditional on the mediation of Israeli 'partnerships', or agreements with people possessing connections to Israel's government, border bureaucracy, or security establishment. Among other things, these partners moved Palestinian goods through the Israeli export infrastructure as Israeli goods, often securing the necessary intermediary financing as well.[42]

In addition, corruption performed a political function and was an integral part of the patrimonial structure of Palestinian clientele politics and the strong security bias of the regime. Money, nepotism and co-option, as much as policing, helped Arafat to consolidate its regime and reward the loyalty of his Fatah and broader PLO supporters against those who opposed the peace process. And indeed it was no coincidence that, up until the mid-2000s, security officials were all paid in cash. This was an open secret acknowledged and understood by the international community, as will be detailed in Chapter 6. Yet no one was particularly bothered. The international overriding aim of supporting the peace process (with its security-oriented paradigm) took precedence over any desire to see the emergence of a more transparent and accountable PA. As stated by former US Ambassador to Israel Martin Indyk:

> The Israelis came to us and said, basically, 'Arafat's job is to clean up Gaza. It's going to be a difficult job. He needs walking around money', because the assumption was that he would use it to get control of all these terrorists who'd been operating in these areas for decades.[43]

Healthier public finances?

The PA monopolies were thus essentially a joint Israeli–Palestinian venture with a specific economical and political rationale, and initially operated with the blessing of the donors. The exact amount of the funds which were diverted is difficult to ascertain, and may have been grossly exaggerated for sensationalist purposes.[44] However, they seem to have been substantial, and as the decade unfolded the issue became too salient and came to be used as a powerful tool to discredit both the PA and the international community's assistance programme. By the early 2000s, putting order into the PA finances thus became pressing both for the international community – in a context where donors were providing huge amounts of budget support – and also the Israelis, at a time when consolidating Arafat's regime was no longer seen to be in their strategic interest.

Under Minister of Finance Salem Fayyad, and within the broader context of a donor-led reform drive, all public assets and investments held by the PA were brought under the control of the Palestinian Investment Fund (PIF), which undertook an evaluation and transparency diagnosis of the PA's commercial activities. As of mid-2000s, it was too early to assess the impact of these measures. A comprehensive report of all investments remained to be published, although the list of assets, of the bank accounts formally controlled by the PCSC, as well as a valuation by the international consulting firm Standard & Poor's of ten of the PA investments, was made public and posted on the PIF's website. In 2005, several of the ministers and high-ranking civil servants who were accused of corruption in 1997 remained in power under the first government of the Abu Mazen presidency, which was formed in February 2005, warranting caution as to how radically different the post-Arafat era would be. In February 2006, the Palestinian Attorney General reported in an inquiry into widespread official corruption that he had uncovered the theft or misuse of US$700 million of public funds, including the state-owned oil, tobacco and broadcasting corporations. Ahmed al-Meghami noted that billions of dollars may have been misappropriated in total.[45] Finally, in Transparency International's 2004 Corruption Perception Index, the PA ranked 108 out of 145 countries surveyed, which suggested that public perceptions of corruption, if not corruption itself, remained very high. Of course, the arrival of Hamas in part transformed the PA internal workings, and indeed part of the reason for the movement's popularity had to do with the perception among the population at large that it was a much more sober and financially 'clean' political formation than Fatah. The extent to which this perception bears connection with the actual reality is unclear, especially once Hamas led the government. Its ties with charitable Islamic organizations worldwide, including radical formations and countries such as Iran and Syria, would seem to indicate that its financial situation, and thus that of the PA under its leadership, is also extremely opaque.

Security, human rights and domestic opposition

The Palestinian security forces

While Israel retained overall security responsibility under Oslo, the Cairo Agreement stipulated the establishment of a 'strong police force' of a maximum of 7,000 recruits to guarantee 'public order and internal security within the jurisdiction of the Palestinian Authority'.[46] The Agreement also established a number of joint security arrangements between the Israelis and the Palestinians, such as the Joint Security Coordination and Cooperation Committee for Mutual Security Purposes (JSC), the District Coordination Offices (DCOs) and the Joint Civil Affairs Coordination and Cooperation Committee (CAC), as well as Joint Patrols and Joint Mobile Units. Oslo II increased the agreed number of policemen to no more than 30,000 (12,000 for the West Bank and 18,000 for Gaza), but on the eve of the agreement it was estimated that the Palestinian police force had already reached 22,000 in Gaza and Jericho alone.[47] By 1998, it was thought to comprise anything between 30,000 and 40,000, a figure which reached 50,000 in 2000 and 53,000 by 2003.[48] According to Oslo, the police would constitute the 'only Palestinian security authority', form 'one integral unit under the control' of the PLC, and have six main divisions – civil, public security, preventive security, Presidential Guard, emergency services and rescue, and intelligence. In reality, however, many more divisions were established although the exact number remains a matter of controversy.

In the late 1990s, the PA security forces were estimated to amount to a dozen operational branches, a figure which increased to more than 15 by 2004, although some of them were more or less active and influential. They included: the General Intelligence, the Preventive Security Organization, the Presidential Guard/Force 17, the National Security Force, the Special Forces, the Special Security, Civil Police, Military Intelligence, the Military Liaison Force, the Coastal Police, the External Security Office, the Office of the National Security Advisor, the Aerial Guard, the Disciplinary Police, the Civil Defence, the Fatah Hawks (dissolved in 1995 but replaced by Fatah's own militia, the Tanzim).[49]

The majority of the Palestinian security forces arrived in the oPt in 1994 and, for most, had served until then in the Palestinian Liberation Army (PLA) throughout the Arab world. According to Graham Usher, Palestinian security forces performed essentially three main functions: enforce law and public order (civil police) in Area A (except when Israeli citizens are concerned, as explained in Chapter 2); deal with the issue of Palestinian collaboration with Israel; ensure the preservation of the regime and fulfil PA security requirements towards Israel (i.e. combating terrorism, violence and incitement, notably through preventive actions against Islamists) in coordination with the Israelis. As noted,

> given the internal security bent of both the Cairo and Oslo II agreements, a strong and massive Palestinian intelligence force is an indispensable condition for the Oslo-inspired peace process. It is not so much tolerated by Israel as Israel's precondition for Palestinian movement towards self-rule.[50]

Security, patronage and regime stability

Throughout the 1990s and early 2000s, security remained the preserve of the Israelis and Americans (with influential but ad hoc inputs by the British and Egyptians), as seen most forcibly in the fact that the international Task Force on Palestinian Reform established in July 2002 deliberately excluded Security Sector Reform from donor purview at a time when Palestinian security and the 'war against terror' dominated the Israeli–Palestinian and global agenda. Security was not included in any other existing multilateral donor mechanisms and dialogue between the PA and donors and the international financial institutions on this issue has been negligible, in so far as it has existed at all. As compared to the multitude of official publications on the Palestinian socio-economic situation, reports on the internal Palestinian security environment have been few, and to the extent that some donors have been interested in those issues, they have addressed them as a parallel track, not as part as the overall donor strategy, which very much focused on the economic and fiscal situations (and despite the fact that Security Sector Reform worldwide became a fashionable donor 'item' from the late 1990s, and, in the oPt, donor fiscal stabilization policies very much impacted on the PA security and political dynamics, and corruption was prevalent within Palestinian security forces).[51] Nonetheless, the general picture which emerges for most of the decade is one of proliferation of semi-clandestine, unaccountable security branches competing against one another – and at times physically clashing – with weak institutionalization, no clear division of labour between them, blurred responsibilities and jurisdictional distinctions, and no unified chain of command. As noted in a report prepared for the UK Department for International Development (DFID) in 2006:

> The PASF [Palestinian National Authority Security Forces] lack a monopoly over the means of violence. Israel continues to control significant

portions of the West Bank. Communications between West Bank and Gaza are difficult. Command and control of the PASF is factionalized and personalized. There are overlapping responsibilities among the different services and no unifying doctrine. The security services have limited political support, and there is an inadequate legislative framework to guide them. The judiciary is weak. Parliamentary and other forms of oversight are virtually non-existent.[52]

For example, at the end of the 1990s, eight different bodies were believed to be dealing with intelligence and anti-opposition related activities.[53] Although in theory all security services were part of the Higher Council of National Security, in practice each 'fiefdom's' chief reported directly, and separately, to the President who, up until the early 2000s, paid the salaries of the security forces directly and in cash. In practice, there was no PLC oversight of the budgets in the security sector. They constituted the backbone of Arafat's patronage system. In this way, he also managed to prevent the creation of one cohesive and powerful organization, which could have posed a threat to his authority.

Crucially, the lack of inter-force coordination, duplication and competition between the different Palestinian security forces fed into, and reinforced, the territorial and political fragmentation of the WBGS. In the 1990s, armed clashes occurred mainly between the security services and the IDF, or between the security services and the Palestinian opposition: one of the most serious incidents – 'Black Friday' – took place in November 1994 when Palestinian police fired live ammunition at civilian demonstrators in Gaza (killing 13 and wounding another 200) following a demonstration by Hamas in protest at the arrest of a number of Islamists by the PA.[54] A significant crackdown on Hamas also occurred in the spring of 1996 following a series of suicide bombings. However, with the *intifada*, and within the context of a growing crisis of PA authority and legitimacy, rivalries and power struggles among Palestinian security services intensified and increasingly deteriorated into clan warfare, extrajudicial executions and internecine struggle, not only between Hamas and Fatah but actually predominantly within Fatah. From 2006 onwards, internal chaos and fighting degenerated a step further, especially in the Gaza Strip, with Hamas and Fatah once again violently clashing against one another.

By 1999, it was estimated that the PA police and security apparatus represented the single largest item in PA recurrent expenditure, accounting for about 30 per cent of the general budget.[55] In addition, the security agencies also had their own budgets that were not included in the overall PA budget, as well as having established their own systems of protection and extortion through such activities as illicit tax collection and commercial activities, notably within the context of the monopolies.[56] As with other positions in the public sector, hiring in the security services had a social and political function. As pointed out by Mohammed Dahlan, the PA Preventive Security Chief in Gaza, in April 1997:

> We have 36,000 people of whom we only need 10,000. This huge number is a burden in the PA and a burden on the security organ. We view it as a social issue because I cannot tell a prisoner who spent 15 years in jail that I have no job for him.[57]

In fact, evidence suggests that a decade after their establishment, their principal *raison d'être* remained their social function. The oPt may have one of the highest security personnel to civilians ratio in the world, but, by the mid-2000s, the actual capacity and capability of these forces were assessed as 'extremely weak', in addition to suffering from professional apathy and a degree of low self-esteem and public status, largely the result of years of inability to protect the Palestinian civilian population against Israeli military operations.[58]

Human rights violations

Since their establishment, Palestinian security forces have been engaged in widespread arbitrary behaviour, human rights violations and misuse of power. This has been extensively documented and denounced by Palestinian civil society, the Palestinian Independent Commission for Citizens' Rights, and international human rights NGOs. In its 1997 report on the human rights situation under the PA, Human Rights Watch summarized the situation as follows:

> Hundreds of arbitrary detentions were carried out that violated defendants' most elemental due-process rights. Those who were interrogated were commonly tortured. Physical abuse caused or contributed to many of the 14 deaths that occurred in custody [between 1994 and 1997]. The Palestinian state security courts have tried and sentenced scores of persons in secret summary proceedings replete with procedural violations. The PA has interfered with the Palestinian press, threatening and arresting journalists and human rights activists, encouraging self-censorship and creating a climate of fear and intimidation.

The situation did not improve as the decade unfolded.[59] On 30 August 1998, the PA for the first time resorted to the death penalty, executing by firing squad two brothers, both members of Military Intelligence in Gaza, after their summary trial by a military court and only three days after they were charged with committing the killings of another two brothers during a dispute between their families. They were denied any right to appeal.[60]

During the *intifada*, the human rights situation remained precarious, although the number of Palestinians arrested, detained and tried on security grounds was substantially lower during these years as compared to the mid-1990s. In addition, in July 2003, under considerable international pressure, Arafat abolished the State Security Courts which he had established by decree in February 1995 under pressure from Israel and the US, urging him to do more to prevent and punish violence against Israelis.[61] But summary trials continued, and the death penalty remained in place. One further difference between the 1990s and the *intifada* years is that the number of extrajudicial executions drastically increased in the early 2000s, as the result of the conflict and collapse of internal order and security in several West Bank and Gaza towns. For instance in 2001, more than 20 Palestinians suspected of collaboration with Israel were unlawfully killed or extra-judicially executed, mainly by members of the Palestinian security forces but also by members of armed groups such as the Al-Aqsa Martyr Brigades. The PA never investigated those killings and none of the perpetrators were brought to justice.[62]

Those arrested, imprisoned, tortured and, in some cases, sentenced to death fell into two main categories: those suspected of collaborating with Israel, and members of the opposition, principally Islamists, including members of armed groups. Other categories of people who were regularly detained, harassed or intimidated were human rights activists, academics, political figures from the secular opposition and journalists. Newspapers were also often closed down.[63] Up until the early 2000s, Islamists were perhaps the single group most targeted by the PA security apparatus. For example, in the spring of 1996, following an unprecedented wave of suicide attacks, the preventive security forces dismantled Hamas' military wing (the Qassam Brigades), arrested over 1,000 Islamists and raided, ransacked and closed down several Islamic social welfare organizations. In addition to repression, however, Arafat also pursued a strategy of co-option.[64] On occasion, the PA negotiated with the Islamists, as seen in the 1996 deal that Hamas would not disrupt the electoral process (despite boycotting it) or the countless ceasefires or *hudna* concluded during Oslo and the *intifada*. Needless to say, the tense if ambiguous relationship between Fatah and Hamas during the 1990s and the treatment of the latter by the PA then controlled by Fatah goes a long way in explaining the violent clashes between the two parties which erupted after Hamas assumed power in 2006 and reached open warfare by mid-2007.

The failure to rein in domestic opposition

By the time Arafat died, however, if authoritarianism, patronage and the prominence of security had played a key role in maintaining his regime and neutralizing the domestic threats to the 'peace process', the political system as a whole had become increasingly less legitimate and popular. The power and authority of the PA had become substantially eroded, and Fatah was increasingly fragmented geographically and organizationally, and unable to mobilize Palestinians behind a coherent national political programme. As explained by Palestinian political analyst George Giacaman:

> The Arafat system [of patronage and clientelism based on clans and families ties] has purposely worked for and resulted in a thorough

process of de-institutionalization of Palestinian society, dividing up and fragmenting society at all levels.... This was the same policy of divide and rule as the one pursued by Israel vis-à-vis Israeli Palestinians, dealing with Christians, Druzes and Muslims separately as if they are different minorities rather than one national group.... This led to a process of 'denationalization of the Palestinians'. Before 1994, even if the same system of patronage and corruption existed within the PLO, its identity was national in the context of a national liberation struggle aimed, since 1988, at establishing a Palestinian state in the WBGS.[65]

In addition to the PA being 'bankrupt', Israel began to target the PA infrastructure directly, most notably during Operation Defensive Shield in the spring 2002. Security installations (including Arafat's presidential compound, the Muqata'a), PA ministries and civil institutions – most of which had been constructed with donor money over the previous eight years – were either looted, seriously damaged or deliberately targeted in IDF operations. Private houses, public buildings, municipal offices, roads, solid waste equipment, electricity stations, street lighting and water networks were also destroyed. For example, the offices of 21 PA ministries and agencies were entered and ransacked in Ramallah at an estimated replacement and repair cost of US$8 million in that city alone.[66]

As the central authority virtually collapsed (although not conceding its formal power and responsibilities despite increasing speculation that the PA might choose to 'dissolve itself') and fragmentation intensified, Palestinian politics became increasingly localized: mayors and governors, family clans, tribes, political groups and armed militias gained in power and authority, competing against one another, often about narrower political interests.[67] The crisis of authority and legitimacy in the PA reached a peak in spring/summer 2004 following Prime Minister Sharon's announcement that Israel would disengage itself unilaterally from Gaza. This triggered a premature escalation in the internecine struggles for power and position within Fatah in both the West Bank and Gaza, degenerating into armed clashes and showdowns, kidnappings and assassinations, pitting Fatah and other Palestinian security branches against one another, and along a multitude of loyalty lines which varied according to locality and kinship networks.[68]

This crisis was also symptomatic of a rift which had become more pronounced since 2000 between Arafat's 'Tunisian' loyalists and the Fatah Tanzim, a grassroots organization around personalities of the 'inside' (those leaders who were living in the oPt prior to Oslo and had often been active during the first *intifada*) such as Mohammed Dahlan in Gaza and Marwan Barghouti, Jibril Rajub and Husam Khader in the West Bank. In this respect, the second *intifada* was in part sustained by this younger generation of Fatah leaders of the first *intifada*, some of whom were prominent in the PLC and security apparatus. Indeed, when the PA was established in 1994, they had either been co-opted into the security forces or initially sidelined, as Arafat set up his regime largely through an alliance of his cadres from Tunis and the WBGS traditional land aristocracy.[69]

While the PA experienced complete mayhem (and was more or less reduced to an 'employment agency') and Fatah lost direction, Hamas gained support. It is estimated that around 10 per cent of the population supported Hamas in 1996, but in the early 2000s this had risen to between 20 and 25 per cent.[70] By 2006, Hamas had imposed itself as the dominant force in Palestinian politics, as seen by its landslide victory in the PLC elections in January 2006, winning 76 out of the 132 seats of the PLC. Arguably, its steadily growing influence was not primarily due to its strict Islamic conservatism or its hardline military tactic of suicide attacks against Israel. Rather, since it was established in 1987 during the first *intifada*, the movement had developed as an indigenous social movement providing much needed welfare services, thus not only establishing a strong popular base but also becoming deeply rooted in Palestinian society across ideological and class divides.[71]

During Oslo, Hamas distinguished itself from the PA by remaining a grassroots organization with a clear and unambiguous 'resistance' message, very attuned to the popular mood, and offering some of the most effective welfare, medical, social, cultural and education services in the oPt. Its leaders were respected for their professionalism and modest lifestyles, sharply contrasting with the perception of a corrupt and self-centred PA leadership. Above all, its stature among Palestinians derived from the fact that it remained the only organization that challenged Fatah's political monopoly and continued resistance to Israeli occupation and colonization, whereas the PA was bound by Oslo not to endanger the Israeli presence (and admittedly, this was also made possible because up until 2006 Hamas never had any formal political responsibility for determining the future of the Palestinians). Hamas thus came to be seen as the sole remaining bearer of the Palestinian national liberation struggle for self-determination and, more generally, the recovery of Palestinian national rights.

This is not to underestimate the significance of Hamas' refusal to recognize Israel, and its long-term objectives of liberating Palestine through *jihad* and establishing an Islamic state on the whole of historical Palestine.[72] Its impact and support, however, cannot be explained with reference to the appeal of its ideology alone. Moreover, Hamas also proved tactically flexible and not necessarily opposed to participating in the building of a Palestinian polity, as seen for instance in the 1996 internal debate on whether it should participate in the general elections (in effect transforming itself into a political party). This was a position which at the time was favoured by the leadership inside the WBGS, but the view of Hamas in exile, who argued that this would mean legitimizing the PA and endorsing the Oslo process, ultimately prevailed. Yet a decade later, and following some substantial success in the partial municipal elections of December 2004 and January 2006, Hamas participated in the PLC elections.[73]

Similarly, Hamas stated on many occasions that it would accept a 'temporary peace' with Israel within the 1967 borders, including East Jerusalem.[74]

Conclusion

Several reasons have been put forward to explain the nature of the PA and Palestinian political developments after Oslo. A popular conception is that PA authoritarianism and neo-patrimonialism have been culturally determined, the PA merely behaving like other undemocratic Arab and/or Islamic states, in addition to having imported the heavily centralized and patronage-based bureaucratic structure of the revolutionary PLO in exile.[75] Others have laid the blame on Arafat himself, a view which became particularly entrenched in the aftermath of the failure of Camp David when a relentless Israeli PR campaign was launched to discredit the Palestinian President as a valid negotiating partner and interlocutor. From then on, the common-sense understanding or narrative which took hold in Israel, the US and Europe was that Arafat was no longer the partner for peace but the spoiler who had turned down Ehud Barak's 'generous offer' at Camp David, and purposefully unleashed the *intifada*.[76] Within the ideological context of the global 'war on terror' from 2001 onwards, many in Israel and the US also came to see him as the archetypal Palestinian terrorist, the Israeli 'Bin Laden' as coined by Sharon three days after 9/11.[77] This vilification of Arafat, who spent the last two and a half years of his life ostracized and virtually under house arrest in the Muqata'a compound in Ramallah, lasted until his death.[78] It was Israel's main public justification at the time for refusing to re-engage in negotiations with the Palestinians.

While the influence of Arafat's personal leadership style on the nature of the PA regime cannot be ignored, focusing on Arafat alone is overtly simplistic, if not disingenuous. This does not account for the complexity of the domestic and external dimensions of the growth of authoritarianism and a patronage-based system in the oPt during the Oslo period. Several authors have put forward more sophisticated analyses. Glenn E. Robinson has argued that the PA became an authoritarian polity because the exiled leadership of the PLO had to recapture and centralize power in the oPt and marginalize the resident Palestinian political leaders which had emerged in the 1980s with the first *intifada*. Rather than being cultural, the nature of PA rule has a strong domestic political logic.[79] Rex Brynen's approach is in essence very similar although he focuses on the neo-patrimonial, rather than authoritarian, dimension of Palestinian politics. In his view, the neo-patrimonial use of resources is to be understood in the context of the emergence of the new Palestinian elite after Oslo. It stemmed from the necessity to create and hold together a PA political power base in the context of transformation, significant political and social divisions, and the fragmentation of the Palestinian nationalist discourse challenged by an increasingly vibrant Islamist opposition.[80]

Robinson and Brynen have rightly emphasized the importance of internal factors in shaping the nature of the Palestinian regime in the 1990s. In addition, they have both pointed to the role of the international community in creating a *rentier* state and sustaining the Palestinian regime within the context of the Oslo 'security first' imperative. The role played by external factors, however, merits more in-depth examination in a context where the main resources and power control remained with Israel. In this respect, Mushtaq Khan *et al.* have put forward a seminal analysis focusing *inter alia* on the external aspects of the failures of Palestinian state formation and governance.[81] Taking as his starting point the Oslo security architecture and the manifold restrictions imposed on the Palestinians (and in particular Israeli control over movement, trade and revenues), Khan argues that Israel's intention was to create a 'client state' upon which it could continue to exert considerable control and leverage through the rents it distributed to the PA. Palestinian dependence on Israeli-controlled rents was coupled with fragmentation of the territory, and a strategy of asymmetric containment which enabled Israel to maintain Palestinian economic vulnerability, as described in the preceding chapter, and thus put pressure on the PA. In this context, Khan contends, many of the main PA governance failures – executive centralization, strong security apparatus, rent-seeking and corruption, etc. – were the direct result of the Oslo architecture set up by Israel with the support of the donor community, and accepted by the Palestinian leadership.[82]

If the 1990s did not result in the creation of a liberal, democratic and accountable polity in the oPt, it was thus in part also because Oslo was about security and the 'peace process' more than it was about establishing a Palestinian democracy. In this sense, the growth of Hamas must primarily be seen as a resounding indictment of the PA and, with it, of the international donor intervention which facilitated and funded such a regime as will be detailed in Chapter 6. The 'high' politics underpinning the international approach to the WBGS will now be explored. The next chapter examines the relationship between aid and politics, outlining the political stances, aid policies, respective roles of and interaction between the four main international actors which dominated most aspects of the diplomatic and donor processes (the US, the EU, the UN and the Bank).

4

AID INSTEAD OF POLITICS

Multiple actors, fragmented interests, limited influence

The profound process of Palestinian fragmentation described in the preceding two chapters occurred at a time when international engagement and multilateral assistance to the Palestinians were at their highest levels in the history of the Israeli–Palestinian conflict. It also took place within a diplomatic framework where the dominant role was assumed by the United States by virtue of its staunch military, political and economic support to Israel. It is one of the main arguments of this book that the relative diplomatic weakness of other third-party actors, coupled with their desire for participation and visibility, played itself out in part at the level of 'low' donor politics, in the hope that this would in turn influence the Israelis' and Americans' 'high' diplomatic politics.

That international assistance to the oPt was a derivative of the triangular relationship between international donors, the US and Israel (and on all three fronts largely determined by domestic politics back home), rather than linked primarily to a bilateral relationship between donors and the Palestinians as recipients, has had two main, and seemingly contradictory, impacts. First, this resulted in the aid agenda, and the specific composition of assistance provided, being tied primarily to Israeli actions and the latest diplomatic plan, rather than to longer-term Palestinian economic, institution- or state-building needs, as will be detailed in Chapters 5 and 6. At times of breakdown in the bilateral negotiations between the Israelis and Palestinians, or when the US decided to take a back seat, donor politics actually became a political centre of gravity in itself, the main arena for playing out the peace process, even if the aid community, led by the Bank, usually went out of its way to couch donor interventions in technical terms. As pointed out by a senior UN official:

> When the parties did not speak we would arrange for an AHLC to take place. The AHLC provided a high-level forum for breaking the dead-lock in bilateral negotiations – sometimes at a very high level (Barak, Peres, Arafat). The Israelis and Palestinians would normally only stay for the opening session; bilateral negotiations would then take place on the fringe. The diplomatic function of such meetings were often more

important than what could actually happen during the formal sessions which were largely ritualistic.

At such times, and most forcefully during the first few years of the *intifada*, donors displayed a particularly pronounced degree of hyperactivity. In the absence of 'movement' on the diplomatic front, donor initiatives *became* the 'peace process'. As in the case of the plethora of international plans which emerged and went (astray) during the Oslo decade, a vertiginous amount of donor reports, strategic plans and programmes for action were produced, often rapidly superseding one another. In contrast, however, the basic situation on the ground – and most notably, donors' own analyses of the economic fundamental – remained remarkably consistent over the years, as was shown in Chapter 2.

Second, while donors' were fully cognizant of the political factors constraining the impact of their aid programmes, they did not attempt to integrate 'Israel' into their equation for peace and development. As Rick Hooper observed:

> It seemed that the basic impulse among the development specialists, which would continue for some time beyond October 1993, was to treat the West Bank and Gaza Strip similar to poor (sovereign) countries. One implication of this was that development plans for the Palestinian economy and society did not initially take fully into consideration the ramifications of an ongoing negotiations process, and the fact that a third party, namely the government of Israel, would necessarily and inevitably be involved in anything that would happen in the West Bank and Gaza Strip.[1]

This chapter looks at the political stances, involvement and assistance programmes of the US, the EU, the UN and the World Bank. It examines the complex dynamics between these four international actors – and their evolution between 1994 and 2004 – resulting from the extreme intermeshing of aid and diplomacy. It focuses in particular on the relationship between the two main donors, the US and the EU, as an illustration of the way non-American third-party actors have attempted to use the aid agenda to exert influence on the Middle East Peace Process, with limited success. The analysis of the UN and the Bank then highlights two distinct multilateral approaches to dealing with the international balance of power within the context of one common objective: 'remaining part of the process'. The atypical nature of the involvement of these two institutions also underlines the extreme degree of politicization of aid to the Palestinians.

The bilateral protagonists: the US plays, the EU pays

US aid policy

In addition to the prominent diplomatic role it exerted, and the financial resources dedicated to Israel, the US – through its official development assistance agency USAID – has also been a major donor to the Palestinians. As compared to other donors, and with perhaps the exception of Germany, the content of its programme has been more openly a function of its bilateral relationship with Israel, in the words of a US diplomat, a 'domestic issue'. Interestingly, US aid to the Palestinians has been unrelated to the yearly aid package it provides to Israel which continues to be linked to US assistance to Egypt as a legacy of the 1978 Camp David Accord. Israel receives around US$3 billion a year in military and economic aid, but the amount could be higher than US$4 billion, as it was in 2003 when it included US$1 billion as an emergency wartime 'Iraq supplemental' to 'strengthen military and civil defences against regional threats'. Indeed, if loan guarantees and grants are added, the estimate could be that Israel receives from the US as much as US$6 billion annually.[2] Most American aid to Israel consists of a direct cash flow, with some requirements on the military side (mainly, to buy from American companies) but few conditions attached. As explained by one USAID official:

> The money to Israel goes through USAID, but it goes so quickly that if you blink you miss it. The President signs the appropriation bill and then the State Department has one month to write the check. That's it. There is no report, no accountability, no auditing. In many ways, this is the most efficient system for aid. This is the only country in the world where we operate in such a way. The Palestinians often jokingly say that they want to be on our Israeli program.

In contrast, apart from a few occasions when it supported the PA through direct cash transfer, American aid to the Palestinians has been project-based. USAID has operated in the WBGS through USAID contractors and private voluntary organizations (PVOs). It has devoted the bulk of its funds to projects in three main areas: economic interaction; community infrastructure projects; and governance. First, enhanced Israeli–Palestinian economic interaction, and water infrastructure in particular, received more than half of all American funding: as stated by a former US Ambassador: 'the bigger we can increase the pie, the best for everyone including Israel'. Support to trade and private sector development through the promotion of industrial estate schemes and establishing a sound legal and regulatory environment for economic intervention has also been a priority sector for the US. Second, American assistance was directed at improving the living conditions of the population, predominantly through basic community infrastructure projects in health and humanitarian aid, especially during the *intifada.* It also included continued support to UNRWA, which has amounted to roughly US$100 million a year.

Finally, governance projects have also been a substantial component of the USAID programme, mainly through support to the PLC and civil society organizations. According to one USAID official, this 'democracy promotion' element has put the US, at times, in conflict with Israel which considered that the priority was on security more than on democracy. However, 'security first' remained the overriding priority of the Americans throughout the period under review. As pointed out by one staff member from the National Democratic Institute (NDI):

> The international community has had a very short-term perspective. It wanted to support the peace process. It never had the political will to promote Palestinian democracy. It is true, that money went to democratization projects, but at the end of the day, it is about foreign governments pushing issues forward politically. Civil society can implement projects but if the PA at the same time is executing citizens after a 20 minutes trial, the signal sent is very different.

In addition to a yearly budget of approximately US$60–80 million a year between 1993 and 1999, Congress approved an additional US$400 million to facilitate the implementation of the Wye River Memorandum in 1998.[3] During the *intifada*, the USAID budget increased to about US$115–180 million a year, with an additional US$20 million in June 2003 in direct support to the Abu Mazen government and another US$20 million in direct assistance to the PA in December 2004 to pay off overdue Palestinian utility bills to Israeli companies.[4] As for most part the US did not provide direct cash assistance to the PA because of Congressional restrictions, the deterioration of the US–PA relationship in the post-Camp David period did not impact its assistance programme. In fact, as diplomatic ties with President Arafat were cut off from the early 2000s, funds increased to respond to growing emergency needs. That American aid to the Palestinians was largely the product of its relationship with Israel and that there was a close and well-coordinated relationship between USAID and Israeli officials may also explain why American financed projects were only minimally damaged in the course of Israeli military incursions during the *intifada*. According to one estimate, the damage incurred by USAID was about US$0.5 million – as opposed to more than €39 million for the Europeans.[5] However, as observed by one US official:

> Many Europeans believe that Israel damaged the projects they had funded on purpose. I do not agree. I think this has more to do with the different kind of projects funded. European projects, such as the Gaza airport and seaport, are simply more vulnerable. On the other hand, many of the projects funded by USAID, such as the infrastructure ones in the water sector, also benefit the Israelis and are negotiated with them from the outset.

Overall, the US Embassy to Israel estimated that American aid to the Palestinians totalled US$1.27 billion between 1994 and 2004 – or about a third of what Israel receives on a yearly basis. At times the gap was even higher: as an indication for the fiscal year 2003, US per capita assistance to Israel amounted to US$654 while the Palestinians received US$54.[6] Compared to the level of funds channelled to Israel, and other donor expenditure to the WBGS, the amount of American aid to the Palestinians was modest. Above all, it did not match its diplomatic predominance in the peace process. This discrepancy contributed to the widely shared feeling among other donors that 'the Americans conclude deals and then send us the bill'. This was particularly true of the Europeans, who were the main aid provider to the oPt.

The European assistance programme

The European aid programme to the Palestinians gave the EC and EU Member States a 'place at the table' which would otherwise have been much more difficult to secure given Israeli–American predominance, and in spite of powerful European strategic interests in the region.[7] The EU (EC, Member States and the European Investment Bank (EIB) in the 1990s) provided about half of all international aid to the Palestinians through a number of distinct budget lines, including UNRWA (since 1971), special funding for the Middle East Peace Process, the MEDA funds for the implementation of the Euro-Mediterranean Partnership ('Barcelona Process', since 1995) and the EC Humanitarian Aid Department (ECHO). Regional peace process projects have also been an important element of EU assistance, through the Regional Economic Development Working Group (REDWG) inherited from the Madrid track, and so-called 'people to people' projects aimed at fostering cooperation between Israeli and Arab civil society in such sectors as the environment, legal matters, health, economics, education, media, human rights and non-violence.[8]

To the WBGS alone, the EU contributed some €3 billion between 1994 and 2002, one third of which came from the EC, and two-thirds from Member States and the EIB. In addition, during this period, the EU provided €1.2 billion to Palestinian refugees through UNRWA. In the midst of the *intifada*, European aid increased, reaching, for the EC alone, between €250 and €325 per year in 2002–2003.[9] European financing was very important in absolute but also in relative terms. Per capita assistance provided to the Palestinians between 1991 and 1995 was estimated at ECU 258 as compared to ECU 11 per capita for the other countries of the Mediterranean area.[10]

Between 1994 and 1998, about 40 per cent of the EU aid programme went to the construction, infrastructure and the natural resources management sector. Other areas of intervention included support to private sector development, to higher education (by covering the recurrent costs of tertiary education), and to institution-building. Initially the focus of the latter was on its infrastructural component rather than technical assistance (TA) to PA institutions, in addition to the EC being one of the main donors to the 1996 elections.

EC officials concurred that the European assistance programme initially lacked focus. With hindsight, they described the first five years variously as; 'scattered', 'very ad hoc', 'support all over the place' or 'a little bit of whatever'. As of the end of 2004, the EC had yet to produce an operational, multi-annual financial pro-gramming framework in the form of a Country Strategy Paper (overall strategic concept for its assistance) and a National Indicative Programme (types of pro-jects), which it normally uses for other Mediterranean partner countries.[11] Instead, programming of financial assistance to the WBGS was carried out on an annual basis. Lack of clearly defined aid priorities may in large part be explained by the perceived need to retain a maximum degree of flexibility to be able to respond to political events. The priority was to be 'part of the process'. Huge pressures were exerted on the EC by Member States to disburse as much and as fast as possible. Concern for visibility also accounts for European initial focus on concrete infra-structure projects, in line with the overall donor programme in the mid-1990s, as will be described in the following chapter.

During the *intifada*, the EU continued to be active in the same such sectors. However, as the overall aid programme achieved greater strategic focus – mainly because of greater political coherence over time – the balance of sectoral allocation moved away from infrastructure towards institution-building aimed at 'raising the capacity, democratic functioning and the regulatory and organi-zational environment' from which Palestinian institutions operate.[12] The EU also played a leading role in financing and coordinating international support for the Palestinian reform process from 2002. Overall, however, European assistance became increasingly more relief-oriented, notably through providing high levels of budgetary support to the PA – an unusual occurrence in standard Barcelona aid packages. It also significantly increased its humanitarian assistance and launched an important food security programme in partnership with local NGOs and UN agencies, notably WFP, FAO and UNRWA.[13]

The politics of European money

As with many other international donors, the overriding aim of EU assistance to the WBGS was to support the Oslo process through providing a peace dividend to the Palestinian population. Nonetheless, from the outset, and in contrast to the US, European aid also purported to support the PA, seen as the only viable partner for peace and the prime governing structure of a future Palestinian state. According to one EC official:

> Since the Madrid conference, we had started to organize ourselves to deal with Palestinian nation-building. Our sense was that this process would be akin to a decolonization process. We thought that one of the most important things would be to set up the institutional framework which would help Palestinian self-determination as supported in the European 1980 Venice Declaration.

The implementation of this objective became particularly prominent from the late 1990s as a result of greater political coherence in anticipation of Palestinian statehood, as exemplified by the EU 1997 Interim Association Agreement signed with the Palestinians, and the 1999 Berlin Declaration in which, for the first time, the EU gave explicit support to the two-state solution. The later part of the decade also coincided with the broader European enlargement process with the EC focusing on governance and structural adjustment to prepare governments for closer cooperation with Europe. Finally, with the *intifada*, it became increasingly difficult to implement infrastructure projects, as deteriorating security conditions on the ground prevented international experts from moving freely and safely. The fact that European-funded projects incurred significant damage in 2001–2002 also contributed to diminishing European enthusiasm for that sector.

EU extension of support to the PA has been assessed internally as one the most successful aspects of European assistance to the Palestinians. According to an EC evaluation in 2000:

> The Commission, when trying to answer, in its Communication of January 1998, the key question whether the extraordinary amount of Community financial resources devoted to the peace process had worked, concluded that the answer is twofold. From the point of view of economic development and regional integration the result of the effort is unsatisfactory. From the political point of view, however, the European's Union's political input and economic contribution has been the determining element for the survival of the Palestinian Authority, and with it, the peace process.[14]

A similar point was made by the then Commissioner Chris Patten in the midst of the *intifada* in December 2001:

> What we have done is to provide some grounds for hope – and in recent months to prevent further economic misery – and to keep the Palestinian Authority – barely – alive and in place by providing €108 million in budgetary aid over the last 14 months. Some people have criticized us for that, although members of the Israeli government have explicitly supported these efforts in the past. We have worked to maintain the only viable partner in peace that Israel can find and we should continue to support the PA, especially in its fight against terrorism. While the PA has made mistakes and must correct them, the PA is the only structure that can provide stability in the Palestinian territories. It is the provider of necessary basic services and in the end the guarantor for a minimum of security for both the Palestinians and the Israelis. If the PA is disabled, we still face a situation of anarchy where Hamas and *Jihad* will no doubt gather increasing support and local extremist committees will compete in an escalation of violence.[15]

More controversially (to Israel), the EU also funded projects in East Jerusalem to support the Palestinian community and public institutions of the city, and to preserve its Arab cultural heritage.[16] Support to both Jerusalem and the PA reflected the European political vision for the Middle East and set it apart from the US.

Indeed, for the past two decades, the EU view on the Israeli–Palestinian conflict, and its resolution, evolved into a relatively consistent and clear diplomatic position based on two main elements.[17] First, the EU has acknowledged the collective rights of both parties to security and self-determination. Historically, it had recognized the right of Israel to live in peace and security within internationally recognized borders. Since the European Council Venice Declaration of 1980, the EU had also supported the Palestinian right to self-determination, a recognition which in 1999 became an official endorsement for 'the creation of a democratic, viable and peaceful sovereign Palestinian state on the basis of existing agreements and through negotiations…as the best guarantee of Israel's security and Israel's acceptance as an equal partner in the region'.[18] More specifically, the EU vision is that of a Palestinian state on the basis of the 1967 borders (with the possibility of minor adjustments through land swaps), Jerusalem as a shared capital, and a just and acceptable solution to the refugee question.[19] Second, the EU has also repeatedly stressed the importance of upholding human rights and international humanitarian law, notably by condemning Palestinian suicide attacks against Israeli civilians as well as Israeli occupation and violations of the Fourth Geneva Convention as it applies to the oPt.[20]

Simultaneously, the EU gradually sought to expand its political role in the peace process through a variety of transatlantic and multilateral processes and appointments, including: the 'Barcelona Process'; bilateral ties centred around cooperation, financial and technical assistance and political dialogue (contractual ties with both Israel and the PLO/PA through Association Agreements); the appointment of Ambassador Miguel Angel Moratinos as Special Envoy to the Middle East Peace Process in 1996 (replaced by Ambassador Marc Otte in 2003); and membership of the Quartet from 2001. As argued, assistance to the Palestinians, and notably its political, financial and technical support to the PA, was also conceived as leverage to gain more political influence in the peace process, thereby also hoping to increase its standing in the region as a whole. As stated in a 2001 briefing paper calling for more robust European political involvement in the peace process alongside the US:

> The EU and its Member States have already laid the groundwork for a more proactive policy: European aid constitutes the primary source of support for the Palestinian Authority; they have strong historical and political ties to each of the main actors involved and neighboring Arab states; they carry an important weight in international organizations; and they have a record of crisis prevention and management in the

region. Israel's trade with Europe, its technological dependency on the EU and its need to anchor itself in the EU system are real assets for the EU. These and other assets should provide for strong inducements and possible leverage to bring about re-engagement in more credible diplomatic negotiations, the results of which Brussels would be prepared to help and back-up.[21]

Nonetheless, despite greater political cohesion and assertiveness over time, the EU failed to acquire a leading diplomatic role commensurate with its financial contribution. As mentioned, the first reason had to do with the disinclination of both Israel and the US to see any other third-party involvement. Internal turf battles and dissentions among Member States also explain limited European influence.

Intra-European dynamics

First, there is the complex relationship between the European pillar I (EC) and pillar II (Common Foreign Security Policy), which entails political, bureaucratic and personal dimensions. At times this confused the relationship between the offices of Commissioner for External Relations and EU High Representative. There were also occasions when internal cooperation between the EC and the Council was poor, notably at the level of capital and local-level donor coordination, reflecting badly on the EU as a whole.[22] Related was the equally intricate relationship between the EC and Member States. Greater cohesiveness and coordination did emerge over the years. For instance, the early 2000s saw the institutionalization of bi-monthly EC/Consular meetings in Jerusalem. Member States, which have to agree on all EC programmes, never rejected a project proposal. In addition, the EC often assumed collective responsibility for controversial European aid projects to the Palestinians, notably budgetary support to the PA and the financing of Palestinian textbooks.

Nonetheless, persistent diverging opinions and interests of Member States – as they related to their relationship with the US, Israel and the broader Arab Middle East – prevented the building of a stable consensus for action although, on paper, European position on the Israeli–Palestinian conflict was clearly articulated. EU policy continued to be forged by the lowest common denominator. Differences are notoriously important between Germany (a function of its history and 'special' relationship with Israel), France (a legacy of its colonial past and current relationship with both Israel and the Arab world, which strongly affects French domestic politics) and the European countries which have strong transatlantic ties to the US (notably Great Britain but also Denmark and the Netherlands). As noted by one EC official:

The Israeli–Palestinian conflict remains a hot political issue: you have 15 member states with different views; in some countries the Prime

Minister and the Foreign Minister do not even share the same position... So while we all agree on what the solution should be and are all united behind a common vision (which is not always the case as evidenced by the diverging positions concerning Iraq), we have problems in agreeing on the steps. As Commissioner Patten says, 'It's easier to go from A to Z than from A to B.'

Finally, relations between the EC and individual Members of the European Parliament (MEP) were also tense on occasion, although the Parliament as a whole has shown support to the EC assistance programme, always approving the funding requested. Three main 'waves' of allegations were launched by pro-Israel MEPs in Strasbourg in the period under review. In the late 1990s, accusations were made that the EC was funding PA corruption; in the early 2000s, that it was fuelling anti-Semitism because of the Palestinian textbooks it was said to finance (which allegedly contained incitement against Israel); and finally, in 2002–2003, that it was financing terrorism through its direct budgetary support to the PA. Internal and external investigations into these allegations did not find conclusive evidence.[23] However, for EC bureaucrats working on the Israeli–Palestinian file, this made working with the PA ever more complicated and time-consuming, 'taking a toll both professionally and personally'. As explained by one EC official:

The Middle East is incredibly emotional. The previous Commissioner for External Relations, Marine, was under accusations in 1998–1999 on the ground that the EC funded Palestinian corruption. Not a single case of corruption has been proven in the Palestinian dossier. If we ever have been extremely attentive with one partner, this is the one. The Commission is subject to harassment, inspection, scrutinized in minute details, but not a single proof of corruption has been found.... It goes in waves (corruption, textbooks, terrorism). We are bothered but used. It is tiring for the Commissioner and all the staff. We could be spending our energy on real work. But we have accepted that. What we are doing is difficult, but we are proud.

The secondary political role played by the Europeans in the MEPP does not mean no influence at all, however. A case could be made that European involvement – like that of the UN – has indirectly contributed to the diffusion of certain shared values, norms and principles with some impact on the overall international agenda: notably that of the two-state solution as the best outcome to the conflict and the importance of upholding IHL which, in the midst of the humanitarian crisis and as construction of the Barrier began, became an increasingly visible theme on the international aid and political agenda. However, by the mid-2000s there was little indication that this process of 'socialization' had resulted in any fundamental policy change or redefinition of the main actors' interests and identities beyond important – but ultimately insufficient – normative consensus-building. The EU continued to be more of a 'payer than a player'.

American–European rivalry

Low politics: leadership of aid coordination fora

This is a position which the Europeans, understandably, never came to hold dear. As, for the various reasons highlighted above, American–European rivalry could not play itself out easily at the diplomatic level, the tension trickled down to the donor level. As noted in Chapter 1, Norway was chosen as the Chair of the AHLC in 1993 as a compromise to resolve the conflict between the two main donors over leadership of the main aid coordination forum. The AHLC itself had been established in part because the Americans wanted a bilateral structure to deal with assistance to the Palestinians. The Europeans for their part favoured keeping the file within the purview of the Regional Economic Development Working Group which they were chairing under the multilateral Madrid framework. If a compromise was initially reached over the AHLC chairmanship, the Europeans never ceased to question the legitimacy of the Norwegian position.

The issue of chairmanship first resurfaced in the mid-1990s and a new compromise was eventually reached at the AHLC in Frankfurt in 1999: Norway would remain Chair but the host country would be Co-Chair, and meetings would be held mostly in Europe. The next AHLC actually took place in Tokyo (!), as some within the US delegation felt that 'the Europeans should not have the monopoly'. Conveniently, Japan, which also aspired to greater visibility, had suggested holding the next meeting. After this, the issue was nonetheless settled and from 2000, all AHLCs took place in Europe – a couple of them, though, in Oslo, as in April 2002 and December 2004. But the European aspiration to exert greater influence on the Palestinian development effort was not assuaged, and neither was its perception (and that of other third-party actors) that Norway leaned more towards the US than the EU. As one EC official put it:

> There has always existed some sort of a competition between Norway and the EU. They were interested in keeping the chair for themselves but were not balanced between the EU and the US. They would always address US concerns first. The job was a bit too big for the Norwegians. They did a good job as facilitator of the Oslo agreement, but then could not lead unless they were in line with the US.

The Norwegians had always been remarkably close to the Americans, the US being Norway's main ally since the end of the Second World War.[24] Norwegian and American officials have also generally recognized an intimate relationship and like-mindedness between the two countries, notably in terms of approach and agenda. As pointed out by one Norwegian diplomat:

> On substance, the Norwegian position is closer to that of the EU but on process, we understood the dilemmas of the American side. The Americans are the only serious players on the political aspects of the crisis so it is important to be in active dialogue with the US. But then, we had realistic expectations too: sometimes we could contribute, sometimes not.

Even if there is a consensus that overall donor coordination actually functioned pretty well 'despite a little bit of pushing and pulling', the issue of chairmanship continued to plague the relationship between the US and the EU and resurfaced in the early 2000s as discussions emerged within the donor community on whether, and how, to streamline the aid coordination mechanisms in view of their evolution during the *intifada*. As of the mid-2000s, however, there had not been any major overhaul of the Oslo aid coordination structure. One EC official attributed this failure to 'US opposition, Norwegian selfishness and the lack of EU cohesion'. The EU was nonetheless given a greater lead in the new mechanisms established to coordinate donor support to both the PA reform process (TFPR) and the emerging humanitarian situation (HEPG).

High-politics: substance or style?

Some have argued that American–European rivalry, witnessed in disputes about the chairmanship of donor meetings and coordination fora, was an expression of two fundamentally different positions and approaches, principally a function of their relationship with the two parties to the conflict, and with their own internal domestic constituencies. As summed up by one EC official: 'Our different conceptions are summarized in the first lines of the Roadmap: "goal driven" (EU); "performance-based" (US).'

Others believe that the rivalry between the two main players was less about substance than about flags, profile and visibility. After all, an international consensus had emerged over the years, converging around the following key themes: that peace is crucial to the region and to the security interests of the Western world; that aid had a major function to play to support the peace process; that the US is *primum inter pares* and an indispensable partner; that a two-state solution on the basis of the 1967 border is the best solution to the conflict; that the state of Palestine should be democratic and based on free market economics; and that all forms of terrorism and violence against civilians are to be strongly condemned. Moreover, as mentioned, the EU is not a monolithic bloc and the agendas of some Member States coincide more closely to that of the US than to other European countries.

Some international officials have thus argued that the issue was not so much one of conflicting agendas as one of differences in bureaucratic cultures and approaches, and in the mechanisms put in place by the donors to deal with the parties. For instance, the EU supported the PA through direct budgetary assistance while the US only did so on exceptional occasions because of Congressional restrictions; the EU referred to international law to a greater extent than the US; the US was engaged in security issues with both sides on a greater scale than the EU; and the US negotiated its Palestinian aid programme with the GOI while the EU did not. Moreover, due to intra-European dissension and complex politics at the capital level, there was also a sense that while the EU (notably the EC) at the local level could be more openly critical of Israel than either the US or other donors, notably on issues related to obstacles to project implementation, they often did so without adequate political backing from Brussels. As bluntly put by a US State Department Official:

> The EU is more aggressive than the US in public speeches, but it should also recognize its institutional limits – notably the differences between its Member States, like we do *vis-à-vis* the Congress. Sometimes, we have the feeling that the EU is trying to corner the US and the donor community at large into doing public pronouncements that they cannot make on their own and that the US cannot make either. This seems illogical. A lot of this is driven locally: many players are frustrated.

The question of which country held the EU presidency also entered into the equation. Similarly, on the EU side, there is recognition that the quality of the EU–US bilateral relationship also depended on who the interlocutor was on the US side – whether USAID, the White House or the State Department – and also which administration was in office. The relationship between the EC and USAID does not seem to have ever been particularly problematic, especially at the local level where both organizations interacted frequently due to a decentralization of their respective aid programmes. The relationship between the EU and the State Department seems to have been less close during the Clinton period when the US monopolized the diplomatic process more 'aggressively' than during the first term of George W. Bush. By contrast, the EU, the State Department and the other main actors seemed to have worked together more closely in the early 2000s. At that time, however, internal tensions between the White House and the State Department were more noticeable. This led to the incongruous situation of having the EU and other Quartet members actually manoeuvring so as to enhance the standing of the State Department within its own administration. As noted by Dr Tocci:

> Since 2001, most EU activities have been tailored to encouraging the Bush administration's engagement in the peace process. EU policymakers proactively pushed the dossier of Palestinian reform, hoping

that this would remove any reason (or excuse) for persisting US passivity. Likewise, the EU initiated the Roadmap, as a means to give former Secretary of State Powell (viewed as closer to European positions) a tool to reengage the President in the region.[25]

This phenomenon was also evident at other times, and at the local level. From most accounts, relationships between donors and diplomats at the working level have been notoriously good, even when political divergences between capitals were most acute. Perceptions were often closer among international bureaucrats working on the Palestinian file at the local level in Jerusalem or Ramallah than between officials from the same country or the same organization working at the local level on the Israeli file in Tel Aviv, or those located in the capital. The times when coordination between the US and the EU was closest were when interests converged around a clear purpose or a specific initiative. This seems to have been the case in the 'heyday of the AHLC structure' in 1994–1995 when the Oslo process appeared to be moving forward. This was also the case around the launching of the Palestinian reform process in the summer of 2002, when capitals rallied rapidly around the establishment of the TFPR. Donor cooperation was equally tight in the period immediately preceding the publication of the Roadmap, as well as in the lead-up to the Israeli disengagement from Gaza. At other times, when there was less convergence on a particular issue or simply less diplomatic movement, donor coordination was less effective. In these periods, international actors may also have tried to revive the peace process through donor meetings in an attempt 'to catalyze the political process through the economic process'.

Whatever the scale of differences between the US and the EU in terms of substance and style, the frequent tensions between the two main protagonists and the fact that the EU continued to pay for a political process in which it had relatively little say, these did not shatter donors' unity of purpose around the importance of aid to the Palestinians in support of the peace process. This was so, although the *intifada* and the seeming failure of the 'aid for peace' agenda could have provided an opportunity to reassess the grounds for donor intervention. As noted by one Bank official:

> At the first pledging conference in October 1993, the US asked the rest of the world to pay. But what is interesting is the extent to which the disconnect between a very profound political disagreement about Palestinian state between the US government and the EU has led to a very compatible development relationship between the EC and USAID. If you look at aid coordination, you see that the US has been successful at strategically evicting the EC from a dominant position in agenda setting but have kept them engaged financially. It has been very successful from the US point of view, but less so from EU: it pays but its voice is not heard, it does not exert any proper influence.

Another organization which also exerted limited influence, despite an important presence on the ground and a long history of engagement in the Israeli–Palestinian conflict, was the United Nations.

The multilateral sponsors: the UN 'processes', the World Bank leads

The United Nations involvement

The UN has been involved in the history and politics of the Israeli–Palestinian conflict since the organization's inception, when Palestine was still a British protectorate, and has passed a number of related resolutions. Of particular significance are General Assembly (GA) resolution 194 (III) of 1948 acknowledging Palestinian refugees' right of return and the principle of compensation for those not choosing to do so; GA resolution 273 (III) of 11 May 1949 admitting Israel to membership of the UN; GA resolution 302 (IV) of 8 December 1949 establishing UNRWA to provide assistance to Palestinian refugees in the oPt, Jordan, Syria and Lebanon; Security Council (SC) resolution 242 of 22 November 1967, following the 1967 war establishing the principle of 'land for peace' (Israeli withdrawal from territories occupied in the recent conflict in exchange for 'termination of all claims or states of belligerency and respect for and acknowledgement of the sovereignty, territorial integrity and political independence of every State in the area and their right to live in peace within secure and recognized boundaries free from threats or acts of force'); and SC resolution 338 of 22 October 1973, following the 1973 war, reasserting the same principle.

Since the 1991 Madrid process, the UN has continued to support the search for peace in the Middle East on the basis of resolutions 242 and 338. In 1993, the Secretary-General (SG) appointed Chinmaya Gharekhan as his Special Representative (SRSG) to the multilateral talks on Middle East peace. Through the SRSG, the UN took part at the multilateral talks as well as at the first donor conference in October 1993. In June 1994, the Office of the Special Coordinator in the Occupied Territories (UNSCO) was established in Gaza to strengthen the presence, inter-agency coordination and assistance of the UN system in support of the implementation of the DOP. Terje Rød Larsen, who had been one of the key facilitators of the secret Oslo process, was appointed as the first Special Coordinator by SG Boutros-Ghali. He remained in his position until December 2004 (except between 1996 and 1999, when the office was headed by Gharekhan).

Although it reported to the Department of Political Affairs (DPA) in New York, UNSCO's mandate originally focused on coordinating the work and assistance of the UN system in the WBGS. UNRWA was the lead operational UN agency in the region, had both the capacity and experience of nearly half a century, and was also headed by an Under Secretary-General, but it was UNSCO which was to provide overall guidance to the UN programmes and agencies operating on the ground. This set-up – which in itself points to the fact that aid to the Palestinians post-1993 was also envisaged by the UN as eminently political – was unusual. The assistance activities of the UN system are typically coordinated through either a Humanitarian Coordinator in an emergency situation, a UN Resident Coordinator (who is also the UNDP Resident Representative), or fully or partially under the auspices of an SRSG when a peace operation is established by the Security Council. In the case of the WBGS, no complex peace mission was set up and no Resident Coordinator structure was put in place.[26]

UNDP did serve as the umbrella organization for the majority of the UN agencies operating in the oPt, notably on matters relating to the leasing of property, movement permits for staff, customs clearance and vehicle licensing.[27] But despite this role and worldwide procedure, UNSCO was designated the focal point for UN coordination. In this capacity, it chaired regular UN inter-agency meetings and coordinated the agencies' input at the local level for regular reports submitted in New York.[28] UNSCO was also the UN focal point in dealing with the donor community, and the Special Coordinator alone represented the UN at donor coordination meetings at both the capital and local levels. As mentioned in Chapter 1, UNSCO served as the Co-Chair of the LACC and provided Secretariat to the JLC, jointly with the Bank (see also Appendix II, 'The aid coordination structure during Oslo and the *intifada*'). For the benefit of the international donor community as a whole, and up until 2001/2002, it produced regular status reports on the evolution of the socio-economic situation in the oPt. At the request of the parties, the Special Coordinator also supported the implementation of the Oslo Accords. For instance, in the mid-1990s, and at the request of the PA, UNSCO assisted in the coordination of the training of the Palestinian Police Force and gave support to UNRWA through which police salaries were initially transferred.[29]

In September 1999, UNSCO's mandate was broadened to encompass 'good offices' functions and a regional dimension, largely in response to the sense of greater political opportunity that characterized the end of the decade. From being the Office of the Special Coordinator in the Occupied Territories, it became the Office of the Special Coordinator for the Middle East Peace Process (still known as UNSCO) headed by the Personal Representative of the SG to the PLO and PA. The Special Coordinator came to represent the SG with the international community and the two parties in all matters related to the diplomatic and socio-economic aspects of the Middle East Peace Process including in multilateral and bilateral regional talks, as well as in acting as UN focal point for UN assistance to Jordan, Lebanon and Syria.[30] At the same time, however, while Rød Larsen was officially mandated to mediate and negotiate between the parties, he also continued to act as the UN coordinator for assistance to the Palestinians. UNSCO premises remained in Gaza up until 2002–2003, when the diplomatic and donor centre of gravity moved from Gaza to the West Bank and UNSCO's international staff was relocated to Jerusalem.

The politics of UN involvement

Despite its long-standing and multifaceted involvement in the Israeli–Palestinian conflict, the continued prominence of the Middle East on the SC agenda throughout the period under review and numerous GA resolutions, and the reconfiguration of UNSCO in 1999, the UN failed to exert a leading political role. The issue was not so much that it did not play a role commensurate with its financial disbursements, as was the case for the EU – although the UN system as a whole was a major aid provider to the Palestinians. Rather, unlike other major international conflicts, diplomatic activities never evolved to a truly multilateral process, for similar reasons to those which accounted for the EU's marginal diplomatic role: Israeli preference for a US-led process and disinclination to see the internationalization of the conflict, notably given its own poor record in complying with UN SC and GA resolutions but also in view of the domestic perceptions of UN GA pro-Arab bias; US eagerness to retain leadership; and lack of consensus among Member States, and notably within the SC, as to what position to adopt vis-à-vis the Middle East Peace Process and the two parties to the conflict.

Despite the limitations on the diplomatic role the UN could exert, the SG and his Special Coordinator were nonetheless keen to be 'part of the process', which was understandable in view of the personal contribution of Larsen to Oslo. The decision was thus taken to privilege the UN's aspirations to play a mediating role in the peace process over that of the organization's responsibilities in providing assistance and protection to the Palestinians or in upholding the principles of its Charter, its GA and SC resolutions, international law, human rights and, more specifically, the Palestinian right to self-determination.

The cultivation of UNSCO's position within the donor community – historically, the UN's 'foot in the door' – and Rød Larsen's personal input resulted in the UN gaining a 'seat at the table' by the late 1990s, consolidated in 2001 by its membership in the Quartet. This represented a marked evolution to the beginning of the decade when UNSCO's function was largely confined to aid coordination. Given Israeli power and the reality of a US-dominated process, this had primarily entailed courting the US and Israel, as only they could ensure that the UN became politically relevant. As explained by two UN officials:

> Terje Rød Larsen's argument is that the main problem is Israel so you have to think about how you will change that. Two options: either you oppose it on principled grounds (but his mandate as Special Coordinator would not have allowed) or you try to influence it directly and indirectly by trying to influence the US. Hence he devoted a disproportionate amount of time to dealing with Israel and the US because he thought that these were the main issues. That was a strategy.
>
> Within the context of the current Israeli government, our assumption has been that the UN could not play an important role without a coali-

tion. As Larsen likes to say, it is necessary to have 'power (US), money (EU) and legitimacy (UN)' together so as to manage the crisis and move the peace process forward. Hence the Quartet, as a means to harness American power and get the US government involved and active. Plus, we added the Madrid co-sponsor, Russia.

This strategy had serious implications for the coherence of the UN response as a whole, notably during the *intifada*. In the late 1990s, asserting the UN's good offices role was made easier by the facts that bilateral negotiations were actually occurring and that Rød Larsen had good channels of communication with the Israeli Labour Party from his Oslo days. With the onset of the crisis, the in-built structural tensions within UNSCO's political-aid coordination mandate and, more broadly, between the different UN agencies and functions became more salient. As pointed out by a UN official:

> A mission that wants to be a political mission does not fit with a mission which focuses on state-building for Palestinians and which is staffed with Palestinians. This has been a very sensitive issue. UNSCO has been 'a best case scenario office'.... When one purports to play the role of a broker between the two sides, does it make sense to be located in Gaza? When crisis hits, this becomes very obvious.

While it was possible to use the aid and socio-economic agenda as a means to advance political objectives in the 1990s, it was less evidently so in the early 2000s. Reporting on the depth of the economic and humanitarian crisis, the building of the Wall or Israel's more frequent breaches of international law became more difficult to reconcile with the desire to 'court Israel'. Having fought hard to get a seat at the table, the SG and his Special Coordinator had to be careful if they did not want to be locked out of the diplomatic game. This was all the more so in the aftermath of Rød Larsen's public remarks surrounding the destruction by the IDF of Jenin's refugee camp during Operation Defensive Shield in April 2002, which he qualified as 'horrific beyond belief'. Thereafter, his standing with the Israelis, and notably PM Sharon's Office, was at an all-time low.[31]

At various times, the idea was contemplated to separate the UN aid and political components, relocate the Special Coordinator and his political staff to the UN headquarters in New York (as the other Quartet Special Envoys who were based in their respective capitals) and entrust aid coordination to the development and humanitarian agencies physically based on the ground. Yet this never materialized, partly out of bureaucratic inertia, but also because the SG wanted his Special Coordinator to remain in the field. Instead, while UNSCO continued to play a role in aid coordination (by virtue of its mandate), it did so less actively. In addition to being in part due to the fact that the tension between its political and aid mandates became more salient as the result of the emergence of the humanitarian crisis, this was also the result of Larsen's personal predilection for his diplomatic role. So whereas in the 1990s UNSCO played a leading aid coordination role through the analytical work it produced, it progressively ceased to monitor Palestinian socio-economic conditions and to publish status reports. As the task was picked up by the Bank on the economic side, and OCHA on the humanitarian one, UNSCO's visibility, standing and credibility among the donor community at large diminished. Similarly, while it very much wanted to remain in control, it played a less energetic role in UN coordination, leading to the widespread feeling among UN agencies that Larsen was only interested in coordinating the UN family in so far as it could foster his political agenda.

Simultaneously, the large operational UN humanitarian agencies, such as WFP, UNICEF and WHO, geared up their assistance and presence on the ground, starting in the aftermath of Operation Defensive Shield. Most notably, OCHA's capacity was considerably expanded after 2002. It established an information and mapping centre to monitor the closure regime and the humanitarian situation, and became the aid community's focal point for increasingly vocal humanitarian advocacy. UN coordination to respond to the crisis, however, remained the prerogative of UNSCO and UNRWA, a division of labour being worked out (on paper) along a policy (UNSCO) versus operational (UNWRA) line, with OCHA supporting both agencies in their respective roles. Although this arrangement was cumbersome, and the involvement of both agencies de facto encroached on the 'humanitarian space', the consensus view on the ground was that the aid coordination structure in the oPt was already sufficiently complex and enough new *intifada* structures had been created not to add any new ones.[32] The PA was equally not keen to see the establishment of a parallel humanitarian structure that would erode its position further. Moreover, as two Under-Secretaries General were already in the region, the decision was taken early on not to appoint a Humanitarian Coordinator, as would normally be the case in other high-profile emergency crises, so as not to 'crowd the ground further' with another senior UN official.

Despite these carefully negotiated internal arrangements, OCHA's de facto expanded role, and in particular its advocacy function, led to concerns that this would compromise Rød Larsen's political stature. The strain between OCHA and UNSCO was palpable from the outset. It peaked in the autumn of 2003 when a report by OCHA on the consequences of the Separation Barrier got widespread news coverage – including an article in the *New York Times* – just a couple of weeks before the SG was due to release a report prepared by UNSCO on the same topic. So serious was the incident that it was referred to the highest levels in New York, where it fed into a deeper turf battle between OCHA and DPA on their respective roles in UN intervention in conflict and post-conflict environments.

This incident – which resulted in a senior UN mission being sent to Jerusalem in early 2004 to assess the implications of OCHA's role – is revealing in different ways. First, it was testimony to an actual lack of coordination between the two agencies, and the extent to which UNSCO's coordination role had weakened. Second, it reflected the parochial internal UN institutional concern about 'turf'. In 2001–2003, the humanitarian situation and the construction of the Barrier were, together with the PA reform process, the main focus of the international community as no major headway was being made on the diplomatic front. In the absence of any substantial progress on the Middle East Peace Process, and in the context of the mounting humanitarian crisis, the visibility of OCHA was naturally enhanced. This was all the more so as OCHA's maps and reports on closure and the humanitarian situation – which were praised by most within the donor community – filled the information gap left by UNSCO, which had ceased to produce regular socio-economic assessments. Finally, the tension between UNSCO and OCHA exemplified a more fundamental dilemma within the UN and the aid community at large, arising from the attempt to integrate political and humanitarian actions in transitional contexts, as detailed in Chapter 1. As is often the case, the partiality involved in supporting a 'peace process' took precedence. From the spring of 2004, OCHA was requested to focus more narrowly on the humanitarian situation and the coordination of the UN emergency response through the annual Consolidated Appeal Process (CAP), rather than on IHL or humanitarian advocacy. Its reporting came to be heavily scrutinized by UNSCO, and in the process, some would argue, the impartiality of its humanitarian mandate was undermined.

As the UN, as an organization of Member States, is a reflection of global power realities, it is doubtful whether the UN would have been more influential, had it embraced a stronger principled stance based on international law and its own resolutions. This would have led to less frustration among the agencies' personnel on the ground, but would also have probably resulted in even less access to the GOI. As observed by one UN official:

> I am not sure the UNSCO–UN position could have been more successful but it could certainly have been different. But would that have not mainly been a case of making you feel better as Terje Rød Larsen would say? The past four years have been disastrous: 'movement' worked in favour of the Israelis only, so we should maybe have pulled out. . . . Having said that, we are so powerless that I am not sure a different position would actually make much difference and change anything. Israel gets its legitimacy from the US only. The UN is only important in a symbolic way. Its intervention will neither change people's lives nor lead to sovereignty.

On the other hand, precisely because of the weak influence the UN could have on the Israeli–Palestinian conflict, and the inherent limitations of any strategy premised on appeasing Israel (by 2003–2004, the UN had once again become marginalized politically), it could also be argued that it may have been more effective to have attempted to uphold the universal principles of the Charter, IHL, human rights and, more specifically, the Palestinian right to self-determination. Beyond the important 'symbolic' function, this would have gone a long way to enhancing the overall credibility and legitimacy of the world's organization as an 'honest broker' in the process and, more generally, its standing in the Middle East. As further noted by one UN bureaucrat:

> The way things have unfolded has been strange. I always thought UNSCO could have used OCHA precisely to do things that Larsen could not have done himself because of the constraints of its political mandate. But he did not. One thing which I did not realize immediately is that the level of anxiety vis-à-vis Israel is extremely high and filters all the way up to the Secretary-General. It stems in part from their overriding desire to maintain a seat at the table and be involved at all cost. This is a natural instinct and not necessary a wrong strategy. There are enough people to beat the Israelis but this does a lot of bad things to our credibility and compromises our activities as the UN in many areas. Is it worth it? What difference do we make politically? There was a sigh of relief in the UN Secretariat when Brahimi talked about Israeli 'poisonous policies'.[33]

Emphasizing the need to respect basic international norms would have been all the more essential as ten years of 'process-focused' American diplomacy has had adverse effects on the frame of reference and principles that had hitherto governed the international community's approach to the Arab–Israeli conflict in a way that arguably condoned Israel's breaches of IHL and its colonization policy. The evolution of the American position during the Oslo process to endorse officially the Israeli stance with regard to key final status issues, such as settlements and the right of return, is a case in point.[34] As noted by Kathleen Christison:

> Since Israel and the PLO signed the DOP in 1993, the Clinton administration has taken the view that honest mediation prevents the United States from espousing a position on virtually any substantive issue. In its overriding concern to avoid dealing with substance, the administration has even backed away from some of the key positions that had undergirded US policy for decades. This has altered the ground rules, changed the language of negotiations, and in a key way, reframed the objectives of the peace process.... The United States' supposedly neutral position of refraining from voicing opinions on such issues as the status of the land and Israel's occupation practices is actually a position of support to Israel. While ostensibly attempting to create a 'level playing field', the United States has in fact, by ignoring UN resolutions, removed the international guarantees that have been the

Palestinians' principal support. Symbolic and intangible though these guarantees may be, they have been what the Palestinians have had to rely on in a situation in which Israel enjoys the real tangible advantages – a state, physical control of the land, clear military superiority – that the United States itself underwrites.[35]

A similar point has been made by Dr Karma Nabulsi:

> Once we possessed a broad consensus, right across the international community, on the types of mechanisms that were needed to resolve the conflict in the Middle East. These mechanisms relied upon common understandings about the principles and guidelines upon which an approach should be based, and included the relevant UN Security Council and General Assembly resolutions; common rules of engagement and reciprocity; regional and international involvement; and the recognition of human rights and international law. In the past three years most of these common understandings have all but disappeared. The evaporation of these former landmarks has heralded a radical shift in the practical dealings of the international community with the Palestinians: it now operates in a vacuum, no longer moored by the common understandings and principles that had guided its approach since as far back as the Treaty of Westphalia. In the absence of the universalist framework within which the Israeli–Palestinian conflict was formerly viewed and discussed, a variety of forms of particularism have now emerged.[36]

The UN may not have been successful in upholding those standards, but had it made it a matter of concern it might at least have had some normative influence on a process otherwise entirely dictated by *realpolitik* and in which it could in any case not exert any determining political influence. While the close relationship he had cultivated over the years with the US and Israel ensured that Larsen himself remained highly influential as a UN diplomat, the UN as an organization, and more specifically UNSCO, which he had assisted in establishing ten years earlier, became increasingly irrelevant.[37] The appointment of Alvaro de Soto as the new Special Coordinator in 2005 did not result in the UN re-establishing its clout. In contrast, a multilateral institution which did exert ever more influence as the decade unfolded was the World Bank, culminating in the political appointment, in April 2005, of its exiting President, James D. Wolfensohn, as the Quartet's Special Envoy for Gaza Disengagement.

Enter the World Bank

The Bank's involvement in the WBGS is recent compared to that of the UN. In 1992, it was tasked by the organizers of the Madrid multilateral peace process to look into future Palestinian development and economic prospects. The result of this assessment was a six-volume study, *Developing the Occupied Territories: An Investment in Peace*, published within a couple of weeks of the signing of the DOP, and which provided the basis for the first donor pledging conference in October 1993. It also informed the first strategic aid framework, the Emergency Assistance Programme for the Occupied Territories (EAP), which was presented by the Bank to the donor community in April 1994. In the summer of that year, the Bank opened an office in East Jerusalem. In the course of the ensuing decade, the Bank's analytical reporting remained a central component of its activities in the oPt, as the Bank published a great number of macroeconomic studies and sectoral analyses.[38]

These assessments became particularly influential during the *intifada*. Starting in 2002, the Bank produced a series of yearly reports on the Palestinian economic crisis, assessing the impact of Israeli policies, of the international emergency assistance, and of the institutional response of the PA. Together with two seminal studies in 2004 on the economic and technical aspects of Israel's disengagement from Gaza, those reports laid out policy recommendations for donors, the PA and Israel with the aim of fostering Palestinian economic recovery.[39] As during those years UNSCO no longer produced any assessment of the socio-economic conditions and OCHA's reporting focused on the humanitarian situation, the Bank's publications became the international point of reference. Those reports were also the only source of data on aid flows available to the international community as the PA, increasingly incapacitated, ceased to collect any information after 2001. Praised for their timeliness, quality and thoroughness, those reports shaped the response, agenda and allocation of funds of the entire aid community in a way reminiscent of the impact the initial six-volume study and EAP had had on building consensus and forging a common donor strategy in the first few years of the Oslo process.

The credibility conferred by its analytical and policy-setting capacity as well as the fact that the Bank enjoyed the trust of both Israel and the PA is part of the reason why it was able to impose itself as the leading multilateral actor in donor coordination well beyond the more limited role it traditionally plays as convenor of CGs, and despite the fact that it was not a big financial player in the WBGS (due to the restrictions on Bank lending and access to regular funds imposed by the legal status of the oPt).[40] As seen in Chapter 1, the Bank was a member of virtually all coordination bodies, and held key positions in most (see also Appendix II, 'The aid coordination structure during Oslo and the *intifada*'). Other reasons why the Bank came to take on this strong coordination and leadership role include: the weakness of the UN coordination system and in particular the vacuum progressively left by UNSCO; the strong desire, like everyone else, to be 'part of the process'; the pronounced interest in the conflict displayed by its senior management; and the personal commitment of James D. Wolfensohn, the Bank's President between 1995 and 2005. The involvement of the Bank's most senior levels resulted in the organization being not only very active, but also highly creative in devising ways to remain involved in the WBGS, although the Bank's economic clause could have dictated that it ceased to do so, especially during the *intifada*.

The issue of framing the Bank's assistance within the purview of its economic mandate, international law and the parameters of the Israeli–Palestinian agreements surfaced from the outset and required careful legal work, in consultation with both parties. As put forward by one Bank official:

> The issue of the Bank's economic clause is a real issue. As the Bank is not authorized to intervene in politics, you have to use your judgement to determine what is politically correct.... The script is that the World Bank is here at the invitation of the Government of Israel, the international community and the PLO (every grant/credit agreement signed by the PA is underwritten by the PLO) for the benefits of the Palestinian population. Hence the Bank entertains a relationship with all the above and has to be very careful to preserve equidistance. All the reports we produce are a balancing act. It does not always work, and we have come under fierce criticism from the Israelis as for example in April 2002 when we issued a press statement [for the launching of an economic report]. If you speak out in criticism of Israel you have to be very, very careful to frame it in a non-political way. It is a real constraint but gives us clarity too.... There are lots of grey areas because the World Bank here is part of a political process.

As the oPt was neither a sovereign state member country nor a territory for which another member country had expressed interest in acting as guarantor, the Bank was unable to provide direct loans or credit to the PA. To circumvent these legal restrictions and start operating in the WBGS, the Bank established a series of trust funds. Though this mechanism – which was unusual at the time although since then has been replicated in other post-conflict settings such as Bosnia-Herzegovina, East Timor and Afghanistan – the Bank was able to provide financial and technical assistance as well as attract high levels of co-financing.

Between 1993 and 2004, the Bank acted as administrator to four separate funds: the multi-donor Holst Fund, devoted to finance the start-up and recurrent costs of the PA as well as job creation projects; the multi-donor Technical Assistance Trust Fund, which managed US$23 million from 12 donors between 1994 and 2001; the Public Financial Management Reform Trust Fund, which was established in April 2004 to once again provide multi-donor budget support to the PA; and the Trust Fund for Gaza and the West Bank (TFGWB), which has been the cornerstone of the Bank's operational involvement. As of 2004, this Fund's resources totalled over US$500 million, mainly from Bank surplus. Four-fifths of the total had been committed to over 30 projects which in turn mobilized a high level of money in parallel and co-financing. The Bank's portfolio covered a wide range of sectors including emergency reconstruction and rehabilitation, infrastructure, technical assistance, education, health, institutional development, private sector growth and water.[41]

In addition to coordinating resource mobilization through trust funds, the Bank's involvement in the WBGS displayed other atypical features for the organization. First, it was one of the first programmes to occur in a post-conflict environment, and the first again seven years later to operate with full staff in an 'in-conflict' setting. One of the fears was that if the Bank withdrew on the grounds that investment was no longer sustainable (as it would usually do in conflict environments), other donors might follow. Thus, despite the *intifada*, its intervention continued to be internally classified as 'post-conflict'. Second, it was the first programme to be decentralized in 1994 so as to give the country director the flexibility to react fast in a highly volatile environment. Third, in light of PA bankruptcy in 2002, its Executive Board approved a moratorium on the TFGWB service charges to avoid the Bank having to suspend its operations through a payment default. This absolutely unprecedented move in the Bank's history is again testimony to the conflict being high on the agenda of its senior management and to the desire to remain operational and 'part of the process'.

Finally, despite its focus on socio-economic development, the Bank's role was highly political and increasingly so as the decade went on. At the same time, however, its economic mandate dictated that the Bank played down its political role by framing its engagement at the level of technical expertise. So sensitive was the issue that, in reporting on the findings of the policy dialogue it led in 2004–2005 with the GOI and the PA on the economic implications of Israeli disengagement, it felt compelled to elucidate its actions as follows:

> In view of the potential for misunderstanding, the Bank clarified to the parties and to donors that these consultations were *not* intended to substitute for bilateral negotiations, and that the Bank would take final responsibility for the analysis and final conclusions drawn from it. Though technical and economic in intent, these papers would reference the broader frameworks within which the donor community continues to operate: the Road map...[and the] legal agreements defining economic relations between Israel and the Palestinian territories.[42]

In the 1990s, the Bank had already played a key role in supporting the AHLC in monitoring the Tripartite Action Plan between the GOI and the PA, as will be detailed in Chapter 6. More importantly, and as this book argues overall, so political were all the policy choices made by the donor community that by shaping the international aid agenda, the Bank necessarily performed a key political function. This was the case whether it suggested prioritizing infrastructure at the onset of the Oslo process so as to provide a peace dividend to the population, whether it encouraged donors to shift to emergency job creation in the mid-1990s in response to Israeli closure to avert a deeper socio-economic crisis, or whether it supported using the PA essentially as a job-creation machine for the purposes of social pacification, thus resorting to budgetary support on an unprecedented scale in the 1990s and even more forcibly during the *intifada*. In a sense, if the Europeans were made to underwrite the American–Israeli dominated diplomatic process financially, the Bank underwrote it conceptually.

But the Bank's role went even further, culminating in the consultations it led with both parties in the lead-up to the Israeli disengagement from Gaza and the appointment of its outgoing President as the Quartet's Special Envoy for Gaza Disengagement in April 2005. While Wolfensohn's mandate was carefully worked out to entail mainly the coordination of donor assistance to the Palestinians following Israeli withdrawal from the Gaza Strip and parts of the West Bank and excluding the 'military and security aspects of disengagement', he was nonetheless appointed as the 'single international interlocutor at the political level on disengagement'.[43]

The increasingly dominant role exerted by the Bank within the donor community was not to the liking of all other third-party actors. In particular UNSCO, which for most of the decade had had relatively smooth relations with the Bank at both the local and capital levels, considered that its coordination mandate and political role were being undermined by the Bank acting *in solo*. Larsen initially tried to push for the policy dialogue surrounding Israeli disengagement to occur within the trilateral framework of the LACC but he was ultimately unsuccessful. In contrast, the US pushed for increasing the Bank's involvement and visibility (although by the time Wolfensohn quitted his position in mid-2006, he had lost much of the support of his initial sponsors).

There had been a few occasions during the decade where the relationship between the Bank and the US had been strained, most notably in the late 1990s. According to one World Bank official:

> Whenever the Bank tried to be fair to both the US and the EU on silly issues such as where the meeting should be held, we were considered as biased by the Americans; if we were in the middle we were considered as pro-European, so it was not easy.

During the last CG meeting in Frankfurt in 1999, the Israeli delegation walked out in protest at the Palestinian presentation of a development plan which made reference to borders and included East Jerusalem. A huge row ensued between the Bank and the US, and as a result, the Bank lost American confidence in its ability to manage and control such large meetings, and was never given the opportunity to do so again. The fact that CGs ceased to be convened illustrated the extent to which the aid process – mirroring the diplomatic scene at large – was dominated by the US which, from the outset, had preferred the smaller, less inclusive and more easily controllable AHLC structure, as mentioned in Chapter 1. As recalled by one UN official:

> [The presentation] upset the Israelis colossally. The US got absolutely furious with the Bank as well as everyone else including the Palestinians

because they blew up the meeting. That marked the end of the CG meetings. The World Bank CG system collapsed because they did not understand the political fundamentals of what you can say or not; they are good economists but not necessarily politically sensitive. On that occasion, [the World Bank representative] did not understand the Israeli mindset and the red lines you cannot cross. That was the end of the Bank's hegemony. Then only the AHLC were left, hence they became pledging meetings de facto.

But the tension between the State Department and the Bank was largely personalities-driven. As mentioned, the relationship between the US and the EU was also particularly bad at that time. Beyond the relationship between the bureaucrats at the working level, the US remained after all the Bank's biggest stakeholder, and it was the US which in 1993–1994 had pushed for the Bank's prominent place in the aid coordination setting.[44] This was also the broad opinion of other third-party actors, notably the EU, which perceived donor meetings as dominated by the US and the Bank, 'working hand in hand'. With the arrival of the new US administration in 2001, the temporary strain of the late 1990s faded away. And even in the last few years of the Clinton administration, the close relationship between the Americans and President Wolfensohn was never allowed to be disrupted.

Conclusion

Through its technical expertise and the quality of its analytical work, the Bank had, by the mid-2000s, arguably become the most politically influential multilateral organization. Its close relationship to the Americans, the personal commitment of Wolfensohn and the perspicacity of Nigel Roberts, the WBGS Country Director between 2000 and 2005, also explain why the Bank was able to impose itself as a key actor. But at a more fundamental level, this is illustrative of both the bankruptcy of the bilateral Israeli–Palestinian political process, and the extent to which diplomacy had been stifled by the US and Israel. To the extent that there was some politics left more than a decade after the onset of Oslo, this was in the Israeli unilateral Disengagement Plan, and the Bank was the organization entrusted with the mediation between the parties. Within the international community, this perpetuated the illusion that a 'process' was moving, and that third-party actors continued to have a key role to play. Yet in reality this evolution only exemplified the extent to which the Israeli–Palestinian conflict had become 'normalized' and the Palestinian state-building effort de-politicized by a decade of international concentration on assuaging the socio-economic and humanitarian symptoms of the crisis, rather than tackling the root causes and diplomatic challenges and obstacles impeding upon the resolution of the conflict. It is to the multifaceted effects of international donor politics and assistance programmes to the WBGS that we will now turn our attention.

ESPOUSING ISRAELI POLICIES

Supporting the 'peace process'

Donors initially gave generous support to the Oslo process on the basis that economic development in the Palestinian territories would help underwrite the compromises thought necessary for both sides to reach a consensus on a political solution to the conflict. Additionally, Arafat was seen as the only Palestinian leader capable of making the necessary compromises, which from the Israeli perspective entailed *inter alia* forgoing the 'right of return'. The Oslo gambit revolved around a 'do whatever it takes' mentality to clinch the deal. As early as 1994–1995, this also entailed shifting their efforts away from development and more towards relief assistance to compensate for the degrading socio-economic situation, in the vain hope that political and economic conditions would change. The *intifada* led to the near collapse of the PA and the emergence of a severe humanitarian crisis. The donor community remained engaged. It reacted by doubling the level of its assistance to the Palestinians and increasing further the proportion of emergency aid. As pointed out by a Bank official:

> With the *intifada*, the sense was that the Palestinian institutions and economy needed to be prevented from collapsing so there remains something of an economy and institutions when the political process resumes. Underlying this position was the same assumption as during Oslo: that donors should support the peace process and thus that it was worth hanging in to avoid collapse without repair. The *intifada* marks a real turning point in modalities but the underlying philosophy remains the same. For instance, with the Roadmap we now talk about economic separation rather than integration as was the case in the early 1990s. But the vision remains intact. Donors have been very reactive.

Recognizing the power dynamics of the conflict, and the pre-eminence afforded to Israeli (and US) security requirements, how did the international community justify its decisions? What was the nature of the debate? What mechanisms were put in place? As mentioned in Chapter 1, the discussions surrounding international development for the oPt, and the question of how donor funds would be used to support the continuation of the 'peace process', largely took place within a small exclusive group comprising the most influential donors (the 'inner circle': US, EU, Bank, UN, Norway), with ad hoc inputs from other international actors depending on the topic under consideration.

In terms of the specific allocation of funds, individual donors pursued their own objectives within the framework of their national preferences and legal constraints, a function of their relationship to both Israel and the PA. This necessarily led to gaps, overlaps and duplications at the project level, especially since donor coordination through the Sector Working Groups (SWG) remained poor. Competition among donors was also persistent throughout the period. In the absence of significant diplomatic headway, there was a strong pressure to be seen to be at least spending money. As noted by one EIB official:

> The whole Israeli/Palestinian process is so highly 'mediacized'. Everybody wanted to get involved and be visible. The jealousy was enormous among donors. Hence this has led to a lot of irrational behaviour, a lot of competition and a lot of projects delayed as a result.

Despite political divergences, rivalry and issues of coherence and complementarity at the project level, donors remained united in their willingness to do whatever it would take to continue to provide financial support to the Palestinians. On the surface, the sense of opportunity created by the 'ups' in the 'process', the crisis management mode characterizing the involvement of the main players and the sheer amount of work performed by individual civil servants gives the impression that donors were innovative, flexible and responsive to events. This is true in so far as they were able to react quickly to a volatile situation on the ground, and were successful at mobilizing and sustaining an impressive level of funds over the years. However, beneath this veneer of change and hyper-activity, a deeper look at the decade after Oslo highlights a high degree of continuity and recurrence, coupled with a dogged fatalism, in the face of all the evidence, that positive change was just around the corner. Yet the situation did not improve but instead steadily got worse. At the donor level, what actually changed – depending on the intensity of the political and economic disruptions – were the constitutive elements of the emergency response, not the fundamentally reactive and short-term nature of the international intervention.

This chapter reviews the evolution of the aid response and assesses its impact, focusing on the macro level and on the political dimension of the effects of international funds. Ten years of international assistance certainly resulted in some beneficial results for the population, notably in terms of alleviating poverty and meeting immediate humanitarian needs. Nevertheless, in terms of the effectiveness and sustainability of the international effort, the picture is much less positive. Sustaining over time such high levels of emergency assistance to the population of an occupied territory also created some serious dilemmas for donors, including in terms of international legality. Finally, the complexity of

Oslo territorial arrangements, coupled with Israeli restrictions and lack of Palestinian national planning, shaped the repartition and effects of the assistance provided in a way that arguably reinforced Palestinian fragmentation. Taken together, this raises the issue of foreign aid's overall impact on the prospect for peace, reconciliation and the resolution of the conflict.

Short-term fixes, political relief and variation on a similar theme

The strategic orientation of the aid effort was generally endorsed at AHLCs. The meetings were often organized in the wake of a diplomatic event, and were always set against the background of the state of Israeli–Palestinian negotiations and the socio-economic situation in the oPt. Opening remarks and Chair summaries invariably referred to the state of the peace process first, before engaging in other items of concern. Members either deplored the lack of progress on the political front and deterioration in the socio-economic situation on the ground, or praised the new impetus resulting from such and such agreement or from some perceived 'movement' – simultaneously emphasizing any encouraging 'sign' on the ground, and choosing not to underline the fundamentally deteriorating socio-economic trends.

For instance, the AHLC in Frankfurt in February 1999 took place following the Wye River Agreement of October 1998; the AHLC in Tokyo in October 1999 after the Sharm El-Sheikh Memorandum; the AHLC in Lisbon in June 2000 within the context of progress on both the Israeli–Palestinian and the South Lebanon bilateral tracks; and the AHLC in Oslo in December 2004 as dialogue around the Israeli disengagement was taking place. When a political success was recorded, the concern of donors was to keep apace with apparent political change in the hope this would trigger some genuine progress; in time of political crisis, the aim was to ensure that the socio-economic deterioration did not exacerbate disagreements and become an additional point of conflict. At times of breakdown in the diplomatic process, donor meetings could also serve as the informal venue for bilateral negotiations, as mentioned in the preceding chapter.

AHLCs became ritualized in their format (the first day would be devoted to informal bilateral consultations, the second day to plenary sessions), in their agendas (*inter alia*, briefings on the socio-economic and fiscal situation, PA strategy, donor response and intention, obstacles to project implementation, and other Israeli–Palestinian donor issues of concern), and in the stereotypical political messages they conveyed. As an illustration, the Chair's Summary of the AHLC in Lisbon opened as follows:

> The Ad Hoc Liaison Committee met in Lisbon against the backdrop of the resumption of Palestinian–Israeli negotiations with the aim of concluding a framework and a permanent status agreement in the autumn, as well as positive developments in Lebanon, representing a new

impetus in the political process towards a lasting peace in the Middle East. With the parties set to resume negotiations during the week of June 12, members reiterated the crucial importance for the peace process of supporting Palestinian socio-economic development. The development effort remains an integral part of the process as it provides an essential underpinning for securing a lasting peace.[1]

At the informal AHLC meeting in Oslo in Norway in April 2002:

> The Chair opened the meeting by noting that it was taking place at a time of great crisis in Israeli–Palestinian relations and that trust and understanding between the two sides were at the lowest point since the establishment of the AHLC. The Chair observed that sustainable peace depended upon a comprehensive approach that combined simultaneous and parallel security, political and economic tracks. The task of the AHLC and the overall donor effort was to advance this third, economic track. The Chair expressed the hope that the meeting would not only secure donor support for the West Bank and Gaza, but also create opportunities for cooperation and restoration of trust between the two sides to support a re-launch of the political process.[2]

Emergency budget support and job creation, 1994–1997

Within the context of the signing of the Declaration of Principles, the first donor strategy for the WBGS, the Emergency Assistance Programme for the Occupied Territories (EAP) produced by the Bank in April 1994, focused on infrastructure rehabilitation and upgrading key public facilities and services. Out of the US$1.2 billion programme of assistance projected by the Bank for the years 1994–1996, half was to go to public investments, a quarter to private sector development, and the remaining quarter to technical assistance, and start-up and recurrent expenditure support to the PA and NGOs.[3] This programme was based on the Bank's comprehensive analysis of the Palestinian economy, as put forward in its original six-volume study. This report had identified the dilapidated state of Palestinian infrastructure (roads, water and sanitation, sewage, housing, transport and electricity) and the inadequate provision of social services (education and health in particular) as key development challenges, especially in light of the overall political purpose of providing tangible benefits to the population of the WBGS, and improving living conditions so as to reinforce the momentum towards peace.[4]

In addition to improving physical public facilities and service availability, the investments proposed would create employment in the construction sector, which in turn would help reduce the adverse effects of shrinking employment opportunities in Israel. The EAP also included financial and technical assistance to establish PA administrative capacity, at the municipal and central levels, as well as through the Palestinian Economic Council for Development and Reconstruction (PECDAR) which was created in October 1993 to allocate and coordinate international funds *ad interim*, pending the PA institutions becoming operational. In addition, donors stressed the need to balance short-term benefits with laying the foundations for sustainable growth – notably through establishing efficient institutions of self-government and supporting private sector investment and growth, without which adequate employment for the rapidly expanding labour force and sufficient growth in fiscal revenues to sustain government services would not be possible. However, on the whole, the overarching objective in 1993/1994 was on generating an immediate 'peace dividend' to be reaped by the population.

Actual disbursements came to be even more geared towards the short-term than the initial projections of the EAP. As early as 1994, donors shifted away from the more sustainable 'emergency' investment and technical programme they had envisaged towards funds to bail out the PA, which was unable to cover the salaries of its newly staffed (and growing) bureaucracy. By the end of 1995, the infrastructure sector had been allocated only one half of the originally planned funds, while budget support to the PA consumed 2.5 times more than initially expected, and in fact necessitated an extra US$150 million.[5] This shift is explained primarily by the unanticipated inflation of the Palestinian budget deficit resulting from a higher budgetary impact of the transfer of responsibilities from the Civil Administration to the PA,[6] continued tax leakage to Israel owing to delays in negotiating the Interim Agreement, and weak internal PA tax collection capacity and high start-up costs, notably to finance the salaries and equipment of the Palestinian police force.[7] Closure also had a negative impact on the budget by leading to the deterioration of the overall economic activity and decreased revenues for the PA.

In addition to sustaining the financial viability of the PA by providing budget support at a level far higher than originally projected, donors also rapidly shifted their focus from public investment to public consumption spending in an attempt to address rising unemployment and poverty levels. Between 1994 and 1996, almost half of all donor funds (over US$600 million) went to short-term support.[8] From 1996 onwards, the progressive decline in recurrent cost financing and the freeing up of some donor funds did not immediately lead to a return to the type of 'emergency' infrastructure investment and project financing envisaged in the EAP, let alone to longer-term development programmes. Instead, in the context of the first major Palestinian economic recession, loss of jobs in Israel and a near total collapse of private sector economic activities, short-term job-creation projects became a substantial component of the international aid programme.

It was not the first time that the international community resorted to emergency employment-generation programmes in the WBGS. In 1989, UNRWA launched a Shelter Rehabilitation Programme which consisted of building shelters for the poorest families in the refugee camps, and in November 1994,

UNDP initiated a community-based programme to literally 'clean up' Gaza.[9] Through the establishment of the SWG on Employment Generation, a series of job-creation projects were also initiated in Gaza in 1995.[10] Nonetheless, from April 1996, in the context of stringent closure – and complete closure of Gaza – following a wave of suicide attacks in Israel, the donor community – at the request of the PA – put in place a major Emergency Employment Generation Programme (EGP). This programme was 'designed to reduce the risk of social unrest and ease the hardships facing Palestinians by creating jobs and supporting labour-intensive micro-projects'.[11] It was supported by two main channels of assistance.

UNDP, in partnership with PECDAR, extended its programme for an initial amount of US$5 million financed by Norway, Sweden, Japan, Switzerland and the US.[12] Other UN agencies such as UNRWA and the International Labour Organization (ILO) also incorporated employment-generation components into their programmes. In addition, the Holst Fund, a multilateral Trust Fund administered by the Bank which had been established in 1994 to disburse the budget funds to the PA, was reoriented to support labour-intensive infrastructure micro-projects, such as the cleaning of streets, the collecting of solid waste and rubbish, the construction of pavements and the building of irrigation ditches. These projects were implemented by PECDAR, local municipalities and village councils. At the peak of the crisis between April and June 1996, when unemployment affected about two-thirds of the labour force in Gaza, some 40,000 workers were given temporary employment (not more than ten days per month in the West Bank and 18 days in Gaza) at an average wage of NIS30 per day for a total of 600,000 labour days. Although the EGP began as an income-transfer activity through 'make-work' schemes, it evolved through to 2001 into a programme of more sustainable community-based high labour content micro-projects. Overall, US$63.5 million was allocated to the EGP through the Fund between 1996 and 2001.[13]

To stem closure and unemployment – as well as attract foreign and local investment – donors also promoted the establishment of industrial estate schemes. The pilot, supported by the EIB, the International Finance Corporation (IFC), USAID and the Bank, was the Gaza Industrial Estate (GIE), located on the Gaza/Israeli border at Karni, and opened in mid-1999. Other estates were planned across the West Bank, but these initiatives never got off the ground and the GIE ceased to be operational in mid-2001.[14] Finally, donors did not go out of their way to attempt to convince the PA that it should not hire staff well beyond the sustainability of its wage bill. This provided a non-negligible additional source of employment.

Between 1994 and 1998, the donor community thus focused on responding to the PA recurrent cost deficit, and to the mounting socio-economic crisis which jeopardized the stability of Arafat's regime which had been established to deliver on peace. In light of the emergency, donors also stressed the importance of expediting the allocation and disbursement of pledged funds, as the rates were initially well below the targets set by the Bank and, more generally, it took some time for the donors to start implementing their programmes.[15] Despite the actual diversion of donor funds to non-sustainable budget support and employment-generation projects – with very little developmental impact – the PA and the donor community nonetheless repeatedly stressed the need for development efforts not to be entirely side-tracked. This was, for instance, the focus of the Palestinian Public Investment Programme for 1997, which was presented by the PA at the CG meeting in Paris on 20 November 1996.[16] By 1998, donors had stopped funding start-up and recurrent costs on a large scale as the PA managed to steadily increase its revenues. Donors also displayed less and less enthusiasm for this type of assistance amidst growing concern with the transparency of PA public finances.

Ephemeral return to the Emergency Assistance Programme, 1998–2000

As the later part of the decade was marked by relative calm, limited political progress, a relaxed closure regime and a certain degree of economic recovery – although pervasive movement restrictions remained a regular feature of Palestinian life, and living conditions never recovered their pre-1993 level – donors were able to shift their aid towards the more medium-term public investment agenda envisaged in the Bank's *original* EAP. Overall, donor assistance for immediate short-term support dropped off to represent 10 per cent of total assistance in 1998–1999.[17] Budget support in particular declined from 31 per cent of all assistance in 1994–1995 to 20 per cent in 1996–1997 and to less than 4 per cent in the second quarter of 1998–1999.[18] However, job creation and the need to reduce high unemployment rates remained on the donor agenda through to 2000. As mentioned in Chapter 2, the two principal sources of new employment from 1998 onwards were the Israeli labour market and the PA, neither of which provided a long-term alternative to achieving sustainable growth in employment, which required *inter alia* job growth in the private sector and, above all, free movement of people and goods, and unfettered access to external markets.

Three priority areas were outlined by the Bank at the CG meeting of 14–15 December 1997 and subsequently followed by other donors[19]: support for the private sector as the engine for economic growth and job creation (which entailed the enactment of an appropriate regulatory framework, legislation and institutional capacity to attract investors but also access to external markets); support for social programmes, notably in the area of service delivery (health, education, water and infrastructure); and the establishment of a governance system. In effect, the donor focus had not significantly evolved since the EAP, and would remain constant until the beginning of the *intifada*, although the internal balance between these priority areas slightly shifted as the decade unfolded in response to the evolving situation on the ground. For instance, in the mid-1990s, emphasis was put on the need to encourage private sector growth in light of the deterioration in the Palestinian economic situation. This was reflected in an increase in the level of disbursements in this area, from US$31 million in 1996 to US$49 million in 1998.[20]

Similarly, support for infrastructure development increased in relative proportion (but not in absolute terms) in the later part of the decade from 19 per cent in 1994–1995 to 39 per cent of donor support in 1998–1999.[21] The importance of infrastructure as one of the most effective ways to provide 'tangible' benefits to the Palestinian population – and commensurate visibility for the donor – was reflected, for instance, in UNDP spending. About two-thirds of the approximately US$450 million mobilized by UNDP for assistance to the Palestinians between 1993 and 2004 went to the infrastructure sector – with the further intent to help generate jobs. Undertaking capital investment projects is very unusual for UNDP, as the agency does not typically do so but provides technical assistance in the five practice areas of governance, poverty reduction, environment and energy, HIV/AIDS and crisis prevention and recovery.[22] This again is an illustration of the highly political nature of aid to the oPt. In addition to infrastructure, a progressively greater international focus was also placed on improving Palestinian public resource management and institutions.[23]

These priority areas were also broadly in accordance with the PA 's own focus, as outlined in the Palestinian Development Programme (PDP) for 1998–2000 presented at the same CG meeting, and subsequently in the Palestinian Development Programme for 1999–2003, made public at the AHLC in Frankfurt in February 1999. The PDP of 1999 emphasized four priority sectors: infrastructure and natural resources management (calculated to be 49 per cent of the overall assistance, or exactly the amount the EAP had recommended five years earlier); human resources and social development; productive development and institutional capacity building. One important difference was that in addition to creating jobs in the private and infrastructure sectors, the PA also emphasized the importance of reviving the agricultural sector, which was neglected in the 1990s. Indeed, that sector remained of very little interest to the international community throughout the period under review, largely for political reasons related to the issues of land and natural resources, as will be detailed. According to the PA, agriculture's share of the GDP declined from 40 per cent in 1988 to 22 per cent in 1995.[24]

At the second pledging conference for the WBGS, the Conference to Support Peace and Development in the Middle East, which took place in Washington DC on 30 November 1998 just a month after the Wye River Memorandum, donors demonstrated their continuing commitment to the implementation of the DOP by pledging US$3 billion for the next five years. Following this agreement, and the Sharm El-Sheikh Memorandum in September 1999, large-scale construction projects were undertaken, such as the Gaza international airport which opened in 1999, the GIE which was inaugurated the same year, the construction of the Gaza Sea Port which was well under way by mid-2000, and the Bethlehem 2000 project which involved renovating the city and its tourist and transport facilities in anticipation of the millennium celebrations. Together with the establishment of the southern safe passage route in 1999 to link Gaza to the West Bank, and other medium-term projects in the infrastructure and social services sectors, these activities generated significant investment and employment opportunities and provided resources for PA public investment programmes as laid out in the PDP. Those projects were also of particular significance because, once completed, they were meant to ease Palestinian access to external markets. However, they came to a halt with the *intifada*. Those which were under construction were never finished, and those which had been completed (such as the airport or the safe passage) ceased to be operational and often incurred significant damage.

Emergency budget support, job creation, cash assistance and humanitarian aid, 2000–2005

The *intifada* resulted in the international donor community returning to the kind of assistance that had characterized the first years of the aid effort. However, if the composition of assistance was reminiscent of the early to mid-1990s, the scale differed. In light of the severe economic recession, total collapse of PA revenues and mounting social and humanitarian needs, overall disbursements increased sharply. On a yearly basis, donors disbursed nearly double what they had provided in the 1990s.[25] In 2001, 70 per cent of the disbursements went to budgetary support and emergency funding, while only 19 per cent of donor assistance was allocated to medium-term development activities.[26] At the peak of the crisis in 2002, support to all forms of emergency assistance rose to 81 per cent (US$ 829 million), out of which 50 per cent went to budget support (US$519 million).[27]

According to the Bank, the ratio between emergency and development aid in commitment terms, which had been approximately 7:1 in favour of development assistance in 2000, had shifted by 2002 to 5:1 in favour of emergency assistance.[28] Furthermore, 'although overall commitments increased by 57 per cent in the period, development assistance declined by 70 per cent (while emergency assistance increased by a factor of 10)'.[29] In 2003, however, donors reintroduced more medium-term support. Budget support declined by 44 per cent compared with its 2002 peak, and humanitarian and emergency assistance fell by 28 per cent. In contrast, spending on medium-term rehabilitation projects, notably in the infrastructure sector, increased. Nonetheless, by 2003, budget support and welfare emergency assistance combined continued to amount to 60 per cent of overall external support, at US$528 million.[30]

In addition to budgetary support to the PA and municipalities, emergency assistance included the following main categories: basic service delivery, private sector support, employment and welfare, physical reconstruction, support to UNRWA and student scholarships. Three principal welfare instruments were used by donors to disburse those funds: food aid, job-creation programmes and cash assistance.[31] Of the estimated US$713 million spent in 2002–2003 on these three instruments, the Bank calculated that some 97 per cent was donor-financed.[32] This also highlights the extent to which during the *intifada* the Palestinian economy came to depend excessively on external assistance.

In 1994, donors had anticipated that after an initial emergency period, funds would transition to fostering long-term development and institution-building. Yet this never materialized as hoped, no matter how hard the international community attempted to maintain a veneer of medium-term development focus, to frame its assistance programme within a broader state-building objective, and to incorporate technical assistance and capacity-building components into emergency projects whenever feasible. As noted, the decade after Oslo was not linear. At times, closure was less acute, enabling donors to invest beyond the 'immediate' emergency (but still as per the initial Emergency Assistance Programme). However, contrary to what is commonly assumed, this remained the exception rather than the rule and pre-dated the *intifada*, with unintended but nonetheless far-reaching consequences on the Palestinian population, the effectiveness, sustainability and legality of donor intervention, and, arguably, the prospects for resolving the conflict.

Mitigating the socio-economic and humanitarian crises

Assessing the impact and relevance of international assistance on any recipient country is challenging. It depends on the standard used, and on whether one privileges a qualitative or quantitative approach. This is even more so in a fluid conflict/post-conflict situation where the quality and comparability of existing data is not reliable, and where conditions for development are particularly demanding. At the micro level, methodologies to evaluate the impact of donor projects have become increasingly standardized. Furthermore, recent initiatives have sought to go beyond traditional donor evaluations to develop 'peace and conflict impact assessment' (PCIA) methodologies targeted at development and humanitarian programmes occurring in conflict and peacebuilding contexts.[33] Nevertheless, as noted in Chapter 1, at the more macro level an increasing awareness among international donors of the impact of aid on conflict and peace has yet to lead them to look systematically into the multifaceted effects of their assistance on political processes, peace and stability. The focus of the following two sections is on the macro rather than project level. It is not organized around an exhaustive set of criteria. Rather, they strive to give a broad overview of the impact of foreign assistance with an emphasis on its political dimension (the specific effects on the PA and Palestinian state-building will be reviewed in Chapter 6).

Aid for the Palestinians: meeting basic needs; alleviating poverty

Investments in the social service and infrastructure sectors have had some beneficial effects, in terms of service availability and meeting basic needs, although by 2004 investments in those areas remained unsustainable and dependent on a continuation of donor flows. Furthermore, much of what was built in the 1990s was heavily damaged or destroyed by Israeli military operations during the first few years of the *intifada*. Below is a list of examples drawn from an aid effectiveness study produced by the Bank and Japan in June 2000, and based on data for the period 1994 to mid-1999:

i   Donors disbursed about US$54 million to the energy sector, principally to rehabilitate the electrical distribution network in Gaza, and rehabilitate and extend the electrical grid to rural villages in the West Bank. Between 1995 and 1998, per capita Palestinian electricity consumption increased by 34 per cent to 681 kWh.

ii About US$55 million was allocated to the transportation sector, the bulk of which went to the rehabilitation and expansion of the WBGS road network: at least 264 km of new roads were constructed, and 949 km of existing roads were rehabilitated.

iii The water and sanitation sector received US$293 million, principally to improve the quality of water in Gaza, as well as the quantity available and access to piped water in the West Bank. More than 308 projects were supported in this sector resulting in a wide range of new facilities (reservoirs, water pipes, water pumping stations, sewage lines and better solid waste collection).

iv Donors disbursed US$314 million to the education sector, including budget support for the recurrent expenditure of the Ministries of Education and Higher Education. Together with the NGO/private sector, donors financed the majority of public investment in this sector. For instance, they funded 96 per cent of all capital spending in the 1997 education budget. More than US$97 million was devoted to constructing and renovating schools for a total of at least 3,764 new classrooms. If the overall student:class/room ratio nonetheless remained constant because of high population growth, it was assessed that there has been 'modest but perceptible improvement' in education physical infrastructure, as well as in the student:teacher ratio and student enrolments, notably in kindergarten.

v   US$181 million was spent on the health sector. Foreign aid to this sector led to a modest increase in primary health care clinics and the construction of four new government hospitals, as well as a 38 per cent growth in hospital beds.[34]

During the *intifada*, there is also little doubt that emergency assistance and budget support played a key role in preventing a further decline in humanitarian indicators. For instance, in 2003, the Bank estimated that without the US$119 million allocated by donors to food aid, job-creation programmes and cash assistance, an additional 250,000 persons (a 35 per cent increase above the level at the time) would have fallen under the subsistence poverty line. Moreover, aid was found to be relatively well targeted, over 40 per cent of food aid and about 55 per cent of cash assistance going to the 16 per cent of Palestinians living below the subsistence poverty line.[35] Without donor assistance, living standards in the oPt would have been far worse.

However, beyond this basic emergency rehabilitation/humanitarian function, the beneficial impact of international aid appears much less evident. First, the effects of aid on the population appear even more modest when adopting a 'needs-driven' rather than 'supply-driven' perspective. For instance, if there was some quantitative progress in the physical availability of public health facilities, issues of quality, such as accessibility and increased demand for services, render the overall picture more mixed: for instance, it was estimated that while between 1994 and 2003, 186 new primary health care clinics were created, access to primary health care actually decreased by 31 per cent as the population grew by 1.8 million over the same period. To reach the level of access to primary health care that pre-vailed in 1994, 328 clinics would have had to be built and made operational in 2004.[36] Closure and lack of access also exacerbated regional disparity, with over-supply of health facilities in some areas and under-supply in others, as seen in the marked variation in hospital bed occupancy rates. Restrictions on access to Jerusalem for most Palestinians limited the contribution of East Jerusalem facili-ties (the best available) to the overall health care system and threatened the viabil-ity of some of those institutions.[37] Second, the short-term impact of relief as a whole has also not been that encouraging. As pointed out by the Bank in 2004:

> The last four years exemplify how little donor assistance can achieve in the absence of a positive policy environment – while donor disburse-ments doubled to almost US$1 billion per annum, real personal incomes fell by almost 40 percent in the same period.[38]

Donors instead of Israel: compensating for the deterioration in Palestinian socio-economic indicators

Thus, although the Palestinian population of the WBGS ranks among one of the most assisted and subsidized communities in the world, such high levels of relief assistance failed to avert socio-economic decline, and Palestinian standards of living actually got worse. A fortiori, development efforts have had little macro-economic and institutional impact. As noted by the EC in 2000 prior to the out-break of the *intifada*:

> Preventing the Palestinian economy and society from collapsing was seen by all, including the Government of Israel, as a key contribution to peace. There is consensus that this objective has been achieved. However, not collapsing is a far cry from real sustainable development of the kind that might rally the Palestinian population to wholehearted support for peace. This is what international aid has failed to achieve.[39]

Time and time again, in what became almost formulaic statements in reports and at donor meetings, the international community emphasized that without a modification of Israeli policies – most notably the dismantlement of the closure regime – there would simply be no scope for the donor community to be able to deliver on its economic part of the Oslo deal. As summed up by the Bank at the fifth CG meeting for the WBGS in December 1997:

> Many of you were here at the first CG for the West Bank and Gaza, in December 1993. The atmosphere then was very different. There was a sense of anticipation. We were quite confident that Palestinian economic skills would at last flourish; that sustained growth was feasible; and that a sound economy would make a major contribution to peace. That was almost exactly four years ago. Where do we find ourselves today? Clearly, not where we expected to be. Far from witnessing a renaissance of the Palestinian economy, we have lived through an extended crisis – punctuated by terrorist acts and characterized by severe economic decline.... To put it bluntly: we expected the economic program to succeed, and to strengthen the political process. Instead political conflict has undermined the Palestinian economy and blunted the efforts of the donors.... As donors, it took us time to adapt our procedures to such a fluid environment. On the Palestinian side, too, significant problems persist. But frankly, these donor and PA shortcomings pale in comparison with external political impediments, and in particular border closure. On this well-worn subject I will simply note our rather conservative estimate of economic losses attributable to closure – some 2.8 billion dollars in 1994–1996, roughly double the 1.49 billion in donor disbursements over the same period, and over three times the total in productive expenditures.[40]

In January 1999, an evaluation of the EC's programme of assistance to the WBGS was even blunter:

> The positive assessment regarding the overall relevance of the [European] projects is purely subjective. If we consider the economic evolution between 1994 and 1998 (main economic indicators, GNP per capita, employment, exports ... evolved negatively) we could conclude that the financing did not influence the Palestinian economic situation. Unfortunately, financing (although the banks can provide it) cannot be the only solution to promote economic development. The main real obstacle to this development results from the lack of a safe-passage for the free movement of Palestinians and goods. We are in a situation of an abuse of prevailing economic standing. Since the West Bank and Gaza Strip enjoy no direct transport and communication with the world at large, other than through Israel or subject to Israeli control, the

consequence is an enormous structural dependence of the Palestinian economy on Israel and vulnerability to Israeli policy. Indeed, whatever the importance, the amount and the nature of financing, it is uncertain whether this will ensure effective economic development as long as the Palestinian economy remains under Israeli control.[41]

In March 2003, the Bank noted:

A doubling of donor disbursements to US$2 billion in 2003 and 2004 – something there is no reason to believe can happen – would only reduce the poverty rate by seven percentage points by the end of 2004. On the other hand, if internal closures were removed and exports facilitated, GDP could surge by about 21 per cent in 2003 and poverty could fall by 15 percentage points by the end of 2004.[42]

In June 2004, it warned with regard to the effect of Israeli disengagement from Gaza on Palestinian economic prospects:

Of itself Israel's Disengagement...will have very little impact on the Palestinian economy and Palestinian livelihoods since it only proposes a limited easing of closure. A focus on this over-arching issue is essential if Disengagement is to deliver long-term benefits.... Disengagement will remove internal restrictions in Gaza and in part of the northern West Bank, but Palestinian economic recovery depends on a radical easing of internal closures throughout the West Bank, the opening of Palestinian external borders to commodity trade, and sustaining a reasonable flow of Palestinian labour into Israel...It is important to understand that additional donor money alone cannot solve today's economic problems. Donor disbursements of approximately US$1 billion per annum (or US$310 per person) are already very high. Additional aid in today's economy would help alleviate day-to-day hardship, but would have little lasting impact. As long as the web of Palestinian economic transactions remains shredded by closures, investors will stay away, and short-term gains will not be sustainable.[43]

And in December 2005, following the Agreement on Movement and Access which was supposed to lead to an easing of the movement of Palestinian goods and people being, notably in and out of the Gaza Strip (but which was never really implemented), the Bank stated:

The Agreement is only a first step. A process of reducing internal movement restrictions in the West Bank is proposed in the Agreement but current GOI policy protects settlements and settler access by restricting Palestinian traffic on key highways, and this conflicts with the need to restore movement between towns, villages, and the borders. GOI's policy on Palestinian labor should also be reconsidered. The number of permitted to work in ISI in 2005 was less than half of the 1999 daily average. GOI intends to phase out all Palestinian labor access by the end of 2007, but a longer transition is needed if further serious disruption to the Palestinian economy is to be avoided.[44]

In this respect, it is striking how little the economic fundamentals actually changed in the decade following Oslo, despite the fluctuating intensity of the crises, and a steady deterioration of the situation. Analytical reporting by donors and notably by the Bank, from its initial six-volume study in 1993 to its two 2004 studies on the prospects for economic revival after disengagement as well as subsequent reports in the mid-2000s, was remarkably consistent. Yet despite a clear and consensual diagnosis of the situation – and of the serious limits of aid effectiveness therein – donors nonetheless continued to provide large amounts of funding as stop-gap solutions to compensate for Israeli policies.

The concept of industrial estates is a case in point. As noted by Peter Lagerquist, industrial zones were first envisaged by the GOI in the late 1980s, in the context of a plan for developing the oPt commissioned by the Israeli Ministry of Defence and designed by the Ministry of Finance. Beyond the security rationale of those zones, the purpose was 'to build up a domestic industrial base, first in Gaza and then in the West Bank, which, linked to the Israeli economy, could absorb Palestinian workers', as well as 'provide infrastructure, and easy and secure access to the Israeli markets for investors in the Strip'.[45] The idea was revived during Oslo within the broader 'New Middle East' discourse on economic regional cooperation promoted by the Israeli left around Shimon Peres.[46] However, as he pointed out:

Not mentioned – though widely understood – was the fact that the Palestinian industrial estates would in the best of circumstances be a less-than-second-best means to Palestinian export promotion. As the World Bank was first to note, the most binding constraints on Palestinian trade were Israel's security prerogatives in the territory and control of Palestinian borders. In addition to the difficulties of trading across the Green Line, Palestinian firms faced an onerous and discriminatory Israeli bureaucracy on their international borders, raising the transaction costs to prohibitive levels. Intervening in these 'political issues', however, was beyond the development industry's mandate in the territories. Indeed, the appeal of the estates program was that by creating closure-proof enclaves, it would supposedly allow 'development' in the territories to proceed as if there was no occupation at all – a perfectly plausible proposition within the context of a political process built on similar premises.[47]

In addition to being presented as 'closure-proof' zones, industrial estates were also marketed to potential investors as secure 'havens for good governance'. Estates were thus a palliative not only to Israeli restrictions on the movement of Palestinian workers and goods intended to provide cheap labour and promote Palestinian exports, but also to PA mismanagement practices and lack of a stable legal and regulatory environment, which deterred investors. In addition, it was a lucrative business opportunity for the Israeli security firm NETACS which was selected by the Palestinian Industrial Estates Development Corporation (PIEDCO) to ensure the security of the estate. By the time the *intifada* broke out, the GIE had resulted in the creation of about 1,000 positions in low value-added textile jobs, largely subcontracted by Israeli companies, either directly or indirectly.[48]

Not only was the quality of the jobs created by the GIE poor, but like other employment-generation programmes with high direct labour content funded by the international community in the 1990s and 2000s, the GIE programme had little developmental impact or indirect labour effects, raising doubt as to the long-term economic benefit and sustainability of such schemes for the Palestinians, and regardless of the fact that the *intifada* eventually led to their demise. The same could be said about the impact of the international community's job-creation projects more broadly. As mentioned above, there were some efforts, in the course of the 1990s, to move from short-term direct hire jobs to employment creation as part of a micro-projects programme aimed at rehabilitating municipal and social infrastructure while expanding the existing capacity of Palestinian institutions and mobilizing small Palestinian contractors and local communities. Nonetheless, and despite the fact that, in sheer numerical terms, these programmes resulted in the creation of jobs, they failed to have any significant spill-over effects on either the Palestinian economy or the living conditions of the population.[49]

These dilemmas faced by the international donor community became all the more acute during the *intifada* because of the sizeable humanitarian component of the aid provided, and the concomitant difficulty in claiming that this could yield any developmental impact. As argued, this was actually already the case in the 1990s, but as the Oslo process had just begun and optimism was high, it is easier to understand why donors conceptualized and justified these emergency projects as part of an 'exceptional', short-term response to a particularly complex and volatile situation, rather than actually admitting that it constituted the bulk of their intervention. As recalled by a US diplomat:

> The first closure of 1994 was a shock to everyone; it was perceived by many as a violation of at least the spirit of Oslo which assumed a lot of economic interdependence between Israel and the Palestinian territory (the thinking at the time was not about a 'viable' state), but we thought this would be temporary. This hope was not completely unfounded. Agreements were being signed like the Hebron Protocol. The PA itself

was beginning to take shape and becoming self-sufficient. There was initially some economic growth, especially in Gaza, a bit of investment in the West Bank too. But there was a lot of bad news too. In retrospect, we should have seen the future more clearly. At the time, it was difficult to see what was happening as a trend, and things could have turned very differently too, if Rabin had not been assassinated, if Netanyahu had not come to power, etc.[50]

Although at the time, it may have been 'difficult to see what was happening as a trend, and things could have turned very differently too', the term 'humanitarian' was nevertheless used as early as 1996, at the occasion of serious food shortages in Gaza. On 31 March 1996, a couple of weeks before the AHLC of 12 April 1996 in Brussels, UNSCO released the details of an 'emergency humanitarian plan to improve the social and economic conditions of Palestinians in the West Bank and Gaza Strip'. The plan pointed to the two main priorities of easing closure to allow private sector activity to resume, and creating jobs. Rød Larsen noted that

> the plan is an emergency humanitarian response to the present situation, recognizing that the long-term political and security implications would necessarily have to be addressed by the parties. Our aim is to facilitate allowing Palestinians to return to work in the private sector, to create new job opportunities and ensure that all necessary food and medical supplies are allowed to enter the West Bank and the Gaza Strip'.[51]

Already in the 1990s, donors thus had a clear appreciation of the situation, and of the necessarily sub-optimal nature of their intervention, but they only began fundamentally to question the *bien fondé* of their involvement as the crisis deepened during the *intifada*. Not only did the provision of humanitarian assistance dramatically increase Palestinian household dependence on aid (thereby exacerbating an already high level of overall economic dependency) but it was rapidly understood that under the conditions prevailing in 2000–2004, even a substantial increase in donor funding would not have any major effect on the steadily deteriorating socio-economic situation, and erosion of Palestinian coping strategies.[52] Furthermore, that such high levels of emergency aid had already been sustained for long periods was not only against donor best practice but in itself exceptional, far exceeding the usual lifespan of other high-profile humanitarian crises where assistance peaks and troughs as the crisis passes from the news headlines.

Humanitarian dilemmas and the 'deluxe occupation'

A consensus also emerged in the early 2000s within the international aid community that the crisis was not only one of needs but reflected the failure to respect humanitarian norms, notably the Fourth Geneva Convention which governs the status of civilians under military occupation. This accentuated the donors' dilemma: whether or not to continue providing relief to mitigate the economic and humanitarian symptoms of a man-made crisis, when under IHL, Israel, as the occupying power, should be responsible for delivering assistance and services to the Palestinian population. Moreover, as high contracting parties to the Conventions, donors also have the obligation to ensure compliance with the law. The intricacy of the situation is well captured by Israeli journalist Meron Benvenisti:

> The Palestinians managed to survive thanks to the international aid, but as usual in these cases, the beneficiary of the international community's rallying to the rescue was their Israeli enemy. Moreover, the contributing states' humanitarian enlistment became a safety net, enabling Israel to impose a deluxe occupation in the West Bank – total military domination with no responsibility for running the life of the occupied population, and no price tag attached.[53]

At the operational level, the situation was exacerbated by strict Israeli restrictions on humanitarian access despite clear commitments made personally by Prime Minister Sharon to the UN Envoy Catherine Bertini in August 2002 that Israel would facilitate aid delivery.[54] Instead, the delivery of humanitarian aid and the movement of relief workers were regularly disrupted by unpredictable closures and cumbersome administrative procedures resulting in delays and added costs for agencies. For instance, between October 2000 and November 2003, UNRWA estimated the costs it incurred through operational constraints to be more than US$25 million. For its part, the EC's humanitarian aid agency, ECHO, reported in 2003 that 20 per cent of its US$35 million budget could be lost as the result of obstructions to its operations.[55] Between March and November 2004, only two WFP national staff were able to enter Gaza.[56]

Not only did aid relieve Israel of its responsibilities under international law, but it also clearly helped sustain its occupation and expansionist policy, which would have been much more onerous to maintain had the international community not paid the bill. This is all the more so as evidence suggests that Israel benefited economically from donor funds: in 2003, it was estimated that for every dollar produced in the oPt, 45 per cent came back into the Israeli economy.[57] Despite increased awareness and concerns expressed in private, the prevailing view among donors remained that they had no option but to continue to provide aid. As noted by an American official:

> This is a valid philosophical discussion but practically, donors do not have any choice. The idea that if we leave, Israel will step in is naïve. We cannot play with the lives of civilians. The humanitarian impulse has to take prominence over political considerations.

Less diplomatically put, by a UN official:

> Yes, we are financing the Israeli occupation but we have to respond to
> the humanitarian imperative. However, there is no serious discussion
> with and among donors on what the red line is which should not be
> crossed. We are mounting a huge humanitarian operation while we all
> know that the humanitarian crisis is caused by closure and movement
> restrictions. The problem of malnutrition for instance is mainly the
> result of the fall in agricultural production because Palestinians are not
> allowed to export. But there is no global discussion among donors, no
> adequate and coherent response to the crisis. The occupation remains a
> background issue. What is certainly clear is that the Israelis do not
> participate in alleviating the humanitarian and socio-economic con-
> ditions of the Palestinian population. Internationals do.

It is noteworthy, however, that in November 2003 the ICRC decided to end its
large-scale distribution of relief aid in the West Bank, which since June 2002
had provided 300,000 Palestinians with food aid for a total amount of US$40
million. The official statement read:

> We have always stressed that the relief programmes in the West Bank
> were put in place to deal with an emergency. In the long-term, humani-
> tarian aid cannot be a viable solution to the crisis in the West Bank.
> Israel has legitimate security concerns. Nonetheless, it must make it
> possible for Palestinians to deal with this crisis using their own means.
> Under the Fourth Geneva Convention, it is the primary responsibility of
> Israel, the occupying power, to ensure that the population of occupied
> territories has sufficient access to food, water, health services and edu-
> cation. Any security measures taken by Israel to defend its citizens
> against attacks should not have a disproportionate impact on Palestini-
> ans civilians living in the occupied territories. Palestinians must be
> given the possibility to live as normal a life as possible.[58]

The ICRC's decision was not trivial, but it remained unique among international
organizations. In fact, to compensate for the end of its programme, donors made
more funds available to WFP so it could scale up its own intervention and
provide food to the Palestinian families no longer covered by the Red Cross.
Suspension of aid was thus never seriously on the international agenda, although
on occasion the UN and other international relief agencies issued warnings to
Israel that they would withdraw from the oPt unless the restrictions to their
movement were eased.[59]

   In addition to the issue of whether international aid was subsidizing the occupation, the question also arose as to the legal and political implications of
funding certain types of projects which might inadvertently play into, and

entrench, Israeli policies of destroying Palestinian infrastructure and fragmenting the geographical space of the oPt. For instance, following the devastation brought about by Operation Defensive Shield, donors engaged in a rapid and impressive coordination effort. Through the LACC, they established an *ad interim* Donor Support Group to assess the physical and institutional damage caused by the incursions into the West Bank, discuss reconstruction priorities with local communities, and mobilize funds for repairs.[60] Thanks to this exercise, about US$150 million was pledged in June 2002 (although only US$65 million was eventually disbursed).[61] Yet it was difficult to obscure the incongruity of the situation. Donors had devoted, over the previous years, an unusually high level of assistance to building Palestinian infrastructure and the PA administration. The physical and institutional damage incurred during those couple of months was estimated at US$342 million. This amounted to one third of the total funds which donors had disbursed in 2002, or about three-quarters of what they had disbursed in a year on average for the period 1994–2000.[62]

Similarly, Israel intensified its policy of house demolitions, notably in the Gaza Strip. During Operation Rainbow alone in May 2004, 298 buildings were demolished and 3,800 people lost their homes.[63] Such was the scale of the destruction that it prompted the Security Council at the UN, in an unusual move, to pass a resolution condemning Israeli action and calling on Israel to respect international law.[64] It is the case that extensive and disproportionate destruction of property can amount to a grave breach of humanitarian law, or a war crime.[65] Yet, as the international community at the UN in New York expressed disapproval, the donor HEPG simultaneously met in Jerusalem to assess the damage and look into funding options for reconstruction. As pointed out by Meyer and Shearer:

> Irrespective of whether the demolitions are deemed illegal, Israel as the occupier has the responsibility to repair any damage it causes and to re-house those made homeless. Israel has yet to be asked to do this by donor states. Thus while international law is cited to condemn demolitions, it has yet to influence aid policy. Instead, donors have funded new structures to re-house those who have lost their homes at the request of humanitarian agencies. One month after Operation Rainbow, for example, an appeal for US$15 million by UNRWA for re-housing assistance received a positive response from many donors. The re-housing policy also received the blessing of the Palestinian National Authority. As demolitions look set to continue it is apposite to ask whether funding the construction of new homes might underwrite Israeli willingness to use this as a tactic. If Israel was presented with the US$15 million bill for Rafah's reconstruction – as international law sets out – would it prompt a rethinking of military strategy and encourage other methods of surveillance that cause less harm to civilians and property? Should the legal obligations on Israel – and donors for that matter – be applied before donors reach for their cheque books?[66]

In the period 2002–2005, collective discomfort grew in the context of intensified Israeli military operations and destruction on a large scale. The construction of the Wall and the renewed diplomatic prominence of the settlement issue contributed to making aid actors increasingly aware of Israeli legal responsibilities as well as those of the donors. The ICJ advisory opinion in July 2004 was important in this regard. Not only did the court clearly stipulate that the Barrier was illegal, but it also stated that

> all States are under an obligation not to recognise the illegal situation resulting from the construction of the wall in the occupied Palestinian territory, including in and around Jerusalem. They are also under an obligation not to render aid or assistance in maintaining the situation created by such construction.[67]

Further, it ruled that

> given that the construction... has, inter alia, entailed the requisition and destruction of homes, businesses and agricultural holdings, the Court finds further that Israel has the obligation to make reparation for the damage caused to all the natural and legal persons concerned.[68]

A few donor meetings in Jerusalem, often within the context of the HEPG, were devoted to discussing this set of dilemmas, which strategy to adopt, how to reconcile the humanitarian imperative while simultaneously not breaching IHL, encouraging respect for that law and indicating to Israel that the international community was not simply there to foot the bill. The construction of the Separation Barrier also became a locus of donor attention, notably as the fear emerged that aid projects could encourage Israel's annexation of territory, and alter the demographics of the population near the barrier, contrary to IHL which prohibits the transfer of populations. As explained:

> Depopulation could happen in one of two ways. First, halting funding for projects inside 'closed areas' may accelerate the movement of Palestinians out of them. Unofficially, donors have voiced their reluctance to fund infrastructure projects inside the 'closed areas' because of the uncertainty of their long-term viability. To enter a 'closed area' Palestinians require permits that need to be renewed at least every six months. Residents living in these areas have largely continued to reach their houses – subject to the opening times of the barrier gates. But day labourers, medical workers and family members face increasing difficulty in obtaining permits. Economic life inside these enclaves is liable to become unsustainable and people will then move out. Second, money increasingly targeted at easing life for Palestinians east of the barrier could attract movement

out of 'closed areas', depopulating those areas of the West Bank owned by Palestinians.[69]

In the summer 2004, the GOI also approached the donor community via the Bank and suggested it consider financing the construction or upgrade of 52 roads and 16 under/overpasses in locations throughout the West Bank so as to restore a measure of 'continuous movement'.[70] This was the result of months of intense negotiations at the technical level between the international community (via the Bank) and Israel over the prospects for Palestinian economic revival within the context of Israeli disengagement from Gaza. On the face of it, donors could not but delight in the Israeli intention to facilitate movement and contiguity within the oPt, something it had repeatedly said was a prerequisite for Palestinian economic recovery. However, an examination of the proposal and attached maps revealed that many of those roads were linked either to the location of the Barrier or to settlements.

Consistent with Israeli Prime Minister Sharon's idea of 'transportation continuity' as the basis for a Palestinian state's contiguity, as will be detailed in the conclusion, what Israel was asking the donors to fund was an entirely new road network for Palestinians that passes under and over, through tunnels and bridges, the existing by-pass road network reserved for the settlers. Considering the PA Cabinet's rejection, and aware that accepting this proposal would have been a de facto official recognition and encouragement of the expansion of Israeli settlements and segregated road network in the oPt, the donor community as a whole – including the US, which had funded by-pass roads in the 1990s – declined.[71] Interestingly, the Bank made a specific reference to IHL to explain donor collective refusal of the Israeli plan, an absolute first in a decade of the Bank's reports on the economic situation in the WBGS:

> Israel's 'continuous movement' proposal is not acceptable to the donor community. Donor concerns have been influenced by the recent ICJ Advisory Opinion on the Separation Barrier, which states that the Barrier, its associated regime (which includes the seam zone) and the settlements contravene international law, and warns against providing international assistance that would serve to maintain the current status quo.[72]

Ten years after the onset of Oslo, donors were made to think not only about the sustainability and cost-effectiveness of their projects, but also about their legality. They became slightly more selective in their choice of programmes. The shift was also perceptible in language. Donors became less timid verbally, and grew in assurance. For instance, looking at the Bank's reports, the term 'closure' was described in its 2002 and 2003 analyses as referring to 'the restrictions placed by Israel for security reasons on the free movement of Palestinian goods and labour across borders and within the West Bank and Gaza'. In its 2004 reports, however, the Bank explicitly linked closure to the Israeli settlement enterprise, defining the term as 'a multi-faceted system of restrictions on the movement of Palestinian goods and people designed to protect Israelis in Israel proper and in the settlements'.[73] This was a marked evolution for a primarily 'economic' organization such as the Bank.

However, no concerted political effort to try to influence Israeli actions on the ground came out of these discussions. By the mid-2000s, within the context of regained optimism brought about by the prospect of Israeli disengagement, this set of humanitarian dilemmas had once again largely disappeared from the donor radar screen. The international community continued to indicate its willingness to deliver a huge amount of emergency assistance to support the 'peace process' (now referring to disengagement). Donor funding was even expected to increase, possibly to reach as much as three billion per annum following Israeli withdrawal.[74]

Underwriting the process of Palestinian territorial fragmentation

Beyond the issues of aid effectiveness, sustainability and international legality lies the more fundamental question of who actually benefited from the aid the international community disbursed to the Palestinian population. As noted, at a general level, far from creating tangible improvements, giving Palestinians a stake in a better future and constituting an engine for growth and development, aid turned into life support. When looking into sectoral allocation, and notably those sectors which touch upon the contentious issues of land, territory and control over resources, the influence of Israel on determining the allocation of international funds to the Palestinians is even more significant.

Aid for Israel: allocating aid according to Israeli territorial and strategic resource considerations

In the 1990s, donor disbursements to the energy sector remained low, at under half of the US$108 million envisaged under the Bank's EAP. As compared to such social areas as health and education, the energy sector was unattractive as it lacked visibility. More importantly, it was a complex area to invest in as it involves the issue of land and delineation of territory. One result was that the extension of the electric grid and services to the rural areas in the West Bank (Areas B and C) was particularly limited. Similarly, in the road sector, territorial final status considerations, and Israeli large-scale by-pass road construction in Area C during the 1990s, resulted in the absence of a Palestinian national strategic plan for the transportation sector. Moreover, even if the Palestinian road network improved, notably in Area A, closure and movement restrictions resulted in poor transportation access. Finally, the agriculture sector was largely neglected by donors, also mainly because it touched upon the issues of land and water use (much agricultural land falling within Area C), even if traditional emphasis by IFIs on market economics may also explain the cool attitude of donors towards this sector.

In contrast, it was comparatively easy to mobilize resources in the area of water and sanitation, which attracted roughly 10 per cent of the total donor disbursement to the WBGS between 1994 and mid-1999.[75] More than 20 donors were involved, leading to overlaps, weak coordination and poorly integrated projects. According to the *Aid Effectiveness* study, the attractiveness of the water sector reflected donors' 'widespread recognition that the water sector is of critical economic and social importance. Palestinian water resources are extremely limited – on a per capita basis among the lowest in the developing world – and must be shared with neighbouring countries'.[76] This is certainly correct but acquires full significance when considering that under Oslo, 82 per cent of the West Bank's ground water resources were allocated to Israel.[77] The issue is thus not so much that Palestinian water resources are limited – although the region is depleted by global standards – but rather that they are over-exploited by the Israelis, who also consume much more water than the Palestinians, notably for agricultural purposes. According to one donor estimate in 2003, while in Gaza and the West Bank per capita water consumption is respectively around 60 litres and 80 litres per day, daily per capita water consumption reaches about 235 litres in Israel, and 400 litres in Israeli settlements.

It is not entirely surprising that the two major donors in the water and sanitation sector were the US and Germany, while Japan and the Bank also devoted some non-negligible levels of funding to this area. In the 1990s, Germany disbursed around 80 per cent of the total funds it allocated to the WBGS (*c.* €40–50 million annually) to the water and sanitation sector. Similarly, the water sector constituted the single most important budget item for USAID in the 1990s, amounting to about US$40–45 million annually, or more than one half of its total annual budget. During the *intifada*, the amount allocated to the water sector decreased, but it nonetheless remained the single most important sector of USAID assistance to the WBGS.[78]

Yet, despite considerable funding allocated to this sector, benefits for the Palestinian population were insufficient. As was also the case in other sectors such as energy, transportation and agriculture, this was in large part due to constraints imposed by Oslo which postponed agreement on the allocation and exploitation of water supplies to final status negotiations, thus leaving the overwhelming majority of the resources under Israeli control in the interim period. Moreover, progress was slow because all the donor projects in this sector had to be approved by the Israeli–Palestinian Joint Water Committee, which did not function effectively because of persisting tension between the two parties. Consequently, many projects were rejected or delayed,[79] and those which were approved often matched Israeli interest first. As noted by one UN staff member:

> In the water sector, the Americans were willing to go for big projects, ready to make big investments in Palestinian areas to compensate for

giving up Palestinian rights to the Israelis. For instance, the US funded this huge desalination plant project in Gaza to compensate the Palestinians for the water taken by the Israelis in the West Bank. The water surplus in the West Bank is sufficient to cover Gaza, but the Americans are ready to spend a huge amount of money on constructing a desalination plant (which is not only extremely expensive to build but then also to run, raising issues of project sustainability) so as to let Israel have most of the West Bank water.

Coupled with a complex and fragmented system of territorial authority, ownership and water management in the West Bank as well as drought and water shortages in 1990s, this may explain the Palestinian population's negative appraisal of donor performance in this sector. In 1999, 35 per cent of the Palestinians surveyed for the *Aid Effectiveness* study responded that the provision of drinking water had worsened, although some improvement was reported in sewage systems.[80] In particular, water availability in rural areas remained poor, and the treatment of waste water and solid waste was restricted by the prohibition to do so outside Area A. More generally, given the general emphasis on the social and political imperatives of economic growth, donors paid hardly any attention to environmental issues as a whole despite serious challenges, notably the depletion and declining quality of water resources available due to rapid population growth, poor management and over-utilization. This in turn leads back to the issue of sustainability.

Lack of Palestinian national planning

Overall, donors did not invest strategically in Palestinian productive capacity which could have minimized the huge dependency on Israel, and which would have been one of the first items under international consideration had Palestinian state-building been the main objective.[81] Furthermore, territorial fragmentation, restrictions on Palestinian water use in general and land use in Area C, and the fact that arrangements for territorial and resource control were postponed until a final status agreement, had not only important negative consequences for the population and considerably slowed down project implementation but, more importantly, made strategic national management and planning virtually impossible. Typically, development policy, including Palestinian documents, did not include plans for the infrastructure and management of resources of the WBGS as a whole, and did not mention East Jerusalem.[82] On rare occasions, the PA tried to include Jerusalem, but this invariably led to disputes with Israel and was therefore muffled by the donor community. For instance, the plenary session of one of the first CG meetings in 1994 was postponed because of a dispute during the bilateral sessions on the issue of Jerusalem. Eventually, the plenary meeting took place but as an abridged, shorter session.[83] As noted, five years later, the issue of Jerusalem was also at the heart of the fiasco in Frankfurt that sealed the fate of CGs.

In addition to the limitations imposed by Israel, the PA never managed to articulate a clear strategy for national development, partly because of the weakness of the relevant ministers in the period up to 2002, and partly because the leadership, mirroring the international community at large, was much more interested in the 'high politics' of the peace process. It thus treated development strategy as residual – priority was given to the diplomatic negotiations and ensuring political stability in the oPt so as to secure continuing international financial flows. This, compounded by the lack of a sound implementation and budgetary framework and problems of coordination and communication between PA institutions, meant that line ministries, to whom development was left, had little incentive to put forward clear priorities and to follow official central channels in their dealing with donors: most sector plans remained shopping lists which ignored the resources available, implementation capacity and sustainability, thus leaving it up to donors to lead the prioritization process on a bilateral basis.[84] This in turn reinforced donors' natural tendency to pursue their own political and commercial interests, resulting in lack of complementarity, poor harmonization and the overloading of Palestinian absorptive capacity in the process.

This was all the more the case as, from the outset, there was considerable confusion and rivalry among PA ministries and institutions regarding their respective responsibilities for aid management and coordination. In addition to the tendency for line ministries to seek direct relationships with donors, there was a lot of overlap in the perceived roles of PECDAR and MOPIC. PECDAR had been set up as a transitional institution in the autumn of 1993 to liaise with donors, UN agencies and international NGOs before the PA was established in the summer of 1994 – including the signing of all bilateral and multilateral agreements and the management of the big infrastructure projects launched by the donors as a matter of priority in line with the perceived need to deliver on the peace process. What Arafat allegedly called the 'first Palestinian Cabinet' was supposed to be eventually folded into the ministerial structure.[85]

Yet, by the time MOPIC was established, it had developed its own power base around the veteran PLO figures of Abu Ala and Mohammed Stayyeh, who unsurprisingly were not keen to see their newly acquired authority vanish so rapidly. This was all the more so as Nabil Shaath, another of the most influential PLO Tunisian apparatchiks, was appointed MOPIC's first minister. As rivalry persisted, itself indicative of Palestinian factionalism, of a wider power struggle within the PLO for influence under the new PA structure, and of Arafat's personal divide-and-rule style of government, it was eventually decided to keep PECDAR as a separate entity, specifically to deal with planning, technical assistance, programme management and project implementation. MOPIC would also focus on planning but take the lead in donor coordination and management.[86] This was a sub-optimal, ambiguous and redundant institutional arrangement. Furthermore, the lack of integration and poor communication between the planning and aid management wings of MOPIC, and the further rivalries within

MOPIC between the departments located in Ramallah and those operating from Gaza City, proved particularly problematic. Until it was split into two separate ministries (Ministry of Planning and Ministry of Foreign Affairs) in May 2003, MOPIC remained a divided and dysfunctional institution which had lost the confidence of the donors.

There was thus no overall Palestinian national development vision, no overall policy goals and no real strategic and coordinated allocation of resources to sectors; instead, aid allocation remained driven by a fragmented project approach and characterized by duplication of requests from the PA and overlaps among donors.[87] As noted, with the exception of a few dynamic sectors such as health, education or employment generation, SWGs remained inefficient. Some progress was made towards a medium-term planning system with the Palestinian Development Plan 1999–2003. However, the plan was never backed up by an adequate budget and, in any case, became obsolete with the beginning of the *intifada*. The crisis then witnessed a succession of emergency plans, largely written by the Bank, which became out of date before the ink was dry.[88] Their main function was unfortunately largely cosmetic: the PA had to be able to present 'a plan' at donor meetings so as to ensure continuing financing. That those plans did little to improve planning thus mattered only marginally.

Not only was Palestinian planning and strategy largely reactive and fragmented, but so were donor projects which were restricted to Area A and to a lesser extent Area B. As in the case of the Gaza desalination plant, this often led to bizarre choices. For instance, whereas the traditional heart of Palestinian economic activity is East Jerusalem and the West Bank, donors decided to fund an airport on the very edge of the Gaza Strip, at one of the most peripheral locations possible. Similarly, for symbolic reasons, the EC did fund a few projects in East Jerusalem, but that was not part of any Palestinian national plan with the idea of Palestinian sovereignty and statehood in mind. As explained by one US official:

> The West Bank is a small area. Even if the peace agreements restricted your room for manoeuvre and you devised a project in Nablus, you could think of that project in a wider regional context. Whereas Israel was seamlessly confiscating land and integrating settlements into Israel, nobody was planning for Palestine. The reality of the West Bank is a North–South one, now it has become West–East. Israelis have been planning from Tel Aviv through Ariel to Aman: why did the international donors not help the Palestinians plan and integrate the projects in a North–South reality? Everyone rushed on projects. There was no planning logic with the establishment of a state in mind.

The fact that donors funded projects principally in Area A necessarily also had negative repercussions on the possibility to attract private investments, and on the type of investments which made their way into the oPt. As pointed out by geographer Jan de Jong:

The closure and carving up of Palestinian territories was accepted blindly by everyone. Western states wanted to satisfy both the Israelis and the Palestinians, hence donors invested in Area A, but how can you expect that private investors would throw away money into a carved-up territory? Hence, most private investors put money in unproductive sectors of Area A, like a restaurant in Ramallah, rather than building a factory – even in Area A this was risky as you would have needed to be sure that supply, staff, etc., would have continuous and unfettered access.... Look at the map of the WBGS already in 1995, there was no genuine possibility for investments. This would never have worked, and ten years later, this is even less likely.[89]

Conclusion

By accommodating territorial constraints, the choices made by donors at the project level thus also contributed to reinforcing the Israeli policy of fragmentation and dispossession. While Israel expanded its territorial and demographic control over key strategic areas of the West Bank, Palestinian presence and use of the land diminished, especially in Jerusalem and the areas along to the Green Line and the Jordan Valley. As noted by Christopher Parker:

Uncritical aid giving might only serve to make effective Palestinian disempowerment under the guise of autonomy bearable over the short-term, while Israel pursues its strategic interests of procuring sovereignty over the land and its resources. The irony is that in order to sustain a process which claims to be leading towards the building of a Palestinian state, the tactics which are being used to sustain the process undermine the future ability of that state to sustain itself.[90]

Beyond the key issues of territorial viability, effectiveness, sustainability and legality, the question also arises as to whether international assistance has been 'harmful' to the prospect for peace, reconciliation and the resolution of the conflict. In May 2004, Mary B. Anderson specifically applied her 'Do No Harm' approach to aid in the oPt. She outlined seven principal ways in which donor assistance has had a negative impact on the conflict by reinforcing 'dividers' between Israelis and Palestinians and weakening 'connectors' between the two parties to the conflict. Her observations are worth citing in full:

i   Donor structures: Decisions were taken some time ago in Western capitals that donor representatives should work primarily on the Palestinian side and, with few exceptions, be based in either East Jerusalem or, for those states which did not already have a consulate in East Jerusalem, Ramallah. Interactions relating to Palestinian affairs and to aid issues for the West Bank and Gaza are carried out mainly by or through Western consul generals represented in East Jerusalem and coordinated by a triumvirate headed by the UN Special Coordinator, a representative of the World Bank and the Norwegian representative. Other diplomatic activities in relation to the peace process are managed by diplomats based in Tel Aviv or at capital level. This multifaceted separation between the assistance and the diplomatic branches of donor governments reinforces the separation between the two communities with whom they relate. Consequently, the interactions between the donor community and Israelis often mirror the interactions of Palestinians and Israelis in their negativity.

ii 'Routinization' of the occupation: The ongoing, daily interactions with the occupation (closure, checkpoints, barrier/wall locations, applications for visas and other permissions, etc.) have become so 'normal', and take so much time and attention, that staff of donor agencies have developed an almost routine attitude towards them. Further, these difficulties are dealt with in an ad hoc way, varying from agency to agency and often addressing one issue, then another, then another. The results of this ad hoc approach are twofold. First, people are caught up in particular battles and enjoy small 'victories', such as getting a portion of the Barrier moved by, say, ten metres, rather than remaining focused on the larger issue – the fact that the Barrier is separating two peoples and reinforcing an illegal domination of one group by the other. Second, people lose sight of the cumulative effects of separate decisions. However, it is the accumulation of many 'small' actions that constitutes the occupation and reinforces dividers between the two groups.

iii Relations with the PA and other aspects of Palestinian society: The refusal in the past of one donor to provide any support to the PA reinforces the Israeli claim that 'there is no one with whom to negotiate'. Donor support and insistence upon reform of the PA unintentionally reinforces assertions by the Israelis that the newly formed and still embryonic Palestinian governmental and public administration structures are a failure. This is not necessarily the case. It should not be forgotten that Palestinians have never had a state and lack the administrative experience of running one. Over 90 per cent of the public administration/governmental functions in Gaza and the West Bank were created after the signing of the Oslo agreement, between 1994 and 2000. A prevailing emphasis on weaknesses in Palestinian society seems to reinforce Israeli feelings that Palestinians are 'not ready' to be peace partners. This judgment has not always held: between Oslo and Camp David, the working assumption of the international community was that there was an effective peace partner on the Palestinian side.

iv Non-coordination: Donors' unwillingness or inability to coordinate certain important aspects of their work makes it easier for Israel to move ahead with various aspects of the occupation. When donors use disagreement among themselves as an excuse for not cooperating, they convey the message that it is legitimate not to cooperate with people with whom you disagree, an attitude that pervades Israeli–Palestinian relations.

v Attitudes: Donor expressions of cynicism, frustration, powerlessness, distrust and even of hatred mirror and possibly reinforce Palestinian attitudes that perpetuate and worsen intergroup dividers. Because much of the programming work with Palestinians is undertaken to ameliorate the impacts of actions by Israelis, donor staff often feel the same antipathy towards Israeli policies and practices that Palestinians feel. These reactions to policy are often translated into feelings specifically towards the Israelis who carry out the policies and, by extension, are generalized to all Israelis. The policies and enactors of those policies may deserve such feelings. The point here is not necessarily that these are inappropriate reactions but that donors, by adopting and mirroring these reactions, reinforce dividers between the two societies rather than reduce them.

vi Words and labels: The acceptance and use of the language of occupation can, in some ways, reinforce its 'legitimacy'. Words that sanitize actions – such as 'incursion' to describe dangerous military entries into Palestinian areas where, at best, people are threatened and, at worst, die – reinforce the 'business as usual' feelings on which Israeli policy depends. Further, labels that apply to entire groups of individuals without differentiating among them, such as 'terrorists' or 'settlers', accentuate dividers. Clearly, not all members of Hamas are committed to terrorism; and although some settlers are driven by ideological zeal, others are living in occupied territories as inexpensive 'suburban' neighbourhoods and would, if politics demanded it, be more easily moved back into Israel's pre-1967 war borders. Political solutions become more possible with recognition of differences within seemingly intransigent groups.

vii Use of history: Many Israelis and Palestinians engage in recitations of history as one way of describing their victimization and explaining/excusing their present actions. Donors also recite histories as a way of explaining why nothing new can happen, possibly reinforcing the likelihood that, indeed, nothing will happen.[91]

An examination of the donor approach to Palestinian institution-building more specifically also highlights some of those points.

6

FUNDING PALESTINIAN ADJUSTMENT

Regime creation and the undermining of Palestinian state-building

By the time Hamas was voted into power, a clear international consensus on the concept of a two-state solution as the best option for peace in the Middle East had emerged, as embodied in the Roadmap of April 2003. This new official stance, coupled with the fact that many Israelis, Palestinians and international bureaucrats believed that the Oslo process had always been about creating such a state, have entrenched the perception a posteriori that international support to Palestinian institution-building had been devised with precisely that intent in mind. As noted by one USAID official:

> From 1993, the US assumed that the outcome of final negotiations will be a state although we were cautious of saying that, as a final status issue, this will depend on negotiations between the parties. But we did not see any other good alternative. So we supported Palestinian institution-building with this objective in mind. Bush's speech in 2002 got us out of the closet. We can now talk about it more openly and we no longer have to be so careful with language, although the PA (not PNA) and the Palestinian Council (not PLC) remain the official line.

Whether this was an American assumption in 1993–1994 or that of other third-party actors is difficult to ascertain, but evidence suggests that, if it was, preparing Palestinians for statehood was nonetheless no one's prime purpose. This chapter looks at the approach and evolution of donor attitude towards Palestinian institution-building in the decade following Oslo, focusing on three key themes: donor budget support, the legitimization of the regime, and the concomitant process of Palestinian 'de-democratization', and reform from 2002 onwards. It contends that although the reform agenda pushed on the PA marked a shift in the international attitude towards the Palestinian leadership, it did not herald a change in its approach from 'regime' to 'state' building, even if greater effort was put into funding a more functional and accountable administration.

Rather, the apparent zeal with which the international community embraced the subject of Palestinian governance and democratization – which ironically occurred when the prospects for the emergence of a Palestinian state had all but

141

evaporated, and after eight years of deliberately disregarding such issues – can be explained as a tactical move within the international community immovable 'aid for peace' strategy, to sustain (or indeed revive) the 'peace process' in the short term and within parameters determined by Israel and the US. Donor attitude to Palestinian institution-building, because it is in essence so political, encapsulates perhaps more than any other sector of assistance the underlying themes of this book: American–Israeli pre-eminence; other third-party actors' attempt to use 'low politics' to influence 'high politics'; the Palestinian leadership compliance; and the consequences this yielded for the Palestinian population of the WBGS, for the Palestinian people, and for the prospect of the resolution of the conflict along a two-state paradigm.

Bailing out the PA: budget support, 1994–1998 and 2000–2005

Budget support: first wave, 1994–1998

As seen in the preceding chapter, donors shifted as early as 1994/1995 from the more traditional investment and technical programme they had envisaged under the Bank's EAP to primarily funding the PA, which was being established and was unable to cover the salaries of its staff, including the police. At the time, financing a government's start-up and recurrent expenditures on such a large scale was unprecedented for international donors. Issues of donor visibility, burden-sharing, fiduciary risk and concern about diverting development funds to finance recurrent, non-sustainable costs make this form of assistance generally unpopular and controversial. To placate home parliaments, a multi-donor Trust Fund administered by the Bank (the Holst Fund) was set up in 1994, with strong external auditing mechanisms. Initially, the Bank, which had never had to act as this type of trustee before, was itself reluctant because of the reputational and fiduciary risks involved.[1]

Nonetheless, the Fund went ahead and in the seven years of operation until it was closed down in 2001, it provided US$222.5 million from 27 donors including the US, for recurrent expenditure primarily to cover the salaries of the staff of the Ministries of Health and Education.[2] Additional budget support was also provided through other channels including direct EU bilateral recurrent cost support to the education and universities sector until 1998 and donor support for police salaries via UNRWA until mid-1995.[3] This UN mechanism to finance the police was agreed upon after considerable delay and discussions, as neither individual governments nor the Bank (through the Fund) were willing to take the risk of transferring these payments directly, although all agreed security was a critical priority.[4]

Finally, as mentioned in Chapter 1, a Tripartite Action Plan (TAP) was signed at the AHLC in Paris in April 1995 by Israel, the PLO and Norway, and subsequently revised, updated and monitored through to 2000. It laid out specific commitments by the two parties and the donors to address the solvency of the PA, general financial and fiscal issues, and the longer-term health of the Palestinian economy. Progressively, the PA succeeded in steadily increasing revenue, through strengthening its domestic tax administration capacities, and establishing an effective revenue system with Israel. Through the taxes it collected on the PA's behalf, Israel provided between 60 per cent and two-thirds of the Palestinian total revenue on a monthly basis.[5] According to the IMF, by 1998, the PA recurrent budget was broadly in balance.[6] From then on, donors thus ceased to finance PA recurrent costs (although they continued to fund all capital expenditures and the PA was never able to allocate a portion of its revenues to public investment) partly as the result of the improved budget situation, but also because of growing concern regarding PA financial accountability and transparency. Nonetheless, after the ascension of Israeli Prime Minister Netanyahu in 1996 and warnings that Israel might cease to remit tax revenues to the Palestinians, transfers were actually frozen for a few months in the summer of 1997; the EC established a Special Cash Facility in 1997 which could be activated rapidly in the event of a future freeze of tax transfers, which did not happen again until after the beginning of the *intifada* in December 2000.[7]

Even if criticized by Palestinian NGOs (who saw their own funding shrink),[8] it was logical, within the parameters of Oslo and given aid's political rationale, that donors initially devoted such high levels of funds to budget support, including funds for the Palestinian security apparatus. Again, optimism was running high and Palestinian expenditure mechanisms were in need of a major overhaul after more than two decades under the Israeli Civil Administration. The interim agreements were still being negotiated, and the PA was starting from scratch without sufficient revenues to meet the basic costs of running social services and the nascent administration. In this context, it is difficult to see how the PA would have been able to establish itself or survive the first few years without external financial assistance. Although the Holst Fund took time to start disbursing funds, it allowed for effective donor monitoring through a unified disbursement procedure, thus also easing transaction costs and the administrative burden on the PA.[9] It subsequently became a model for future multi-donor trust funds administered by the Bank in other post-conflict settings such as Bosnia-Herzegovina, East Timor and Afghanistan.[10]

For its part, the TAP was a helpful mechanism for drawing the parties' attention to essential actions needed to be taken in the fiscal, financial and economic spheres, most notably with regard to freedom of movement, accessibility to external markets and PA transparency. However, according to the periodic TAP status reports to the AHLC, most of the provisions, and Israeli and Palestinian commitments, went unfulfilled. Frustration was frequently expressed by donors at the lack of progress but they did not exercise any substantial leverage with either of the parties to ensure compliance.[11] With regard to the Palestinians, the donor community did not weigh in more forcefully on the side of sound, long-term fiscal and institutional development because of immediate pressures to prevent any interruption in the flow of financial support, and because of the political and socio-economic functions of aid. As mentioned, patronage – through public hiring and the provision of 'walking money' – was seen as necessary to ensure the stability of Arafat's regime, even if simultaneously – and in a somewhat contradictory manner – donors repeatedly stated that the consolidation of all public accounts under the control of the Palestinian Ministry of Finance (MoF) 'should be given utmost priority'.[12]

Similarly, despite repeated (and repetitive) emphasis at donor meetings through to 2000 that the fact that nearly all the total of its current expenditures was spent on recurrent costs (and principally salaries) was a 'serious cause of concern', donors did not take firm action beyond declaratory condemnations against the excessive growth of the wage bill and unsustainable public sector hiring.[13] This performed a clear welfare function. As recalled by a World Bank official:

> Very rapidly, it became clear that there would be no real economic opportunity because of closure and a continuation of the occupation. At the same time, the personnel of the PA grew dramatically, diverting money away from investment, but sustaining a patronage system and acting as a job-creation machine. I remember arguing with Arafat about why he was absorbing more and more funds. His reply was: when you see an 18-year-old in the street, do you prefer to let him go to Hamas or enrol him in the police?... This was a huge issue in 1996/1997. We discussed it at LACC, JLC, etc., but donors decided that it was important to stabilize the situation. There was a sense that there was not much of an alternative. But once you allow this principle and let the recruitment of the PA be used as a political and social instrument, then you give up on the notion of professional civil service and police. It became too politicized. In this context, there is no way you could have had an efficient civil service structure.

Donors equally failed to encourage a more participatory budgeting process, and the open legislative scrutiny of the budget by the PLC.[14] No real pressure was exerted on the Palestinians on specific issues of governance such as the rule of law and human rights, even if these were extensively discussed at donor meetings, particularly from the late 1990s.[15] As for the monopolies, there was also little incentive for third parties, concerned as they were with ensuring the continuation of Israeli–Palestinian negotiations, to disrupt what were essentially private Israeli–Palestinian deals. As explained by two American diplomats:

> The monopolies were a derivative of agreements reached between Palestinians and Israelis. There was a recognition that Arafat should have direct control over some funds. From an Israeli point of view, this enabled them to buy Palestinian leadership for political purposes. This

was understood by donors and not directly addressed because this took place between Palestinians and Israelis, at a very high level. What it was all about was clear but we put it on the side even though it ran counter to good governance practice.

PA corruption within the context of the Middle East is qualitatively less than in the rest of the world. It is not as bad as the press made it. On the whole, there was some very good control over donor assistance, a tight Holst Fund monitoring mechanism as well as bilateral donors' audits. Our funds were not mishandled. But there were two big loopholes. First, Mohamed Rashid's arrangements with the Israelis. Donors were aware of the monopolies, although we had no clear sense of what the scale was or even really that it was being used for corrupt practices. Mohamed Rashid's intention was to build up a private resource for the PA and reinvest in other things like casinos and other PA investments abroad. He was very secretive about it all. As early as 1996/1997 donors started to ask questions and demanded information. But Israel was not interested. Corruption was not an issue for the Israelis until they pretended to be convinced that money was being diverted to terrorism. From the late 2000s, Israel suddenly got interested and began to make a fuss.... Second, there was the ability of the security services to extort funds as 'protection rackets'. This the international community could also not monitor.

Furthermore, there was a sense that donors needed to display some leniency vis-à-vis the PA not only because of the difficult socio-economic conditions on the ground, but also to compensate for the absence of progress on peace negotiations. This would also 'assist' the PA to accept lesser political goals. As pointed out by a Bank official:

Donors allowed this to happen because of the prevailing enthusiasm – about being directly involved in the creation of a state – and because it was seen as important to spend a lot of money on institution-building, at least on paper. They did not put enough emphasis on proper financial PA management and did not exert more pressure because of the political games being played here. It is a game of trade-off. The PA was given something in return for Israel not delivering on the peace process. This was a sort of 'gratification' in compensation for Israeli political obstructionism. Donors did not insist on accountability and transparency in part because they felt guilty for not insisting at the political level on a process that Israel had sought to derail. As no state was actually being established, donors poured in ever more money to keep PA officials satisfied and have them accept the status quo. We give you money, you abandon the revolt, the occupation, the liberation. Look at

145

the deals concluded by the PA after 1996 with radical groups. Everyone knew that the money was siphoned off and going to security services and extremist groups for 'political' stability reasons.

The US Congress nonetheless passed legislation in 1996 prohibiting the US from continuing to provide direct budget assistance to the PA. A US official noted:

> At the development level, there was an appreciation of the problems of corruption but the diplomatic level did not provide any backing. Instead of pressuring the PA to do a better job, we simply stopped giving them money. We did not do it with carrots or the aim to have political reform. We simply protected ourselves.

Budget support: the return, 2000–2005

The *intifada* resulted not only in a general compression of the economy resulting from conflict, closure and curfews, but also in Israel withholding PA tax revenues between December 2000 and 2002. As a result, the PA was able to collect an average of US$21 million per month, compared to around US$88 million per month in 2000 and monthly budget needs in 2001 estimated at US$90 million under the austerity plan, enacted following the outbreak of the crisis. Donors responded by resuming budget support but on a much higher scale than in the 1990s.

By mid-2001, Arab League donors were contributing US$45 million a month in budget support (through the Islamic Development Bank) and the EU another US$9 to 10 million.[16] In 2002, 50 per cent of all donor disbursements went to budget support (both the PA and municipalities) for a yearly total of US$519 million (out of which 84 per cent went to salaries)[17] – more than a doubling of what was provided for by the Holst Fund during its entire existence between 1994 and 2001. Budget support continued through 2003, 2004 and 2005. In January 2003, in an atmosphere of overall donor fatigue and a mounting humanitarian crisis and after American intervention, Israel resumed the regular transfer of PA tax revenues and also rebated part of the revenues it had withheld since 2000 which, by the end of 2002, was estimated to be about US$480 million. Fiscal revenues thus increased from then on. However, the PA budget remained strained because of continued macroeconomic recession, the burden of paying outstanding municipal bills to Israeli suppliers, and an expanding wage bill. Public sector employment grew by 5,300 in 2003 (including 3,443 Palestinians hired in the security sector) and public sector salaries went up 15 per cent. As of early 2004, external budget support continued to represent just under a third of all international disbursements to the WBGS.[18]

Such high levels of recurrent cost support were justified both politically (to sustain the PA pending statehood and as a negotiating partner for when the 'peace process' was back on track) and in terms of the maintenance of vital public services.[19] This type of support was considered by the Bank to be the most effective 'welfare' instrument employed by donors, in comparison to food aid, cash payment schemes and job-creation programmes. For instance, the Bank estimated that

> in 2002, some 75,000 households (half a million Palestinians or 15 per cent of the population) were paid their salaries through donor budget support, and that this prevented perhaps 100,000 people from falling into poverty. Civil servants' salaries were also an important part of total consumer demand for goods and services.... Budget support injected in 2002 alone is estimated to represent about 15 per cent of GDP.[20]

Between 1996 and 2002, no US assistance went to the PA directly. A Congressional waiver enabled the government to do so for a one-off payment of US$20 million in early July 2003 to finance utility payments and repair and rehabilitate municipal infrastructure.[21] One US official commented:

> It was the first time ever that we gave money directly to the PA. The context was that of the Roadmap, of the appointment of Abu Mazen as Prime Minister, so the money was intended to push for the Roadmap, give support to Abu Mazen, reward the Palestinians for their progress in the field of financial transparency (led by Minister Fayyad) and for the general improvement of the political situation. It was also the run-up to the Iraqi war, lots of money was being given to everyone including US$50 million to the Palestinians, out of which US$20 million went directly to the PA. We held lots of consultations with Congress and in-house with lawyers. The provision in the legislation that prevents direct aid to the PA includes a presidential 'national security waiver'. It would have taken too long to make the case, so we decided to use section 451 of our Foreign Assistance Act (1961) which provides for 'unanticipated contingency'. This is used rarely, but Congress approved and Abu Mazen was invited to the White House.[22]

In December 2004, President Bush again approved US$20 million in direct assistance to the PA to pay off overdue Palestinian bills to Israeli companies.[23]

In addition to a difference in scale, and to the fact that donors in the 2000s sent their money directly to the MoF (as opposed to individual ministries, as with the Holst Fund), there was another fundamental distinction between the provision of direct budget support in the 1990s, and during the *intifada*. The EC, which after the Arab League was the largest contributor to recurrent costs, and provided on average US$10 million per month between 2000 and 2002 equalling a total disbursement of €246 million, attached conditionality to its support.[24] As will be developed in the last part of this chapter, this should be contextualized within the broader reform effort, initiated by the donor community in mid-2002 and on which the EU had began to focus in the late 1990s well before the widespread interest of the US and other donors. However, conditionality[25] became a necessity, given the numerous allegations by the GOI, pro-Israeli groups in Europe, and MEPs concerning Arafat's misuse of EU funds to finance terrorism.[26] The European Anti-Fraud Office (OLAF) investigated those allegations between February 2003 and March 2005. In August 2004, its intermediary assessment was that there was 'no evidence that the EU non-targeted direct budget assistance was used to finance illegal activities, including the financing of terrorism', a conclusion which was confirmed in 2005.[27]

Nonetheless, the virulence of the attacks was so forceful and so time-consuming for EC bureaucrats working on the Israeli–Palestinian file that it goes some way to explaining why the EU decided to suspend direct budgetary support on a bilateral basis in 2003.[28] The official reasons were that the PA had not met all the required conditions and that Israel had partially resumed tax revenue transfers, which had provided the main rationale for European budget support in the first place.[29] The truth, however, is that by 2003 it had become too risky for the EC to continue to shoulder non-targeted budget support alone, without the full involvement of other international donors and the active monitoring of the IFIs. Political pressures in Brussels and Strasbourg were just too strong.

As the EC withdrew its budget support and a general sense of donor fatigue set in, prospects were bleak that the PA would manage to raise sufficient funds to meet its continuous budgetary needs, and avert a severe crisis. The idea was thus floated to establish a new trust fund to provide multi-donor budget support to the PA. The Public Financial Management Reform Trust Fund, which became operational in April 2004 and was administered by the Bank, built on the EC conditionality mechanisms and the wider international approach to Palestinian reform by establishing a new series of benchmarks to be fulfilled by the PA. These conditions anticipated improved financial transparency and, most critically, the provision of budgetary and fiduciary assurances to donors sufficient to ensure their continued financial support.[30] In 2004, the Reform Trust Fund disbursed US$123.4 million from nine donors, with the EC being the largest contributor. This represented half of the total external budget support provided for in 2004 which amounted to US$352 million.[31]

That the EC continued, through 2004 and 2005, to be the main provider of budgetary assistance suggests that the decision to stop budget support in 2003 had more to do with issues of political risk than with the above-mentioned reasons given at the time. This is all the more clear given that between the time that it discontinued direct budgetary assistance in 2003 and the establishment of the Bank's Reform Trust Fund, the EC in fact continued to fund PA expenses directly. However, it was no longer assistance for general budget expenditure. Instead, a new instrument of targeted support linked to financial reform-related conditions was put in place to enable the PA to pay off its arrears to small and medium-sized enterprises, and for social expenditure: €90 million was allocated to this new facility (including €10 million for TA), or roughly what the EC had disbursed in direct budgetary support from 2000 to 2002, which amounted to between 90 and 100 million yearly.[32] Although the US was one of the most vocal advocates for the creation of the Reform Trust Fund, recognizing that the PA 'desperately needed some money', it did not provide any funds to the Fund. As explained by an American diplomat:

> The 20 million we gave [in 2003] reflected a particular set of circum-stances that allowed us to do so politically. The prospect of aid is con-tingent on both how money is used and the general political situation. It is currently impossible to think about such a move. There is a high degree of frustration vis-à-vis the PA which is unable to deliver on security and comply with the Roadmap. But let's see what happens with Gaza.

The Reform Trust Fund allowed for the continuation of budget support which donors might otherwise have been reluctant to provide, given the overall political atmosphere. But, notwithstanding all the publicity around the establishment of this new mechanism, the benchmarks were not actually new and were narrowly focused on public financial management, as made clear in the title of the Fund. While trans-parency and accountability may have been enhanced, revenues and expenditures continued to expand (largely through a continuously growing civil service wage bill and a large public sector salary increase in 2003), further weakening an already fragile fiscal situation.[33] For instance, in 2004, about 65 per cent of the PA total expenditures – US$1,344 million – were devoted to the PA wage bill.[34]

Furthermore, as with the Holst Fund in the early 1990s, donors did not use the Reform Trust Fund to encourage broader institutional and governance reforms. Officially, this did not happen because the prevailing view was that if benchmarks were to be met, they needed to be limited to priority areas within the purview of the MoF. But equally important was the fact that the political and socio-economic stabilization functions of budgetary support remained the same as in the 1990s, and just as compelling. Moreover, by 2004, the reform effort initiated in mid-2002 had largely lost momentum, with donors focusing by then on the Israeli disengagement. As noted by one Bank official with reference to the establishment of the Fund:

> The idea was just brilliant. It is great for the Israelis. They know the PA will be able to continue to deliver public services without too much noise. Of course, this is very short-term, but this will keep the PA alive for another year or so.

Similar to employment-generation programmes and humanitarian aid, budget support deepened Palestinian dependency on external assistance, and primarily served to alleviate the Palestinian economic and budgetary crises brought about by closure and, between 2000 and 2002, Israel's policy of withholding tax revenues. It is thus perhaps not that surprising that, in the words of a World Bank staff member, 'the only donor which clearly stated from the beginning that it would not participate [the US] in the Trust Fund is the one which was pushing the most for its establishment'.

Legitimizing the regime: de-democratizing Palestinian politics

Conferring legitimacy on the peace process: the 1996 elections

Like all other political mechanisms and institutions established in the oPt in the early 1990s, the 20 January 1996 presidential and legislative elections were a direct outcome of Oslo.[35] Within the context of continuing occupation, and the absence of a state, their prime purpose was not to buttress a political transition to national independence, or to lay the foundations for the development of a democratic entity in the WBGS. Rather, the elections were mainly conceived as a way to confer legitimacy on the PA and the Oslo process. As pointed out by Norwegian election specialist Kåre Vollan:

> The rules and modalities of the Palestinian elections, and the nature of the institutions to be elected, were not decided by a provisional government or a constituent assembly as is normally the case when democratic authority is to be transferred to the indigenous population of a territory. In such cases, voting is an act of sovereign self-determination. Even though the Palestinian elections resemble the act of a sovereign people, and by most Palestinians clearly were regarded as a step *towards* sovereignty, the rules of the game – and consequently the design of the future Palestinian political institutions – were decided as much by the occupying power (Israel) as by the Palestinians themselves.[36]

Legitimizing Oslo meant lending legitimacy to Arafat's regime, consolidating the power base of his political faction, Fatah, and locking out of Palestinian politics opposition groups such as Hamas, Islamic Jihad, the Democratic Front for the Liberation of Palestine (DFLP) and the Popular Front for the Liberation of Palestine (PFLP). This was in the interest of both Israel and the PA, with political and financial backing from the international community. The EC, for instance, allocated ECU17 million in 1995 for the preparation and coordination of the international observation mission.[37] This overriding objective explains the peculiar 'majority' electoral system negotiated between the two parties for the PLC elections. It was a unique and archaic system, seldom employed anywhere else in the world, although it had been used in Jordan until the early 1990s.[38]

The WBGS was divided into 16 constituencies with each constituency having a number of seats according to the size of its population. The 'majority' system comprised open lists in multiple-member districts, as opposed to a classic 'majority' system in a single-member constituency.[39] This meant that voters could vote for as many candidates as the number of seats allocated to that particular constituency, the candidates with the highest number of votes being then elected. Christians and Samaritan Jews were given quotas in five constituencies amounting to seven seats out of a total of 88 available. Despite this proviso and the fact that Fatah decided not to run full lists in all constituencies so as to leave some room for the opposition, the majority system in multiple-member constituencies is biased towards the largest political party and discriminates against minorities and the opposition, leaving them dependent on the goodwill of the majority not to run full lists. As pointed out by Palestinian political analyst Dr George Giacaman:

> Falsifying election results is the least sophisticated way of falsifying elections. Before that, there is a stage where you can actually influence elections by devising an election law in a certain way so as to favour some groups to the detriment of others. The PLC has been weak in large part as a result of the 1995 law. The division into small constituencies has reinforced localism and clannism as well as militated against the formation of national political parties. The majority system (as opposed to proportional representation) meant that those who won only got 30 per cent of the vote cast while those who lost got 60 per cent. Finally, as it could not produce a political parliamentary opposition, the election law made it easier to co-opt individuals....An election law determines the future of a political system, its representiveness, inclusiveness and whether it can play a nation-forming function. It is not surprising that Israel is organized according to a single electoral constituency: the idea is to create a nation.[40]

Out of the 88 seats, 51 Fatah candidates were elected, in addition to around 20 Fatah-affiliated independent candidates. Fatah thus made up between two-thirds and three-quarters of the PLC. Arafat was elected President with 88.2 per cent of the vote. The non-participation of the Islamic parties, the PFLP and the DFLP, largely accounts for this result. However, had the opposition parties decided to run, the electoral system would not have guaranteed their fair representation.

Assessed against their own yardstick and that of the international community, the 1996 elections were a success. They resulted in the outcome they had been designed to produce, confirmed Arafat's mandate, and consolidated the political power of Fatah and the PA leadership.[41] Although there were serious allegations of fraud, donors gave the elections their stamp of legitimacy.[42] However, contrary to the optimistic comments of some members of the donor community, the Palestinian elections, which had not been intended to mark a retreat from authoritarianism, did not usher in a democratization process within the oPt.[43] Rather, they reinforced Arafat's authoritarianism and one-party rule: PFLP member Ryad al-Malki called the elections 'the Fatah primaries' and, indeed, in the absence of opposition parties they were mainly about Fatah leaders and activists competing for positions in the new Palestinian administration.[44] This is not to minimize the centrality of the event, nor the enthusiasm it generated. Voter turnout was impressive and so was the number of candidates who decided to run.[45] But given the elections' engineering and the context of continuing occupation, it was hard to view it as a first step towards Palestinian democracy.

De-democratization: the marginalization of the Palestinians from outside

In fact, the elections in the oPt could be said to epitomize the profound Palestinian de-democratization process that occurred in the 1990s. This was the result of the creation of the PA which inevitably led to the fragmentation of the PLO. In the words of Edward Said:

> The PLO has transformed itself from a national liberation movement into a kind of small-town government with the same handful of people still in command. PLO offices abroad – all of them the result of years of costly struggle whereby the Palestinian people earned the right to represent themselves – are being deliberately neglected, closed, or sold off. For the over 50 per cent of the Palestinian people who do not live in the Occupied Territories – 350,000 stateless refugees in Lebanon, nearly twice that number in Syria, many more elsewhere – the plan may be the final dispossession.[46]

The 1995 Palestinian election law stipulated that PLC members shall be considered members of the PNC, a symbolic attempt to uphold the rights in Palestine of all Palestinians irrespective of whether they live in the oPt, or as refugees in the diaspora.[47] Nonetheless, the first Palestinian elections did focus Palestinian energies, and the world's attention, on the WBGS and excluded the majority of the Palestinians from voting. In so doing, they lent force to the broader process of marginalization of the concerns and institutions of the Palestinians from 'outside' and the fragmentation of the Palestinian body politic which accentuated in the 1990s.[48] This process was particularly acute for the Palestinian refugees who are estimated to represent some two-thirds of the Palestinian people, and are living mostly outside the oPt.[49]

As the refugee question was to be tackled during permanent status negotiations, and because it is perceived as one of the most politically sensitive and emotionally charged bilateral issues, the international community simply excluded the refugees as a distinct group with specific rights and needs from the Oslo peace process.[50] As a legacy of the Refugee Working Group (RWG), which had been initiated in 1991–1992 as part of the Madrid peace framework, a number of informal or 'track II' workshops on Palestinian refugees took place in the 1990s and 2000s under the leadership of Canada as Chair of the multilateral RWG.[51] Other more private and confidential meetings on refugees were also convened as part of various informal channels, such as the 'Stockholm track' in the months leading to the Camp David Summit in July 2000.[52]

However, from the outset, this work remained positioned at the margins of official donor intervention. Furthermore, donors focused on the technical, relief and socio-economic dimension of the refugee question: for example, compensation, absorption and resettlement. The fundamentally political nature of the issue – and the implications not only for the resolution of the Israeli–Palestinian conflict but also for Palestinian institution- and state-building, not to mention Palestinian refugees' own needs and aspirations – was left unaddressed.[53] The general supposition was that it would ultimately be resolved through the charity of the international community. According to one EC diplomat:

> The basic assumption was that the refugees would stay where they are except in Lebanon. A solution for Lebanon would have to be found. The symbolic aspect is also very important…The solution would entail an admission of Israeli responsibility that would not carry with it a return but compensation. But then the second obstacle was: who would pay and how much? The moral damage is relatively easy to cost but what about confiscated property? The EC did a survey and concluded that nearly all properties were traceable back to their rightful owners. This means gigantic sums of money. There were some vague expectations that the international community would pay.

And indeed, this is what is reported to have been mulled over by the two sides in the course of the 'Swedish channel' meetings, and formed the basis of both the last Clinton proposal of 23 December 2000 and the unofficial peace plan of 2003 (Geneva Accord) – a vaguely worded declaratory statement on the right of return accompanied by a detailed mechanism to implement and fund what essentially would be the Palestinian refugees' non-return.[54] According to Israeli journalists Uriya Shavit and Jalal Bana:

> The idea was that the international community would contribute US$20 billion over a period of 15 to 20 years to settle all claims of the refugees. The funds would be given as compensation to refugee households and as an aid grant to countries that would rehabilitate refugees. The refugees would be given three options: to settle in the Palestinian state, to remain where they were, or to immigrate to countries that would voluntarily open their gates to them such as Canada, Australia and Norway.[55]

As further noted by Dr Karma Nabulsi:

> A vast wave of policy-oriented academic research was undertaken after 1993, guides by an unspoken understanding that a final settlement would comprehensively ignore refugee rights. It focused instead upon developing mechanisms that would impose this settlement through a system combining compensation, absorption of existing refugee camps in the West Bank and Gaza into local neighbourhoods and of the refugees into host and third-party countries, and the resettlement of some into the West Bank. This was to be done by mutual arrangement between Arab host nations and those members of the international community involved in the peace process. They were to present it to an unresisting refugee population inside and outside the West Bank and Gaza as a legitimate agreement negotiated by the PNA acting in the name of the PLO whose presence and signature would guarantee its legitimacy. Under this policy the PNA became the primary client of the international donor community, and the exclusive focus of both attention and external pressure. The refugees as a group were assessed, surveyed, quantified, classified and tested, and their living standards, housing conditions, and economic and social interests became the objects of study. The refugees themselves, as a people, were nowhere to be found.[56]

As the refugee population did not figure prominently on the political agenda of the international community, neither did funding to sustain their living conditions. This is clearly illustrated by the decline of donor support to UNRWA's regular budget, despite population growth, the rise in the local cost of living and, above all, a substantial increase of overall foreign aid to the Palestinians from 1993. According to Harish Parvathaneni, Chief of the UNRWA Policy Analysis Unit between 2000 and 2005, 1993 marked 'a watershed in the decline of the agency's income'. In effect, UNRWA's general budget remained basically flat in the 1990s. Based on donor pledges to the regular budget, the agency annual increase of income between 1993 and 1999 was about US$1.7 million, as compared to an average annual increase of income of US$12.3 million during the period 1985–1992.[57]

This decline was essentially the result of donors' shifting strategic priorities. As shown, from 1993, assistance to the Palestinians was primarily directed at the PA, and projects in the WBGS as the locus for the peace process. Project assistance directly to the oPt provided more visibility than budget support for a UN agency. The assumption in the early and mid-1990s was also that UNRWA would eventually transfer its personnel and facilities to the PA as the result of the completion of final status negotiations on the refugee question – as made clear by the move of UNRWA headquarters from Vienna to Gaza City in July 1996.[58] So although the PA's territorial jurisdiction was limited to the oPt, and

UNRWA assisted a far greater proportion of the Palestinian population living in the Middle East, donor annual contributions to UNRWA ranged between US$259 and US$341 million between 1994 and 1999, as compared to annual disbursements to the PA between US$420 and US$526 million during the same period. The agency's income based on donor pledges to its non-regular projects (mainly covering field operations and infrastructure projects) also declined after 1993. By 1998, it had fallen below that of any year between 1985 and 1993.[59] Shortfall in UNRWA funding resulted in a variety of austerity and cost-reduction measures as well as in a decline in the standards of the social services provided to the refugees.

The political and financial marginalization of the refugees was primarily the outcome of the fact that the Oslo gradualist approach relegated the question to final status negotiations, itself the result of the fact that the 'ethnic cleansing' and dispossession of more than half of Palestine's native population of 1948 remain to this day unspoken about in Israeli society, and the 'right of return' a non-issue as it is considered as tantamount to the end of the Jewish State.[60] Although the international community's intention was not necessarily malign (to eliminate the Palestinian refugee issue by deliberately writing off UNRWA, as some have argued), the outcome was nonetheless politically damaging, in addition to harming the refugees' standards of living. As with the issue of territory and settlements, the result has also been that a decade later, the international community's collective understanding of the issue is now much closer to the Israeli conception than to that of the Palestinians and international law. In his speech of 14 April 2004 on the occasion of America's official endorsement of Sharon's Disengagement Plan, President Bush stated:

> It seems clear that an agreed, just, fair and realistic framework for a solution to the Palestinian refugee issue as part of any final status agreement will need to be found through the establishment of a Palestinian state and the settling of Palestinian refugees there, rather than Israel.[61]

In addition to prejudging final status negotiations, the exclusion of refugee concerns from the political process was harmful to the Palestinian state-building process. As pointed out by a UN official:

> The political structures set up by the political structures set up after Oslo did not tackle the refugees, which is the overwhelming majority of the population. How do you expect that the created institutions would become the basis for the state?

Reforming the regime, 2002–2005

The origins: the 1999 international task force report on strengthening Palestinian public institutions

The first international attempt to tackle the issue of Palestinian institution-building comprehensively came in 1998. From the outset, Palestinian intellectuals, civil society organizations, reformist PLC members and international human rights NGOs had denounced the nature of the PA. Since the mid-1990s, donors themselves had closely monitored (if not acted upon) the evolution of the PA fiscal situation and institution-building at the MoF through the TAP mechanism and had expressed concerns about the lack of fiscal and financial public management. At times, more general issues of governance were also raised, such as a weak legislative process, the absence of the rule of law and human rights abuses. But as mentioned, the peace process required that donors refrain from criticizing both parties. As recalled by the former American Consul-General in Jerusalem, Edward Abington:

> The Palestinians started pushing for reforms in 1996 with the PLC investigation into PA public finances. But the major reason donors did not do so until later on in the decade was that the focus of the US and Israel in their dialogue with the PA was on security entirely. But, by the late 1990s, the system was clearly under strain and there were a lot of suicide bombings. I held many discussions with Arafat on transparency, the rule of law, enabling legislation, etc., but even then [in the late 1990s] there was no serious pressure on Arafat to reform…Neither the State Department nor the White House mentioned reform in their discussions with him, so Arafat did not take the issue seriously.

Moreover, aside from budgetary and financial and political support for the Palestinian elections, donor projects in the institution-building domain were scarce, and even less expressly targeted at democracy promotion. As an illustration, as late as January 1999, out of the four EU projects under way in this area, three had not been implemented and the last one had not even started, although technical assistance (TA) was provided to some PA institutions such as Palestinian credit agencies and the Ministry of Higher Education under different sectoral classifications.[62] More generally, up until the late 1990s, there had been no 'systematic assessment of the institutions of the PA, its structure and procedures, its ability to set priorities and to allocate resources, and its transparency and accountability'.[63]

With the funding of the EC and the government of Norway, the New York-based Council on Foreign Relations under the initiative of Henry Siegman put together an independent Task Force made up of 17 distinguished international figures, under the chairmanship of former French Prime Minister Michel

Rocard, and 24 experts, most of whom were Palestinians based in the oPt. The principal authors of the 90-page report, which came out in June 1999, were Yezid Sayigh and Khalil Shikaki. The Rocard–Siegman report offered a diagnosis of the state of Palestinian governance, and laid out recommendations to improve the effectiveness and credibility of the PA and its institutions in the areas of constitutionality, the executive, legislative and judicial branches of government, public administration, personnel, planning, public finance, social services, the economy and the police force. The primary audience for the report, which was also available in Arabic, was intended to be the Palestinians themselves (the PA but also civil society) while the international donor community was the second main target, which is partly why a panel of distinguished personalities was set up. As recalled by Henry Siegman:

> The Task Force members were necessary to provide political support and influence not only vis-à-vis the PA but also with regards to donors. But the people who did the work were mainly Palestinians, about 25 people on the ground. The main challenge was for Arafat not to block the initiative. So I went to see him and he agreed that we go ahead. Had he known the results, I am not sure he would have agreed, and indeed when he saw the first draft of the report he tried to kill it and asked me not to publish it. Nabil Shaath [PA Minister of Planning and International Cooperation] called me in NYC and I had to fly to see Arafat. After a long and difficult discussion, I managed to convince him that he should buy into it and that the study will strengthen him in the long run. Eventually, he agreed to embrace it rather than to fight it.

The report was comprehensive in its assessment of Palestinian institutions, provided detailed recommendations, and was fairly balanced in its evaluation of the PA and the various external constraints under which it had to operate. It also rightly emphasized that the main challenge facing the development of sound, accountable, transparent institutions was political rather than technical or financial. However, very little was said about the role played by both Israel and the international community in establishing and bankrolling the PA regime. The onus was on the PA to reform, because it was necessary in and of itself, but also because by the late 1990s it had become apparent to donors that it was politically increasingly difficult and counterproductive to continue to support such a regime. The PA was more and more frequently under attack domestically, in Israel and abroad (where EU allegations of PA corruption had just surfaced). While international support for the peace process had encouraged the creation of such a regime in 1994–1998, the same objective now seemed to dictate assistance to build more efficient institutions. The link was made explicit by the Task Force, although it was not until three years later that it would come to be acknowledged by all donors, especially the US:

Confidence in the Palestinian Authority's institutions affects its contest for legitimacy with elements that reject the Oslo Accords and claim to do a better job than the Palestinian Authority in delivering certain services to the Palestinian people. This confidence bears on the Palestinian Authority's ability to negotiate with Israel and affects Israel's confidence in the Palestinian Authority's ability to implement agreements. Good governance is therefore a necessary condition for the success of the peace process.[64]

However, despite increasing international interest in the late 1990s in Palestinian institution-building, the need to reinforce the democratic legitimacy of the PA, the first explicit international references to a Palestinian 'state', and some modest signs of progress in the financial and economic sphere,[65] the political will to reform was not strong enough, either on the part of Arafat and the PA, or on the part of the donor community, especially the US. Optimism had resurfaced after three years of deadlock in the peace process. Israeli Labour Party Chairman Ehud Barak was elected Prime Minister in May 1999, the Palestinian economy showed signs of revival, political negotiations resumed, and President Clinton was in the last years of his second term and keen to go down in history as the American President who had brought peace to the Middle East. Following the Wye River Memorandum of October 1998, the US approved a US$400 million funding package in addition to its annual pledge to WBGS, intended to ensure that the PA delivered on its security and political commitments and to deter Palestinian unilateral declaration of a state upon expiry of the Oslo process in May 1999. The time was thus not ripe to exert too much pressure on the PA. As explained by a State Department diplomat:

> The Europeans were the first to start pushing. We tended to resist. The argument was that the things we were asking the Palestinians to do on the political level were already difficult enough, so we should not push too hard. Reform became an issue after 2000.... The US did not want to get rid of Arafat until after Camp David and then after the Bush administration came into power. During the Clinton years, the centralization of everything to do with the Israeli–Palestinian peace process was in the hands of Dennis Ross. Some frustration was expressed within the State Department as traditionally it is the Bureau for Near East Affairs which runs that part of the world rather than political appointees. Reform was not a huge issue then, we worked well with Arafat right until Camp David. There was no effort to sideline him, although there was some interest in improving PA financial transparency for the PA's own sake but also to cover ourselves from Congressional criticisms.

Although the US and Israel publicly welcomed the Task Force report, it is reported that they were not particularly thrilled about the perceived interference of such prominent international figures into what they considered to be their *chasse gardée*. But even the Europeans, who displayed more commitment, were not ready to push either.

The onset of the *intifada* resulted in 18 months where emergency assistance was all that the international community was prepared to provide. The gravity of the situation on the ground, coupled with intense Israeli pressure on Arafat, undercut whatever leverage the international community, and reformists within the PA, may have had. The question of Palestinian institution-building did not entirely disappear during those years. The EC, through the conditionality it attached to its budget support from 2001, kept the issue alive. The Bank's *Fifteen Months* assessment of March 2002 refocused donor attention on the importance of enhancing public sector management which it had first exhaustively developed in 1999.[66] However, up until the end of May–June 2002, reform did not figure prominently on the donor agenda. Above all, it lacked high-level international political backing.

The international task force on Palestinian reform, 2002–2005

On 10 July 2002, international donor representatives meeting in London formed a Task Force on Palestinian Reform (TFPR) composed of Quartet representatives plus Japan, Norway, the Bank and the IMF. Its purpose was to guide donors and to monitor the implementation of a fairly ambitious Palestinian reform agenda, as outlined by the PA in its 100 Days Plan approved by the Palestinian Cabinet on 23 June.[67] In London, it was agreed that seven donor reform support groups (RSG) would be created in the areas of financial accountability, market economics, civil society, public administration and civil service reform, local government, elections and the judiciary. These RSGs, in consultation with the relevant Palestinian counterparts, would be responsible for highlighting specific Palestinian commitments, determining benchmarks and identifying areas for donor support. Their input would be compiled into action plans and progress reports on the Palestinian reform programme that would be presented to the TFPR members at both local and capital levels. These reports bore a strong resemblance to the status reports and matrixes produced in the 1990s to monitor the implementation of the TAP, even if they covered more ground. Noticeably, security reform, which was identified as one of the key elements of this reform process, was left outside the purview of the TFPR: it was not even debated that it would not remain an exclusively Israeli/US matter.[68]

The London meeting had been organized in haste. In a matter of weeks, PA reform – and the main recommendations of the 1999 Task Force Report on Strengthening Palestinian Public Institutions – was taken down from the shelf and became priority number one for the Quartet and the international donor community. In the 20 or so days that separated the 100 Days Reform Plan and the London meeting, the Bank was able to put together a detailed matrix fleshing out the PA reform programme and implementation commitments as per the PA plan, which donors would consider as specific indicative benchmarks of success and for which external support would be forthcoming, if achieved. This was the first of a fairly long series of donor action plans and matrixes. Although essentially a Bank document, this first plan was entitled 'Reform Agenda of the Palestinian Government'.[69]

This dual sense of urgency and utmost political importance was largely brought about by the active concern and involvement of the US at the diplomatic level. At the London meeting, the State Department sent Elizabeth Cheney (daughter of US Vice-President Dick Cheney) and then Deputy Assistant Secretary for Near East Affairs, to chair the meeting, highlighting the political significance attached by the White House to the issue of Palestinian governance. Indeed, PA reform had suddenly emerged as a key, self-serving component of America's new Middle East diplomacy. On 24 June 2002, just a couple of weeks before the London meeting, President George W. Bush made a keynote speech in the Rose Garden at the White House outlining his 'vision of two states, living side by side, in peace and security'.[70] But his *vision* was strictly qualified. A 'provisional state of Palestine' would be created only after 'a new and different Palestinian leadership' emerges and 'entirely new political and economic institutions' are established. As he stated:

> Peace requires a new and different Palestinian leadership, so that a Palestinian state can be born. I call on the Palestinian people to elect new leaders, leaders not compromised by terror...and when the Palestinian people have new leaders, new institutions and new security arrangements with their neighbors, the United States of America will support the creation of a Palestinian state, whose borders and certain aspects of its sovereignty will be provisional until resolved as part of a final settlement in the Middle East....A Palestinian state will never be created by terror. It will be built through reform. And reform must be more than cosmetic change or a veiled attempt to preserve the status quo. True reform will require entirely new political and economic institutions based on democracy, market economics and action against terrorism...America's pursuing this reform along with key regional states. The world is prepared to help, yet ultimately these steps toward statehood depend on the Palestinian people and their leaders. If they energetically take the path of reform, the rewards can come quickly. If Palestinians embrace democracy, confront corruption and firmly reject terror, they can count on American support for the creation of a provisional state of Palestine.[71]

The creation of the TFPR in July 2002 thus served the broader US objective of regime change and the removal of President Arafat, who had become *persona non grata*. For the next year and a half, political progress (i.e. a return to negotiations with the prospect of perhaps the emergence of a state in the future) would be conditioned on PA reform. Beyond the focus on the removal of Arafat and broader regional considerations, there are several views on how to explain the sudden American fervour with Palestinian reform. In the view of one American official, regime change and reform were in part linked to the necessity to reinvigorate the peace process. In the absence of any meaningful peace process, this was one way for international actors to re-engage politically.

> The EC was the first to push for reform in the late 1990s. We were at the time concerned with building credible institutions but we never made an explicit link to statehood because it was a final status issue. Then the US got a new administration with new priorities. The peace process was not happening on the ground, so the issue was how to get it back on track. We understood the Palestinians needed a political horizon. On 24 June 2002, Bush spelled out the two-state solution; this was the first time the US said so publicly but the underlying assumption was that the Palestinians would have to earn that state. There was a direct linkage between the June 24 speech and the July 10 meeting in London creating the TFPR. The Palestinians rejected the US position vis-à-vis Arafat, but they were on board with the broader need for reform. Our interests also converged with those of the other donors; we all had the same agenda.

A contrasting and much more cynical view prevalent among international observers was that, far from being a means to return to the peace process, reform was actually a means to delay any real progress on the political front, dictated by Israel's interest in removing Arafat and procrastinating on the peace process. This could also be seen as a tactic to defuse international attention away from Israel and back to the PA. As mentioned, the reform process was launched in the wake of the biggest Israeli military operation in the West Bank and at a time when Israel was under intense international scrutiny and the media spotlight. As put forward by Henry Siegman:

> The US shift on Palestinian reform came with President Bush as an expression of support for the position taken by Sharon. It was an expedient way to prevent and delay a peace process that the Israeli government did not want as it became increasingly clear that any political process ran the risk of forcing Israel to go back to 1967. This is something that they want to delay as much as possible so as to create as many facts on the grounds as possible. So the context was a very dishonest one...Palestinians understood it. Certainly Arafat did. And he was not prepared to deal seriously with the issue of terror without any assurance that there would be a return to 1967. By the same token, Palestinian reformers were never able to mobilize properly because of

the political situation. They did not want to be seen as serving Sharon government's agenda of regime change.

Scepticism was indeed warranted, not only because the US had until then exhibited very little interest in the way Palestinians were governed, but also because their enthusiasm for PA reform would be relatively short-lived, except in the area of security sector reform. Other Quartet members and donors who had displayed a more long-standing commitment to reform since the late 1990s had less narrowly defined goals. They actually distanced themselves from the US call for leadership change, as seen, for instance, in the different emphasis found in the various Quartet statements at the time. These statements framed the reform effort within the general context of 'implementing the vision of two states, Israel and an independent, viable and democratic Palestine, living side by side in peace and security', but made no reference to the need for new Palestinian leaders.[72] Yet they had strong extraneous motivations to embrace the US reform agenda beyond the more genuine attempt to curb violence and establish sound institutions as a prerequisite for the governance of a future Palestinian state. Going along with the American-led reform agenda – while distancing themselves from its regime-change rhetoric – was first and foremost a way for other Quartet members to ensure continued American engagement in the peace process. As mentioned in Chapter 4, this was something that both the EU and UN saw as paramount and was one of the main *raisons d'être* of the Quartet.

But there were more specific reasons too. For the EC and EU Member States, PA reform took on three additional objectives. First, given Israeli arguments that it had no negotiating partner on the Palestinian side and perceived prejudice of the US-led regime change agenda, reform came to be acknowledged by the EU as a precondition for rebuilding trust between the parties to ensure a return to political negotiations and therefore re-energize a moribund peace process. The result was that the EU also ended up linking reform with advancing the peace process, but more as a reaction to the Israeli–American position than as a straightforward endorsement of the linkage. Put bluntly by an external observer of European politics in Brussels, 'it was the EU response to Israeli and American arguments that the Palestinians are a bunch of terrorists'. The EU also emphasized that reform will only succeed if the effort is part of a broader political framework – hence the importance of linking the TFPR to the Quartet (political) rather than to the Oslo–AHLC (donor) structure. Reform and the peace process were thus seen as mutually reinforcing.

Second, as developed in the earlier part of this chapter, reform has to be understood in light of the European assistance programme and budget support to the PA, which the EC needed to protect against increasingly virulent accusations that EU taxpayers' money was financing Palestinian corruption and terrorism. There was also a belief that reform, especially of the financial sector, would enhance aid effectiveness across the board. Finally, reform was also a way for the EU to attempt to use the leverage provided by its budget support to the PA to influence the political process, which at that particular time was very much limited to the reform process. This was all the more so as the TFPR was one of the only aid coordination structures where the EU had acquired a non-negligible leadership role. In short, from a European point of view, the reform agenda was necessary for the continuation of its assistance programme, the peace process and its own involvement therein. As recalled by a EC bureaucrat:

> In late 2000/2001, when we first were internally talking about attaching conditions to our budgetary support, the EC local office in Jerusalem tried to push Brussels for fairly tough conditions. Brussels' position back then was that we should be smooth. Thus, for instance, the number of conditions negotiated on the ground for the 2002 aid package was then cut by half by Brussels although they had already been agreed upon with the PA. And then there was the Bush speech, the 100 Days Plan and we could not be tough enough! The current emphasis on reform and conditionality at the headquarters level does not reflect a real strategic shift but is a response to the American/Israeli agenda. It is a pity because we as Europeans could have done the same for a long time and better supported the establishment of credible, transparent institutions.

Between the first TFPR meeting in London in July 2002 and the early 2005s, five meetings took place at the capital level in Paris in August 2002, at the Dead Sea in Jordan in November 2002, in London in February 2003, in Rome in December 2003 and then in Oslo in December 2004. While the local TFPRs were donor-only gatherings, capital-level TFPRs were trilateral meetings, bringing together international members with an Israeli and a Palestinian delegation. Typically, donors would first meet on their own to review the measures accomplished by the PA in each reform area, determine the overall progress achieved since the previous capital-level meeting, and set the priorities for the period ahead. Donors would also examine and discuss the measures taken by Israel to facilitate the Palestinian reform process, principally in terms of easing movement restrictions, easing the PA financial situation and improving the humanitarian conditions on the ground. From 2003, the meetings were convened back-to-back with the AHLCs. As time went by, they also occurred with much less frequency and were shorter in duration, from a two-day meeting in Paris to half a day in Rome and Oslo.

Following the initial excitement surrounding the establishment of the TFPR, the central issue became how to sustain the momentum of the reform process, both on the part of the PA and also on the part of the international community. Significant reform measures did occur between 2002 and 2004, especially in the field of financial transparency, economic legislation and elections, the most noteworthy steps including: the signing of the Basic Law and the Law on the Independence of the Judiciary; the establishment of the position of a Palestinian

Prime Minister in March 2003; the consolidation of all PA revenues into a single treasury account controlled by the MoF; the strengthening of the budget process and of the internal and external auditing mechanisms; the consolidation of PA commercial activities into the PIF; the payment of public servants' salaries (including that of the security services) through bank transfers rather than cash; the partial streamlining of the security services into six sectors; the *de jure* abolition of State Security Courts (which had been established under the pressure of Israel and the US in 1995); the passing of enabling legislation in economic sphere; the beginning of the streamlining of the PA central and local public administration structures; and the establishment of the Central Elections Commission (CEC).

Overall, however, and with the exception of the financial domain, the reform process yielded disappointing results, above all when compared to the international fanfare surrounding its launch, and despite considerable funding in support of its implementation. In addition, until Arafat's death, many of the measures actually accomplished on paper – and thus marked off as successfully achieved benchmarks – remained largely cosmetic. The creation of the post of Prime Minister (under strong Israeli and American pressure as a way to marginalize Arafat) did not lead to its effective empowerment as Arafat retained control. Similarly, despite significant progress in the financial sector, Arafat held on to approximately 8 per cent of the budget for the President's Office. For its part, the law on the judiciary, although passed, was never fully implemented, and after the *de jure* abolition of the State Security Courts, a few instances of summary executions were nonetheless recorded. In fact, one area where almost no substantial progress was recorded was in the area of judicial reform and the rule of law. Finally, although the PA had initially announced that elections would take place in January 2003, they were regularly postponed until the death of Arafat made it an imperative for presidential elections to occur.

The reasons underlying the failure of the reform effort are manifold. First, as international donors recognized time and time again, the environment on the ground and deterioration of the status quo were not conducive to the process. There were the issues, constantly raised with the GOI, of withheld revenues and movement restrictions.[73] For the whole of 2003, the PLC was not able to meet in plenary session except twice, to approve the government presented by Prime Minister Abu Mazen and receive the latter's resignation. In these circumstances, it was difficult to see how any serious progress on legislative matters could occur. The same was true for other PA officials involved in the reform process in simply performing their civil servants' duties, such as judges, election experts and police. Despite video-conferencing facilities, their work – and the implementation of the reform programme – required that they move freely within the WBGS and between the two areas. Furthermore, while the PA was under considerable pressure to reform its finances, the IDF raided four branches of Palestinian banks in Ramallah on 25 February 2004, undermining the stability of the banking system, the credibility of those Palestinian officials working on financial reform and the overall trust of the population in the PA's ability to preserve a minimum level of economic stability.[74]

Faced with far more pressing matters, the Palestinian population consistently ranked the reform process as being one of its lowest priorities, although this did not mean that it did not see the need for reform. Credibility depended on whether the process made a difference to their daily lives or yielded political progress, and neither occurred. As an indication, a poll in October 2003 showed that although 61.4 per cent evaluated the performance of the PA as 'bad' to 'very bad', 58.7 per cent believed that the political situation obstructed the success of the reform effort.[75] Moreover, the ability of any Palestinian leader to quell violence in the absence of significant improvement in the conditions on the ground was questionable. The same opinion poll indicated that 76.8 per cent remained supportive of continuing the *intifada*, while 67.9 per cent believed that Palestinian military operations against Israeli targets were a suitable response during the current political situation.[76] More generally, there also remained the fundamental question of how much institution-building could actually be achieved in the context of a military occupation:

> For a large number of Palestinians, the idea of modernizing the PA and instruments of governance – while under military occupation – is either impossible or meaningless; to them the primary goal of institutional transformation therefore should be to strengthen the Palestinian capacity to challenge the Israeli occupation.[77]

The second reason concerned the issue of timing and the general international attitude toward Palestinian institution-building. As long as the peace process was moving, the international community, including the EU, refrained from criticizing the PA even if there was growing domestic discontent. Donors began to show some commitment to reform at the time when the US that was mainly interested in making Arafat politically irrelevant. This explains why there was considerable external pressure to create a position of Prime Minister, and why the international community disproportionately emphasized reforming the PA finances and security apparatus – the two areas upon which Arafat's power rested. Reform in the financial sphere was also of paramount importance because it directly impacted on the ability of donors to continue their assistance. In the end, the international intervention led by the US discredited the whole process and caused unease even among those within the Palestinian political establishment who had long called for more democratization and better governance. The frontal attacks on Arafat were particularly damaging, since they so intimately mirrored the Israeli 'demonization' of the President. The public perception was thus that reform was externally driven to serve the Israeli–American regime-change agenda, something which in turn was used by Arafat and his supporters to portray the reforms as hurting Palestinian national interests, and to block any real progress.[78]

The issue of elections is a case in point. At the time the TFPR was established, elections were presented as the centrepiece of the reform process alongside financial and security sector reform. Such was the initial importance attached to this area that two separate pre-election assessment missions were financed during the same month of July 2002, one by USAID and the other by the EC.[79] The EC also made known that it would earmark about €10 million (by mid-2003 totalling around €13 million) to finance the process.[80] The date envisaged for national elections was early 2003. Elections at all levels were also identified by civil society and reform-oriented PLC and PA members as the overriding priority in terms of the renewal of the Palestinian political process, legitimatization and accountability.[81] The last legislative elections had taken place in 1996 and there had not been any municipal elections since 1976. Moreover, there was widespread belief that elections would serve as a catalyst for broader reform. However, it soon became apparent that elections within the circumstances prevailing on the ground in 2002–2004 would lead to the re-election of Arafat and considerable gains for Hamas at the local level.[82] Moreover, voter registration turned out to be a sensitive political issue as restrictions on movement hindered the process, and Israel opposed the registration of voters in Jerusalem. Over time, donors, and in particular the US, thus displayed less and less interest, all the more so since there was no progress on the part of the PLC in the drafting of a new electoral law that was needed for elections to be held. The CEC continued to be supported technically and financially, and made some progress on voter registration and its overall operational plan. Yet elections as a political priority disappeared from the international agenda. They were only reactivated after the death of Arafat in November 2004.

From the outset the reform process was conceived as a short-term technocratic exercise rather than a longer-term in-depth political process that should be owned by the Palestinians and address fundamental issues of Palestinian statebuilding. In this respect, it is striking that many Palestinians identified the issue of reform within Fatah as the key to reform the political system, because of the need not only to elect, renew and democratize the Palestinian leadership, but also to build a clearer political programme and make the transition from a national liberation movement to a political party. Yet this issue was never seriously considered by the international donor community, who chose not to engage in the Palestinian political and social arenas. Similarly, very little was done to improve the organizational capacity and performance of Palestinian political parties. This leads us to the third main reason that explains why the reform process hardly got off the ground: there remained strong internal Palestinian resistance, primarily on the part of Arafat and his supporters within the PA. Prime Minister Abu Mazen, who initially tried to move forward on the reform agenda, ran into direct conflict with Arafat. The reform process became highly politicized, especially within Fatah. This was one of the reasons Abu Mazen resigned six months after having been appointed. His replacement, Abu Ala, was keen not to repeat the same mistake as his predecessor and showed only nominal support for the process.[83]

Conclusion

Given the mainly instrumental objectives of the reform agenda, it was perhaps not surprising that by the time Arafat died, only limited measures had been achieved in the key donor strategic areas of security and finance. Palestinian political life had not become more democratic (indeed, legislative elections continued to be postponed through 2005 as the partial municipal elections of the end of 2004/early 2005 had resulted in considerable gains for Hamas), the rule of law had not improved, the 'de-democratization' process which occurred in the 1990s had not been reversed, and Palestinians were not any closer to statehood. Under these conditions, it was also not surprising that the TFPR lost steam, replaced as it was by the new 'game in town', Gaza disengagement. This was all the more so since, from 2004, donor concerns about financial accountability (the key to their own programme survival) were being addressed by the new Bank-administered Reform Trust Fund which, like the Holst Fund ten years earlier, continued to disburse a vast amount of unsustainable budgetary support.

CONCLUSION

At least up until the electoral victory of Hamas in January 2006, when the oPt progressively descended into ever more chaos, violence and political in-fighting and the West imposed an embargo on the democratically elected government bringing about the actual death of the PA, many continued to believe that, for all its governance failings, the creation of the PA and a decade of institution-building had laid the foundation for the emergence of a Palestinian state. As noted by one UN official:

> We started at zero, there were no institutions of their own. The Pales-
> tinians had no experience in managing their administration. Now, the
> structures are in place, whether good or whether there is scope for
> improvement is a different story, but there was nothing before. Devel-
> opment should not be overemphasized; we did not start with no elec-
> tricity, no schools, no transport. . . . The main difference as compared to
> 93 is less the number of hospital beds, the number of classrooms and of
> mobile phones than the whole question of ownership. For the first time
> ever, truly Palestinian-owed structures were put in place.

In reality, this book has shown that not only was the PA's capacity strictly circumscribed by the Oslo agreements and continuing Israeli military occupation,
but its functioning has also been almost entirely reliant on funds remitted by
Israel or charitably made available by donors. It should be re-emphasized that
from its establishment to this day, the PA has never been able to contribute its
own resources to public investment and the provision of public services. The
entire public investment programme has been financed by donors, with the
exception of a unique contribution by the PA in 2000 of US$13 million – a
meagre sum compared to the more than US$8 billion provided by the inter-
national community between 1994 and the beginning of 2006.[1] This raises issues
of acute vulnerability and sustainability, especially given heavy demographic
pressures, and has been exposed most forcibly following the decision of Western
donors to suspend direct cash flows to the PA after 2006.

Beyond the wishful aspirations that one day it may transform itself into the governing structure of an inferred Palestinian state, the PA was not conceived and established for that purpose. In practice, it principally acted as a service and job provider for the non-refugee population of the oPt and as a sub-contractor of security for the Israelis within the interim arrangements of self-rule. It was also assumed that, with sufficient co-optation and enticements, Yasser Arafat would deliver on the peace process, notably by forgoing the Palestinian demand for full sovereignty and the right of return: that is to say, that the nature of Palestinian internal politics would evolve from a national liberation movement into a compliant administration without addressing the main issues and grievances which had been the *raison d'être* of this movement in the first place.

Arafat and his clique within the Fatah leadership accepted those terms of engagement. They spent the ensuing decade competing against one another for favours – both internally as part of Arafat's patronage system, and with the Israelis for movement permits, security transactions and business deals, etc. – to maintain positions of power and build their own personal wealth. Thus, for structural, bilateral and internal reasons, the Palestinian regime which emerged in WBGS after 1994 was authoritarian, unaccountable and repressive. Up until Hamas' legislative victory, such a regime was effectively subsidized and maintained by the international community, and in fact since 2006 the same has continued to be the case at even higher levels, although as will be highlighted below, donors have used different channels to disburse funding.

Continuity amidst fragmentation

To this day, there is little indication that the oPt is evolving beyond a permanently sub-sovereign political status. Instead, both Israeli discourse and policy on the ground over the last 14 years has pointed to Israel's resistance to, and active undermining of, a viable two-state solution. Sovereign Palestinian statehood seems as far off as ever. Progressively, Palestinians have been spatially confined to – and now literally fenced off within – areas of high population density from which Israel has been disengaging itself while at the same time maintaining security control and retaining as much strategic land and settlers as possible, especially along the Green Line, in the Jordan Valley and in Jerusalem. As mentioned in Chapter 2, the process of collective dispossession, territorial and demographic expansion which continued to occur in the 1990s and to this day bears striking similarities with the Allon Plan of 1967, whereby large portions of the oPt were to be annexed to Israel while the Palestinians would live in autonomous enclaves. At the time, the idea was that these pockets would have an administrative link to Jordan. After Oslo, the PA was created to police and cater for the basic needs of the population, but the overall vision remained very much akin.

In this respect, Ariel Sharon's conception of a Palestinian 'state', as articulated over the last few years when he was Israeli Prime Minister, is telling because it laid out what a contemporary version of the Allon Plan may look like.

For Sharon, a Palestinian state did not imply a return to the 1967 armistice line, nor did it entail full Palestinian sovereignty, and certainly not over East Jerusalem. It was based on 'transportation' rather than 'territorial' contiguity, and was essentially made up of Gaza and isolated pockets of territory in the West Bank forming three main demographic enclaves, separated from one another by the Separation Barrier delineating the main settlement blocs (the Ariel, Jerusalem and Etzion blocs) and linked through tunnels or bridges, and with no joint external border on the east with Jordan (Israel retaining control of the Jordan Valley as well as all land transit points and airspace). Sharon's conception of a Palestinian 'state' was in fact not so different from either Rabin's conception of Palestinian self-rule or the quasi-sovereign 'Bantustan' model of apartheid South Africa, a comparison which he is reported to have made himself in private.[2] As pointed out by Israeli political columnist Akiva Eldar:

> Such semantic exercises [such as 'transportation contiguity'] serve Sharon in bridging between the aspiration that Israel hold on to at least half the West Bank, the international consensus that the Palestinians deserve an independent state, and Israel's demographic interest. After the Oslo Accords, Sharon gradually recognized that terms like 'self-government' and 'autonomy' had become outmoded as models for long-term solution. He realized that the interim agreement had in fact turned areas A into autonomous regions, and that under final status it would be necessary to go one step further.[3]

In this context, it was not surprising that Sharon publicly described Gaza disengagement as 'a blow to the Palestinians, in that it will force them to give up on their aspirations [to statehood] for many years to come'.[4] And indeed, far from being the first step to a return to the Roadmap towards a supposed two-state solution, the Israeli unilateral move proceeded from the exact same logic. As stated by Sharon on the eve of the withdrawal: 'Gaza cannot be held on to forever. Over one million Palestinians live there, and they double their numbers with every generation.'[5] A few days before, the Israeli daily *Ha'aretz* published a leading article entitled 'For First Time, Jews Are No Longer a Majority Between the Jordan and the Sea'. It showed that the proportion of Jews living in the 'territories under Israel's control' (Israel, WBGS) stood at 49 per cent, but would jump to 56.8 per cent following disengagement. This would ensure 'a Jewish majority within Israeli territories [Israel, West Bank] for the next 20 years', according to Israeli demographic expert Professor Sergio Della Pergolla.[6]

In addition, as the world extolled Israel's evacuation of about 8,000 settlers from Gaza in the summer of 2005, the settler population in the West Bank has continued to expand. In the first nine months of 2005 alone, the number of Jewish settlers in the West Bank increased by an estimated 12,800.[7] By 2008, it is estimated that about 270,000 settlers live in the West Bank, in addition to approximately 200,000 Israelis living in East Jerusalem. Finally, the Wall's construction is proceeding rapidly and Israel is consolidating its control over a vast area in and around Jerusalem.[8] These continuing developments on the ground were consistent with a new Israeli unilateral disengagement initiative as articulated in the spring of 2006, Prime Minister Ehud Olmert's 'Convergence Plan', which proposed to settle Israeli final borders unilaterally over the next few years, along a perimeter defined by the Barrier and including major areas in East Jerusalem, including the historic and religious sites, the main West Bank settlement blocs and the Jordan Valley.[9]

Fragmentation and the creation of a demographic and territorial fait accompli is testimony to the fact that the traditional Israeli national narrative and policy towards the Palestinians was not fundamentally altered after Oslo. If the Declaration of Principles led to the recognition by Israel of the PLO as the representative of the Palestinian people, in part the result of an acknowledgment of the demographic reality in the WBGS and the need to begin separating both peoples so as to preserve the Jewish character of the State of Israel, it did not lead to the recognition that the Palestinians also had legitimate and equal national rights to either the land or a sovereign state. Oslo did not entail a shift in the Israeli national consciousness from the mythical Zionist vision of the Jewish homeland as 'vacant' at the time of the return of the 'nation' towards the acknowledgment of the 'bi-nationality' of the land.[10] Tragically, as perceptively observed by Israeli historian Ilan Pape in his recent book on the 1948 war:

> The ideology that enabled the depopulation of half of Palestine's native people in 1948 is still alive and continues to drive the inexorable, sometimes indiscernible, cleansing of those Palestinians who live here today. It has remained a powerful ideology today, not only because the previous stages in Palestine's ethnic cleansing went unnoticed, but mainly because, with time, the Zionist whitewash of words proved so successful in inventing a new language to camouflage the devastating impact of its practices. It begins with obvious euphemisms such as 'pullouts' and 'redeployment' to mask the massive dislocations of Palestinians from Gaza and the West Bank that have been going on since 2000.[11]

For its part, the Palestinian leadership must also acknowledge its role in the deterioration of the situation. Arafat made some poor strategic choices, first and foremost, it could be argued, by undermining his own negotiators in Washington in the early 1990s and opening up the Oslo Channel.[12] Thereafter, he exerted the limited powers he had been granted under the interim agreements by acting as if the autonomous areas were his own property, the funds he received from Israel and the international community were his own personal wealth, and the Palestinian population were his lawful subjects. He divided and ruled, distributed favours and rents to those who helped him stay in power, and simultaneously repressed and tried to co-opt those who challenged his authority. He was reactive to Israeli and international diplomatic initiatives and did little to develop a national strategic vision which could have guided donors in their support for Palestinian development. He also failed to rein in violence and stop terrorism against Israelis. He succeeded in maintaining his position, but his regime – and his party Fatah – grew increasingly unpopular and unstable, in a context where it had failed to uphold Palestinian resistance and national revendications, to ensure the basic safety needs and protection of the population under its jurisdiction, as well as to deliver on peace, socio-economic development, the recovery of Palestinian national rights and the creation of an independent state. We are reminded here of Rousseau's famous passage in the *Contrat Social*:

> The strongest man is never strong enough to be master all the time, unless he transforms force into right and obedience into duty.... To yield to force is an act of necessity, not of will; it is at best an act of prudence...Since no man has any natural authority over his fellows, and since force alone bestows no right, all legitimate authority among men must be based on convenants.[13]

As a result, Palestinian violence against Israelis was rekindled on a large scale and domestic politics was gravely radicalized. Furthermore, while the PA leadership was concerned with high politics and its personal survival, Hamas broadened its appeal as an organization not only resisting Israeli occupation but also very much attuned to the needs of the Palestinian population, notably through its extensive social network of charitable Islamic organizations. Nevertheless, if the PA bears a share of responsibility for the way events unfolded, the international framework arguably remains the determining parameter. As seen, the situation is acutely asymmetrical, given the imbalance of power and Israel's disproportionate control over every aspect of Palestinian life and territory.

'High' versus 'low' politics

Despite suffocating and consistently deteriorating Palestinian conditions on the ground which became increasingly more discernible as the decade unfolded, international donors chose to remain steadfastly engaged, even if these conditions imposed critical limitations on the avowed political purpose, effectiveness, sustainability and legality of their intervention.

This book has argued that a main reason for this misguided policy has been that the provision of aid to the Palestinians was above all a function of their relationship to Israel and to the US. Furthermore, one overriding consideration has been donors' desire to be and to remain involved in the resolution of one of the most high-profile conflicts of the planet. Within the current power configuration, assistance to the Palestinians has provided a means to be part of a process from which donors would otherwise have been excluded, because of the Israeli–American pre-eminence and the inability of other states, notably in Europe and in the Arab world, to agree on a common policy. As Israel and the US dominated the diplomatic arena, effectively stifling the development of any alternative political vision and discourse, foreign aid remained the one level of intervention accessible to other third-party actors.

Although the specific reasons why bilateral donors and international organizations proceeded the way they did have been manifold, and a function of each actor's complex relationship to each party to the conflict and to the other international players, at the general level there has thus been an inverted relationship between political influence on the peace process and financial investments in the WBGS. The less access actors had to 'high politics', the more they pushed for a place in 'low politics'. Of course, it was not an entirely cynical enterprise. The hope was that the provision of assistance and funds to the Palestinians would in turn give donors ammunition to influence American unilateral mediation efforts and Israeli policies on the ground. But it did not. Courting the US and appeasing Israel only just about enabled donors to stay relevant – by doggedly adhering to a process characterized by excessive pragmatism and diplomatic accommodation – and to show the world (or, if not that, then convince themselves) that 'something' was being done for the Palestinians. Over time, classic sunk-cost arguments of the type found at the time of the European decolonization process and based on the notion that past investments could not be allowed to be wasted were also used to justify continued support. In short, aid to the Palestinians has only marginally been about the Palestinians and their needs. It has first and foremost been about donors themselves, and about them and Israel.

Devastating consequences

However, by using aid to the Palestinians as a 'fig leaf' for the absence of progress in a diplomatic process and their inability to exert any determining political influence, donors have been complicit in some of the major structural defects of the peace process itself and, above all, in some of its perverse consequences. Aid has performed a critical emergency relief function and temporarily acted as a social and political safety valve. But by sustaining such high levels of funds over such a long period, donors also bankrolled a poorly run and increasingly disliked Palestinian regime, subsidized Israeli military occupation, and indirectly encouraged the continuing colonization and fragmentation of the oPt, as well as the broader process of Palestinian dispossession.

In so doing, Israel was absolved of its obligations vis-à-vis the Palestinian civilian population as the Occupying Power under the Fourth Geneva Convention. Furthermore, aid has contributed to normalizing the conflict: while humanitarian symptoms were assuaged and a semblance of stability was maintained, there has been less incentive to resolve it. In the process, ODA also acted as a diversion. As the international community focused on aid to the Palestinians, it simultaneously gave Israel the diplomatic space to pursue its policies on the ground, reinforcing further the asymmetrical nature of the conflict. Finally, the cognitive gap between Israelis and Palestinians has arguably widened during the

Oslo years, by raising to ever more extreme thresholds both populations' perceptions as to the compromises that might be necessary to resolve the conflict.

As witnessed in other regions of the world, aid is a poor substitute for politics, particularly in transitional and conflict settings. In the absence of a political strategy for ending a conflict and bringing peace, the transformative impact of international assistance is extremely limited, if not negligible. As mentioned in Chapter 1, one major lesson learned from other crises is that uncritical aid-giving may actually exacerbate and prolong a conflict. In this particular case, the *intifada* clearly showed that cushioning the harmful impacts of Israeli policies on Palestinian territory, economy and society – by giving money to the Palestinians – encouraged, rather than disheartened, Israeli measures. Donors did not even manage to prevent Israel from destroying much of the infrastructural and institutional projects they had financed in the WBGS between 1994 and 2001.

Renewed violence, chaos and lawlessness in the oPt also exposed the pitfalls of having facilitated the establishment of a dysfunctional interim institution such as the PA without the independent authority or resources to maintain effective control and raise its own finances. As donor attitudes to the Palestinian regime and notably its internal management practices rested largely on Arafat's compliance and progress in the peace process, they were eventually altered in the post-Camp David period. But the reform initiative came late. It was superficial, self-serving and narrowly conceived. It rapidly lost steam and became one additional, rapidly forgotten, international initiative to further the Middle East Peace Process (superseded by the new, equally rapidly forgotten 'games in town': Gaza disengagement, Hamas government and so on).

At the same time, however, the *intifada* did not induce a similar determination on the part of international actors to intervene politically or economically to exert pressure on Israel or use comparable conditionality to influence Israel's policies. Again, this can be explained in large part by the current international balance of power, divisions among Western states, and the dismal nature of domestic politics in the Arab or Islamic world. At a level of analysis further down, this is to be linked to the influence of domestic politics on foreign policy and to the powerful effects of the deliberate instrumentalization of anti-Semitism and the Holocaust by some. The virulence of the attacks unleashed by extreme elements within the pro-Israel camp against individuals and institutions that disapprove of the actions of the Israeli government publicly paralyses and silences many in the policy-making and media circles. By the time Hamas was elected into government, the PA thus remained the primary client of the international donor community, even though more than a decade of peace implementation had demonstrated that exclusive focus on the PA – in a dual context of conflict and occupation where it was merely the 'recipient' of aid but neither sovereign nor 'host' – had resulted in a set of disastrous outcomes.

174

Epilogue: aid to the Palestinians after Hamas' electoral victory

At first glance, the electoral victory of Hamas seems to have drastically altered the situation. It has led Western donors – primarily the EU as the largest contributor – to suspend direct budgetary support to the PA because they consider Hamas to be a terrorist organization. This decision certainly represents a marked departure from the Arafat era, not least for the state of the PA's coffers and the inability of the new government to pay the salaries of its staff and therefore the livelihoods of a great proportion of the Palestinian population. The World Bank estimated in May 2006 that with about 172,000 persons receiving some sort of payment from the PA (with about 150,000, including security personnel, directly on its payroll), 30 per cent of the Palestinian population were dependent on the PA.[14]

Yet despite the newness of the situation, the discussions which took place at the diplomatic and donor levels sounded remarkably familiar. They have revolved, as most donor discussions had over the previous 12 years, around how the international community could continue to channel funds to the WBGS regardless of the legal and political challenges facing donor countries who were directly or indirectly involved in the 'war on terror'. In the post-January 2006 situation, the trick became how to assist the Palestinian *people* while by-passing the democratically elected Palestinian *government* in order to circumvent donors' own legislation.[15] Several ideas were floated. In the early months of 2006, there were talks about how to boost the role of the President's Office so as to disempower the authority of the office of the Hamas Prime Minister Ismail Haniyeh – the very same office that the PA had been pressurized to establish three years earlier as one of the conditions for continuing international aid flows. A proposal for establishing a multilateral funding mechanism, such as a Bank-administered Trust Fund akin to the Holst Fund of the early 1990s, was also considered. Finally, donors pondered the option of substantially increasing the funding of UN agencies and NGOs.

On 9 May 2006, the Quartet announced the establishment of a 'temporary international mechanism that is limited in scope and duration, operates with full transparency and accountability, and ensures direct delivery of any assistance to the Palestinian people'.[16] The EU was entrusted with working out the modalities of such a mechanism (TIM) with the help of the Bank. Six weeks later, the Europeans made their first contribution to the TIM of €105 million to facilitate the direct delivery of assistance to the population of the WBGS through the mechanism's three 'windows' (health, utilities, social allowances) and technical assistance.[17] This sum broadly corresponded to the annual amount the EC spent in direct budgetary assistance between 2001 and 2005. At the same time, the EC also increased its funding to UNRWA and WFP to provide food aid and cash subsidies.[18] And indeed, it is estimated that despite Western donors suspending direct financial assistance to the PA, an unprecedented US$1.2 billion was disbursed to the WBGS for the year 2006. Out of this total, some US$700 million transited directly through the office of President Abbas, the rest through international agencies, whether the United Nations or non-governmental organizations. Not only did this effectively mean the death of the PA and the institutional structure established by the international community, but it also raised, more than ever before, issues of transparency and accountability as these resources were transferred without any legislative scrutiny.

Thus, donors did not use the opportunity brought about by the new Palestinian political configuration to fundamentally reassess their failed 'aid for peace' strategy. The story of the previous 12 years, and especially the surreal situation in which they found themselves on the eve of Palestinian elections in 2006 – providing short-term, unsustainable emergency assistance and pumping large sums of money into an ever more aid-dependent territory which was becoming steadily less viable, politically, economically and geographically – could have acted as a cautious reminder. Instead, third-party actors chose to continue with the well-trodden path of humanitarian and socio-economic 'stop-gap' solutions. As in the 1990s, the TIM initiative and continuing donor assistance has been accompanied by strong international hopes. This time, the initial wish was that, starved of its resources and isolated diplomatically, the PA would accept the political conditions set out by the Quartet immediately after Hamas' electoral victory.[19]

As of the first months of 2008, this wish had not materialized. Instead, and as one might have expected, politically and financially boycotting the elected Hamas government and its administration, while boosting the office of the Fatah president exacerbated the power struggle between the two movements, and between the legislative and the executive branches of the government. This resulted in ever more armed violence between the two clans, the collapse of the national unity government, and the effective seizure of Gaza by Hamas in June 2007 while the centre of power in the West Bank remained controlled by Fatah. Palestinian political fragmentation could not be more conspicuous.

Suspending such high levels of aid; bringing politics back in

If peace cannot be bought, what can be done? The Israeli–Palestinian conflict is complex but arguably no more than other seemingly intractable conflicts. What set it apart from other conflicts are its intricate international, regional, domestic, religious and historical dimensions, not the presumed *sui generis* nature of the conflict itself (one land, two peoples). It is essential to bring substance and politics back in. A diplomatic process is a necessary prerequisite to any negotiated, sustainable peace agreement but only as a means to an end and a vehicle to advance a policy, not as an end in itself in the absence of a coherent policy.

A comprehensive international strategy that addresses the totality of concerns – the security, political, legal, socio-economic and even symbolic aspects of the conflict – in turn implies breaking up the vicious aid circle and suspending such high levels of aid to the Palestinians, while simultaneously stepping up international efforts to protect the civilian population of the WBGS as well as the physical integrity of the occupied territory. It means an integrated and coherent international peace and negotiations strategy linking economic assistance to a clear set of security, political and human rights goals leading to a permanent status agreement and an end to the conflict but, more importantly, an evenly balanced incentive structure towards *both* parties, rather than solely the Palestinians.

This in turn necessitates addressing head-on the root causes of the conflict, the key permanent status issues which Oslo sought to eschew (borders, Jerusalem, refugees, settlements, security and so on). Isaac Deutscher perceptively observed four decades ago:

> A man once jumped from the top floor of a burning house in which many members of his family had already perished. He managed to save his life; but as he was falling to the ground, he hit a person standing down below and broke the person's legs and arms. The jumping man had no choice; yet to the man with the broken limbs he was the cause of his misfortune. If both behaved rationally, they would not become enemies...But look what happens when these people behave irrationally. The injured man blames the other for his misery and swears to make him pay for it. The other one, afraid of the crippled man's revenge, insults him, kicks him and beats him up whenever they meet. The kicked man again swears revenge and is again punched and punished. The bitter enmity, so whimsical at first, hardens and comes to overshadow the whole existence of both men and to poison their minds.[20]

Aid has not been and cannot be the antidote to the Israeli–Palestinian conflict. Going back to Hannah Arendt's injunction at the beginning of this book, only an 'unpremeditated, attentive facing up to, and resisting of, reality' may help the two parties and the rest of the international community to find a durable cure. Beyond the cessation of violence on both sides and addressing the core issues to the conflict, reconciliation will require a critical re-examination of the historical record, notably recognition by Israel of its role in dispossessing half of the Palestinian population of 1948 and in the four decades of occupation of East Jerusalem, the West Bank and the Gaza Strip, and attendant humiliation, oppression and suffocation of the Palestinian population of the oPt. It will also require an acceptance by the Palestinians of the reality of the State of Israel and an unconditional renunciation to indiscriminate violence against Israeli civilians. In short, it will require a critical re-examination of the Israeli and Palestinian respective national narratives, acknowledging the 'bi-nationality' of the land, even if the resolution of the conflict itself need not necessarily end in one, single, bi-national state (but could if the two populations so wished).[21] This entails respecting international law and the rights – collective and individual – of both peoples, notably to address Palestinian grievances and national aspirations, as well as Israel's deep-seated feeling of insecurity in the Middle East. In fact, it may require going back to the pre-Oslo multilateral and rights-based regional approach to solving the Israeli–Arab conflict.

APPENDIX I

Overview of foreign aid to the occupied
Palestinian territory, 1994–2004

These figures and tables on international assistance are drawn from two World Bank reports: *Four Years – Intifada, Closures and Palestinian Economic Crisis – an Assessment* (Jerusalem: World Bank, October 2004) and, for the year 2004, *Stagnation or Revival? Israeli Disengagement and Palestinian Economic Prospects* (Jerusalem: World Bank, December 2004). For the period up until 2003, the information was first compiled and published in Michael Keating, Anne Le More and Robert Lowe (eds), *Aid, Diplomacy and Facts on the Ground: The Case of Palestine* (London: Chatham House, 2005).

* Approximately US$7 billion was disbursed in the West Bank and Gaza between 1994 and 2004, excluding support to UNRWA's regular budget. According to the World Bank, this represents the highest sustained rate of per capita disbursements to an aid recipient in the world since the Second World War.
* Between 1994 and 2000, annual donor disbursements averaged approximately US$500 million per year, or US$150 per capita. After the outbreak of the *intifada*, this figure doubled, reaching the average of US$308 per capita in 2001–2002 and US$258 per capita in 2003. A comparison with other 'high-profile' post-conflict cases makes the amplitude of the aid disbursed to the WBGS clear. In the 1990s, per capita assistance for Bosnia over five years was estimated at US$215 per year, and for East Timor over a two-year period at US$235. Even more contrasting, the net global Official Development Aid disbursement average in 2004 stood at US$13 per capita. (Table A1.1.)

Table A1.1 Donor commitments and disbursements, 1998–2004 (US$ million)

	1998	1999	2000	2001	2002	2003	2004
Commitments:							
Regular (development) support	667	692	852	473	261	326	
Emergency and budgetary support	0	0	121	755	1,266	1,078	
Total commitments	667	692	973	1,228	1,527	1,404	
Total disbursements	419	482	549	929	1,026	883	900

Source: Ministry of Planning and World Bank staff calculations.

Note
Excludes support to UNRWA's regular budget.

• The ratio of emergency to development aid in disbursement terms in 2002 was 4:1, up from 3:2 in 2001. In 2003, the ratio was 3:2, with emergency assistance still in the lead, although budget support disbursements halved in that year (from US$464 million to US$264 million). (Table A1.2.)

Table A1.2 Breakdown of donor disbursements 2001–2003

	2001	%	2002	%	2003	%
Total Disbursements (per capita)	929	100	1,026	100	891 (248)	100
	(300)		(315)	45	264	30
Budget support	540	58	464	36	264	30
Emergency/welfare	214	23	365	19	355	40
Development Aid	175	19	197			
Total without budget support	389		562		619	

Source: World Bank for 2001 and 2002; MoP data and staff calculations for 2003.

• In 2003, the three major donors also ranked highest for contributions to the PA budget, humanitarian aid and development assistance. (Table A1.3.)

Table A1.3 Top ten donors, 2002 and 2003 compared (US$ million)

Donor	2002 disbursements	Donor	2003 disbursements
League of Arab States	316	USAID	224
European Commission	217	European Commission	187
USAID	194	League of Arab States	124
Norway	44	Norway	53
World Bank	37	World Bank	50
Italy	32	United Kingdom	43
Germany	21	Italy	40
Denmark	18	Sweden	32
Sweden	16	Germany	27
Canada	14	Spain	17
Other	117	Other	94
Total	1,026	Total	891
Share of top 3 donors (%)	71	Share of top 3 donors (%)	55

Source: MoP data, World Bank staff calculations.

APPENDIX II

The aid coordination structure during Oslo and the *intifada*

The aid coordination structure as of 2000[1]

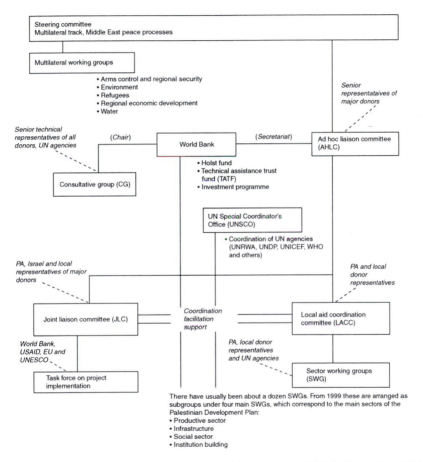

Figure A2.1 The aid coordination structure as of 2000 (source: AHLC, September 1999; Mokoro Ltd, Oxford, July 2003).

The evolution of the coordination structure after 2000

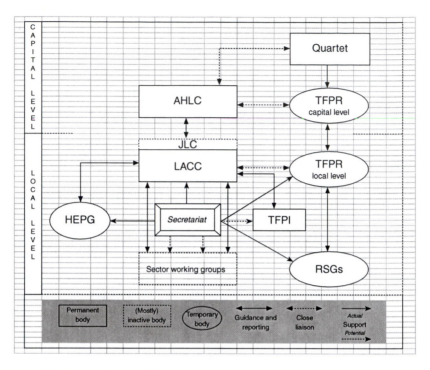

Figure A2.2 The evolution of the coordination structure after 2000 (source: Consultants' interpretation of de facto situation, April 2003; Mokoro Ltd, Oxford, July 2003).

NOTES

INTRODUCTION

1 For instance, in 2004, the World Bank estimated that per capita assistance to the West Bank and Gaza averaged US$310. By comparison, the net global Official Development Assistance disbursement average in 2004 stood at US$13 per capita. World Bank, *Disengagement, the Palestinian Economy and the Settlements* (Jerusalem: 23 June 2004) ii. We may note nonetheless that the level of combined international assistance to the Palestinians is negligible compared to what the US alone allocates bilaterally to Israel. If one includes military and economic aid, loans guarantees and grants, hard and soft money, it is estimated that bilateral American aid to Israel could reach as much as US$6 billion a year.

2 Yasser Arafat died on 11 November 2004. He had been one of the founding leaders of the Fatah movement in the late 1950s, had become the Chairman of the Executive Committee of the PLO in 1969, and was elected President of the PA in 1996, which he remained until his death.

3 As of the mid-2000s, the population of the WBGS was estimated at about 3.8 million (2.4 for the West Bank; 1.4 for the Gaza Strip). This included about 920,000 UNRWA-registered refugees in Gaza and 665,000 in the West Bank, out of a total of 4.1 million refugees registered by UNRWA in its five areas of operation (West Bank, Gaza, Jordan, Syria and Lebanon). The PLO's Department of Refugee Affairs estimated that there were 5.8 million Palestinian refugees worldwide. CIA, *World Factbook* (Washington DC: CIA, 2006). UNRWA, 'UNRWA in Figures', Gaza, March 2004. International Crisis Group, *Palestinian Refugees and the Politics of Peacemaking* (Amman/Brussels: ICG, 5 February 2004) i, 2.

4 Such attributes include few or no functioning institutions, the inability to deliver on basic public goods, the inability to maintain a monopoly over the legitimate use of force in its territory and assure security for its citizens, and the loss of legitimacy. See Sebastian von Einsiedel, 'Policy Responses to State Failure', in Simon Chesterman, Michael Ignatieff and Ramesh Thakur, eds, *Making States Work. State Failure and the Crisis of Governance* (Tokyo: United Nations University Press, 2005) 15.

The distinction is made throughout this book between a 'state' and a 'regime'. Without entering into an epistemological debate on the definition of a state, it is worth keeping in mind both the notion of a 'social contract' as the basis for legitimate state–society relationships in the tradition of Hobbes, Rousseau and Locke, and the classic Weberian conception of a state as a human community associated with a given territory which possesses an administrative and legal order and can claim with success the monopoly of legitimate use of force. The working distinction used throughout this book refers to that proposed by William Zartman in his introduction to *Beyond Coercion: The Durability of the Arab State.* According to him, 'state' refers to a sovereign and authoritative institution which is the receptacle of political legitimacy, power and a set of rules, and is associated with a recognized territory. 'Regime', on the other hand, refers to the group of people who run the state at a given time: 'regimes, administrations or leaders may rise and fall, but only when the nature of the organization and its structures change, can one say a state has been altered'. Regimes are not only linked to a group of people but also to political rules and the way institutions function. Adeed Dawisha and William I. Zartman, eds, *Beyond Coercion: The Durability of the Arab State* (London: Croom Helm, 1988) 8. See also: Jean-Jacques Rousseau, *The Social Contract* (London: Penguin, 1762 (1968 for edition)); Max Weber, *Le Savant et le politique* (Paris: Plon, 1959) 100–101.

5 The Declaration of Principles of September 1993 stipulated a two-stage process whereby the central political issues between the two parties (including borders, Jerusalem, refugees, settlements and security arrangements) would be dealt with in 'final status' negotiations after a five-year transitional period, in the course of which it was hoped confidence between the Israelis and Palestinians would be built. Final status talks never occurred. For an alternative to the Oslo gradualist approach, see International Crisis Group, *Middle East Endgame II: How a Comprehensive Israeli–Palestinian Peace Settlement Would Look* (Amman/Brussels: ICG, 16 July 2002).

6 Conference to Support Middle East Peace, Co-Sponsors' Summary, Washington DC, 1 October 1993, in 'Documents and Source Material', *Journal of Palestinian Studies* XXIII, 2 (Winter 1994), 128.

7 The two-state solution as the basis for a permanent and just resolution of the Palestine question was first articulated by the UN in 1947 and had been the Palestinian leadership's official demand since 1988. However, it was not until the late 1990s, and most forcibly the early 2000s, that an international consensus emerged – at the declaratory level at least – around the notion of a two-state solution as the best option for peace in the Middle East. In 1999, the European Union, which since the Venice Declaration in 1980 had pronounced itself in favour of a Palestinian right to self-determination, gave explicit support for two states. In June 2002, the two-state solution officially became US policy when President Bush spelled out his 'vision [of] two states, living side by side, in peace and security'. This vision then underpinned the international Roadmap for Peace developed by the Quartet in 2002–2003. The Israeli government also indicated in the early 2000s that it was in favour of the creation of a Palestinian state. It should nonetheless be acknowledged that not all members of the international community necessarily subscribed to the same 'vision' of an independent Palestinian state. Indeed, remarkably little thought was given throughout the decade to the attributes – physical and otherwise – of such a state and to what would be its relationships to either Israel or the Palestinian people or nation.

8 The Quartet was established in September 2001 and has since then been the highest multilateral diplomatic forum for the Palestinian–Israeli peace process. It comprises the United States, the European Union, the United Nations and Russia.

9 Avi Shlaim, *The Iron Wall. Israel and the Arab World* (London: Allen Lane, Penguin, 2000) 516–520.

10 This line of thought was particularly popular among Israeli scholars and Labour politicians, Israeli Foreign Minister Shimon Peres being one of the strongest proponents of such an approach, which he developed in his book *The New Middle East*, published in 1993. It was also disseminated in the literature published at the time on behalf of the international community. See World Bank studies such as World Bank, *Developing the Occupied Territories: An Investment in Peace* (Washington DC: 1993); World Bank, *The West Bank and Gaza: The Next Two Years and Beyond*

(1994). However, many Arab economists were a lot more sceptical. See Markus E. Bouillon, *The Peace Business. Money and Power in the Palestinian–Israeli Conflict* (New York: I.B. Tauris, 2004) 1–2.

11 The Roadmap for Peace was developed by the Quartet and presented to the government of Israel (GOI) and PA on 30 April 2003. It was a performance-based, goal-driven plan, with clear phases, timelines and benchmarks, and involved reciprocal steps in the political, security, economic and humanitarian fields with the aim of reaching a final and comprehensive settlement by 2005. It was officially accepted by both parties in May 2003. However, the GOI expressed 14 reservations concerning its implementation, which denoted a departure from not only the wording but also the broad intent of the plan. In any event, implementation of the Roadmap never began.

12 Anne Le More, 'Killing with Kindness: Funding the Demise of a Palestinian State', *International Affairs* (October 2005).

13 To this day, there is no international agreement on what a 'viable' Palestinian state would entail. By a 'viable' state is meant here *inter alia* a sovereign state attached to a given territory, the oPt east of the 1949 Armistice Line ('Green Line') (i) with East Jerusalem at its capital; (ii) whose territory is contiguous such that Palestinians can move freely within it (i.e. within and between the West Bank, the Gaza Strip and East Jerusalem); (iii) which has sovereign control over the movement of goods and people across its national borders; and (iv) which has independent control over its natural resources.

14 The potent narrative which took hold in Israel, the US and Europe after the summit was that President Arafat had spoiled the peace process by turning down Ehud Barak's 'generous offer' at Camp David and purposefully unleashing the *intifada*. This narrative was transmitted to, and uncritically reproduced in the media by, Prime Minister Barak in his final statement of 25 July 2000. See also his statement on his return from Camp David to Israel dated 26 July 2000. This one-sided version remained unquestioned until a year later when Robert Malley, the former Special Assistant to President Bill Clinton who participated in the summit, published a piece in *The New York Review of Books* dispelling the myth of the 'Israeli generous and historic offer'. Other articles on this issue were published around the same time. See Robert Malley and Hussein Agha, 'Camp David: The Tragedy of Errors', *The New York Review of Books*, 9 August 2001; Deborah Sontag, 'Quest for Mideast Peace: How and Why It Failed', *New York Times*, 26 July 2001; Aluf Benn, 'The Selling of the Summit', *Ha'aretz*, 27 July 2001. Clayton E. Swisher, *The Truth about Camp David. The Untold Story about the Collapse of the Middle East Peace Process* (New York: Nation Books, 2004). For an excellent, nuanced and comprehensive analysis of the history of the failure of the peace negotiations during the Oslo years, see Charles Enderlin, *Le Rêve Brisé. Histoire de l'échec du processus de paix au Proche-Orient 1995–2002* (Paris: Fayard, 2002).

15 It is estimated that close to 800,000 people had been uprooted in 1948 (figure cited by Ilan Pappe). Since the late 1980s, the Israeli 'new' historians have critically reassessed what they themselves call 'Israel's foundational myths' and in particular the traditional Zionist narrative of the 1948 war and its aftermath. This group includes scholars such as Professor Avi Shlaim, Dr Ilan Pape and Dr Simha Flapan. Their 'revisionist' analysis was made possible in large part by the declassification of the GOI archives which are governed by the 30-year rule. See, for instance, Eugene L. Rogan and Avi Shlaim, eds, *The War for Palestine. Rewriting the History of 1948* (Cambridge: CUP, 2001). Shlaim, *The Iron Wall. Israel and the Arab World*. Zeev Sternhell, *Aux origines d'Israel. Entre nationalisme et socialisme* (Paris: Fayard, 1996). Ilan Pappe, *The Ethnic Cleansing of Palestine* (Oxford: One World, 2006).

16 On the fragmentation of the Palestinian body politic after Oslo, see Karma Nabulsi,

'The State-Building Project: What Went Wrong', in Michael Keating, Anne Le More and Robert Lowe, eds, *Aid, Diplomacy and Facts on the Ground: The Case of Palestine* (London: Chatham House, 2005) 117–128.

17 *Yediot Aharonot*, 7 September 1993. Quoted in Graham Usher, *Palestine in Crisis: The Struggle for Peace and Political Independence after Oslo* (London: Pluto Press, 1995) 71–72.

18 According to Mushtaq Khan, 'rents' refer to a politically generated income that exists only through some specific rights, subsidies or transfers, artificially maintained through a political process, that aim at influencing or capturing the state. 'Monopoly profits, subsidies, transfers, unnecessary job creation in the public sector are all examples of rent-creation.' Within the liberal, 'good governance' model, rent-seeking is portrayed as economically damaging and a cause for under-development (especially in its most extreme version, corruption) in so far as it stifles competition, often works through patron–client networks, and consolidates the power of privileged groups. Mushtaq Khan, 'Evaluating the Emerging Palestinian State. Good Governance versus Transformation Potential', in Mushtaq Husain Khan, ed., with George Giacaman and Inge Amundsen, *State Formation in Palestine. Viability and Governance during a Social Transformation* (London: RoutledgeCurzon, 2004).

19 'Neo-patrimonialism', as coined by Shmuel Eisenstadt with reference to African states and based on the classic Weberian notion of patrimonialism, refers to states whose main characteristics are the personalization of power and a weak distinction between the public and the private good. The state is the 'property' of the leader, who rules by distributing favours and rents to his 'clients' who help him remain in power. As a result, the rule of law is weak, and clientelism and corruption are endemic. See Shmuel Noah Eisenstadt, *Traditional Patrimonialism and Modern Neo-Patrimonialism* (London: Sage, 1973). The neo-patrimonial model has often been used with reference to Arafat and the PA, notably by Rex Brynen. See Rex Brynen, 'The Neopatrimonial Dimension of Palestinian Politics', *Journal of Palestinian Studies* XXV, no. 1 (Autumn 1995).

20 Khan, ed., *State Formation in Palestine. Viability and Governance During a Social Transformation*, 51.

21 John J. Mearsheimer and Stephen M. Walt, 'The Israel Lobby and US Foreign Policy', *Faculty Research Working Papers Series*, Harvard University, John F. Kennedy School of Government (March 2006). Michael Massing, 'The Storm over the Israeli Lobby', *The New York Review of Books*, 8 June 2006.

22 Dennis Ross, *The Missing Peace. The Inside Story of the Fight for Middle East Peace* (New York: Farrar, Straus and Giroux, 2004) 6–7.

23 Ibid. 327–494.

24 Kathleen Christison, 'Bound by a Frame of Reference, Part I.I.I: US Policy and the Palestinians, 1988–98', *Journal of Palestine Studies* XXVII, no. 4 (Summer 1998): 54, 59.

25 'Sharon Invokes Munich in Warning US in Appeasement', *New York Times*, 5 October 2001, 'Defiant Sharon Losing Support in White House', *Washington Post*, 11 April 2002. Avi Shlaim, 'America and the Israeli–Palestinian Conflict', in Ken Booth and Tim Dunne, eds, *Worlds in Collision: Terror and the Future of Global Order* (Basingstoke/New York: Palgrave, 2002).

26 Eliot Abrams was perhaps the most influential in terms of the Israeli–Palestinian conflict and MEPP. Appointed Special Assistant to the President and Senior Director on the National Security Council for Near East and North African Affairs during Bush's first term in office, and promoted to Deputy National Security Advisor during Bush's second term, Abrams was the key official interlocutor between the US, the Israelis and the Palestinians. See also Mearsheimer, 'The Israel Lobby and US Foreign Policy'.

27 Transcript of remarks by Bush and Sharon on Israel, *New York Times*, 14 April 2004.

28 The American approach to the Arab–Israeli conflict has been characterized by a procedural bias for process over substance since the late 1960s. William B. Quandt, *Peace Process. American Diplomacy and the Arab–Israeli Conflict since 1967* (Washington DC, Berkeley: Brookings and UCP, 2005; third edition).

29 Bias and self-censorship are also prevalent in the media, in particular in the US. This sensitive issue has been the subject of a number of recent books and articles. See Norman G. Finkelstein, *Beyond Chutzpah. On the Misuse of Anti-Semitism and the Abuse of History* (Berkeley, Los Angeles: University of California Press, 2005); Pascal Boniface, *Est-il permis de critiquer Israel?* (Paris: Robert Laffont, 2003); Mearsheimer, 'The Israel Lobby and US Foreign Policy'; Tony Judt, 'The Country That Wouldn't Grow Up', *Ha'aretz*, 5 May 2006; Michael Massing, 'The Storm over the Israeli Lobby', *The New York Review of Books*, 8 June 2006.

30 World Bank, *Emergency Assistance Program for the Occupied Territories* (Washington DC: World Bank, April 1994) 7.

31 Israel does not qualify for ODA due to its high level of per capita income and GDP. However, since 1978, the US has provided both Israel and Egypt with substantial bilateral military and economic assistance as part of the peace agreement known as the Camp David Accords.

32 On these issues, see for instance Benoit Challand, *Civil Society, Autonomy, and Donors: International Aid to Palestinian NGOs* (Florence: Institut Universitaire Européen, 2006); Benoit Challand, 'The Power to Promote and Exclude: External Support for Palestinian Civil Society' (unpublished PhD, Florence, Institut Universitaire Européen, 2005): Salah Abdel Shafi, *Civil Society and Political Elites in Palestine and the Role of International Donors: A Palestinian View* (Lisbon: EuroMeSCo, July 2004); Sari Hanafi and Linda Tabar, 'Donor Assistance, Rent-seeking and Elite Formation', in Khan, ed., *State Formation in Palestine. Viability and Governance during a Social Transformation*; International Crisis Group, *Islamic Social Welfare Activism in the Occupied Palestinian Territories: A Legitimate Target?* (Amman/Brussels: ICG, 2 April 2003); Sari Hanafi, 'ONGs palestiniennes et bailleurs de fonds: la formation d'un agenda', in Sarah Ben Nefissa, ed., *Pouvoirs et associations dans le monde arabe* (Paris: CNRS, 2002).

33 Jeff Coulter, 'Remarks on the Conceptualization of Social Structure'. Quoted in Alexander Wendt, 'Anarchy Is What States Make of It: The Social Construction of Power Politics', *International Organization* 46, no. 2 (1992): 406. See also P.M. Haas, 'Epistemic Communities and International Policy Coordination', *International Organization* 46, no. 1 (Winter 1992).

1 AID BECAUSE OF POLITICS: THE ANALYTICAL, LEGAL AND INSTITUTIONAL FRAMEWORKS

1 An accepted definition of 'foreign aid' is the one provided by the Development Assistance Committee (DAC) of the Organization for Economic Cooperation and Development (OECD), the organization's norm-setting committee which coordinates donor countries' activities by defining parameters, establishing guidelines, assessing performance and compiling data on aid flows. According to the DAC, foreign aid or Official Development Assistance (ODA) is defined as grants or loans to developing countries undertaken by the official sector with the promotion of economic development and welfare as the main objective, and at concessional financial terms of at least 25 per cent. This definition encompasses humanitarian assistance and emergency relief.

2 For good general accounts on foreign aid, see Roger Riddell, *Foreign Aid Reconsidered* (Baltimore/London: Johns Hopkins University Press/ODI, 1987); Olav Stokke,

ed., *Foreign Aid Towards the Year 2000: Experiences and Challenges* (London: Frank Cass in association with the EADI, Geneva, 1996); Peter J. Burnell, *Foreign Aid in a Changing World* (Buckingham: Open University Press, 1997).

3 See Olav Stokke, *Aid and Political Conditionality* (London: Frank Cass, 1995); Thomas Carothers, *Aiding Democracy Abroad: The Learning Curve* (Washington DC: Carnegie Endowment for International Peace, 1999); Peter J. Burnell, ed., *Democracy Assistance. International Cooperation for Democratization* (London: Frank Cass, 2000).

4 For a good summary of the terms of the debate see Joanna Macrae and Nicholas Leader, *Shifting Sands: The Search for 'Coherence' between Political and Humanitarian Responses to Complex Emergencies, HPG Report* (London: Overseas Development Institute, August 2000); Devon Curtis, *Politics and Humanitarian Aid: Debates, Dilemmas and Dissension, HPG Report* (London: Overseas Development Institute, April 2001).

5 *Joint Evaluation of Emergency Assistance to Rwanda, The International Response to Conflict and Genocide: Lessons from the Rwanda Experience: Synthesis Report* (Steering Committee of the Joint Evaluation of Emergency Assistance to Rwanda, 1996).

6 Mary B. Anderson, *Do No Harm. How Aid Can Support Peace or War* (Boulder, London: Lynne Rienner, 1996 and 1999) 1. On this debate see also: Michael Maren, *The Road to Hell: The Ravaging Effects of Foreign Aid and International Charity* (New York, London: Free Press, 1997); Peter Uvin, *The Influence of Aid in Situations of Violent Conflict* (Paris: OECD, September 1999); Neil MacFarlane, *Politics and Humanitarian Action* (Providence: Watson Institute, Brown University, 2000); Neil MacFarlane, *Humanitarian Action: The Conflict Connection* (Providence: Watson Institute, Brown University, 2001).

7 On aid and economic agendas in civil wars, see David Keen, *The Economic Functions of Violence in Civil Wars, Adelphi Paper 320* (Oxford: OUP, 1998); David Shearer, 'Aiding or Abetting? Humanitarian Aid and its Economic Role in Civil War', in Mats Berdal and David M. Malone, eds, *Greed and Grievance: Economic Agendas in Civil Wars* (London, Ottawa: Lynn Rienner, 2000).

8 For a fascinating account of the way foreign aid inadvertently laid the groundwork for the Rwandan genocide, see Peter Uvin, *Aiding Violence. The Development Enterprise in Rwanda* (West Hartford: Kumarian Press, 1998) 3. For similar issues in the Afghani context, see also Antonio Donini, Norah Niland and Karin Wermester, eds. *Nation-Building Unraveled? Aid, Peace and Justice in Afghanistan* (Bloomfield: Kumarian Press, 2004).

9 OECD, *Conflict, Peace and Development Co-Operation on the Threshold of the 21st Century* (Paris: OECD, 1998) 45.

10 Uvin, *The Influence of Aid in Situations of Violent Conflict* 4.

11 *The Geneva Conventions of August 12, 1949* (International Committee of the Red Cross, Geneva); *Protocols Additional to the Geneva Conventions of 12 August 1949* (International Committee of the Red Cross, Geneva, 1977).

12 See for instance UNDG/ECHA Working Group on Transition Issues, *Report* (New York: United Nations, February 2004).

13 Macrae and Leader, *Shifting Sands: The Search for 'Coherence' between Political and Humanitarian Responses to Complex Emergencies* 25.

14 OECD, *Conflict, Peace and Development Co-Operation on the Threshold of the 21st Century* 22.

15 For a good and concise analysis of the role of the international financial institutions (IFIs) in peace-related activities, see Jonathan Stevenson, *Preventing Conflict: The Role of the Bretton Woods Institutions, Adelphi Paper 336* (Oxford: OUP for the

International Institute for Strategic Studies, 2000). See also Stephan Klingebiel, *The OECD, World Bank and International Monetary Fund: Development Activities in the Crisis Prevention and Conflict Management Sphere* (unpublished; Bonn, January 2001); International Monetary Fund, *A Macroeconomic Framework for Assistance to Post-Conflict Countries* (Washington DC: IMF, 1996). World Bank, *Post Conflict Reconstruction. The Role of the World Bank* (Washington DC: World Bank: 1998). World Bank, *The Role of the World Bank in Conflict and Development. An Evolving Agenda* (Washington DC: World Bank, 2003).

16 The World Bank's Exclusionary Clause, Article IV, Section 10 of its Articles of Agreement, states:

> The Bank and its officers shall not interfere in the political affairs of any member; nor shall they be influenced in their decisions by the political character of the member or members concerned. Only economic considerations shall be relevant to their decision, and these considerations shall be weighted impartially in order to achieve the purposes stated in Article I.

17 James Boyce has argued that given the overlap between economics and politics, especially in conflict/post-conflict situations:

> the exclusionary clause in the World Bank's charter can be read in either of two ways: as excluding all political considerations regardless of their economic importance, or as ruling out only those political considerations that are economically irrelevant. In postconflict settings, the absurdity of the first reading is particularly apparent.
>
> (James K. Boyce, 'Beyond Good Intentions: External Assistance and Peace Building', in S. Forman and S. Patrick, eds, *Good Intentions. Pledges of Aid for Postconflict Recovery* (London: Lynne Rienner, 2000) 380)

18 Alvaro de Soto and Graciana del Castillo, 'Obstacles to Peacebuilding', *Foreign Policy* (Spring 1994).

19 Klingebiel, *The OECD, World Bank and International Monetary Fund: Development Activities in the Crisis Prevention and Conflict Management Sphere* 10.

20 Boyce, 'Beyond Good Intentions: External Assistance and Peace Building', 369.

21 Joanna Macrae, 'The Politics of Coherence: The Formation of a New Orthodoxy on Linking Aid and Political Responses to Chronic Political Emergencies'. Paper presented at a conference on Politics and Humanitarian Aid, ODI, London, 1 February 2001, 11.

22 Ibid.

23 Nicholas Leader and Joanna Macrae, *Terms of Engagement: Conditions and Conditionality in Humanitarian Action*, HPG Report (London: Overseas Development Institute, July 2000) 4.

24 Elizabeth M. Cousens, Chetan Kumar and Karin Wermester, *Peacebuilding as Politics: Cultivating Peace in Fragile Societies* (Boulder, London: Lynne Rienner, 2001) 10.

25 Ibid. 184.

26 United Nations, *World Summit Outcome Document*, 15 September 2005. The inaugural meeting of the PBC took place on 23 June 2006. See also Michael Barnett, Hunjoon Kim, Madalene O'Donnell and Laura Sitea, 'Peacebuilding: What Is in a Name?' *Global Governance* 13, no. 1 (2007).

27 Ashraf Ghani, Claire Lockhart and Michael Carnahan, 'An Agenda for State-Building in the Twenty-First Century', *The Fletcher Forum of World Affairs* 30, no. 1 (Winter 2006); Stephen Krasner and Carlos Pascual, 'Addressing State Failure', *Foreign Affairs* (July/August 2005).

28 Israel has put forward various arguments to support its claim that the Fourth Geneva

Convention is inapplicable *de jure* to the oPt, the central one being that the sovereignty over the WBGS was disputed at the time Israel assumed control and thus was not the territory of another 'High Contracting Party' to whom it could be returned (this argument is based on Israeli interpretation of Article 2 of the Fourth Geneva Convention). What Israel refers to as 'Judea, Samaria and Gaza' or the 'territories' has thus, according to Israel, a status *sui generis* (neither part of Israeli territory nor formally occupied territory). However, although Israel objects to the *de jure* application of the Fourth Geneva Convention, it recognizes the *de facto* application of some parts of the Convention, which the government of Israel (GOI) has labelled its 'humanitarian provisions' but without ever defining them. The Israeli Supreme Court also recognizes the GOI in the oPt as bound by the customary 'Laws of War', mainly the Hague Regulations of 1907. *Review of the Applicability of International Humanitarian Law to the Occupied Palestinian Territory. Briefing Paper* (Program on Humanitarian Policy and Conflict Research, Harvard University, January 2004) 3–5.

29 The number of resolutions by the various organs of the UN affirming the *de jure* applicability of the Geneva Conventions to the oPt is extensive. See also Conference of High Contracting Parties to the Fourth Geneva Convention, *Declaration*, Geneva, 5 December 2001.

30 See PLO Negotiations Affairs Department, 'Permanent Status Issues, Borders'.

31 See UN General Assembly resolution 3236 (XXIX), 22 November 1974. This resolution 'reaffirms the inalienable rights of the Palestinian people in Palestine, including: (a) The right to self-determination without external interference; (b) The right to national independence and sovereignty'. The rights of the Palestinians, as set forth by the General Assembly in 1974, have been reaffirmed every year since.

32 Allison Hodgkins, *Israeli Settlement Policy in Jerusalem* (Jerusalem: PASSIA, December 1998) 3. Basic Law, Jerusalem, Capital of Israel, 30 July 1980.

33 *The Geneva Conventions of August 12, 1949.* Art. 47.

34 Ibid., *Protocols Additional to the Geneva Conventions of 12 August 1949.*

35 Under the Agreement on the Gaza Strip and Jericho of May 1994, Israel withdrew from parts of the Gaza Strip and the town of Jericho. Under the Israeli–Palestinian Interim Agreement on the West Bank and the Gaza Strip of September 1995 (or Oslo II), Israel withdrew from six further Palestinian cities (Tulkarem, Qalqilya, Jenin, Nablus, Ramallah and Bethlehem). It withdrew from the area H1 of Hebron in January 1997 following the signing of the Hebron Protocol. Finally, Israel redeployed from more territory in March 2000 following the Sharm El-Sheikh agreement.

36 Prior to Oslo, the Civil Administration within the Office of the Coordinator of Government Activities in the Territories (COGAT) under the Israeli Ministry of Defence, was responsible for administering all civilian affairs and economic matters including, *inter alia*, granting licences and permits, regulating trade, collecting taxes, organizing public infrastructure and services and supervising the operations of local governments. Those tasks were transferred for the most part to the PA in 1994. Nonetheless, COGAT has continued to exist, dealing with matters such as the issuing of movement permits. See World Bank, *Developing the Occupied Territories: An Investment in Peace* (Washington DC: 1993).

37 The percentage of areas as of after the redeployment of March 2000. B'Tselem, *Land Grab. Israel's Settlement Policy in the West Bank* (Jerusalem: B'Tselem, May 2002) 82.

38 See Geoffrey R. Watson, *The Oslo Accords: International Law and the Israeli-Palestinian Agreements* (Oxford: OUP, 2000) 115–121.

39 Information provided over the phone by the ICRC Legal Adviser, Tel Aviv Delegation, 21 July 2004.

40 'PM to Tell UN: Israel's Responsibility for Gaza is Over', *Ha'aretz*, 13 September

2005. 'Legal Aspects of Israel's Disengagement Plan under International Humanitarian Law (IHL)', Policy Brief, International Humanitarian Law Research Initiative, Harvard University, 30 August 2004.

41 See UNSCO, *Economic and Social Conditions in the West Bank and Gaza Strip, Quarterly Report* (Gaza: UNSCO, various years 1996–1999). See also United Nations Office of the Special Coordinator (UNSCO), *Report on the Palestinian Economy* (Gaza: UN, Spring 2001). 'Occupied Palestinian Territory' is mentioned on p. ii.

42 Mary B. Anderson, 'Do No Harm: The Impact of International Assistance to the Occupied Palestinian Territory', in Michael Keating, Anne Le More and Robert Lowe, eds, *Aid, Diplomacy and Facts on the Ground: The Case of Palestine* (London: Chatham House, 2005) 147.

43 There is some debate as to whether Israeli settlement policy constitutes a 'grave breach' (i.e. a war crime) of the Geneva Convention; regardless of the view one adopts on settlements, Israel allegedly committed war crimes during the *intifada*, *inter alia* through the 'extensive destruction and appropriation of property, not justified by military necessity and carried out unlawfully and wantonly' (Article 147, Fourth Geneva Convention). See for instance, Human Rights Watch, *Jenin: IDF Military Operations*, May 2002; United Nations, 'Special Rapporteur on Occupied Territories Horrified at Israeli Action in Gaza', Press Release HR/4760, 19 May 2004; Amnesty International, *Israel and the Occupied Territories. Under the Rubble: House Demolition and Destruction of Land and Property* (London: May 2004).

44 *Beit Sourik Village Council v. The Government of Israel and the Commander of the IDF Forces in the West Bank*, HCJ 2056/04 (30 June 2004) para. 35. Cited in David Shearer and Anuschka Meyer, 'The Dilemma of Aid Under Occupation', in Keating, ed., *Aid, Diplomacy and Facts on the Ground: The Case of Palestine* 170.

45 Aluf Benn, 'AG Urges Sharon to Consider Adopting Geneva Convention', *Ha'aretz*, 24 August 2004.

46 An explanatory graph of the aid coordination system in the 1990s is provided in Appendix II, 'The aid coordination structure during Oslo and the *intifada*'.

47 Stephen Lister and Anne Le More, *Aid Management and Coordination during the Intifada. Report to the LACC Co-Chairs* (July 2003); Stephen Lister and Raisa Venäläinen, *Improvement of Aid Coordination for West Bank and Gaza* (20 September 1999).

48 The AHLC membership is composed of the US, the EU, Russia, Norway, Japan, Saudi Arabia and Canada. Associated members are the PLO/PA, Israel, Egypt, Jordan, Tunisia and the UN. It is chaired by Norway and, since 1999, co-chaired by each meeting's host. The Bank acts as its Secretariat.

49 AHLC, 5 November 1993.

50 Rick Hooper, *The International Politics of Donor Assistance to the Palestinians in the West Bank and Gaza Strip, 1993–1997* (Research in Middle East Economics 3, Greenwich: JAI Press, 1999) 68.

51 See Stephen Lister and Raisa Venäläinen, *Improvement of Aid Coordination for West Bank and Gaza*. Until 2000, meetings were held on average twice a year, usually in the US or Europe although Japan hosted the AHLC in 1999. Since the beginning of the *intifada*, meetings have been convened in Europe, and on average only once a year.

52 Hooper, *The International Politics of Donor Assistance to the Palestinians in the West Bank and Gaza Strip, 1993–1997* 67.

53 Lister and Anne Le More, *Aid Management and Coordination during the Intifada. Report to the LACC Co-Chairs* Annex D: Aid Coordination Bodies.

54 The JLC membership was composed of the US, the EU, Japan, Israel, the PA (Chair), Norway (Secretariat) and UNSCO and the Bank as Co-Secretariat.

55 Tripartite Action Plan on Revenues, Expenditures and Donor Funding for the Pales-tinian Authority, AHLC, Paris, 27 April 1995. See for instance the updating of the Tripartite Action Plan on Revenues, Expenditures and Donor Funding for the Pales-tinian Authority, AHLC, Tokyo, 15 October 1999.

56 Joint Liaison Committee, *Terms of Reference* (revised version), 3 November 1998.

57 Comprising four members: UNSCO, the Bank, the EU/EC and USAID, with the Chair rotating every six months.

58 Task Force on Project Implementation, *Terms of Reference*, 3 November 1998.

59 Lister and Anne Le More, *Aid Management and Coordination during the Intifada. Report to the LACC Co-Chairs* Annexes D and E.

60 Hooper, *The International Politics of Donor Assistance to the Palestinians in the West Bank and Gaza Strip, 1993–1997* 68.

61 The UN representative did not participate in the proceedings on 4 November while members resolved this issue.

62 Hooper, *The International Politics of Donor Assistance to the Palestinians in the West Bank and Gaza Strip, 1993–1997* 67–68. With the creation of the local aid coordination structures, in which UNSCO played a significant role as Co-Chair of the LACC, the UN role at the capitals' level also expanded: from 1995, UNSCO would informally work with the Bank and Norway in the preparations of AHLCs. In so doing, it almost acted as Co-Secretariat, although this was never formalized.

63 Ibid. 69–70.

64 Rex Brynen, *Aid Management and Coordination during the Intifada. Report to the LACC Co-Chairs. Peer Review and Commentary* (July 2003).

65 An explanatory graph of the aid coordination system during the *intifada* is provided in Appendix II, 'The aid coordination structure during Oslo and the *intifada*'.

66 It is comprised of Norway (Convener), the Quartet members, Japan, Canada, the Bank and the IMF.

67 The HEPG is chaired by the EU/EC, UNSCO is the Deputy Chair and its other members are the US, Norway and the Bank. The LACC Secretariat is also the HEPG Secretariat, with the support of OCHA, and participation can be extended to other countries or organizations according to the topic under discussion. Topics covered by the HEPG include access negotiations, contacts with COGAT, review of ongoing relief efforts and other humanitarian matters.

68 Lister and Anne Le More, *Aid Management and Coordination during the Intifada. Report to the LACC Co-Chairs* 20.

2 ISRAELI POLICIES: THE TERRITORIAL, DEMOGRAPHIC AND SOCIO-ECONOMIC FRAGMENTATION OF THE OCCUPIED PALESTINIAN TERRITORY

1 Avi Shlaim, *The Iron Wall. Israel and the Arab World* (London: Allen Lane, Penguin, 2000) 11, 352.

2 The Allon Plan, proposed by senior Labour Party official Yigal Allon just after the June 1967 war, called for Israel's annexation of up to half of the West Bank, with the areas densely populated by Palestinians forming two unconnected areas to the north and south to become part of a Jordanian–Palestinian state. B'Tselem, *Land Grab. Israel's Settlement Policy in the West Bank* (Jerusalem: B'Tselem, May 2002) 7. See also Shimon Peres, *The New Middle East* (New York: Henry Holt, 1993) 163–179.

3 Peter Ezra Weinberger, 'Co-opting the PLO: A Critical Reconstruction of the Oslo Accords, 1993–1995' (unpublished PhD, London School of Economics and Political Science, 2002) 10–11.

4 The document stated that any agreement with the Palestinians must be guided by three key principles: the need to reach a permanent agreement which will entail 'the establishment of a Palestinian entity whose status will be determined in negotiations between the sides and limits of sovereignty will be detailed in the following section'; the need to uphold Israel's and Israeli citizens' security; and the need to maintain Israeli settlements 'in the Western Land of Israel'. The following sections stated *inter alia* that there will be no return to the 1967 borders, that settlements will not be dismantled, that the Jordan River will be the security border of Israel, and that Jerusalem will remain the eternal and unified capital of Israel. Importantly, in the section entitled 'Status of the Palestinian Entity and Limits on its Sovereignty', the document mentioned that 'if the Palestinian entity subjects itself to the limits presented in this document, its self-determination will be recognized. According to an alternative opinion it will be regarded as an enlarged autonomy, and according to another opinion, as a state.' 'Beilin-Eitan Agreement: National Agreement Regarding the Negotiations on the Permanent Settlement with the Palestinians', 26 January 1997.

5 West Bank and Gaza ID holders travel in cars with green licence-plates; Jerusalem ID holders and Israelis (including settlers) travel in cars with yellow plates. Since 1994, green-plated cars can enter neither East Jerusalem nor Israel. In addition, since the beginning of the *intifada*, the main roads of the West Bank have been for the sole use of Israeli cars, Israeli military vehicles and diplomatic/UN cars and trucks (white licence-plates). Palestinian cars are prohibited, apart from a few shared taxis and collective buses.

6 Amira Haas, 'Israel's Closure Policy: An Ineffective Strategy of Containment and Repression', *Journal of Palestinian Studies* XXXI, no. 3 (Spring 2002).

7 Blandine Destremau, 'Israël-Palestine: L'espace en miettes ou l'appropriation identitaire du territoire', *Monde Arabe – Maghreb Machrek*, no. 150 (Octobre– Décembre 1995): 5.

8 Haas, 'Israel's Closure Policy: An Ineffective Strategy of Containment and Repression', 8.

9 UN Report of the Secretary-General submitted in accordance to GA resolution ES-10/2, 26 June 1997. SC, item Agenda 5, para. 22.

10 OCHA Bi-weekly Update, 16 October–31 October 2003.

11 Ibid. p. 23.

12 Curfews in H-2 apply only to the approximately 30,000 Palestinian inhabitants who have been living under virtual house arrest; the 400–500 Israeli settlers in H-2 have been allowed to leave their homes at any time. Between October 2000 and January 2001, a 24-hour curfew was in force almost continuously; it was only lifted for a few hours every three to four days to allow residents to go shopping. See Amnesty International, *Broken Lives – A Year of Intifada* (London: Amnesty International, 2001) 82.

13 OCHA, *United Nations 2004 Humanitarian Plan of Action for the Occupied Palestinian Territory (CAP)* (New York and Geneva: OCHA, November 2003) 15.

14 B'Tselem, *Forbidden Roads: The Discriminatory West Bank Road Regime* (Jerusalem: B'Tselem, August 2004) 20, 29.

15 Brigadier General Paz, Head of Civil Administration, June 2004, quoted in ibid. 34.

16 Haas, 'Israel's Closure Policy: An Ineffective Strategy of Containment and Repression', 4, 9.

17 Quoted in *Ha'aretz*, 2 November 2001.

18 Universal Declaration of Human Rights, adopted and proclaimed by General Assembly resolution 217 A (III) of 10 December 1948. See in particular Articles 13, 23, 25 and 26.

19 Amnesty International, *Israel and the Occupied Territories. Surviving under Siege:*

The Impact of Movement Restrictions on the Right to Work (London: Amnesty International, September 2003) 22.

20 Israel uses several methods to seize control of Palestinian land in the oPt: the declaration and registration of land as 'state land', requisition for military needs, declaration of land as abandoned property and the expropriation of land for public needs. The level of incentives varies but includes the definition of most settlements as 'national priority areas', business and housing grants, land, construction and tax discounts, free schooling and extra support to local authorities. The per capita budget available to local authorities in the WBGS in the 1990s was more than 40 per cent higher than the national average. For a comprehensive historical, legal and bureaucratic account of the expansion of Israeli settlements in the WBGS, including Jerusalem, see Jean-François Legrain, 'Judaisation et démembrement: politiques israéliennes du territoire en Cisjordanie-Gaza (1967–1995)', *Monde Arabe – Maghreb Machrek*, no. 152 (Avril–Juin 1996); B'Tselem, *Land Grab. Israel's Settlement Policy in the West Bank*. International Crisis Group, *The Jerusalem Powder Keg* (Amman/Brussels: ICG, 2 August 2005).

21 Israeli–Palestinian Interim Agreement on the West Bank and the Gaza Strip, Washington DC, 28 September 1995 (Oslo II), Chapter V, Article XXXI (7), in 'Special Document File', *Journal of Palestinian Studies*, XXV, no. 2, Winter 1996.

22 'Israel and the Occupied Territories: The Issue of Settlements Must Be Addressed According to International Law', Amnesty International report, 8 September 2003.

23 *Report on Israeli Settlement in the Occupied Territories*, Foundation for Middle East Peace (Washington DC: FMEP, November–December 2002).

24 Information provided by Peace Now Settlement Watch Officer Dror Ektes, 3 November 2003.

25 B'Tselem, Press Release, 15 May 2002.

26 Haas, 'Israel's Closure Policy: An Ineffective Strategy of Containment and Repression', 4.

27 *Ha'aretz*, 23 September 2003.

28 Applied Research Institute Jerusalem (ARIJ), 'An Overview of the Geopolitical Situation in the Palestinian Areas', May 2001. B'Tselem, *Land Grab. Israel's Settlement Policy in the West Bank*.

29 Allison Hodgkins, *Israeli Settlement Policy in Jerusalem* (Jerusalem: PASSIA, December 1998) 80–83. International Crisis Group, *The Jerusalem Powder Keg*.

30 B'Tselem, *Land Grab. Israel's Settlement Policy in the West Bank* 103.

31 See in particular, Hague Regulations annexed to the 1907 Hague Convention and the Fourth Geneva Convention, Article 49.

32 B'Tselem, *Hebron, Area H-2: Settlements Cause Mass Departure of Palestinians* (Jerusalem: B'Tselem, August 2003).

33 Article 49, 'Geneva Convention Relative to the Protection of Civilian Persons in Time of War', in *The Geneva Conventions of August 12, 1949* (International Committee of the Red Cross, Geneva) 172.

34 'Hebron's H2 Area is Being Cleansed of Palestinians', *Ha'aretz*, 16 February 2004.

35 For a comprehensive account of the expansion of by-pass roads in the West Bank and how it is linked to the growth of settlements, see B'Tselem, *Forbidden Roads: The Discriminatory West Bank Road Regime*.

36 Special supplement on 'The price of settlements', *Ha'aretz*, 26 September 2003, 27.

37 House demolitions also occur in the context of large-scale Israeli military operations, not necessarily connected to settlement expansion. This was for instance the case during Operation Defensive Shield in April 2002 when 400 homes were destroyed in the Jenin refugee camp, leaving 2,000 people homeless. See OCHA, 'Rafah Status Report', 23 October 2003.

38 Jeff Halper, 'The 94 Percent Solution. A Matrix of Control', *Middle East Report* 216 (Fall 2000): 2.

39 United Nations' Report of the Secretary-General prepared pursuant to General Assembly resolution ES-10/13, 24 November 2003, 3–4.

40 Israel's Cabinet Decision 2077, 23 June 2002, in United Nations' Report of the Secretary-General prepared pursuant to General Assembly resolution ES-10/13, 24 November 2003, 3.

41 B'Tselem, *Behind the Barrier. Human Rights Violations as a Result of Israel's Separation Barrier* (Jerusalem: B'Tselem, March 2003) 6–7.

42 The first phase of the continuous barrier concerned the north-western governorates of Jenin, Tulkarem, Qalqilia and Salfit and in Bethlehem and Jerusalem.

43 Humanitarian and Emergency Policy Group (HEPG) of the Local Aid Coordination Committee (LACC), *The Impact of Israel's Separation Barrier on Affected West Bank Communities* (May 2003) 3.

44 See ibid. and subsequent updates (31 July 2003, 30 September 2003 and 30 November 2003) and United Nations' Report of the Secretary-General prepared pursuant to General Assembly resolution ES-10/13, 24 November 2003.

45 'Despite US Deal, Israel Starts Ariel Fence', *Ha'aretz*, 16 June 2004.

46 HEPG (OCHA/UNRWA), *The Humanitarian Impact of the West Bank Barrier on Palestinian Communities. Update 4.* (Jerusalem: HEPG, September 2004) 3.

47 United Nations' Report of the Secretary-General prepared pursuant to General Assembly resolution ES-10/13, 24 November 2003, 3.

48 For more recent estimates, see for instance OCHA, 'Preliminary Analysis of the Humanitarian Implications of the February 2005 Projected Route', February 2005.

49 International Court of Justice, 'Legal Consequences of the Construction of a Wall in the Occupied Palestinian Territory', Press Release 2004/28, 9 July 2004.

50 'Permanent residents' are the only Palestinians entitled to live in the zone. Palestinians not residing in the closed zone but whose land, business or work is situated inside the seam area also need to obtain permits to enter the enclave – the so-called 'green' permits.

51 Humanitarian and Emergency Policy Group (HEPG) of the Local Aid Coordination Committee (LACC), *The Impact of Israel's Separation Barrier on Affected West Bank Communities*. Update 1, 31 July 2003, 16–23.

52 Mustafa Barghouti, Director of the Health, Development, Information, and Policy Institute (HDIP), Press Conference at the occasion of the release of the report 'Health and Segregation: the Impact of the Israeli Separation Wall on Access to Health Care Services', HDIP, Ramallah, 28 January 2004.

53 International Crisis Group, *The Jerusalem Powder Keg* i.

54 Humanitarian and Emergency Policy Group (HEPG) of the Local Aid Coordination Committee (LACC), *The Impact of Israel's Separation Barrier on Affected West Bank Communities* 14. The Palestinian Environmental NGOs Network (PENGON), *Stop the Wall in Palestine. Facts, Testimonies, Analysis and Call to Action* (Jerusalem: PENGON, June 2003) 160.

55 In 2005, the Head of the Knesset Economics Committee estimated that the Barrier will cost $3.4 billion. See OCHA, 'Preliminary Analysis of the Humanitarian Implications of the February 2005 Projected Route', February 2005.

56 Yedioth Ahronoth, 23 May 2003, quoted in OCHA, *The West Bank Wall. Humanitarian Status Report: Northern West Bank Trajectory* (Jerusalem: OCHA, July 2003) 2.

57 This was stated on many occasions. See for instance Prime Minister Olmert's Address to the Knesset on Presentation of the 31st Government, 4 May 2006.

58 United Nations' Report of the Secretary-General prepared pursuant to General

Assembly resolution ES-10/13, 24 November 2003, Annex II: Summary legal position of the Palestinian Liberation Organization.

59 Special Rapporteur of the Commission on Human Rights, John Dugard, *Report on the Situation of Human Rights in the Palestinian Territories Occupied by Israel since 1967, Submitted in Accordance with Commission Resolution 1993/2 A* (September 2003) 6.

60 See all the UNSCO and World Bank reports on the Palestinian economy, 1994–2006. See also Samir Abdullah and Clare Woodcraft, 'Israeli Closure Policy: Sabotaging Sustainable Development', in Sara Roy, ed., *The Economics of the Middle East: A Reassessment* (Stamford: Jay Press, 1999).

61 Sharif Elmusa and Mahmud El-Jaafari, 'Power and Trade: The Israeli–Palestinian Economic Protocol', *Journal of Palestinian Studies* XXIV, no. 2 (Winter 1995): 16–17.

62 Sara Roy, *The Gaza Strip. The Political Economy of De-Development* (Washington DC: Institute for Palestine Studies, 1995) 4. See also various articles in George Abed, ed., *The Palestinian Economy. Studies in Development under Prolonged Occupation* (London, New York: Routledge, 1988).

63 Independent Task Force sponsored by the Council on Foreign Relations, *Strengthening Palestinian Public Institutions (The Rocard Report)* (New York: UN, June 1999) 58. World Bank and UNSCO, *Donor Investment in Palestinian Development 1994–1998* (Jerusalem: World Bank/UNSCO, 1999) 10. See also Major General Shlomo Gazit, *The Carrot and the Stick. Israel's Policy in Judea and Samaria, 1967–68* (Washington DC: B'nai B'rith Books, 1995).

64 Ishac Diwan, and Radwan A. Shaban, *Development under Adversity. The Palestinian Economy in Transition* (Jerusalem: Palestine Economic Policy Research Institute (MAS) and World Bank, 1999) 5, Sara Roy, 'De-Development Revisited: Palestinian Economy and Society since Oslo', *Journal of Palestinian Studies* XXVIII, no. 3 (Spring 1999): 69.

65 Christopher Pissarides, ed., *Evaluating the Paris Protocol. Economic Relations between Israel and the Palestinian Authorities* (Report commissioned for and financed by the European Commission, July 1999) 4.

66 Elmusa, 'Power and Trade: The Israeli–Palestinian Economic Protocol', 19.

67 World Bank, *Developing the Occupied Territories: An Investment in Peace*, six vols, Vol. 1 (Washington DC: World Bank, September 1993) 4.

68 See for instance, Pissarides, ed., *Evaluating the Paris Protocol. Economic Relations between Israel and the Palestinian Authorities*; and World Bank, *Long-Term Policy Options for the Palestinian Economy* (Jerusalem: World Bank, July 2002).

69 World Bank, *Long-Term Policy Options for the Palestinian Economy* xii, xiv.

70 International Monetary Fund, *West Bank and Gaza: Economic Performance and Reform under Conflict Conditions* (Washington DC: IMF, 2003) 63.

71 Cited in UNSCO, Statement to the AHLC, Tokyo, October 1999. See also Markus E. Bouillon, *The Peace Business. Money and Power in the Palestinian–Israeli Conflict* (New York: I.B. Tauris, 2004).

72 Julie Trottier, *Hydropolitics in the West Bank and Gaza Strip* (Jerusalem: PASSIA, 1999) 66.

73 Claude Bruderlein, 'Human Security Challenges in the oPt', in Michael Keating, Anne Le More and Robert Lowe, eds, *Aid, Diplomacy and Facts on the Ground: The Case of Palestine* (London: Chatham House, 2005) 81.

74 See International Monetary Fund, *West Bank and Gaza Strip. Economic Developments in the Five Years since Oslo* (Washington DC: IMF, 1999) 13. World Bank, *Twenty Seven Months – Intifada, Closures and Economic Crisis – An Assessment* (Jerusalem: World Bank, May 2003) 2.

75 'International Community Reaffirms Support for Palestinian Development', Press Release, World Bank, Paris, 15 December 1997.

76 World Bank, *Fifteen Months – Intifada, Closures and Palestinian Economic Crisis – An Assessment* (Jerusalem: World Bank, March 2002) 13.

77 United Nations Office of the Special Coordinator (UNSCO), *Economic and Social Conditions in the West Bank and Gaza Strip. Quarterly Report* (Gaza: UNSCO Autumn 1996) i.

78 World Bank and Japan, *Aid Effectiveness in the West Bank and Gaza* (Jerusalem: World Bank, June 2000) 13.

79 Diwan, *Development under Adversity. The Palestinian Economy in Transition* 7.

80 World Bank, *Long-Term Policy Options for the Palestinian Economy* xviii; World Bank and Japan, *Aid Effectiveness in the West Bank and Gaza* 14.

81 World Bank and Japan, *Aid Effectiveness in the West Bank and Gaza* 14.

82 Diwan, *Development under Adversity. The Palestinian Economy in Transition* 2.

83 Chair's Summary, Ad Hoc Liaison Committee, Tokyo, 15 October 1999.

84 World Bank, *Four Years – Intifada, Closures and Palestinian Economic Crisis – An Assessment.* (Jerusalem: World Bank, October 2004) 18.

85 World Bank, *Twenty Seven Months – Intifada, Closures and Economic Crisis – An Assessment* 7–8.

86 World Bank, *Four Years – Intifada, Closures and Palestinian Economic Crisis – An Assessment.* 24.

87 United Nations Conference on Trade and Development (UNCTAD), *Report on UNCTAD's Assistance to the Palestinian People* (28 July 2003) 5.

88 World Bank, *Four Years – Intifada, Closures and Palestinian Economic Crisis – An Assessment.* 16. World Bank, *Stagnation or Revival? Israeli Disengagement and Palestinian Economic Prospects* (Jerusalem: World Bank, December 2004) 7.

89 OCHA, *A Report on the Deteriorating Humanitarian Situation in the Gaza Strip* (Jerusalem: OCHA, 1 October 2004) 2.

90 World Bank, *Fifteen Months – Intifada, Closures and Palestinian Economic Crisis – An Assessment* v.

91 World Bank, *Twenty Seven Months – Intifada, Closures and Economic Crisis – An Assessment* 52. See also International Monetary Fund, *West Bank and Gaza: Economic Performance and Reform under Conflict Conditions* 59–81.

92 World Bank, *Four Years – Intifada, Closures and Palestinian Economic Crisis – An Assessment.* 33–35.

93 Sara Roy, 'Palestinian Society and Economy: The Continued Denial of Possibility', *Journal of Palestinian Studies* XXX, no. 4 (Summer 2001): 9–10.

94 Leila Farsakh, 'Palestinian Labor Flows to the Israeli Economy: A Finished Story?' *Journal of Palestinian Studies* XXXII, no. 1 (Autumn 2002): 14.

95 World Bank, *Four Years – Intifada, Closures and Palestinian Economic Crisis – An Assessment.* 52–54.

96 These figures compare with a far lower decline in the number of workers in areas less closed off and enclosed as of 2003, namely a decline of only 13 per cent in the number of workers from Jericho between 1999 and 2003, 14 per cent in the number of workers from Jerusalem and 33 per cent in the number of workers from Bethlehem. Palestinian Centre Bureau of Statistics (PCBS), Labour Flows Data, Various rounds, 1999–2003.

97 United Nations Special Coordinator's Office (UNSCO), 'Fragmentation and the Non-Viability of the West Bank Economy Due to the Separation Barrier and Other Closure Measures', January 2004 (unpublished).

98 World Bank, *Stagnation or Revival? Israeli Disengagement and Palestinian Economic Prospects* 6.

99 World Bank, *Disengagement, the Palestinian Economy and the Settlements* (Jerusalem: World Bank, 23 June 2004) i.

100 World Bank and Japan, *Aid Effectiveness in the West Bank and Gaza* 13.

101 World Bank, *Fifteen Months – Intifada, Closures and Palestinian Economic Crisis – An Assessment* iv, 34–36; World Bank, *Twenty Seven Months – Intifada, Closures and Economic Crisis – An Assessment* 7.

102 OCHA, *Preliminary Humanitarian Damage Assessment and Humanitarian Action Plan (May–December 2002)* (Jerusalem: OCHA, June 2002) 8.

103 World Bank, *Four Years – Intifada, Closures and Palestinian Economic Crisis – An Assessment.* 42.

104 FAFO, *Paying a Price. Coping with Closure in Jericho, Gaza City and in Two Palestinian Villages* (Oslo: FAFO, 2001). Combined summary of the three studies.

105 World Bank, *Twenty Seven Months – Intifada, Closures and Economic Crisis – An Assessment* 32.

106 According to the FAO,

> food insecurity exists when people are undernourished due to the physical unavailability of food, their lack of social or economic access, and/or inadequate food utilization. Food insecure people are those individuals whose food intake falls below their minimum calorie (energy) requirements, as well as those who exhibit physical symptoms caused by energy and nutrient deficiencies resulting from an inadequate or unbalanced diet, or from inability of the body to use food effectively because of infection or disease. An alternative view would define the concept of food insecurity as referring only to the consequence of inadequate consumption of nutritious food, considering the physiological utilization of food by the body as being within the domain of nutrition and health.
>
> (FAO, 'Guidelines for National Food Insecurity and Vulnerability Information and Mapping Systems (FIVIMS): Background and Principles', Committee on World Food Security, 24th Session, Rome, 2–5 June 1998)

OCHA, *United Nations 2005 Humanitarian Plan of Action for the Occupied Palestinian Territory (CAP)* (New York and Geneva: OCHA, November 2004) 7.

107 Cited in World Bank, *Four Years – Intifada, Closures and Palestinian Economic Crisis – An Assessment.* 48.

108 UNSCO, 'Update on the Socio-economic Situation', AHLC meeting in Rome, 10 December 2003. OCHA, *United Nations 2004 Humanitarian Plan of Action for the Occupied Palestinian Territory (CAP)* 18–19.

109 David Shearer, *The Humanitarian Crisis in the Occupied Palestinian Territory, Humanitarian Exchange Nb 28* (London: Overseas Development Institute, November 2004) 3.

110 UNRWA/OCHA, 'Rafah Humanitarian Needs Assessment', 6 June 2004.

111 Jean-Luc Siblot, Genevieve Wills and Tareq Abu ElHaj, *Food Security in the Occupied Palestinian Territory, Humanitarian Exchange Nb 28* (London: Overseas Development Institute, November 2004) 26.

112 UNSCO, 'Update on the Socio-economic Situation', AHLC meeting in Rome, 10 December 2003.

113 Mustafa Barghouti, ed., *Health and Segregation. The Impact of Israeli Separation Wall on Access to Health Care Services* (Ramallah: HDIP, January 2004).

114 OCHA, *United Nations 2005 Humanitarian Plan of Action for the Occupied Palestinian Territory (CAP)* 7.

115 UNSCO, Update on the socio-economic situation, AHLC meeting in Rome, 10

December 2003. OCHA, *United Nations 2004 Humanitarian Plan of Action for the Occupied Palestinian Territory (CAP)* 18–19.

116 OCHA, *Preliminary Humanitarian Damage Assessment and Humanitarian Action Plan (May–December 2002)* 17.

117 UNRWA, Press Release, 22 January 2004. OCHA, *Report to the LACC on Humanitarian Consequences of Israeli Defence Forces Operations in Rafah, Southern Gaza Strip* (Jerusalem: OCHA, 28 January 2004) 2. OCHA, *A Report on the Deteriorating Humanitarian Situation in the Gaza Strip* 2.

118 OCHA, *A Report on the Deteriorating Humanitarian Situation in the Gaza Strip* 2.

119 UNSCO, *Draft Fact Sheet: Occupied Palestinian Territory*, 19 February 2007.

3 PALESTINIAN ADJUSTMENT: THE RISE AND FALL OF ARAFAT'S REGIME

1 Edward W. Said, *Peace and Its Discontents. Gaza–Jericho, 1993–1995* (London: Vintage, 1995) 2.

2 The internet domain '.ps' was officially launched in April 2005.

3 Said, *Peace and Its Discontents. Gaza–Jericho, 1993–1995* 5, 8–9.

4 Mushtaq Husain Khan, ed., with George Giacaman and Inge Amundsen, *State Formation in Palestine. Viability and Governance during a Social Transformation* (London: RoutledgeCurzon, 2004) 2.

5 For a comprehensive analysis of the role and workings of the PLC in the 1990s, see Bernard Botiveau, 'Le Conseil Législatif Palestinien: du conseil de l'autonomie au parlement des territoires', *Monde Arabe – Maghreb Machrek*, no. 161 (Juillet–Septembre 1998); Jerusalem Media and Communication Centre, *The Palestinian Council* (Jerusalem: JMCC, January 1998); David Schenker, *Palestinian Democracy and Governance: An Appraisal of the Legislative Council* (Washington DC: The Washington Institute for Near East Policy, 2000).

6 Inge and Basem Ezbidi Amundsen, 'PNA Political Institutions and the Future of State Formation', in Mushtaq Husain Khan, with George Giacaman and Inge Amundsen, eds, *State Formation in Palestine. Viability and Governance during a Social Transformation* (London: RoutledgeCurzon, 2004), 145.

7 Indeed, in the 1990s, there were Ottoman, British, Jordanian (in the West Bank), Egyptian (in Gaza) and Israeli legal codes simultaneously in force in the oPt. For a detailed study on the Palestinian legal and judicial systems, see Viktoria Wagner, *Palestinian Judiciary and the Rule of Law in the Autonomous Areas. An Introduction* (Jerusalem: PASSIA, November 2000).

8 Khan, ed., *State Formation in Palestine. Viability and Governance during a Social Transformation* 86.

9 Independent Task Force sponsored by the Council on Foreign Relations, *Strengthening Palestinian Public Institutions (The Rocard Report)* (New York: June 1999) 30–31.

10 Ziad Abu-Amr, 'The Palestinian Legislative Council: A Critical Assessment', *Journal of Palestinian Studies* XXVI, no. 4 (Summer 1997): 91–92, Azmi Shu'aybi, 'A Window on the Workings of the PA: An Inside View', *Journal of Palestinian Studies* XXX, no. 1 (Autumn 2000): 91.

11 Independent Task Force sponsored by the Council on Foreign Relations, *Strengthening Palestinian Public Institutions (The Rocard Report)* 33.

12 Ibid. 34.

13 Jean-François Legrain, 'The Successions of Yasir Arafat', *Journal of Palestinian Studies* XXVIII, no. 4 (Summer 1999): 5.

14 Shu'aybi, 'A Window on the Workings of the PA: An Inside View', 89, 91.

15 There were about 23,000 staff in the Israeli Civil Administration (most of who were

Palestinians) at the time of the Oslo Accords. Independent Task Force sponsored by the Council on Foreign Relations, *Strengthening Palestinian Public Institutions (The Rocard Report)* 18.

16 International Monetary Fund, *West Bank and Gaza: Economic Performance and Reform under Conflict Conditions* (Washington DC: IMF, 2003) 64.

17 Independent Task Force sponsored by the Council on Foreign Relations, *Strengthening Palestinian Public Institutions (The Rocard Report)* 46–47. Shu'aybi, 'A Window on the Workings of the PA: An Inside View', 89–90.

18 World Bank, *Twenty Seven Months – Intifada, Closures and Economic Crisis – An Assessment* (Jerusalem: World Bank, May 2003) xiii.

19 World Bank, *Four Years – Intifada, Closures and Palestinian Economic Crisis – An Assessment.* (Jerusalem: World Bank, October 2004) 21.

20 Quoted in AMAN, Coalition for Accountability and Integrity, Project Proposal, Ramallah, 2003.

21 David Sewell, *Governance and the Business Environment in West Bank/Gaza* (Washington DC: World Bank, May 2001) 7–8.

22 PLC Special Committee Corruption Report, Summer 1997, in Jerusalem Media and Communication Centre, *The Palestinian Council* 133–170. See also 'Arafat's Rampant Corruption', Mid-East Realities, 6 September 1997; Ilan Halevy, 'Self-Government, Democracy, and Mismanagement under the Palestinian Authority', *Journal of Palestinian Studies* XXVII, no. 3 (Spring 1998): 37.

23 PLC Special Committee Corruption Report, Summer 1997, in Jerusalem Media and Communication Centre, *The Palestinian Council* 133–170.

24 Sara Roy, 'Alienation or Accommodation?' *Journal of Palestinian Studies* XXIV, no. 4 (Summer 1995): 80.

25 Cited in Peter Lagerquist, 'Privatizing the Occupation: The Political Economy of an Oslo Development Project', *Journal of Palestinian Studies* XXXII, no. 2 (Winter 2003): 26.

26 Independent Task Force sponsored by the Council on Foreign Relations, *Strengthening Palestinian Public Institutions (The Rocard Report)* 60.

27 Ibid.

28 When eventually a revised version of the 1999 budget was presented to the PLC including all revenues, it appeared that about US$126 million had been deposited into bank accounts abroad. Shu'aybi, 'A Window on the Workings of the PA: An Inside View', 93–94.

29 International Monetary Fund, *West Bank and Gaza: Economic Performance and Reform under Conflict Conditions* 74.

30 Sewell, *Governance and the Business Environment in West Bank/Gaza* 9–10.

31 PLC Special Committee Corruption Report, Summer 1997, reproduced verbatim in Jerusalem Media and Communication Centre, *The Palestinian Council* 133–170. See also Mohamed M Nasr, 'Monopolies and the PNA', in Mushtaq Husain Khan, ed., with George Giacaman and Inge Amundsen *State Formation in Palestine. Viability and Governance During a Social Transformation* (London: RoutledgeCurzon, 2004), 184.

32 World Bank and Japan, *Aid Effectiveness in the West Bank and Gaza* (Jerusalem: World Bank, June 2000) 51.

33 Palestinian Investment Fund, Press Release, 3 March 2003.

34 Lagerquist, 'Privatizing the Occupation: The Political Economy of an Oslo Development Project', 14–15.

35 'La Justice Israélienne et le Mossad se penchent sur les comptes secrets de Yasser Arafat à l'étranger', *Le Temps*, 7 December 2002.

36 International Monetary Fund, *West Bank and Gaza: Economic Performance and Reform under Conflict Conditions* 88–89.

37 Markus E. Bouillon, *The Peace Business. Money and Power in the Palestinian–Israeli Conflict* (New York: I.B. Tauris, 2004) 96.

38 Rex Brynen, 'Donor Aid to Palestine: Attitudes, Incentives, Patronage and Peace', in Michael Keating, Anne Le More and Robert Lowe, eds, *Aid, Diplomacy and Facts on the Ground: The Case of Palestine* (London: Chatham House, 2005) 138.

39 Nasr, 'Monopolies and the PNA', 168–169.

40 Sewell, *Governance and the Business Environment in West Bank/Gaza* 9.

41 Nasr, 'Monopolies and the PNA', 186.

42 Lagerquist, 'Privatizing the Occupation: The Political Economy of an Oslo Development Project', 14.

43 'Arafat's Billion', transcript, 60 minutes, CBS, 9 November 2003.

44 In July 2002, for example, the Israeli daily *Yediot Aharonot* reported that Arafat allegedly sent a yearly pension of US$5.1 million to his wife Suha, who was opulently residing in Paris. Quoted in 'La justice israélienne et le Mossad se penchent sur les comptes secrets de Yasser Arafat à l'étranger', *Le Temps*, 7 December 2002.

45 Chris McGreal, 'Palestinian Authority "May Have Lost Billions"', *Guardian*, 6 February 2006.

46 Agreement on the Gaza Strip and the Jericho area, 4 May 1994, Articles VIII and IX, Annex I.

47 The Israeli–Palestinian Interim Agreement on the West Bank and Gaza Strip, 28 September 1995, Annex I. See also Graham Usher, 'The Politics of Internal Security: The PA's New Intelligence Services', *Journal of Palestinian Studies* XXV, no. 2 (Winter 1996): 23.

48 Jocelyn Grange, 'Les Forces de sécurité palestiniennes. Contraintes d'Oslo et quête de légitimité nationale', *Monde Arabe – Maghreb Machrek* 161 (Juillet–Septembre 1998): 22 ; Shu'aybi, 'A Window on the Workings of the PA: An Inside View', 89 ; Task Force on Palestinian Reform (TFPR), Progress Report, September 2003.

49 For a detailed analysis and history of Palestinian security forces, see Strategic Assessments Initiative, *Planning Considerations for International Involvement in the Palestinian Security Sector* (Report Sponsored by the Royal Netherlands Ministry of Foreign Affairs and The International Development Research Center of Canada, Washington DC: SAI, July 2005) 25–31. See also Gal Luft, 'The Palestinian Security Services: Between Police and Army', *Middle East Review of International Affairs* 3, no. 2 (June 1999).

50 Usher, 'The Politics of Internal Security: The PA's New Intelligence Services', 25–26.

51 One should note that the issue of the Palestinian security sector and the role donors could play in facilitating its reform attracted increasingly more interest from the mid-2000s within the context of Israel disengagement from Gaza. See for instance Strategic Assessments Initiative, *Planning Considerations for International Involvement in the Palestinian Security Sector*. Nicole Ball, Peter Bartu and Adriaan Verheul, 'Squaring the Circle: Security-Sector Reform and Transformation and Fiscal Stabilisation in Palestine' (Report prepared for the UK Department for International Development, London, 16 January 2006).

52 Ball, 'Squaring the Circle: Security-Sector Reform and Transformation and Fiscal Stabilisation in Palestine' 19.

53 Luft, 'The Palestinian Security Services: Between Police and Army', 4.

54 *New York Times*, 19 November 1994.

55 Independent Task Force sponsored by the Council on Foreign Relations, *Strengthening Palestinian Public Institutions (The Rocard Report)* 81.

56 Amundsen, 'PNA Political Institutions and the Future of State Formation', 150. Rex Brynen, 'Donor Aid to Palestine: Attitudes, Incentives, Patronage and Peace' in Keating, ed., *Aid, Diplomacy and Facts on the Ground: The Case of Palestine* 136.

57 Interview with Mohammed Dahlan in *Al-Quds Al-Arabi* (London, 25 April 1997). Cited in Human Rights Watch, *Palestinian Self-Rule Areas: Human Rights under the Palestinian Authority* (New York: Human Rights Watch, September 1997).

58 Strategic Assessments Initiative, *Planning Considerations for International Involvement in the Palestinian Security Sector* 31.

59 See for instance Amnesty International, *Annual Report. Palestinian Authority* (London: Amnesty International, 1998).

60 The Palestinian Independent Commission for Citizens' Rights, *Fourth Annual Report. 1 January 1998 to 31 December 1998* (Ramallah: PICCR, 1999) 122. See also Amnesty International, Public Statement, 'Amnesty International Shocked by the Palestinian Authority's First Use of the Death Penalty', 1 September 1998.

61 On 24 March 1996, US Vice President Al Gore, on an official visit to the PA, supported Arafat's establishment of the courts. A month later, as evidence surfaced of the courts' lack of due-process safeguards, he added: 'I know there has been some controversy over the Palestinian security courts, but I personally believe that the accusations are misplaced and that they are doing the right thing in progressing with prosecutions'; cited in Israel/Occupied West Bank and Gaza Strip, Human Rights Watch Report, 1996. See also the Palestinian Independent Commission for Citizens' Rights, *Second Annual Report. 1 July 1995 to 31 December 1996* (Ramallah: PICCR, 1997). Amnesty International, *Annual Report. Palestinian Authority* (London: Amnesty International, 2003), Amnesty International, *Annual Report. Palestinian Authority* (London: Amnesty International, 2004).

62 Amnesty International, *Annual Report. Palestinian Authority* (London: Amnesty International, 2002).

63 For instance, in July 1994, the daily *Al-Nahar* was closed for displaying pro-Jordanian views, the main Palestinian daily *Al Quds* was temporary banned from publishing in 1995 for being too critical of Oslo and the PA, and Hamas' weekly *Al Watan* was closed in the spring of 1996. Amal Jamal, 'The Palestinian Media: An Obedient Servant or a Vanguard of Democracy?' *Journal of Palestinian Studies* XXIX, no. 3 (Spring 2000).

64 International Crisis Group, *Dealing with Hamas* (Amman/Brussels: ICG, 26 January 2004) 9–10.

65 Interview, George Giacaman, Ramallah, 22 November 2003.

66 Local Aid Coordination Committee (LACC) – Donor Support Group, *Physical and Institutional Damage Assessment. West Bank Governorates, March–May 2002. Summary Report* (Jerusalem: 23 May 2002). Overall, the physical and institutional damage incurred during these months was estimated at US$342 million.

67 International Crisis Group, *Who Governs the West Bank? Palestinian Administration under Israeli Occupation* (Amman/Brussels: ICG, 28 September 2004) i.

68 Arnon Regular, 'The Coming Civil War', *Ha'aretz*, 7 March 2004; James Bennet, 'A West Bank Town's Absolute State of Chaos', *New York Times*, 15 July 2004; Danny Rubinstein, 'Arafat is Teetering but Surviving', *Ha'aretz*, 18 July 2004; Arnon Regular and Gideon Alon, 'HQ of Arafat's Nephew Hit as Gaza Clashes Intensify', *Ha'aretz*, 19 July 2004; Joseph Berger 'Gauging the Price of Peace in Gaza. Discord among Palestinians Raises a New Set of Questions', *New York Times*, 21 July 2004.

69 For an analysis of the 'old versus young guard' divide, see Khalil Shikaki, 'Palestinians Divided', *Foreign Affairs* 81, no. 1 (Jan./Feb. 2002). See also Graham Usher, 'Facing Defeat: The Intifada Two Years On', *Journal of Palestinian Studies* XXXII, no. 2 (Winter 2003).

70 According to a poll conducted in December 2003 by the Palestine Centre for Policy and Survey Research, Hamas' level of popular support had reached 20 per cent, behind Fatah with 25 per cent (Poll 10). See also International Crisis Group, *Dealing*

with Hamas 3. Hamas has dominated the opposition; the Islamic Jihad, through active in its armed attacks against Israel, is minuscule and does not command the support of a large proportion of the population. The secular opposition has remained marginal in its influence on the ground.

71 Hamas' support at the national level as recorded in opinion polls has largely been a function of the state of the peace process. In the immediate aftermath of Oslo II and the redeployment of the Israeli army, it reached its lowest point at about 10 per cent; until then, Hamas' support had averaged 13 per cent of the population. All along, however, local election results in professional associations, trade unions, student councils, chambers of commerce, etc., put Hamas to anywhere between 30 and 45 per cent of the popular vote. Ziad Abu-Amr, 'Hamas: A Historical and Political Background', *Journal of Palestinian Studies* XXII, no. 4 (Summer 1993): 15; Wendy Kristiansen, 'Challenge and Counterchallenge: Hamas's Response to Oslo', *Journal of Palestinian Studies* XXVIII, no. 3 (Spring 1999): 35; Shaul Mishal and Avraham Sela, *The Palestinian Hamas* (New York: Columbia University Press, 2000).

72 See Hamas' Charter, 18 August 1988.

73 'En Palestine, le Hamas se convertit au bulletin de vote', *Libération*, 14 March 2005.

74 This idea of a temporary peace has been pondered by the Hamas leadership since the late 1980s. See Kristiansen, 'Challenge and Counterchallenge: Hamas's Response to Oslo'; Mishal, *The Palestinian Hamas*. Most recently, it was reiterated by Hamas' founder and spiritual leader, Sheikh Ahmed Yassin. In an interview with the German Press Agency on 9 January 2004, Yassin stated: 'Hamas is prepared to accept a temporary peace [with Israel] if a Palestinian state is established in the West Bank and Gaza Strip. The rest of the territories [Israel proper] will be left to history'; *Jerusalem Post*, 9 January 2004. This position was repeated by Hamas' Damascus-based political leader Khaled Meshaal in the aftermath of the 2006 legislative elections and again in 2007 where he talked of 'Israel as a reality' and stated that 'there will remain a state called Israel, this is a matter of fact'. 'Hamas "Ready to Talk to Israel"', interview, BBC News, 8 February 2006; 'Mershal: Hamas Accepts State of Israel is a Reality', *Ha'aretz*, 10 January 2007.

75 On the lack of democracy in the Arab world, see for instance Elie Kedourie, *Democracy and Arab Political Culture* (London: Frank Cass, 1994); Oliver Schlumberger, 'The Arab Middle East and the Question of Democratization: Some Critical Remarks', *Democratization* 7, no. 4 (Winter 2000); United Nations Development Programme (UNDP), *Arab Human Development Report 2002* (New York: UN, 2002). For a culturalist interpretation of Middle Eastern neo-patrimonialism, see Hisham Sharabi, *Neopatriarchy. A Theory of Distorted Change in Arab Society* (Oxford, New York: OUP, 1988).

76 For a critical analysis of the Israeli narrative of Yasser Arafat's responsibility for the failure of the Camp David Summit, see Introduction to this volume, note 14.

77 Brian Whitaker, 'Sharon Likens Arafat to Bin Laden', *Guardian*, 14 September 2001.

78 Arafat did not leave his compound between May 2002 and 29 October 2004, when he was flown to Paris for medical treatment two weeks before he died on 11 November 2004. 'Frail Arafat in Paris Hospital', BBC News, 29 October 2004.

79 Glenn E. Robinson, *Building a Palestinian State: The Incomplete Revolution* (Bloomington: Indiana University Press, 1997); Glenn E Robinson, 'The Growing Authoritarianism of the Arafat Regime', *Survival* 39, no. 2 (Summer 1997).

80 Rex Brynen, 'The Neopatrimonial Dimension of Palestinian Politics', *Journal of Palestinian Studies* XXV, no. 1 (Autumn 1995). See also Rex Brynen, 'The Dynamics of Palestinian Elite Formation', *Journal of Palestinian Studies* XXIV, no. 3 (Spring 1995).

81 Khan, ed., *State Formation in Palestine. Viability and Governance during a Social Transformation.*

82 Ibid. 52–53.

4 AID INSTEAD OF POLITICS: MULTIPLE ACTORS, FRAGMENTED INTERESTS, LIMITED INFLUENCE

1 Rick Hooper, *The International Politics of Donor Assistance to the Palestinians in the West Bank and Gaza Strip, 1993–1997* (Research in Middle East Economics 3, Greenwich: JAI Press, 1999) 64.
2 These estimates are based on information informally provided by US officials. See also US Embassy to Israel, 'US Assistance to Israel: 1949–2004 Total', 20 November 2005.
3 The Wye River Memorandum, signed by both parties at the White House on 23 October 1998, was an agreement to implement the 1995 Interim Agreement and other previous accords, such as the Hebron Protocol of 1997. It foresaw Israeli redeployment from a further 13 per cent of the West Bank (12 per cent from Area C to B), included a number of security and economic provisions, and reiterated the parties' commitment to reach a permanent status agreement by May 1999. Most of those provisions went unfulfilled.
4 USAID, 'West Bank and Gaza, Budget 1993–2004'. See also Congressional Research Service (CRS) Report for Congress, 'US Aid to the Palestinians', 2 February 2006.
5 Estimate based on information provided by a USAID Official and on 'Physical Damages Inflicted by IDF Attacks to EU-Funded Development Projects', Table compiled by the EC Office in Jerusalem, 14 December 2002.
6 US Embassy to Israel, 'US Assistance to Israel: 1949–2004 Total', 20 November 2005, and 'US Assistance to Israel', 2004.
7 Since 2003, resolving the conflict has explicitly become an integral part of the EU's own security interests. European Council, *A Secure Europe in a Better World: European Security Strategy* (Brussels: European Council Publishers, 12 December 2003).
8 Ambassador Miguel Angel Moratinos, 'European Union – Middle East: Developing Societies for Peace', European Institute, Florence, 23 March 2000.
9 'European Aid to Palestine 2002–2003', EC Office in Jerusalem, 4 April 2004.
10 'Evaluation of the European Community's Programme of Assistance to the West Bank and Gaza Strip', European Court of Auditors Special Report, Brussels, January 1999, 7.
11 A Country Strategy Paper for 2000–2006 and a National Indicative Programme for 2000–2002 were completed in 2000 but never implemented because of the onset of the *intifada*. European Commission, *Euro-Mediterranean Partnership Country Strategy Papers, 2000–2006, West Bank and Gaza Strip* (Brussels: EC, 2000). European Commission, *National Indicative Programme, West Bank and Gaza Strip, 2000–2002* (Brussels: EC, 2000).
12 European Commission, *Euro-Mediterranean Partnership Country Strategy Papers, 2000–2006, West Bank and Gaza Strip* 19.
13 European Commission's Office in the West Bank and Gaza Strip, *The European Commission and the Palestinians, Three Decades of Partnership* (Gaza/Jerusalem: EC, June 2003).
14 European Commission, *Euro-Mediterranean Partnership Country Strategy Papers, 2000–2006, West Bank and Gaza Strip* 18.
15 Speech by European Commissioner Chris Patten before the European Parliament, 'Situation in the Middle East', 2 December 2001.
16 European Commission's Office in the West Bank and Gaza Strip, *The European Commission and the Palestinians, Three Decades of Partnership* 7, 27.
17 Nathalie Tocci, *The Widening Gap between Rhetoric and Reality in EU Policy Towards the Israeli–Palestinian Conflict* (Working Document no. 217, Brussels: CEPS, January 2005).
18 Declaration by the European Council on the Situation in the Middle East,

Venice, 12–13 June 1980. Conclusions of the European Council, Berlin, 24–25 March 1999.

19 European Commission's Office in the West Bank and Gaza Strip, *The European Commission and the Palestinians, Three Decades of Partnership* 7.

20 Ibid. See also 'Declaration by the Presidency on Behalf of the European Union on the Situation in the Middle East', Brussels, 11 September 2003, and 'Presidency Conclusions', Brussels: European Council, 16/17 October 2003.

21 Volker Perthes, *The Middle East Peace Process: An Opportunity for the EU?* (Brussels: Stiftung Wissenshaft und Politik (SWP), May 2001) 7.

22 One such occasion was the capital-level TFPR meeting at the Dead Sea in November 2002 where a side meeting was organized at the last minute to discuss overall donor coordination. The EU Special Envoy attended but not the EC, which had the expertise and knowledge of the file, *de facto* limiting European input and reflecting badly on its overall capacity to assume greater leadership.

23 In fact, the EC never financed any Palestinian textbook. Some Member States did, but it was nonetheless the Commission which came under attack. 'The Palestinian Textbooks Controversy. Discussion about Palestinian Textbooks in the Light of the Peace-Building Process', EC, West Bank and Gaza Strip, January 2005. The 2000s allegations regarding 'terrorism' will be addressed in Chapter 6.

24 Hilde Henriksen Waage, *Peacemaking is a Risky Business. Norway's Role in the Peace Process in the Middle East, 1993–96* (Oslo: International Peace Research Institute (PRIO), 2004) 240–241.

25 Tocci, *The Widening Gap between Rhetoric and Reality in EU Policy Towards the Israeli–Palestinian Conflict* 14.

26 The United Nations Truce Supervision Organization (UNTSO), which was set up in 1948 to 'supervise the observance of the truce in Palestine' and since 1949 has mainly been supervising the Armistice Agreements, has continued to operate, but its role is strictly circumscribed.

27 In 2004, for instance, UNDP acted as an administrative umbrella for 19 out of the 25 UN agencies operating in the oPt. Agencies for which UNDP did not perform any such function included UNSCO, UNRWA, UNESCO, the World Bank and the IMF.

28 For instance, the report of the SG on 'Assistance to the Palestinian People' is submitted on a yearly basis to the GA through the Economic and Social Council.

29 Rex Brynen, *A Very Political Economy: Peacebuilding and Foreign Aid in the West Bank and Gaza* (Washington DC: United States Institute of Peace Press, 2000) 174.

30 United Nations, *The Question of Palestine and the United Nations* (New York: Department of Public Information, March 2003) 49.

31 'Jenin Camp "Horrific Beyond Belief"', BBC News, 18 April 2002. See also 'Ben-Eliezer: Larsen Guilty of "Incitment" Against Israel' and 'A-G Moots Declaring UN Envoy Larsen "Persona Non Grata"', *Ha'aretz*, 21 April 2004.

32 Ms Catherine Bertini, Personal Humanitarian Envoy of the Secretary-General, Mission Report, 11–19 August 2002, 23, 24.

33 In an interview with a French radio station in April 2004, Lakhdar Brahimi, the then UN Envoy to Iraq and special adviser to Kofi Anan, described the Israeli 'policy of domination and the suffering imposed on the Palestinians' as the 'great poison' in the region, prompting strong protest by the Israeli mission to the UN and leading the SG publicly to distance himself from the remarks of his special adviser. 'UN Envoy Condemns Israeli Policy', BBC News, 23 April 2004.

34 Transcript of remarks by Bush and Sharon on Israel, *New York Times*, 14 April 2004.

35 Kathleen Christison, 'Bound by a Frame of Reference, Part I.I.I: US Policy and the Palestinians, 1988–98', *Journal of Palestine Studies* XXVII, no. 4 (Summer 1998): 60.

36 Karma Nabulsi, 'The Peace Process and the Palestinians: A Road Map to Mars', *International Affairs* 80, no. 2 (March 2004): 221.

37 In January 2005, Larsen was appointed Special Envoy for the implementation of Security Council resolution 1559 on Lebanon and the withdrawal of all non-Lebanese forces from Lebanon, and remained one of the closest advisors to the SG on the Middle East.

38 A full listing of the reports produced by the Bank in the 1990s is available on the Bank's website as well as in World Bank (Operations Evaluation Department), *West Bank and Gaza: An Evaluation of Bank Assistance* (Washington DC: World Bank, March 2002).

39 World Bank, *Fifteen Months – Intifada, Closures and Palestinian Economic Crisis – An Assessment* (Jerusalem: World Bank, March 2002). World Bank, *Twenty Seven Months – Intifada, Closures and Economic Crisis – An Assessment* (Jerusalem: World Bank, May 2003). World Bank, *Four Years – Intifada, Closures and Palestinian Economic Crisis – An Assessment* (Jerusalem: World Bank, October 2004). World Bank, *Disengagement, the Palestinian Economy and the Settlements* (Jerusalem: World Bank, 23 June 2004). World Bank, *Stagnation or Revival? Israeli Disengagement and Palestinian Economic Prospects* (Jerusalem: World Bank, December 2004).

40 For a discussion of the legal issues arising from the fact that the oPt is not a sovereign country, see Ibrahim F.I. Shihata, I. Hadi Abushakra and Hans-Jürgen Gruss, 'Legal Aspects of the World Bank's Assistance to the West Bank and Gaza Strip', *Palestine Yearbook of International Law (1992–1994)* (Boston: Brill, 1995).

41 World Bank (Operations Evaluation Department), *West Bank and Gaza: An Evaluation of Bank Assistance*. Anne Le More, 'Twelve Years of World Bank's Assistance to the West Bank and Gaza', May 2005 (Draft).

42 World Bank, *Stagnation or Revival? Israeli Disengagement and Palestinian Economic Prospects* 9.

43 World Bank, 'Wolfensohn Honoured by Special Envoy Appointment', Press Release, Washington DC, 14 April 2005.

44 As pointed out by one Bank official: 'What happens on our board is a reflection of what happens internationally. The US is driving the agenda.'

5 ESPOUSING ISRAELI POLICIES: SUPPORTING THE 'PEACE PROCESS'

1 Chair's Summary, Ad Hoc Liaison Committee, Lisbon, 8 June 2000.

2 Chair's Summary, Informal Ad Hoc Liaison Committee, Oslo, 25 April 2002.

3 World Bank, *Emergency Assistance Program for the Occupied Territories* (Washington DC: World Bank, April 1994) 4.

4 World Bank, *Developing the Occupied Territories: An Investment in Peace*, six vols, Vol. 1 (Washington DC: World Bank, September 1993).

5 Barbara Balaj, Ishac Diwan and Bernard Philippe, 'Aide Extérieure aux Palestinians: ce qui n'a pas fonctionné', *Politique étrangère* 3/95 (Autumn 1995): 755.

6 As noted by one EC official, 'when Israel left, it also left the bills'.

7 Balaj, 'Aide Extérieure aux Palestinians: ce qui n'a pas fonctionné', 756.

8 World Bank (Operations Evaluation Department), *West Bank and Gaza: An Evaluation of Bank Assistance* (Washington DC: World Bank, March 2002) 4–5.

9 Rex Brynen, *A Very Political Economy: Peacebuilding and Foreign Aid in the West Bank and Gaza* (Washington DC: United States Institute of Peace Press, 2000).

10 United Nations Office of the Special Coordinator (UNSCO), *Emergency Employment Programme* (Gaza: UNSCO, 31 August 1996) 3.

11 World Bank, *Holst Peace Fund. Supporting Development in the West Bank and Gaza* (Washington DC: World Bank, 2002) 6.

12 United Nations Office of the Special Coordinator (UNSCO), *Emergency Employment Programme*.

13 World Bank, *Holst Peace Fund. Supporting Development in the West Bank and Gaza* 6, 9.

14 Peter Lagerquist, 'Privatizing the Occupation: The Political Economy of an Oslo Development Project', *Journal of Palestinian Studies* XXXII, no. 2 (Winter 2003): 9, 17.

15 Brynen, *A Very Political Economy: Peacebuilding and Foreign Aid in the West Bank and Gaza* 113–114.

16 Palestinian National Authority, the Palestinian Public Investment Programme (PIPP) for 1997, presented to the CG Meeting, Paris, 19–20 November 1996.

17 World Bank (Operations Evaluation Department), *West Bank and Gaza: An Evaluation of Bank Assistance* 4.

18 World Bank and Japan, *Aid Effectiveness in the West Bank and Gaza* (Jerusalem: World Bank, June 2000) 19.

19 For instance, in its planned assistance programme for 2000–2006, the EC focused on the same three areas, though worded slightly differently and in different order, namely: infrastructure and natural resources management, institutional capacity building and private sector development. European Commission, *Euro-Mediterranean Partnership Country Strategy Papers, 2000–2006, West Bank and Gaza Strip* (Brussels: EC, 2000) 19.

20 World Bank and Japan, *Aid Effectiveness in the West Bank and Gaza* 47.

21 Ibid. 19, 22.

22 United Nations Development Programme (UNDP), *UNDP in the Occupied Palestinian Territory. Programme Review 2005* (New York: UNDP, 2005) 25–30.

23 See for instance Chair's Summary, Ad Hoc Liaison Committee, Tokyo, 15 October 1999 and Lisbon, 8 June 2000.

24 Palestinian National Authority, *Palestinian Development Plan 1999–2003* (January 1999) 58–59.

25 For details on the amount and repartition of foreign aid, see Appendix I, 'Overview of Foreign Aid to the Occupied Palestinian Territory, 1994–2004'.

26 World Bank, *Fifteen Months – Intifada, Closures and Palestinian Economic Crisis – An Assessment* (Jerusalem: World Bank, March 2002) 65–66.

27 World Bank, *Twenty Seven Months – Intifada, Closures and Economic Crisis – An Assessment* (Jerusalem: World Bank, May 2003) 52.

28 As explained above, what was *a posteriori* counted as 'development' was in fact the type of assistance which was envisaged in the Bank's Emergency Assistance Programme.

29 World Bank, *Twenty Seven Months – Intifada, Closures and Economic Crisis – An Assessment* 51.

30 World Bank, *Four Years – Intifada, Closures and Palestinian Economic Crisis – An Assessment* (Jerusalem: World Bank, October 2004) 66–67.

31 World Bank, *Twenty Seven Months – Intifada, Closures and Economic Crisis – An Assessment* 54–55.

32 World Bank, *Disengagement, the Palestinian Economy and the Settlements* (Jerusalem: World Bank, 23 June 2004) 3.

33 For an overview of these methodologies, see Mark Hoffman, 'Peace and Conflict Impact Assessment Methodology: Evolving Art Form or Practical Dead End?' in David Bloomfield, Martina Fischer and Beatrix Schmelzle, eds, *Berghof Handbook for Conflict Transformation* (Berlin: Berghof Research Centre for Constructive Conflict Management, September 2001).

34 All data from World Bank and Japan, *Aid Effectiveness in the West Bank and Gaza* 30–46.

35 World Bank, *Four Years – Intifada, Closures and Palestinian Economic Crisis – An Assessment* xvii.

36 Claude Bruderlein, 'Human Security Challenges in the Occupied Palestinian Territory', in Michael Keating, Anne Le More and Robert Lowe, eds, *Aid, Diplomacy and Facts on the Ground: The Case of Palestine* (London: Chatham House, 2005) 81.

37 World Bank and Japan, *Aid Effectiveness in the West Bank and Gaza* 42–46.

38 World Bank, *Stagnation or Revival? Israeli Disengagement and Palestinian Economic Prospects* (Jerusalem: World Bank, December 2004) 1.

39 European Commission, *Euro-Mediterranean Partnership Country Strategy Papers, 2000–2006, West Bank and Gaza Strip* 16.

40 'The Donor Experience and the Way Ahead', statement by the World Bank, Fifth Consultative Group Meeting for the West Bank and Gaza, Paris, 15–17 December 1997.

41 'Evaluation of the European Community's Programme of Assistance to the West Bank and Gaza Strip', European Court of Auditors Special Report, Brussels, January 1999, 7.

42 World Bank, *Twenty Seven Months – Intifada, Closures and Economic Crisis – An Assessment* xv.

43 World Bank, *Disengagement, the Palestinian Economy and the Settlements* (Jerusalem: World Bank, 23 June 2004) i, ii.

44 World Bank, *The Palestinian Economy and the Prospects for Its Recovery* (Jerusalem: World Bank, December 2005) 3.

45 Lagerquist, 'Privatizing the Occupation: The Political Economy of an Oslo Development Project' 7.

46 See Introduction, note 10, for further details.

47 Lagerquist, 'Privatizing the Occupation: The Political Economy of an Oslo Development Project' 9.

48 Ibid. 10–11, 15–17.

49 World Bank, *Holst Peace Fund. Supporting Development in the West Bank and Gaza* 6–9.

50 In January 1997, Israel and the PLO signed the Protocol Concerning the Redeployment in Hebron, dividing the city between two zones: H1 which was placed under PA control, and the centre of the city (H2), home of about 30,000 Palestinians and 400–500 Israeli settlers, which remained under Israeli control.

51 United Nations Office of the Special Coordinator (UNSCO), 'United Nations Special Coordinator Releases Details of Emergency Humanitarian Plan to Improve Economic Situation in the West Bank and Gaza Strip', Press Release, Gaza, 31 March 1996. See also United Nations Relief and Work Agency (UNRWA), 'Economic Effects of the Closure and Implications for UNRWA's Food Distribution Policy', Gaza, 12 March 1996.

52 The Bank even estimated that with a population growing at 5 per cent a year, the humanitarian situation would worsen, predicting that poverty levels would climb to 56 per cent in 2006, reaching 72 per cent in Gaza. World Bank, *Disengagement, the Palestinian Economy and the Settlements* 31.

53 Meron Benvenisti, 'International Community Supports a Deluxe Occupation' *Ha'aretz*, 11 September 2003.

54 Ms Catherine Bertini, Personal Humanitarian Envoy of the Secretary-General, Mission Report, 11–19 August 2002.

55 David Shearer and Anuschka Meyer. 'The Dilemma of Aid Under Occupation', in Keating, ed., *Aid, Diplomacy and Facts on the Ground: The Case of Palestine* 169.

56 Jean-Luc Siblot, Genevieve Wills and Tareq Abu ElHaj, *Food Security in the Occupied Palestinian Territory, Humanitarian Exchange Nb 28* (London: Overseas Development Institute, November 2004) 27.

57 UNCTAD, *Report on UNCTAD's Assistance to the Palestinian People* (Geneva: UN, 28 July 2003) 8.
58 International Committee of the Red Cross, 'New Strategy for the West Bank', 20 November 2003.
59 See for instance, 'Aid Donors Warn Israel on Occupied Territories', *Financial Times*, 29 November 2003.
60 Stephen Lister and Anne Le More, *Aid Management and Coordination during the Intifada. Report to the LACC Co-Chairs* (July 2003) 6.
61 World Bank, *Twenty Seven Months – Intifada, Closures and Economic Crisis – An Assessment* 56.
62 Local Aid Coordination Committee (LACC) – Donor Support Group, *Physical and Institutional Damage Assessment. West Bank Governorates, March–May 2002. Summary Report* (Jerusalem: LACC, 23 May 2002).
63 OCHA and UNRWA, 'Rafah Humanitarian Needs Assessment: Submission to the Local Aid Coordination Committee', 6 June 2004.
64 UN Security Council resolution 1544 of 19 May 2004, S/Res/1544 (2004).
65 *The Geneva Conventions of August 12, 1949* (International Committee of the Red Cross, Geneva). Fourth Convention Art. 147.
66 David Shearer and Anuschka Meyer. 'The Dilemma of Aid Under Occupation', in Keating, ed., *Aid, Diplomacy and Facts on the Ground: The Case of Palestine* 174–175.
67 International Court of Justice, *Legal Consequences of the Construction of a Wall in the Occupied Palestinian Territory* (9 July 2004) Para. 159.
68 Ibid. Para. 152.
69 David Shearer and Anuschka Meyer. 'The Dilemma of Aid Under Occupation', in Keating, ed., *Aid, Diplomacy and Facts on the Ground: The Case of Palestine* 172.
70 World Bank, *Stagnation or Revival? Israeli Disengagement and Palestinian Economic Prospects* 9.
71 Amira Haas, 'Donor Countries Won't Fund Israeli-Planned Separate Roads for Palestinians', *Ha'aretz*, 30 November 2004.
72 World Bank, *Stagnation or Revival? Israeli Disengagement and Palestinian Economic Prospects* 9.
73 Compare World Bank, *Fifteen Months – Intifada, Closures and Palestinian Economic Crisis – An Assessment*. World Bank, *Twenty Seven Months – Intifada, Closures and Economic Crisis – An Assessment*. World Bank, *Four Years – Intifada, Closures and Palestinian Economic Crisis – An Assessment*.
74 World Bank, *Stagnation or Revival? Israeli Disengagement and Palestinian Economic Prospects* 3. See also *Ha'aretz*, Sunday 10 July 2005.
75 World Bank and Japan, *Aid Effectiveness in the West Bank and Gaza* 33.
76 Ibid.
77 Julie Trottier, *Hydropolitics in the West Bank and Gaza Strip* (Jerusalem: PASSIA, 1999) 66.
78 USAID West Bank and Gaza Programme Budget, 1993–2004.
79 Fadia Daibes, ed., *Water in Palestine. Problems, Politics, Prospects* (Jerusalem: PASSIA, 2003) 33–35.
80 World Bank and Japan, *Aid Effectiveness in the West Bank and Gaza* 67.
81 Contrast, for example, with World Bank, *Afghanistan: State-building, Sustaining Growth, and Reducing Poverty* (Washington DC: World Bank, January 2005).
82 For instance, Jerusalem did not figure in the Palestinian Development Plan 1998–2000 presented by the Palestinians at the CG meeting of December 1997. See European Commission Statement, Consultative Group Meeting for West Bank and Gaza, Paris, 14–15 December 1997.

83 Chairman's Statement, Consultative Group Meeting for West Bank and Gaza, Paris, 9 September 1994.
84 See, for instance, MOPIC, 'Development Planning Strategy and Funding Programme', October 1996; 'The Palestinian Public Investment Programme (PIPP) for 1997', November 1996.
85 Interview, Dr Mohammed Stayyeh, Jerusalem, 24 January 2004.
86 Interview, World Bank official, Washington DC, 27 April 2004.
87 These themes have been explored in more detail in Anne Le More, 'Foreign Aid Strategy', in Numan Kanafani, and David Cobham, eds, *The Economics of Palestine: Economic Policy and Institutional Reform for a Viable Palestinian State* (London: Routledge, 2004).
88 See, for instance, the Emergency Public Investment Plan 2003, endorsed by donors at the London AHLC in February 2003; the Quick Impact Intervention Programme July–December 2003, presented by the Palestinian Ministry of Planning to the donors at the LACC in July 2003; the Palestinian Socio-Economic Stabilization Plan for 2004–2005 and the Medium-Term Development Plan 2004–2005 of September 2003, presented at the AHLC, Rome, in December 2003.
89 Interview, Jan de Jong, Jerusalem, 17 July 2004.
90 Christopher Parker, *Resignation or Revolt? Socio-Political Development and the Challenges of Peace in Palestine* (London, New York: I.B. Tauris, 1999) 226.
91 Mary B. Anderson, 'Do No Harm: The Impact of International Assistance to the Occupied Palestinian Territory', in Keating, ed., *Aid, Diplomacy and Facts on the Ground: The Case of Palestine* 145–147.

6 FUNDING PALESTINIAN ADJUSTMENT: REGIME CREATION AND THE UNDERMINING OF PALESTINIAN STATE-BUILDING

1 World Bank (Operations Evaluation Department), *West Bank and Gaza: An Evaluation of Bank Assistance* (Washington DC: World Bank, March 2002) 27.
2 World Bank, *Holst Peace Fund. Supporting Development in the West Bank and Gaza* (Washington DC: World Bank, 2002) 3, 9.
3 Rex Brynen, *A Very Political Economy: Peacebuilding and Foreign Aid in the West Bank and Gaza* (Washington DC: United States Institute of Peace Press, 2000) 174, 79.
4 Bilateral donors also provided equipment via the Coordinating Committee for International Assistance to a Palestinian Police Force (COPP) headed by Norway. Barbara Balaj, Ishac Diwan and Bernard Philippe, 'Aide Extérieure Aux Palestinians: ce qui n'a pas fonctionné', *Politique étrangère* 3/95 (Autumn 1995): 762.
5 International Monetary Fund, *West Bank and Gaza: Economic Performance and Reform under Conflict Conditions* (Washington DC: IMF, 2003) 63. World Bank, *Fifteen Months – Intifada, Closures and Palestinian Economic Crisis – An Assessment* (Jerusalem: World Bank, March 2002) v.
6 International Monetary Fund, *West Bank and Gaza: Economic Performance and Reform under Conflict Conditions* 67.
7 'Proposition de financement: fonds spécial de trésorerie', Commission Européenne, Brussels, 1997 (unpublished). Interview, EC official, Brussels, 18 June 2003.
8 According to the Bank, in the early 1990s, NGOs were receiving between US$140 and $200 million in yearly external assistance. In 1994, external support decreased to about US$90 million to stabilize at US$60 million by 1995–1996; World Bank and Japan, *Aid Effectiveness in the West Bank and Gaza* (Jerusalem: World Bank, June 2000) 20.
9 World Bank (Operations Evaluation Department), *West Bank and Gaza: An Evalu-*

ation of Bank Assistance 27. OED also noted that 'there is no indication that funds were diverted or improperly used'.

10 Salvatore Schiavo-Campo, *Financing and Aid Management Arrangements in Post-Conflict Situations* (World Bank Conflict Prevention and Reconstruction Unit Working Paper No. 6, Washington DC: World Bank, June 2003) 6.

11 See for instance 'Statement on Behalf of the AHLC Chair', Consultative Group for the West Bank and Gaza, Paris, 14–15 December 1997; Chair's Summary, Ad Hoc Liaison Committee, Frankfurt, 4 February 1999; Chair's Summary, Ad Hoc Liaison Committee, Lisbon, 8 June 2000.

12 See for instance, International Monetary Fund, *West Bank and Gaza Strip. Fiscal Developments since Oslo and Future Challenges* (Washington DC/Jerusalem: IMF, February 1999) 7. Report presented at the Ad Hoc Liaison Committee in Frankfurt on 4 February 1999.

13 For instance, the issue of PA governance and financial accountability figured prominently on the agenda of the fifth meeting of the World Bank Consultative Group held in December 1997 in Paris. Little was achieved by the time donors met at the AHLC in Frankfurt in February 1999, nor was there much progress recorded by June 2000 when donors gathered in Lisbon. See Chairman's Summary, Consultative Group for the West Bank and Gaza, Paris, 14–15 December 1997; Chair's Summary, Ad Hoc Liaison Committee, Frankfurt, 4 February 1999; Chair's Summary, Ad Hoc Liaison Committee, Tokyo, 15 October 1999. Chair's Summary, Ad Hoc Liaison Committee, Lisbon, 8 June 2000. See also, International Monetary Fund, 'West Bank and Gaza – Report on Fiscal developments in January–June 1999', 10 August 1999. See also United Nations Office of the Special Coordinator (UNSCO), *The Economy of the West Bank and Gaza Strip: A Retrospective on the 1990s and Future Challenges* (January 1999) 14.

14 Schiavo-Campo, *Financing and Aid Management Arrangements in Post-Conflict Situations* 11.

15 See, for instance, Chair's Summary, Ad Hoc Liaison Committee, Lisbon, 8 June 2000.

16 World Bank, *Fifteen Months – Intifada, Closures and Palestinian Economic Crisis – An Assessment* v.

17 World Bank, *Twenty Seven Months – Intifada, Closures and Economic Crisis – An Assessment* (Jerusalem: World Bank, May 2003) 52.

18 World Bank, *Four Years – Intifada, Closures and Palestinian Economic Crisis – An Assessment* (Jerusalem: World Bank, October 2004) 64.

19 World Bank, *Twenty Seven Months – Intifada, Closures and Economic Crisis – An Assessment* 85. European Commission's Office in the West Bank and Gaza Strip, *The European Commission and the Palestinians, Three Decades of Partnership* (Gaza/Jerusalem: EC, June 2003) 8–9.

20 World Bank, 'West Bank and Gaza: Public Financial Management Reform Trust Fund', Washington DC, April 2004 (unpublished) 2.

21 'State Department Summarizes Assistance to Palestinian Authority: Regular and Supplemental Aid Total More Than US$120 million in 2003', US State Department, Press Release, 11 November 2003.

22 PM Mahmoud Abbas was welcomed into the White House on 25 July 2003. He was the first Palestinian leader to be invited since President Bush was sworn into office in January 2001. 'Abbas Wins White House Red Carpet', BBC News, 25 July 2003.

23 Congressional Research Service (CRS) Report for Congress, 'US Aid to the Palestinians', 2 February 2006.

24 European Union, Working Group on Budgetary Assistance to the Palestinian Authority, 'Draft Conclusions', March 2004 (unpublished).

25 For example: consolidation of PA revenue into a Single Treasury Account (STA) monitored by the IMF; PA payroll managed by the MoF; a freeze on public sector hiring; reinforcement of financial control and audit capacities; evaluation of all PA commercial investments and their consolidation under the PIF; the passing and application of the Basic Law and the Law on the Independence of the Judiciary.

26 See for instance, 'Israel Says Papers Link EU Funds to Terror', *The Times*, 6 May 2002, and 'EU Funding to the Palestinian Authority: Commissioner Patten Responds to a Letter from Mr Laschet, MEP', Brussels, 6 February 2003.

27 European Anti-Fraud Office (OLAF), 'OLAF Investigation into EU Budget Assistance for the Palestinian Authority', Press Release, Brussels, 10 August 2004; and 'OLAF Investigation into EU Assistance to the Palestinian Authority Budget', Press Release, Brussels, 17 March 2005.

28 One EC official remarked that at the peak of the campaign in 2002–2003 he was spending around 80 per cent of his time dealing with those allegations.

29 Interview, EC official, Brussels, 17 June 2003. European Commission's Office in the West Bank and Gaza Strip, *The European Commission and the Palestinians, Three Decades of Partnership* 9.

30 World Bank, *West Bank and Gaza: Public Financial Management Reform Trust Fund* 4.

31 As of 2005, the donors to the Trust Fund had been Australia, Canada, the EC, France, Japan, Korea, Norway, the UK and the World Bank. World Bank, West Bank and Gaza, 'Public Financial Management Reform Programme and Trust Fund, Joint Supervision Report, 28 February–3 March 2005', 4, 31

32 'EU to Support Reform of Palestinian Authority with New Forms of Aid', EC Press Release, Brussels, 30 April 2003.

33 On the improvements in the public financial management system of the WBGS, see the Bank's report 'West Bank and Gaza Country Financial Accountability Assessment', June 2004. On the need for fiscal stabilization, see World Bank, *Stagnation or Revival? Israeli Disengagement and Palestinian Economic Prospects* (Jerusalem: World Bank, December 2004) 20.

34 World Bank, West Bank and Gaza, 'Public Financial Management Reform Programme and Trust Fund, Joint Supervision Report, 28 February–3 March 2005', 4.

35 The decision to hold elections was contained in Article III of the 1993 Declaration of Principles and the central provisions included in Chapter 1 and Annex II of the Interim Agreement.

36 Nils and Kåre Vollan Butenchøn, eds, *Interim Democracy. Report on the Palestinian Elections January 1996* (Oslo: Norwegian Institute of Human Rights, May 1996) 20.

37 'Evaluation of the European Community's Programme of Assistance to the West Bank and Gaza Strip', European Court of Auditors Special Report (Brussels: January 1999) 19.

38 A majority system was also adopted for the presidential elections but it was a straightforward one, the President being elected by a simple majority with the WBGS being considered as one constituency.

39 The two most common electoral systems used for parliamentary elections are the proportional system and the majority system in a single-member constituency.

40 Interview, Dr George Giacaman, Ramallah, 22 November 2003. The Israeli electoral system is based on nation-wide proportional representation, with Israel being a single electoral district.

41 National Democratic Institute for International Affairs and the Carter Center, *The January 20, 1996 Palestinian Elections* (Washington DC and Atlanta: NDIIA/Carter Center, 1997) 84. Glenn E Robinson, *Building a Palestinian State: The Incomplete Revolution* (Bloomington: Indiana University Press, 1997) 196. Adir Waldman,

'Negotiated Transitions to Democracy: Israel and the Palestinians as a Case Study', *Democratization* 7, no. 2 (Summer 2000): 124.

42 European Union, Electoral Unit, Joint Statement by Heads of International Observer Delegations, Ramallah, 21 January 1996, annexed in Butenchøn, ed., *Interim Democracy. Report on the Palestinian Elections January 1996* 127. The local observers, who included members of Palestinian NGOs and human rights organizations, did not reach the same conclusions as their international colleagues. In a press conference on 25 January, they actually called for a re-vote throughout the oPt, citing interference by Palestinian security forces, missing ballot boxes and their exclusion from the vote-counting. Quoted in Lamis Andoni, 'The Palestinian Elections: Moving toward Democracy or One-Party Rule?' *Journal of Palestinian Studies* XXV, no. 3 (Spring 1996): 14. According to Dr Mustafa Barghouti,

> the international community refused to look into the issue of fraud, although it might have been very big in places such as Gaza, Ramallah or Hebron. This touched at least 20/25 PLC members or maybe even one quarter of the Council but no one was interested.
> (Interview, Dr Mustafa Barghouti, Ramallah, 22 November 2003)

43 For instance, the US-based NDI and Carter Center stated that

> the Palestinian elections of January 20, 1996, marked a historic step in the MEPP that built upon the 1979 Camp David Accords and the 1993 Oslo Accords. The elections provided Palestinians living in the West Bank, Gaza Trip and East Jerusalem an opportunity to participate in building their own democratic self-governing polity for the first time.
> (National Democratic Institute for International Affairs and the Carter Center, *The January 20, 1996 Palestinian Elections* vii)

44 Ryad al-Malki, quoted in Andoni, 'The Palestinian Elections: Moving toward Democracy or One-Party Rule?' 8.

45 Ballots were cast by 73.5 per cent of registered voters. There were 676 candidates, mostly independent, running for the 88 available seats. National Democratic Institute for International Affairs and the Carter Center, *The January 20, 1996 Palestinian Elections* vii.

46 Edward W. Said, *Peace and Its Discontents. Gaza–Jericho, 1993–1995* (London: Vintage, 1995) 2.

47 Butenchøn, ed., *Interim Democracy. Report on the Palestinian Elections January 1996* 22.

48 Karma Nabulsi, 'The State-Building Project: What Went Wrong?' in Michael Keating, Anne Le More and Robert Lowe, eds, *Aid, Diplomacy and Facts on the Ground: The Case of Palestine* (London: Chatham House, 2005) 121–122.

49 For figures on refugees, see note 3 in the Introduction. Basing this on UNRWA-registered refugees alone, amounting to 4.1 million, only 38 per cent live in the WBGS. 'UNRWA in Figures', Public Information Office, UNRWA Headquarters, Gaza, March 2004.

50 On the issue of Palestinian refugees, see Ilan Pappe, *A History of Modern Palestine. One Land, Two Peoples* (Cambridge: CUP, 2004) 139. Ilan Pappe, *The Ethnic Cleansing of Palestine* (Oxford: One World, 2006). Eugene L. Rogan and Avi Shlaim, eds, *The War for Palestine. Rewriting the History of 1948* (Cambridge: CUP, 2001). Joint Parliamentary Middle East Councils Commission of Enquiry – Palestinian Refugees, *Right of Return* (London: Labour Middle East Council, March 2001). Tanya Reinhart, *Israel/Palestine: How to End the War of 1948* (New York: Seven Stories Press, 2002) 51–60. International Crisis Group, *Palestinian Refugees and the*

Politics of Peacemaking (Amman/Brussels: ICG, 5 February 2004) i. The refugee question remains taboo although many analysts – Israeli, Palestinian (including refugees) and international – have recognized that the Palestinian demand that the principle of their right of return be recognized by Israel did not automatically imply restitution in kind and did not necessarily prejudge the outcome of a negotiated compromise between the parties on the practical implementation of such a right.

51 This constituted the so-called 'Ottawa process' financed by CIDA in collaboration with the Canadian Department of Foreign Affairs and International Trade. Half a dozen workshops took place between 1997 and 2003, some in Ottawa and some in Minster Lovell (UK) organized jointly with the Centre for Lebanese Studies at Oxford and the Royal Institute for International Affairs. See the Canadian Expert and Advisory Services Fund (www.crdi.ca/en/ev-26770-201-1-DO_TOPIC.html).

52 Uriya Shavit and Jalal Bana, 'Everything You Wanted to Know about the Right to Return but Were Too Afraid to Ask', *Ha'aretz* magazine, 6 July 2001.

53 For an overview of Palestinian needs and aspirations as determined by the Palestinian refugees and exiles themselves, see the results of a comprehensive participatory civic needs assessment undertaken in 2004 and 2005. Civitas Project, *Palestinian Register: Laying Foundations and Setting Directions* (University of Oxford: Nuffield College, 2006).

54 See for instance Robert Malley and Hussein Agha, 'Camp David: The Tragedy of Errors', *The New York Review of Books*, 9 August 2001; and Charles Enderlin, *Le Rêve Brisé. Histoire de l'échec du processus de paix au Proche-Orient 1995–2002* (Paris: Fayard, 2002) 332–333.

55 Uriya Shavit and Jalal Bana, 'Everything You Wanted to Know about the Right to Return but Were Too Afraid to Ask', *Ha'aretz* magazine, 6 July 2001.

56 Karma Nabulsi, 'The Peace Process and the Palestinians: A Road Map to Mars', *International Affairs* 80, no. 2 (March 2004): 229–230.

57 Harish Parvathaneni, 'The Impact of the Oslo Accords on UNRWA's Funding', in Keating, ed., *Aid, Diplomacy and Facts on the Ground: The Case of Palestine* 90–93.

58 Jalal Al-Husseini, 'UNRWA and the Palestinian Nation-Building Process', *Journal of Palestinian Studies* XXIX, no. 2 (Winter 2000): 61.

59 Harish Parvathaneni, 'The Impact of the Oslo Accords on UNRWA's Funding', in Keating, ed., *Aid, Diplomacy and Facts on the Ground: The Case of Palestine* 94–96.

60 The issue is not just about demographics. At a deeper level, any recognition – even symbolic – of the right of return signifies an acknowledgment of Israel's responsibility for the dispossession of a large proportion of the Palestinians and the ensuing creation of the refugee problem, in the words of Tanya Reinhart that 'Israel's birth was in sin', something which challenges what remains today the official Israeli national narrative. Reinhart, *Israel/Palestine: How to End the War of 1948* 51–60. Since the late 1980s, the Israeli 'new' historians have critically reassessed what they themselves call 'Israel's foundational myths' and in particular the traditional Zionist narrative of the 1948 war and its aftermath. See note 15 in the Introduction. This group includes scholars such as Professor Avi Shlaim, Dr Ilan Pape and Dr Simha Flapan. Their 'revisionist' analysis was made possible in large part by the declassification of the GOI archives which are governed by the 30-year rule. See, for instance, Rogan, ed., *The War for Palestine. Rewriting the History of 1948*; Avi Shlaim, *The Iron Wall. Israel and the Arab World* (London: Allen Lane, Penguin, 2000) ; Zeev Sternhell, *Aux Origines d'Israel. Entre nationalisme et socialisme* (Paris: Fayard, 1996). Pappe, *The Ethnic Cleansing of Palestine*.

61 'Transcript of Remarks by Bush and Sharon on Israeli Disengagement Plan', *New York Times*, 14 April 2004.

62 'Evaluation of the European Community's Programme of Assistance to the West Bank and Gaza Strip' 32–34.

63 Independent Task Force sponsored by the Council on Foreign Relations, *Strengthening Palestinian Public Institutions (The Rocard Report)* (New York: UN, June 1999) 3.

64 Ibid.

65 See World Bank, *West Bank and Gaza: Strengthening Public Sector Management* (Jerusalem: World Bank, 1999). Some important PA reform commitments were also made in the context of the revised TAP of October 1999 presented at the AHLC in Tokyo in October 1999. In addition, the Economic Policy Framework, prepared by the PA in collaboration with the IMF, was presented at the AHLC in Lisbon in June 2000. These reform initiatives were restricted to restructuring PA's economic, financial and banking sectors and, as of the beginning of the *intifada*, it was too early to record substantial progress. It may be noted, however, that for the first time the issue of rule of law figured prominently on the agenda of the AHLC in Lisbon, testifying to increased international interest in broader Palestinian governance. See Chair's Summary, Ad Hoc Liaison Committee, Tokyo, 15 October 1999, and Lisbon, 8 June 2000.

66 World Bank, *Fifteen Months – Intifada, Closures and Palestinian Economic Crisis – An Assessment* 93–98.

67 The 100 Days Reform Plan was published on 26 June 2002. See also PLC, 'A Statement Issued by the Palestinian Legislative Council towards Development and Reform of the PNA Institutions', 16 May 2002.

68 'Advancing Palestinian Reform', Meeting of the Task Force on Reform, London, 10 July 2002.

69 Following the 100 Days Plan, the PA worked, *inter alia*, towards implementing a 60-Day Action Plan in 2003 and a Six-Month Reform Plan in the first half of 2004, and put forward a One-Year Reform Action Plan in September 2004.

70 President George W. Bush, 'Statement Outlining his "Vision" for a Solution to the Middle East Conflict', White House, 24 June 2002. It should be noted that it would take another three years before the American President made the leap from a 'vision' of two states to endorsing the 'creation of a peaceful, democratic Palestinian state'. 'Statement Welcoming Palestinian President Mahmoud Abbas to the White House', 26 May 2005.

71 President George W. Bush, 'Statement Outlining his "Vision" for a Solution to the Middle East Conflict', White House, 24 June 2002.

72 'Quartet Joint Statement', US Department of State, Office of the Spokesman, New York, 16 July 2002. See also the following Quartet Statement of 17 September 2002.

73 The transfer of tax revenues it collected on the behalf of the PA was resumed in January 2003; however, as of early 2005, about NIS 1 billion of clearance revenues remained attached by Israeli court orders and held by the Israeli government. After the arrival of Hamas in 2006, Israel once again ceased to transfer funds to the PA.

74 'Security Forces nab "Terror Funds" in Ramallah Banks', *Ha'aretz*, 26 February 2004.

75 Jerusalem Media and Communication Centre (JMCC), Public Opinion Poll Unit, Poll 49, October 2003.

76 Ibid.

77 International Crisis Group, *The Meanings of Palestinian Reform* (Amman/Washington DC: ICG, 12 November 2002) 2.

78 Ibid.

79 IFEs, IRI and NDI, 'Palestinian Elections. A Pre-Election Assessment Mission Report', August 2002; and European Commission, 'Palestinian Territories of West Bank and Gaza Strip. Presidential, Legislative Council and Local Government Elections January–March 2003', EC Election Exploratory Mission Findings, 14–24 July 2002, Brussels, 13 August 2002.

80 European Commission's Office in the West Bank and Gaza Strip, *The European Commission and the Palestinians, Three Decades of Partnership* 11.

81 See, for instance, Hanan Ashrawi and Ian Urbina, 'Reforming from Within', *Guardian*, 6 June 2002.

82 See, for instance, Jerusalem Media and Communication Centre (JMCC), Public Opinion Poll Unit, Poll 49, October 2003, 4.

83 Independent Task Force on Strengthening Palestinian Public Institutions sponsored by the Council on Foreign Relations, *Reforming the Palestinian Authority: An Update* (New York: ITF, April 2004).

CONCLUSION

1 International Monetary Fund, *West Bank and Gaza: Economic Performance and Reform under Conflict Conditions* (Washington DC: IMF, 2003) 66.

2 Chris McGreal, 'Sharon in Palestine State U-Turn', *Guardian*, 28 February 2003; Akiva Eldar, 'Sharon's Palestinian "State" – in the Eyes of the Beholder', *Daily Star*, 21 June 2004.

3 Ibid.

4 Prime Minister Ariel Sharon, Interview, *Ha'aretz*, Pesach Supplement, 5 April 2004.

5 Sharon's Speech on Gaza Pullout, 15 August 2005.

6 'For First Time, Jews Are No Longer a Majority Between the Jordan and the Sea', *Ha'aretz*, 11 August 2005.

7 'State: West Bank Settler Population Grew by 12,800 in Past Year', *Ha'aretz*, 26 August 2005.

8 International Crisis Group, 'The Jerusalem Powder Keg', Middle East Report 44, 2 August 2005; and 'PM Ordered E1 Police HQ Built Two Months Ago', *Ha'aretz*, 26 August 2005.

9 'Olmert Vows to Set Final Borders', BBC News, 13 February 2006; 'Mofaz Presents Israel's Final Borders', *Jerusalem Post*, 21 March 2006.

10 Amnon Raz-Krakotzkin, 'A Peace without Arabs: The Discourse of Peace and the Limits of Israeli Consciousness', in George Giacaman and Dag Jorund Lonning, eds, *After Oslo. New Realities, Old Problems* (London: Pluto Press, 1998) 62. Amal Jamal, 'The Palestinians in the Israeli Peace Discourse: A Conditional Partnership', *Journal of Palestinian Studies* XXX, no. 1 (Autumn 2000). Peter Ezra Weinberger, 'Co-Opting the PLO: A Critical Reconstruction of the Oslo Accords, 1993–1995' (unpublished PhD, London School of Economics and Political Science, 2002).

11 Ilan Pappe, *The Ethnic Cleansing of Palestine* (Oxford: One World, 2006) 260.

12 Rashid Khalidi, *The Iron Cage. The Story of the Palestinian Struggle for Statehood* (Boston: Beacon Press, 2006) 161–164, 80.

13 Jean-Jacques Rousseau, *The Social Contract* (London: Penguin, 1968 [1762]) 52–53.

14 World Bank, 'The Impending Palestinian Fiscal Crisis: Potential Remedies', 7 May 2006.

15 See, for instance, Benita Ferrero-Waldner, European Commissioner for External Relations and European Neighbourhood Policy, 'Suspension of Aid to the Palestinian Authority Government', European Parliament Plenary, Brussels, 26 April 2006.

16 Quartet Statement, UN, New York, 9 May 2006.

17 'EU Contributes €105 Million to the Temporary International Mechanism for the Palestinians', Press Release, EC, Brussels, 23 June 2006.

18 'Commission Provides €20 Million Food Aid to the Palestinians', Press Release, EC, Brussels, 17 July 2006.

19 The three main conditions are: renounce violence; recognize Israel; and recognize all previous agreements reached between Israel and the PLO, mostly in relation to Oslo.

20 Isaac Deutscher, *New Left Review*, 20 June 1967.
21 In recent years, there has been a renewed interest in the idea of a one-state solution as the result of the growing realization that the prospect of two states is increasingly less likely. See Khalidi, *The Iron Cage. The Story of the Palestinian Struggle for State-hood* 206–217; Tony Judt, 'Israel: The Alternative', *The New York Review of Books*, 23 October 2003.

APPENDIX II: THE AID COORDINATION STRUCTURE DURING OSLO AND THE *INTIFADA*

1 The two figures contained in this Appendix are drawn from Stephen Lister and Anne Le More, *Aid Management and Coordination during the Intifada. Report to the LACC Co-Chairs* (Oxford: Mokoro, July 2003) 4, 11.

BIBLIOGRAPHY

The Geneva Conventions of August 12, 1949. International Committee of the Red Cross, Geneva.

Protocols Additional to the Geneva Conventions of 12 August 1949. International Committee of the Red Cross, Geneva, 1977.

Review of the Applicability of International Humanitarian Law to the Occupied Palestinian Territory. Briefing Paper. Program on Humanitarian Policy and Conflict Research, Harvard University, January 2004.

Abdel Shafi, Salah. *Civil Society and Political Elites in Palestine and the Role of International Donors: A Palestinian View.* EuroMeSCo Paper 33, Lisbon: EuroMeSCo, July 2004.

Abdullah, Samir and Clare Woodcraft. 'Israeli Closure Policy: Sabotaging Sustainable Development'. In *The Economics of the Middle East: A Reassessment,* edited by Sara Roy. Stamford: Jay Press, 1999.

Abed, George, ed. *The Palestinian Economy. Studies in Development under Prolonged Occupation.* London, New York: Routledge, 1988.

Abu-Amr, Ziad. 'Hamas: A Historical and Political Background'. *Journal of Palestinian Studies* XXII, no. 4 (Summer 1993): 5–19.

—— 'The Palestinian Legislative Council: A Critical Assessment'. *Journal of Palestinian Studies* XXVI, no. 4 (Summer 1997): 90–97.

—— 'Report from Palestine'. *Journal of Palestinian Studies* XXIV, no. 2 (Winter 1995): 40–47.

Al-Husseini, Jalal. 'UNRWA and the Palestinian Nation-Building Process'. *Journal of Palestinian Studies* XXIX, no. 2 (Winter 2000): 51–64.

Allison, Graham. *Essence of Decision: Explaining the Cuban Missile Crisis.* Boston: Little, Brown, 1971.

Amnesty International. *Annual Report. Palestinian Authority.* London: Amnesty International, 1998.

—— *Amnesty International Annual Report.* London: Amnesty International, 2000.

—— *Broken Lives – A Year of Intifada.* London: Amnesty International, 2001.

—— *Annual Report. Palestinian Authority.* London: Amnesty International, 2001.

—— *Annual Report. Palestinian Authority.* London: Amnesty International, 2002.

—— *Annual Report. Israel and the Occupied Territories.* London: Amnesty International, 2003.

—— *Annual Report. Palestinian Authority.* London: Amnesty International, 2003.

—— *Israel and the Occupied Territories. Surviving under Siege: The Impact of Movement Restrictions on the Right to Work.* London: Amnesty International, September 2003.

—— *Annual Report. Palestinian Authority.* London: Amnesty International, 2004.

—— *Israel and the Occupied Territories. Under the Rubble: House Demolition and Destruction of Land and Property.* London: Amnesty International, May 2004.

Amundsen, Inge and Basem Ezbidi. 'PNA Political Institutions and the Future of State Formation'. In *State Formation in Palestine. Viability and Governance during a Social Transformation*, edited by Mushtaq Husain Khan, with George Giacaman and Inge Amundsen. London: RoutledgeCurzon, 2004.

Anderson, Mary B. *Do No Harm. How Aid Can Support Peace or War.* Boulder, London: Lynne Rienner, 1996 and 1999.

Andoni, Lamis. 'The Palestinian Elections: Moving Toward Democracy or One-Party Rule?' *Journal of Palestinian Studies* XXV, no. 3 (Spring 1996): 5–16.

Annan, Kofi. *The Causes of Conflict and the Promotion of Durable Peace and Sustainable Development in Africa.* New York: United Nations, April 1998.

Arendt, Hannah. *The Origins of Totalitarianism.* San Diego, New York, London: Harcourt Brace, 1951.

Bailey, F.G. *Stratagems and Spoils. A Social Anthropology of Politics.* Oxford: Blackwell, 1969.

Balaj, Barbara, Ishac Diwan and Bernard Philippe. 'Aide Extérieure aux Palestinians: ce qui n'a pas fonctionné'. *Politique étrangère* 3/95 (Autumn 1995): 753–767.

Ball, Nicole and Tammy Halevy. *Making Peace Work: The Role of the International Development Community.* Washington DC: Overseas Development Council, 1996.

Ball, Nicole, Peter Bartu and Adriaan Verheul. 'Squaring the Circle: Security-Sector Reform and Transformation and Fiscal Stabilisation in Palestine'. Report prepared for UK Department for International Development, London, 16 January 2006.

Barghouti, Mustafa, ed. *Health and Segregation. The Impact of Israeli Separation Wall on Access to Health Care Services.* Ramallah: HDIP, January 2004.

Barnett, Michael, Hunjoon Kim, Madalene O'Donnell and Laura Sitea. 'Peacebuilding: What Is in a Name?' *Global Governance* 13, no. 1 (2007): 35–59.

Beilin, Yossi. *The Path to Geneva. The Quest for a Permanent Agreement, 1996–2004.* New York: RDV Books, 2004.

Berdal, Mats and David M. Malone, eds. *Greed and Grievance: Economic Agendas in Civil Wars.* London, Ottawa: Lynn Rienner, 2000.

Birzeit University/UNDP. *Palestine Human Development Report.* Ramallah : Birzeit University/UNDP, June 2002.

Boniface, Pascal. *Est-il permis de critiquer Israel?* Paris: Robert Laffont, 2003.

Borzel, Tanja and Thomas Risse. 'When Europe Hits Home: Europeanization and Domestic Change'. *European Integration online Papers (EIoP)* 4, no. 15 (2000).

Botiveau, Bernard. 'Le Conseil Législatif Palestinien: du conseil de l'autonomie au parlement des territoires'. *Monde Arabe – Maghreb Machrek*, no. 161 (Juillet–Septembre 1998): 8–17.

Bouillon, Markus E. *The Peace Business. Money and Power in the Palestinian–Israeli Conflict.* New York: I.B. Tauris, 2004.

Boutros Ghali, Boutros. *An Agenda for Peace. Preventive Diplomacy, Peacemaking and Peace-Keeping.* New York: United Nations, 1992.

Boyce, James K. 'Beyond Good Intentions: External Assistance and Peace Building'. In *Good Intentions. Pledges of Aid for Postconflict Recovery*, edited by Shepard Forman and Stewart Patrick. London: Lynne Rienner, 2000.

—— *Investing in Peace: Aid and Conditionality after Civil Wars, Adelphi Paper 351.* Oxford: OUP for the International Institute for Strategic Studies, 2002.

Brynen, Rex. 'The Dynamics of Palestinian Elite Formation'. *Journal of Palestinian Studies* XXIV, no. 3 (Spring 1995): 31–43.

—— 'The Neopatrimonial Dimension of Palestinian Politics'. *Journal of Palestinian Studies* XXV, no. 1 (Autumn 1995): 23–36.

—— *A Very Political Economy: Peacebuilding and Foreign Aid in the West Bank and Gaza.* Washington DC: United States Institute of Peace Press, 2000.

—— 'Aid Management and Coordination during the Intifada. Report to the LACC Co-Chairs. Peer Review and Commentary'. World Bank, July 2003.

B'Tselem. *Land Grab. Israel's Settlement Policy in the West Bank.* Jerusalem: B'Tselem, May 2002.

—— *Al Mawasi, Gaza Strip. Intolerable Life in an Isolated Enclave.* Jerusalem: B'Tselem, March 2003.

—— *Behind the Barrier. Human Rights Violations as a Result of Israel's Separation Barrier.* Jerusalem: B'Tselem, March 2003.

—— *Hebron, Area H-2: Settlements Cause Mass Departure of Palestinians.* Jerusalem: B'Tselem, August 2003.

—— *Not All It Seems. Preventing Palestinian Access to Their Lands West of the Separation Barrier in the Tulkarm-Qalqiliya Area.* Jerusalem: B'Tselem, June 2004.

—— *Forbidden Roads: The Discriminatory West Bank Road Regime.* Jerusalem: B'Tselem, August 2004.

Buchanan, Andrew S. *Peace with Justice. A History of the Israeli–Palestinian Declaration of Principles on Interim Self-Government Arrangements.* London/New York: Macmillan, 2000.

Burnell, Peter J. *Foreign Aid in a Changing World.* Buckingham: Open University Press, 1997.

—— ed. *Democracy Assistance. International Cooperation for Democratization.* London: Frank Cass, 2000.

Butenchøn, Nils and Kåre Vollan, eds. *Interim Democracy. Report on the Palestinian Elections January 1996.* Oslo: Norwegian Institute of Human Rights, May 1996.

Carothers, Thomas. *Aiding Democracy Abroad: The Learning Curve.* Washington DC: Carnegie Endowment for International Peace, 1999.

Carter, Jimmy. *Palestine. Peace Not Apartheid.* New York: Simon and Schuster, 2006.

Challand, Benoit. 'The Power to Promote and Exclude: External Support for Palestinian Civil Society. Florence'. Unpublished PhD. Institut Universitaire Européen, 2005.

—— *Civil Society, Autonomy, and Donors: International Aid to Palestinian NGOs.* Working Paper. Florence: Institut Universitaire Européen, 2006.

Chesterman, Simon, Michael Ignatieff and Ramesh Thakur, eds. *Making States Work. State Failure and the Crisis of Governance.* Tokyo: United Nations University Press, 2005.

Christison, Kathleen. 'Bound by a Frame of Reference, Part I.I.I: US Policy and the Palestinians, 1988–98'. *Journal of Palestine Studies* XXVII, no. 4 (Summer 1998): 53–64.

—— *Perceptions of Palestine. Their Influence on US Middle East Policy.* Berkeley and Los Angeles: University of California Press, 1999.

CIA. *The World Factbook*. Washington DC: CIA, 2006.

Civitas Project. *Palestinian Register: Laying Foundations and Setting Directions*. Oxford: Nuffield College, University of Oxford, 2006.

Cousens, Elizabeth M. and Charles K. Cater. *Toward Peace in Bosnia: Implementing the Dayton Accords*. International Peace Academy Occasional Paper Series, Boulder, London: Lynne Rienner, 2001.

Cousens, Elizabeth M., Chetan Kumar and Karin Wermester. *Peacebuilding as Politics: Cultivating Peace in Fragile Societies*. Boulder, London: Lynne Rienner, 2001.

Cox, Robert W. 'Social Forces, States and World Orders: Beyond International Relations Theories'. In *Neorealism and Its Critics*, edited by Robert O. Keohane. New York: Columbia University Press, 1986.

Crawford, Gordon. *Foreign Aid and Political Reform: A Comparative Analysis of Democracy Assistance and Political Conditionality*. Basingstoke: Palgrave, 2001.

Curtis, Devon. *Politics and Humanitarian Aid: Debates, Dilemmas and Dissension, HPG Report*. London: Overseas Development Institute, April 2001.

Daibes, Fadia, ed. *Water in Palestine. Problems, Politics, Prospects*. Jerusalem: PASSIA, 2003.

D'Alançon, François. 'The EC Looks to a New Middle East'. *Journal of Palestine Studies* XXIII, no. 2 (Winter 1994): 41–51.

Darby, John and Roger MacGinty. *The Management of Peace Processes*. Basingstoke: Macmillan, 2000.

Dawisha, Adeed and William I. Zartman, eds. *Beyond Coercion: The Durability of the Arab State*. London: Croom Helm, 1988.

de Jong, Jan. 'The Geography of Politics: Israel's Settlement Drive after Oslo'. In *After Oslo. New Realities, Old Problems*, edited by George Giacaman and Dag Jorund Lonning. London, Chicago: Pluto Press, 1998.

de Soto, Alvaro and Graciana del Castillo. 'Obstacles to Peacebuilding'. *Foreign Policy* (Spring 1994): 69–74.

Debié, Franck and Sylvie Fouet. *La Paix en miettes. Israel et Palestine (1993–2000)*. Paris: PUF, 2001.

Destremau, Blandine. 'Israël–Palestine: l'espace en miettes ou l'appropriation identitaire du territoire'. *Monde Arabe – Maghreb Machrek*, no. 150 (Octobre–Décembre 1995): 13–18.

Diehl, Paul F. *International Peacekeeping*. Baltimore; London: Johns Hopkins University Press, 1993.

Diwan, Ishac, and Radwan A. Shaban, *Development under Adversity. The Palestinian Economy in Transition*. Jerusalem: Palestine Economic Policy Research Institute (MAS) and World Bank, 1999.

Donini, Antonio, Norah Niland and Karin Wermester, eds. *Nation-Building Unraveled? Aid, Peace and Justice in Afghanistan*. Bloomfield: Kumarian Press, 2004.

Doyle, Michael W. *Peacebuilding in Cambodia, IPA Policy Briefing Series*. New York: International Peace Academy, 1996.

Durch, William J. *UN Peacekeeping, American Politics and the Uncivil Wars of the 1990s*. Basingstoke: Macmillan, 1997.

Eisenstadt, Shmuel Noah. *Traditional Patrimonialism and Modern Neo-Patrimonialism*. London: Sage, 1973.

Elmusa, Sharif and Mahmud El-Jaafari. 'Power and Trade: The Israeli–Palestinian Economic Protocol'. *Journal of Palestinian Studies* XXIV, no. 2 (Winter 1995): 14–32.

Enderlin, Charles. *Le Rêve Brisé. Histoire de l'échec du processus de paix au Proche-Orient 1995–2002*. Paris: Fayard, 2002.

—— *Les Années Perdues. Intifada et guerres au Proche-Orient 2001–2006*. Paris: Fayard, 2006.

European Commission. *The Palestinians and the European Union*. Jerusalem: EC, 1999.

—— *Euro-Mediterranean Partnership Country Strategy Papers, 2000–2006, West Bank and Gaza Strip*. Brussels: EC, 2000.

—— *National Indicative Programme, West Bank and Gaza Strip, 2000–2002*. Brussels: EC, 2000.

European Commission's Office in the West Bank and Gaza Strip. *The European Commission and the Palestinians, Three Decades of Partnership*. Gaza/Jerusalem: EC, June 2003.

European Court of Auditors 'Evaluation of the European Community's Programme of Assistance to the West Bank and Gaza Strip'. Special Report, Brussels, January 1999.

FAFO. *Paying a Price. Coping with Closure in Jericho, Gaza City and in Two Palestinian Villages*. Oslo: FAFO, 2001.

Farsakh, Leila. 'Palestinian Labor Flows to the Israeli Economy: A Finished Story?' *Journal of Palestinian Studies* XXXII, no. 1 (Autumn 2002): 14–15.

Finkelstein, Norman G. *Beyond Chutzpah. On the Misuse of Anti-Semitism and the Abuse of History*. Berkeley, Los Angeles: University of California Press, 2005.

Forman, Shepard and Stewart Patrick. *Good Intentions: Pledges of Aid for Postconflict Recovery*, Center on International Cooperation Studies in Multilateralism. Boulder, London: Lynne Rienner, 2000.

Foster, Mick and Fozzard, Adrian. *Aid and Public Expenditure: A Guide*. London: Overseas Development Institute, October 2000.

Fouet, Sylvie. 'Le Contrôle des mouvements comme enjeu de pouvoir'. *Monde Arabe – Maghreb Machrek*, no. 161 (Juillet–Septembre 1998): 28–42.

Freund, Julien. *L'Essence du politique*. Paris: Dalloz, 1965.

Galtung, Johan, and C.G. Jacobsen. *Searching for Peace: The Road to Transcend*. London: Pluto, 2000.

Gazit, Major General Shlomo. *The Carrot and the Stick. Israel's Policy in Judea and Samaria, 1967–68*. Washington DC: B'nai B'rith Books, 1995.

George, A. 'From Groupthink to Contextual Analysis of Policy-Making Groups'. In *Beyond Groupthink: Political Group Dynamics and Foreign Policy-Making*, edited by P. Hart, E. Stern and B. Sundelius. Michigan: University of Michigan Press, 1997.

Ghani, Ashraf, Claire Lockhart and Michael Carnahan. 'An Agenda for State-Building in the Twenty-First Century'. *The Fletcher Forum of World Affairs* 30, no. 1 (Winter 2006): 101–124.

Goldstein J. and Robert O. Keohane, eds. *Ideas and Foreign Policy. Beliefs, Institutions and Political Change*. Ithaca: Cornell University Press, 1993.

Goulding, Marrack. 'The Evolution of United Nations Peacekeeping'. *International Affairs* 69, no. 3 (1993): 451–464.

Grange, Jocelyn. 'Les Forces de sécurité palestiniennes. Contraintes d'Oslo et quête de légitimité nationale'. *Monde Arabe – Maghreb Machrek* 161 (Juillet–Septembre 1998): 21–24.

Gresh, Alain. *OLP histoire et stratégies. Vers l'etat Palestinien*. Paris: SPAG, 1983.

Haas, Amira. 'Israel's Closure Policy: An Ineffective Strategy of Containment and Repression'. *Journal of Palestinian Studies* XXXI, no. 3 (Spring 2002): 5–20.

Haas, P.M. 'Epistemic Communities and International Policy Coordination'. *International Organization* 46, no. 1 (Winter 1992): 1–35.

Halevy, Ilan. 'Self-Government, Democracy, and Mismanagement under the Palestinian Authority'. *Journal of Palestinian Studies* XXVII, no. 3 (Spring 1998): 35–48.

Halper, Jeff. 'The 94 Percent Solution. A Matrix of Control'. *Middle East Report* 216 (Fall 2000):14–19.

Hanafi, Sari. 'ONGs palestiniennes et bailleurs de fonds: la formation d'un agenda'. In *Pouvoirs et associations dans le monde arabe*, edited by Sarah Ben Nefissa. Paris: CNRS, 2002.

Harik, Iliya. 'The Origins of the Arab State System'. In *The Foundations of the Arab State*, edited by Ghassan Salamé. London: Croom Helm, 1987.

HEPG (OCHA/UNRWA). *The Humanitarian Impact of the West Bank Barrier on Palestinian Communities. Update 4*. Jerusalem: HEPG, September 2004.

Hirschman, Albert O. *The Passions and the Interests. Political Arguments for Capitalism before Its Triumph*. Princeton: Princeton University Press, 1977.

Hodgkins, Allison. *Israeli Settlement Policy in Jerusalem*. Jerusalem: PASSIA, December 1998.

Hoffman, Mark. 'Peace and Conflict Impact Assessment Methodology: Evolving Art Form or Practical Dead End?' In *Berghof Handbook for Conflict Transformation*, edited by David Bloomfield, Martina Fischer and Beatrix Schmelzle. Berlin: Berghof Research Center for Constructive Conflict Management, September 2001.

Hollis, Martin and Steve Smith. *Explaining and Understanding International Relations*. Oxford: Clarendon, 1990.

Hooper, Rick. *The International Politics of Donor Assistance to the Palestinians in the West Bank and Gaza Strip, 1993–1997*: Research in Middle East Economics 3. Greenwich: JAI Press, 1999.

Human Rights Watch. *Palestinian Self-Rule Areas: Human Rights under the Palestinian Authority*. New York: Human Rights Watch, September 1997.

Humanitarian and Emergency Policy Group (HEPG) of the Local Aid Coordination Committee (LACC). *The Impact of Israel's Separation Barrier on Affected West Bank Communities*. New York: UN, May 2003.

Independent Task Force on Strengthening Palestinian Public Institutions sponsored by the Council on Foreign Relations. *Reforming the Palestinian Authority: An Update*. New York: April 2004.

Independent Task Force sponsored by the Council on Foreign Relations. *Strengthening Palestinian Public Institutions (The Rocard Report)*. New York: June 1999.

International Court of Justice. *Legal Consequences of the Construction of a Wall in the Occupied Palestinian Territory*. The Hague: ICJ, 9 July 2004.

International Crisis Group. *The Meanings of Palestinian Reform*. Amman/Washington DC: ICG, 12 November 2002.

—— *Islamic Social Welfare Activism in the Occupied Palestinian Territories: A Legitimate Target?* Amman/Brussels: ICG, 2 April 2003.

—— *Dealing with Hamas*. Amman/Brussels: ICG, 26 January 2004.

—— *Palestinian Refugees and the Politics of Peacemaking*. Amman/Brussels: ICG, 5 February 2004.

—— *Who Governs the West Bank? Palestinian Administration under Israeli Occupation*. Amman/Brussels: ICG, 28 September 2004.

—— *The Jerusalem Powder Keg*. Amman/Brussels: ICG, 2 August 2005.

International Monetary Fund. *A Macroeconomic Framework for Assistance to Post-Conflict Countries*. Washington DC: IMF, 1996.

—— *West Bank and Gaza Strip. Economic Developments in the Five Years since Oslo*. Washington DC: IMF, 1999.

—— *West Bank and Gaza: Economic Performance and Reform under Conflict Conditions*. Washington DC: IMF, 2003.

—— *West Bank and Gaza Strip. Fiscal Developments since Oslo and Future Challenges*. Washington DC/Jerusalem: IMF, February 1999.

International Task Force on Palestinian Reform (TFPR). *Progress Report*. Jerusalem: TFPR, March–June 2004.

Jamal, Amal. 'The Palestinian Media: An Obedient Servant or a Vanguard of Democracy?' *Journal of Palestinian Studies* XXIX, no. 3 (Spring 2000): 45–59.

—— 'The Palestinians in the Israeli Peace Discourse: A Conditional Partnership'. *Journal of Palestinian Studies* XXX, no. 1 (Autumn 2000): 36–51.

Janis, Irving. *Groupthink*. Boston: Houghton Mifflin, 1982.

Jeong, Ho-Won. *Approaches to Peacebuilding*. Basingstoke: Palgrave Macmillan, 2002.

Jerusalem Media and Communication Centre. *The Palestinian Council*. Jerusalem: JMCC, January 1998.

—— *Foreign Aid and Development in Palestine*, Jerusalem: JMCC, March 1999.

Joint Parliamentary Middle East Councils, Commission of Enquiry – Palestinian Refugees. *Right of Return*. London: JPMEC, March 2001.

Kaufman, Edy, Walid Salem and Juliette Verhoeven, eds. *Bridging the Divide – Peacebuilding in the Israeli–Palestinian Conflict*. Boulder: Lynn Rienner, 2006.

Keating, Michael, Anne Le More and Robert Lowe, eds. *Aid, Diplomacy and Facts on the Ground: The Case of Palestine*. London: Chatham House, 2005.

Kedourie, Elie. *Democracy and Arab Political Culture*. London: Frank Cass, 1994.

Keen, David. *The Economic Functions of Violence in Civil Wars. Adelphi Paper 320*. Oxford: OUP, 1998.

Keohane, Robert. O. 'International Institutions: Two Approaches'. In *International Rules*, edited by R.J. Beck, A.C. Arend and R.D. Vander Lugt. Oxford: OUP, 1996.

Khalidi, Rashid. *The Iron Cage. The Story of the Palestinian Struggle for Statehood*. Boston: Beacon Press, 2006.

Khan, Mushtaq Husain, ed., with George Giacaman and Inge Amundsen. *State Formation in Palestine. Viability and Governance during a Social Transformation*. London: RoutledgeCurzon, 2004.

Klingebiel, Stephan. 'The OECD, World Bank and International Monetary Fund: Development Activities in the Crisis Prevention and Conflict Management Sphere'. Bonn, January 2001 (unpublished).

Krasner, Stephen and Carlos Pascual. 'Addressing State Failure'. *Foreign Affairs* (July/August 2005): 153–163.

Kristiansen, Wendy. 'Challenge and Counterchallenge: Hamas's Response to Oslo'. *Journal of Palestinian Studies* XXVIII, no. 3 (Spring 1999): 19–36.

Kühne, Winrich, Peter Cross and Tanja Schümer. *Winning the Peace: Concept and Lessons Learned of Post-Conflict Peacebuilding*. Ebenhausen: Stiftung Wissenschaft und Politik, 1996.

Kumar, Krishna. *Rebuilding Societies after Civil War: Critical Roles for International Assistance*. Boulder, London: Lynne Rienner, 1997.

—— *Postconflict Elections, Democratization, and International Assistance.* Boulder, London: Lynn Rienner, 1998.

Kumar, Krishna, David Tardif-Douglin and Carolyn Knapp. *Rebuilding Postwar Rwanda: The Role of the International Community, USAID Evaluation Special Study; Report No. 76.* Washington DC: USAID, 1996.

Lagerquist, Peter. 'Privatizing the Occupation: The Political Economy of an Oslo Development Project'. *Journal of Palestinian Studies* XXXII, no. 2 (Winter 2003): 5–20.

Le More, Anne. 'Foreign Aid Strategy'. In *The Economics of Palestine: Economic Policy and Institutional Reform for a Viable Palestinian State*, edited by Numan Kanafani and David Cobham, London: Routledge, 2004.

—— 'Killing with Kindness: Funding the Demise of a Palestinian State'. *International Affairs* 81, no. 5 (October 2005): 981–999.

—— 'The Dilemma of Aid to the PA after the Victory of Hamas'. *International Spectator* (June 2006): 87–95.

Leader, Nicholas and Joanna Macrae. *Terms of Engagement: Conditions and Conditionality in Humanitarian Action, HPG Report.* London: Overseas Development Institute, July 2000.

Legrain, Jean-François. 'Judaisation et démembrement: politiques israéliennes du territoire en Cisjordanie-Gaza (1967–1995)'. *Monde Arabe – Maghreb Machrek*, no. 152 (Avril–Juin 1996): 42–75.

—— 'The Successions of Yasir Arafat'. *Journal of Palestinian Studies* XXVIII, no. 4 (Summer 1999): 5–20.

Lister, Stephen and Anne Le More. *Aid Management and Coordination During the Intifada. Report to the LACC Co-Chairs.* Oxford: Mokoro, July 2003.

Lister, Stephen and Raisa Venäläinen. *Improvement of Aid Coordination for West Bank and Gaza.* Oxford: Mokoro, 20 September 1999.

Local Aid Coordination Committee (LACC) – Donor Support Group. *Physical and Institutional Damage Assessment. West Bank Governorates, March–May 2002. Summary Report.* Jerusalem: LACC, 23 May 2002.

Luft, Gal. 'The Palestinian Security Services: Between Police and Army'. *Middle East Review of International Affairs* 3, no. 2 (June 1999): 39–42.

Lumsdaine, David Halloran. *Moral Vision in International Politics: The Foreign Aid Regime, 1949–1989.* Princeton: Princeton University Press, 1993.

MacFarlane, Neil. 'The Role of the United Nations in Contemporary World Politics: In Pursuit of the Possible'. Inaugural Lecture, University of Oxford, 11 February 1997.

—— *Politics and Humanitarian Action.* Providence: Watson Institute, Brown University, 2000.

—— *Humanitarian Action: The Conflict Connection.* Providence: Watson Institute, Brown University, 2001.

Macrae, Joanna and Nicholas Leader. *Shifting Sands: The Search for 'Coherence' between Political and Humanitarian Responses to Complex Emergencies, HPG Report.* London: Overseas Development Institute, August 2000.

Maren, Michael. *The Road to Hell: The Ravaging Effects of Foreign Aid and International Charity.* New York, London: Free Press, 1997.

Massad, Joseph A. *The Persistence of the Palestinian Question. Essays on Zionism and the Palestinians.* London: Routledge, 2006.

Mearsheimer, John J. and Stephen M. Walt. 'The Israel Lobby and US Foreign Policy'.

Faculty Research Working Papers Series, Harvard University, John F. Kennedy School of Government (March 2006).

Mishal, Shaul and Avraham Sela. *The Palestinian Hamas*. New York: Columbia University Press, 2000.

Moore, Jonathan. *Hard Choices: Moral Dilemmas in Humanitarian Intervention*. Oxford: Rowman and Littlefield, 1998.

Nabulsi, Karma. 'The Peace Process and the Palestinians: A Road Map to Mars'. *International Affairs* 80, no. 2 (March 2004): 221–231.

Nasr, Mohamed M. 'Monopolies and the P.N.A'. In *State Formation in Palestine. Viability and Governance During a Social Transformation*, edited by Mushtaq Husain Khan, with George Giacaman and Inge Amundsen. London: RoutledgeCurzon, 2004.

National Democratic Institute for International Affairs and the Carter Center. *The January 20, 1996 Palestinian Elections*. Washington DC and Atlanta: NDIIA/Carter Center, 1997.

Neufeld, Mark. 'Reflexivity in International Relations Theory'. *Millennium* 22, no. 1 (Spring 1993): 53–76.

OCHA. *Preliminary Humanitarian Damage Assessment and Humanitarian Action Plan (May–December 2002)*. Jerusalem: OCHA, June 2002.

—— *The West Bank Wall. Humanitarian Status Report: Northern West Bank Trajectory*. Jerusalem: OCHA, July 2003.

—— *United Nations 2004 Humanitarian Plan of Action for the Occupied Palestinian Territory (CAP)*. New York and Geneva: UN, November 2003.

—— *Report to the LACC on Humanitarian Consequences of Israeli Defence Forces Operations in Rafah, Southern Gaza Strip*. Jerusalem: OCHA, 28 January 2004.

—— *A Report on the Deteriorating Humanitarian Situation in the Gaza Strip*. Jerusalem: OCHA, 1 October 2004.

—— *United Nations 2005 Humanitarian Plan of Action for the Occupied Palestinian Territory (CAP)*. New York and Geneva: UN, November 2004.

OECD. *Shaping the 21st Century: The Contribution of Development Co-Operation*. Paris: OECD, 1996.

—— *Conflict, Peace and Development Co-Operation on the Threshold of the 21st Century*. Paris: OECD, 1998.

O'Neill, William G. *A Humanitarian Practitioner's Guide to International Human Rights Law*. Providence: Watson Institute, Brown University, 1999.

Otunnu, Olara A. and Michael W. Doyle. *Peacemaking and Peacekeeping for the New Century*. Lanham, Oxford: Rowman and Littlefield, 1998.

Palestine Liberation Organization, Negotiations Support Unit. *Israeli Settlements and International Law*, March 2000.

Palestinian National Authority. *Palestinian Development Plan 1999–2003*, January 1999.

Palestinian National Authority, Ministry of Planning and International Cooperation (MOPIC). *The 3rd and 4th Quarterly Monitoring Report of Donors' Assistance of the Year 2001*, December 2001.

Pappe, Ilan. *A History of Modern Palestine. One Land, Two Peoples*. Cambridge: CUP, 2004.

—— *The Ethnic Cleansing of Palestine*. Oxford: One World, 2006.

Paris, Roland. 'International Peacebuilding and the "Mission Civilisatrice"'. *Review of International Studies* 28 (2002): 637–656.

—— 'Peacebuilding and the Limits of Liberal Institutionalism'. *International Security* 22 (Fall 1997): 54–89.

Parker, Christopher. *Resignation or Revolt? Socio-Political Development and the Challenges of Peace in Palestine*. London, New York: I.B. Tauris, 1999.

Parsons, Nigel. *The Politics of the Palestinian Authority. From Oslo to Al-Aqsa*. London: Routledge, 2005.

Peck, Connie. *Sustainable Peace: The Role of the UN and Regional Organizations in Preventing Conflict*. Lanham, Oxford: Rowman and Littlefield, 1998.

Peres, Shimon. *The New Middle East*. New York: Henry Holt, 1993.

Perthes, Volker. *The Middle East Peace Process: An Opportunity for the EU?* Brussels: Stiftung Wissenshaft und Politik (SWP), May 2001.

Pictet, Jean S., ed. *Commentary: Fourth Geneva Convention Relative to the Protection of Civilian Persons in Time of War*. Geneva: International Committee of the Red Cross, 1958.

Pissarides, Christopher, ed. *Evaluating the Paris Protocol. Economic Relations between Israel and the Palestinian Authorities*. Report commissioned for and financed by the European Commission, July 1999.

Putnam, Robert D. 'Diplomacy and Domestic Politics: The Logic of Two Level Games'. *International Organization* 42, no. 3 (Summer 1988): 427–460.

Qouta, S., R.L. Punamaki and E. El-Sarraj. 'Prevalence and Determinants of PTSD among Palestinian Children Exposed to Military Violence'. *European Children and Adolescent Psychiatry* (2003): 135–156.

Quandt, William B. *Peace Process. American Diplomacy and the Arab–Israeli Conflict since 1967*. Washington DC/Berkeley: Brookings and UCP, 2005 (third edition).

Ratner, Steven R. *The New UN Peacekeeping: Building Peace in Lands of Conflict after the Cold War*. Basingstoke: Macmillan, 1995.

Raz-Krakotzkin, Amnon. 'A Peace without Arabs: The Discourse of Peace and the Limits of Israeli Consciousness'. In *After Oslo. New Realities, Old Problems*, edited by George Giacaman, and Dag Jorund Lonning. London: Pluto Press, 1998.

Reinhart, Tanya. *Israel/Palestine: How to End the War of 1948*. New York: Seven Stories Press, 2002.

—— *The Roadmap to Nowhere. Israel/Palestine since 2003*. London, New York: Verso, 2006.

Riddell, Roger. *Foreign Aid Reconsidered*. Baltimore/London: Johns Hopkins University Press/ODI, 1987.

Robinson, Glenn E. *Building a Palestinian State: The Incomplete Revolution*. Bloomington: Indiana University Press, 1997.

—— 'The Growing Authoritarianism of the Arafat Regime'. *Survival* 39, no. 2 (Summer 1997): 42–56.

Rogan, Eugene L. and Avi Shlaim, eds. *The War for Palestine. Rewriting the History of 1948*. Cambridge: CUP, 2001.

Ross, Dennis. *The Missing Peace. The Inside Story of the Fight for Middle East Peace*. New York: Farrar, Straus and Giroux, 2004.

Rousseau, Jean-Jacques. *The Social Contract*. London: Penguin, 1968 [1762].

Roy, Sara. *The Gaza Strip. The Political Economy of De-Development*. Washington DC: Institute for Palestine Studies, 1995.

—— 'Alienation or Accommodation?' *Journal of Palestinian Studies* XXIV, no. 4 (Summer 1995): 73–82.

—— 'De-Development Revisited: Palestinian Economy and Society since Oslo'. *Journal of Palestinian Studies* XXVIII, no. 3 (Spring 1999): 64–82.

—— *Failing Peace. Gaza and the Israeli–Palestinian Conflict*. London: Pluto Press, 2007.

—— 'Palestinian Society and Economy: The Continued Denial of Possibility'. *Journal of Palestinian Studies* XXX, no. 4 (Summer 2001): 5–20.

Said, Edward W. *Peace and Its Discontents. Gaza–Jericho, 1993–1995*. London: Vintage, 1995.

—— 'The Real Meaning of the Hebron Agreement'. *Journal of Palestinian Studies* 21, no. 3 (1997): 31–36.

Sayigh, Yezid. *Armed Struggle and the Search for State: The Palestinian National Movement, 1949–1993*. Oxford: Clarendon Press, 1997.

—— 'Arafat and the Anatomy of a Revolt'. *Survival* 43, no. 3 (Autumn 2001): 46–60.

Schenker, David. *Palestinian Democracy and Governance: An Appraisal of the Legislative Council*. Washington DC: The Washington Institute for Near East Policy, 2000.

Schiavo-Campo, Salvatore. *Financing and Aid Management Arrangements in Post-Conflict Situations*. World Bank Conflict Prevention and Reconstruction Unit Working Paper No. 6, Washington DC: World Bank, June 2003.

Schlumberger, Oliver. 'The Arab Middle East and the Question of Democratization: Some Critical Remarks'. *Democratization* 7, no. 4 (Winter 2000): 104–132.

Sewell, David. *Governance and the Business Environment in West Bank/Gaza*. Washington DC: World Bank, May 2001.

Sharabi, Hisham. *Neopatriarchy. A Theory of Distorted Change in Arab Society*. Oxford, New York: OUP, 1988.

Shearer, David. *The Humanitarian Crisis in the Occupied Palestinian Territory, Humanitarian Exchange Nb 28*. London: Overseas Development Institute, November 2004.

Shikaki, Khalil. 'The Palestinian Elections: An Assessment'. *Journal of Palestinian Studies* XXV, no. 3 (Spring 1996): 17–22.

—— 'Palestinians Divided'. *Foreign Affairs* 81, no. 1 (January/February 2002): 89–105.

Shlaim, Avi. *The Iron Wall. Israel and the Arab World*. London: Allen Lane, Penguin, 2000.

—— 'America and the Israeli–Palestinian Conflict'. In *Worlds in Collision: Terror and the Future of Global Order*, edited by Ken Booth and Tim Dunne. Basingstoke/New York: Palgrave, 2002.

—— 'Israeli Politics and Middle East Peacemaking'. *Journal of Palestinian Studies* XXIV, no. 4 (Summer 1995): 21–31.

Shu'aybi, Azmi. 'A Window on the Workings of the PA: An Inside View'. *Journal of Palestinian Studies* XXX, no. 1 (Autumn 2000): 88–97.

Siblot, Jean-Luc, Genevieve Wills and Tareq Abu ElHaj. *Food Security in the Occupied Palestinian Territory, Humanitarian Exchange Nb 28*. London: Overseas Development Institute, November 2004.

Special Rapporteur of the Commission on Human Rights, John Dugard. *Report on the Situation of Human Rights in the Palestinian Territories Occupied by Israel since 1967, Submitted in Accordance with Commission Resolution 1993/2 A*, September 2003.

Stedman, Stephen John. 'Spoiler Problems in Peace Processes'. *International Security* 22, no. 2 (Fall 1997): 5–53.

Sternhell, Zeev. *Aux origines d'Israel. Entre nationalisme et socialisme*. Paris: Fayard, 1996.

Stevenson, Jonathan. *Preventing Conflict: The Role of the Bretton Woods Institutions,*

Adelphi Paper 336. Oxford: OUP for the International Institute for Strategic Studies, 2000.

Stokke, Olav. *Aid and Political Conditionality.* London: Cass, 1995.

—— ed. *Foreign Aid towards the Year 2000: Experiences and Challenges.* London: Frank Cass in association with the EADI, Geneva, 1996.

Strategic Assessments Initiative. *Planning Considerations for International Involvement in the Palestinian Security Sector.* Report Sponsored by the Royal Netherlands Ministry of Foreign Affairs and the International Development Research Center of Canada. Washington DC: SAI, July 2005.

Swisher, Clayton E. *The Truth about Camp David. The Untold Story about the Collapse of the Middle East Peace Process.* New York: Nation Books, 2004.

Taraki, Lisa, ed. *Living Palestine. Family Survival, Resistance, and Mobility under Occupation.* Syracuse, New York: Syracuse University Press, 2006.

The Palestinian Environmental NGOs Network (PENGON). *Stop the Wall in Palestine. Facts, Testimonies, Analysis and Call to Action.* Jerusalem: PENGON, June 2003.

The Palestinian Independent Commission for Citizens' Rights. *Second Annual Report. 1 July 1995 to 31 December 1996.* Ramallah: PICCR, 1997.

The Palestinian Independent Commission for Citizens' Rights. *Fourth Annual Report. 1 January 1998 to 31 December 1998.* Ramallah: PICCR, 1999.

Tocci, Nathalie. *The Widening Gap between Rhetoric and Reality in EU Policy towards the Israeli–Palestinian Conflict.* CEPS Working Document no. 217, Brussels: CEPS, January 2005.

Trottier, Julie. *Hydropolitics in the West Bank and Gaza Strip.* Jerusalem: PASSIA, 1999.

UNDG/ECHA Working Group on Transition Issues. *Report.* New York: United Nations, February 2004.

UNICEF. *Humanitarian Action Occupied Palestinian Territory – Donor Update.* Jerusalem: UNICEF, 19 November 2003.

United Nations. *The Question of Palestine and the United Nations.* New York: Department of Public Information, March 2003.

United Nations Conference on Trade and Development (UNCTAD). *Report on UNCTAD's Assistance to the Palestinian People.* Geneva: UNCTAD, 28 July 2003.

United Nations Development Programme (UNDP). *Arab Human Development Report 2002.* New York: UNDP, 2002.

—— *UNDP in the Occupied Palestinian Territory. Programme Review 2005.* New York: UNDP, 2005.

United Nations Office of the Special Coordinator (UNSCO). *Emergency Employment Programme.* Gaza: UNSCO, 31 August 1996.

—— *Economic and Social Conditions in the West Bank and Gaza Strip. Quarterly Report.* Gaza: UNSCO, Autumn 1996.

—— *Economic and Social Conditions in the West Bank and Gaza Strip. Quarterly Report.* Gaza: UNSCO, Spring 1998.

—— *The Economy of the West Bank and Gaza Strip: A Retrospective on the 1990s and Future Challenges.* Gaza: UNSCO, January 1999.

—— *Economic and Social Conditions in the West Bank and Gaza Strip. Quarterly Report.* Gaza: UNSCO, Spring 1999.

—— *Report on the Palestinian Economy. Special Focus: Donor Disbursements and Public Investment.* Gaza: UNSCO, Autumn 1999.

—— *Report on the Palestinian Economy.* Gaza: UNSCO, Spring 2001.

—— A Briefing on the Economic and Social Impact of Recent Events in the West Bank. Ramallah: UNSCO, 16 April 2002.

Usher, Graham. Palestine in Crisis: The Struggle for Peace and Political Independence after Oslo. London: Pluto Press, 1995.

—— 'The Politics of Internal Security: The PA's New Intelligence Services'. Journal of Palestinian Studies XXV, no. 2 (Winter 1996): 21–34.

—— Dispatches from Palestine: The Rise and Fall of the Oslo Peace Process. London: Pluto, 1998.

—— 'Facing Defeat: The Intifada Two Years On'. Journal of Palestinian Studies XXXII, no. 2 (Winter 2003): 21–40.

Uvin, Peter. Aiding Violence. The Development Enterprise in Rwanda. West Hartford: Kumarian Press, 1998.

—— The Influence of Aid in Situations of Violent Conflict. Paris: OECD, September 1999.

Waage, Hilde Henriksen. Peacemaking Is a Risky Business. Norway's Role in the Peace Process in the Middle East, 1993–96. Oslo: International Peace Research Institute (PRIO), 2004.

Wagner, Viktoria. Palestinian Judiciary and the Rule of Law in the Autonomous Areas. An Introduction. Jerusalem: PASSIA, November 2000.

Waldman, Adir. 'Negotiated Transitions to Democracy: Israel and the Palestinians as a Case Study'. Democratization 7, no. 2 (Summer 2000): 113–141.

Watson, Geoffrey R. The Oslo Accords: International Law and the Israeli–Palestinian Agreements. Oxford: OUP, 2000.

Weber, Max. Le Savant et le politique. Paris: Plon, 1959.

Weinberger, Peter Ezra. 'Co-Opting the PLO: A Critical Reconstruction of the Oslo Accords, 1993–1995'. Unpublished PhD. London School of Economics and Political Science, 2002.

Wendt, Alexander. 'Anarchy Is What States Make of It: The Social Construction of Power Politics'. International Organization 46, no. 2 (1992): 391–425.

Williams, Emma. It's Easier to Reach Heaven Than the End of the Street. A Jerusalem Memoir. London: Bloomsbury, 2006.

Woods, Ngaire. 'Groupthink, the IMF, the World Bank and Decision Making About the 1994 Mexican Crisis'. In Decision-Making in International Organizations, edited by Bob Reinalda and Bertjan Verbeek. London: Routledge, 2003.

World Bank. Developing the Occupied Territories: An Investment in Peace. Six vols. Vol. 1. Washington DC: World Bank, 1993.

—— Emergency Assistance Program for the Occupied Territories. Washington DC: World Bank, April 1994.

—— The West Bank and Gaza: The Next Two Years and Beyond, Washington DC: World Bank 1994.

—— A Background Note on the Economy for the Fourth Meeting of the Consultative Group for the West Bank and Gaza Strip. Jerusalem: World Bank, November 1996.

—— Assessing Aid: What Works, What Doesn't and Why. Oxford: World Bank, 1998.

—— Post Conflict Reconstruction. The Role of the World Bank. Washington DC: World Bank, 1998.

—— West Bank and Gaza: Strengthening Public Sector Management. Jerusalem: World Bank, 1999.

—— 'West Bank and Gaza: Public Expenditure Review'. Unpublished, April 1999.

—— *Holst Peace Fund. Supporting Development in the West Bank and Gaza.* Washington DC: World Bank, 2002.

—— *Fifteen Months – Intifada, Closures and Palestinian Economic Crisis – an Assessment.* Jerusalem: World Bank, March 2002.

—— *Long-Term Policy Options for the Palestinian Economy.* Jerusalem: World Bank, July 2002.

—— *The Role of the World Bank in Conflict and Development. An Evolving Agenda.* Washington DC: World Bank, 2003.

—— *Twenty Seven Months – Intifada, Closures and Economic Crisis – an Assessment.* Jerusalem: World Bank, May 2003.

—— 'West Bank and Gaza: Public Financial Management Reform Trust Fund'. Unpublished, April 2004.

—— *Disengagement, the Palestinian Economy and the Settlements.* Jerusalem: World Bank, 23 June 2004.

—— *Four Years – Intifada, Closures and Palestinian Economic Crisis – an Assessment.* Jerusalem: World Bank, October 2004.

—— *Stagnation or Revival? Israeli Disengagement and Palestinian Economic Prospects.* Jerusalem: World Bank, December 2004.

—— *The Palestinian Economy and the Prospects for Its Recovery.* Jerusalem: World Bank, December 2005.

World Bank and Japan. *Aid Effectiveness in the West Bank and Gaza.* Jerusalem: World Bank, June 2000.

World Bank and UNSCO. *Donor Investment in Palestinian Development 1994–1998.* Jerusalem: World Bank/UNSCO, 1999.

World Bank Operations Evaluation Department. *West Bank and Gaza: An Evaluation of Bank Assistance.* Washington DC: World Bank, March 2002.

INDEX

References to notes are prefixed by *n*.
Italic page numbers indicate tables and figures not included in the text page range.